THE BIBLIOPHILE'S
DICTIONARY

2,054 MASTERFUL WORDS & PHRASES
by Miles Westley

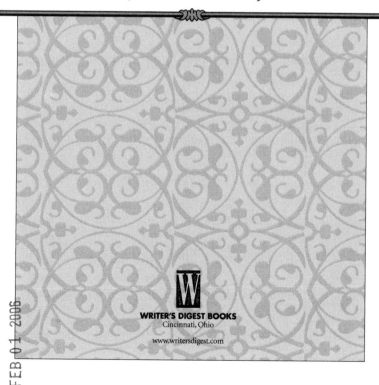

WRITER'S DIGEST BOOKS
Cincinnati, Ohio

www.writersdigest.com

09 08 07 06 05   5 4 3 2 1

Distributed in Canada by Fraser Direct, 100 Armstrong Avenue, Georgetown, ON, Canada L7G 5S4. Tel: (905) 877-4411.

Distributed in the U.K. and Europe by David & Charles, Brunel House, Newton Abbot, Devon, TQ12 4PU, England. Tel: (+44) 1626 323200, Fax: (+44) 1626 323319. E-mail: mail@davidandcharles.co.uk

Distributed in Australia by Capricorn Link, P.O. Box 704, Windsor, NSW 2756 Australia. Tel: (02) 4577-3555

Library of Congress Cataloging-in-Publication Data

Westley, Peter Miles.

The bibliophile's dictionary : 2,054 masterful words and phrases / by Peter Miles Westley.-- 1st ed.

p. cm.

Includes bibliographical references and index.

ISBN 1-58297-356-3 (hardcover : alk. paper)

1. English language--Dictionaries. 2. English language--Terms and phrases. 3. Vocabulary. I. Title.

PE1630.W47 2005

423--dc22

2005011176

Edited by Amy Schell
Cover and interior design by Claudean Wheeler
Production coordinated by Robin Richie

F+W PUBLICATIONS, INC.

PERMISSIONS

ACKNOWLEDGMENTS

*This book could not have been written without
the help and support of many people:*

GENE BRISSIE - my agent at James Peter Associates, who took on this project with an enthusiasm that helped turned the project from a labor of love into something that I became convinced would actually be published. Thanks for your support and guidance through this whole process.

AMY SCHELL - my editor at Writer's Digest Books, who helped me turn a somewhat unwieldy manuscript of several thousand terms and tens of thousands of citations into what you now hold. Thanks also for your help navigating the murky waters of "fair use" standards and the permissioning process with other publishers.

JACKIE JENKINS - for reviewing and refining all two thousand plus definitions in the book. Thanks for helping me keep my sanity during the last days of this effort.

CYNTHIA LAUFENBERG - for providing the essential pronunciation guide.

All of the authors and publishers who inspired this effort and generously allowed me to reprint materials from their works. If you liked the citations, I encourage you to read the whole documents; I recommend them all.

To my wife and daughters for putting up with all of the endless hours that it took to get the book in its final form; I never could have done it without your understanding and patience.

To all of my family and friends who encouraged me and supported this crazy effort: Mom, Dad, Nick, Monica, Camille, Edna Mashihara, Tom Dossena, Carol Roberts, Dyer Grote, Rob Edington, Sue and Jack Terrell, Teena Berman, Owen Hart, Vicky Gaetz, Amy Milani, Shelley Brown, Dan Vasquez, Stacey and Steve Katz, Michael Tunstal, Manisha Choksi Eckton, Shantha Farris, Kaeti Bradley, Joanne Madden, Ann Hood, Aimee and Greg Price, Susi and Kamran Ghiasi, and Mimi Towle.

Finally, to two of my dearest relatives who passed away during the writing of this book but who were great inspirations and who were always with me in spirit, Dan Mashihara and Tony Cartwright.

ABOUT THE AUTHOR

Peter Miles Westley was born in the San Francisco bay area to parents who had recently emigrated from England. He grew up in Mountain Lakes, New Jersey and contemplated a variety of creative professions. Although he has pursued a career in finance, he has always had a series of creative side projects. This is his first book.

Westley is a cum laude graduate of Dartmouth College and has an MBA from the Stanford University Graduate School of Business. He has had a successful career as an investment banker; first advising and investing in troubled companies, then advising and raising capital for media and Internet companies. Westley is married with two daughters and lives in Tiburon, California.

For Lisa, Sydney, and Alexandra;
and for aspiring writers everywhere

TABLE OF
CONTENTS

INTRODUCTION

I guess I've always been a bit of a collector. Like many kids, I had my brief stints collecting coins and stamps. As I got a little older, I became a comic collector, particularly Marvel Comics of the 1960s and 1970s. Many of these comics were written by Stan "The Man" Lee, the man who first opened my eyes to the fun and power of a few well-selected words. Stan came from the P.T. Barnum school of bombastic phrasemaking. Here are a few samples from a ten-page story featuring a hero named Dr. Strange in the late 1960s: "starting one of his myriad death-battles"; "penciled & inked by the prestidigitator Steve Ditko"; "A cosmos shudders, as the delicate balance of its most inviolable laws is upset"; "the cataclysmic impact of their clash threatens to destroy them both!"; "a fierce maelstrom rips across the void!" To a young kid from the suburbs, this was eye-opening stuff. I remember going to my dictionary to figure out what the heck this guy was talking about. It never seemed like work, though. In fact, figuring out Stan's meaning was part of the fun, and it felt like I was becoming part of a secret society that knew about this hidden world of fantasy and excitement. I understood that this overblown vocabulary was used tongue-in-cheek, with a wink and a nod to his audience.

Not long after I was introduced to some more down-to-earth terminology in the pages of *Mad* magazine, sprinkled liberally with yiddish terms—meshuggener this, furshlugginer that, and farshtinkener the other one. The words sounded funny and comical and just right, somehow, even if I didn't know exactly what they meant. I also remember thoroughly enjoying a Monty Python skit in which a family enjoyed great sensual pleasure from "woody" words like *sausage, bound, vole, caribou, erogenous zone, concubine, vacuum*, and the nonsense word *gorn* and seemed to physically reel in pain when anyone said a "tinny" word like *newspaper, litter bin, leap*, and *recidivist*.

I had some English teachers in high school who emphasized vocabulary. I remember one in particular, Mrs. Smith, who loved the alliteration of a poem that referred to "dark, dank bungalows"—the rest of the poem is lost to me now. My mother also appreciated poetry, great books and the possibilities of the English language. My father used to enjoy playing the "Dictionary Game" in which we made up hypothetical definitions for unfamiliar words. My liberal arts education at Dartmouth College, which emphasized reading and writing, also enhanced my appreciation for clear, concise prose that said exactly what the author intended.

Somewhere along the way I became enamored of the writing style of pulp-fiction author Robert E. Howard. He had an ability to create a mythical world and atmosphere over the course of a paragraph or two. One of Howard's tricks in accomplishing this feat

1

was his use of words that were descriptive but also evoked a certain time and place. You will find many of his favorites included herein.

As I was growing to appreciate Howard, I started to think that I might want to take a shot at writing someday. One logical step seemed to be expanding my vocabulary, which would increase my ability to say exactly what I meant to convey and also set the mood for a story. So I started collecting words. At first, it was a simple list of definitions and citations. As the list grew over the years, however, it seemed to make sense to organize the list into categories that might serve me as a writer. Many of the words appeared in more than one category. For other words, I only included interesting, but less common, definitions and uses. Some words I knew well but wanted to make note of because I liked them and wanted to remember to use them when I did start writing.

Most of the words in this book are followed by the citations in which I found them. Words without citations typically are used in the definitions for other words in the book.

So what, then, is this book? It is a hybrid, a kind of literary hippogriff—part dictionary, part thesaurus, and part encyclopedia. Unlike that ungainly mythical creature, however, this effort has two clear goals. The first is to provide some additional colors to the author's palette—subtle shades of nuance that may have been unfamiliar previously and that will help put the finishing touches on the written masterpiece in development. The second goal is to provide examples to be an inspiration to the working writer. The book aims to make clear the power of specificity—the way the right turn of phrase or literary reference can make a passage more powerful. Hopefully the book also provides the nonwriter with a fun source for improving his or her vocabulary and brushing up on a little history, mythology, and literary allusions.

I should make it clear that this book was initially a personal tool. It obviously reflects my interests and reading materials. It also shows my personal gaps of knowledge in certain areas. More than many reference works, typically prepared by committee, this one is quirky, subjective, idiosyncratic, and reflective of the preferences and whims of its author. It was only after showing the book to a few friends that I was convinced it might be of interest to others. Hopefully you will be in that group.

Peter Miles Westley
Tiburon, California
April 2005

"I had declared in public my desire to be a writer ... I wanted to develop a curiosity that was oceanic and insatiable as well as a desire to learn and use every word in the English language that didn't sound pretentious or ditzy."

—PAT CONROY, *MY LOSING SEASON*

"He wanted nothing, for the time being, except to understand ... Without advice, assistance or plan, he began reading an incongruous assortment of books; he would find some passage which he could not understand in one book, and he would get another on that subject ... There was no order in his reading; but there was order in what remained of it in his mind."

—AYN RAND, *THE FOUNTAINHEAD*

1. PERSONALITY TRAITS

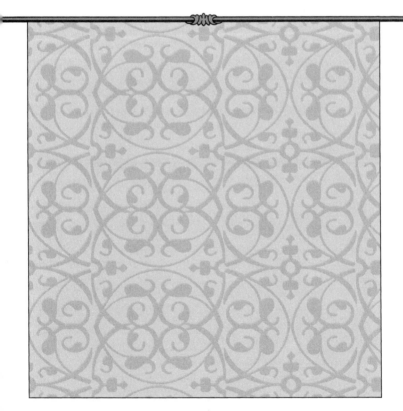

TALKERS AND QUIET TYPES

garrulous (GAR uh lus, also GAR yuh lus) - *adj.* pointlessly or tiresomely talkative.

The *American Heritage Dictionary* states that "loquacious usually implies a disposition to talk incessantly or to keep up a constant flow of chatter—a loquacious mood; garrulous implies a wearisome loquacity about trivial matters—a garrulous old man; voluble suggests a continuous flow of glib talk—a voluble oration."

> "I heard the waves still lapping on the beach, **garrulously** attesting the fury of the night." –JACK LONDON, *The Sea Wolf*

laconic (luh KAH nik) - *adj.* expressing something with as few words as possible; minimum use of words (Lakonikos is Greek for Spartan).

> "'Won't work, Jack,' Ricky said **laconically**." –MICHAEL CRICHTON, *Prey*

loquacious (lo KWAY shus) - *adj.* excessively talkative; fond of talking.

> "[J.M.W. Turner] was a poet as well as a painter and a man of shrewd and vigorous speech, though he was never **loquacious.**" –TIM HILTON, *The New York Times Book Review*, 9/7/03

prolix (PRO liks) - *adj.* overly wordy; verbose; tedious (seems to be used to describe writing more than speaking).

*see other **prolix** entry for citation, p. 106*

quidnunc (KWID nunk) - *n.* an inquisitive, gossipy person; someone who wants to know everything that is happening; a busybody (from the Latin, literally quid = what, nunc = now).

> "Astounding News by Express, via Norfolk! The Atlantic Crossed in Three Days!... The subjoined jeu d'esprit with the preceding heading in magnificent capitals, well interspersed with notes of admiration, was originally published, as matter of fact, in the *New York Sun*, a daily newspaper, and therein fully served the purpose of creating indigestible aliment for the **quidnuncs** during the few hours intervening between a couple of the Charleston mails." –EDGAR ALLAN POE, *The Balloon Hoax*

reticent (RET uh sent) - *adj.* reserved in speech or style; inclined to be silent.

> "In a family of passionately expressive people like Father Herzog and Aunt Zipporah Will had developed a quieter, observant, **reticent** style." –SAUL BELLOW, *Herzog*

sententious (SEN tent shus) - *adj.* expressing much in few words; short and pithy; terse and forceful, 2. full of, or fond of using, maxims, proverbs, etc., esp. in a way that is pompous and moralizing.

> "'A dollar means more grub,' he remarked **sententiously**." –JACK LONDON, *The Apostate*

sesquipedalian (SESS kwuh puh DAL yun) - *adj.* given to using long words, 2. characterized by overly long words.

*see other **sesquipedalian** entry for citation, p. 103*

taciturn (TA suh turn) - *adj.* habitually silent or untalkative.

> "He started out by saying that people were describing me as a **taciturn** and withdrawn person and he wanted to know what I thought. I answered, 'It's just that I don't have much to say. So I keep quiet.'" –ALBERT CAMUS, *The Stranger*

voluble (VOL yuh bul) –*adj.* talkative; characterized by fast or rapid speech.

> "Mundy is more successful with his minor characters... Chullunder Ghose, a fat, emotional, excitable, **voluble** Bengali babu." –L. SPRAGUE DE CAMP, *The Blade of Conan*

GENEROUS AND STINGY

abstemious (ab STEE me us) - *adj.* sparing, especially in the indulgence of the appetite or passions, particularly sparing in the use of alcohol or food.

> "'I can only hope that when you find the path of **abstemious** devotion, you do not entirely forget the friends of your debauched youth.'" –DAVID LISS, *A Conspiracy of Paper*

avarice (A vuh rus) - *n.* an excessive or inordinate desire of gain; greediness after wealth; covetousness; cupidity (*adj.* avaricious).

> "The sailor grinned and passed him a fragment of sea biscuit. He clutched it **avariciously**, looked at it as a miser looks at gold, and thrust it into his shirt bosom." –JACK LONDON, *Love of Life*

chary (CHAR ee, also CHAIR ee) - *adj.* hesitant or cautious; hesitant to grant or expend.

> "The priest listened attentively, but was chary with his **advice**." –FYODOR DOSTOYEVSKY, *The Brothers Karamazov*, transl. by David Magarshack

cupidity (kyu PIH duh tee) - *n.* greed; intense desire for wealth.

> "'We have already offered what will beggar the kingdom to pay. To offer more would further excite Ophir's **cupidity**.'" –ROBERT E. HOWARD, *Black Colussus*

magnanimous (mag NA nuh mus) - *adj.* noble and generous in spirit; tolerant and understanding; forgiving.

> "Brian Sabean listens to Billy's **magnanimous** offer of Mike Venafro; all Billy wants in return is a minor league player." –MICHAEL LEWIS, *Moneyball*

munificent (myu NIH fuh sunt) - *adj.* very liberal in giving or bestowing; lavish.

> "My father gave me ten shillings and my mother five for pocket money and I thought them **munificent**." –SAMUEL BUTLER, *The Way of All Flesh*

parsimonious (PAR suh MO nee us) - *adj.* sparing in expenditure of money; frugal to excess; stingy; miserly.

> "'Why should I be **parsimonious** with this life which is cheap and without value?'"
> —JACK LONDON, *The Sea Wolf*

parsimony (PAR suh MO nee) - *n.* stinginess; frugality; great reluctance to spend money unnecessarily.

> "He drove the boy into treachery by his **parsimony**." —ROBERT E. HOWARD, *Swords of the Purple Kingdom*

penurious (pe NUR ee us) - *adj.* extreme frugality with money and possessions; stinginess (*n.* penury: severe poverty).

> "Tu was **penurious** with him. Always maintained that giving young men money was bad for them." —ROBERT E. HOWARD, *Swords of the Purple Kingdom*

provident (PRAHV uh dunt, also PRAHV uh dent) - *adj.* preparing, providing for future financial needs; economic foresight.

> "The **provident** young person neither ate his bacon immediately nor let it be soaked by the vegetable juices. The **provident** young person evacuated his bacon to the higher ground at the plate's edge and stored it there as an incentive. The provident young person ate his bite of fried onions, which weren't good but also weren't bad, if he needed a preliminary treat." —JONATHAN FRANZEN, *The Corrections*

spendthrift (SPEND thrift) - *n.* one who demonstrates wasteful or extravagant spending (therefore, the opposite of thrifty).

> "This impressed upon the clerk the mediocrity of his own status: he longed to have

epaulettes, decorations and titles. Such things must be to her liking, he suspected, judging by her **spendthrift** ways."
> GUSTAVE FLAUBERT, *Madame Bovary*, transl. by Francis Steegmuller

EMOTIONAL AND UNEMOTIONAL

(ALSO SEE EMOTIONS)

demure (dih MYUR) - *adj.* reserved, modest, 2. affecting a modest or reserved manner; coy.

> "I wish I had saved his letter, but I was so humiliated by its **demure** arguments that I buried it on the bottom of the garbage can." —PAT CONROY, *My Losing Season*

indurate (IN duh rut, also IN dyuh rut, in DUR uht, in DYUH rut) - *v.* to make hard; harden, 2. to render callous, unfeeling, or stubborn, 3. to cause to be firmly established or fixed.

> "So **indurated** was I at that time to the abomination of the place, that I heard without a touch of emotion the puma victim begin another day of torture." —H.G. WELLS, *The Island of Dr. Moreau*

insouciant (in SOO see unt, also ahn soos YAHN) - *adj.* carefree; heedless; indifferent; casually unconcerned.

> "My words all but slapped him in the face, and he collected himself once again to the posture of an **insouciant** buck." —DAVID LISS, *A Conspiracy of Paper*

inure (ih NUR, also ih NYUR) - *v.* to become accustomed to something unpleasant by prolonged exposure.

> "Interspecies hybrids of advertising and entertainment have suddenly become the

norm, remarkably unremarkable. And we have become thoroughly **inured**." –KURT ANDERSON, *The New York Times Magazine*, 12/15/02

lachrymose (LA kruh MOS) - *adj.* tearful, sorrowful, sad.

"'You think you've got something to be afraid about?' Doc Daneeka demanded, lifting his delicate, immaculate dark head up from his chest to gaze at Yossarian irascibly for a moment with **lachrymose** eyes." –JOSEPH HELLER, *Catch-22*

lugubrious (luh GOO bree us, also luh GYOO bree us) - *adj.* mournful, gloomy; dismal; comically or ridiculously doleful.

"...the long **lugubrious** howl..." –JACK LONDON, *Batard*

obdurate (OB duh rut, also ob DUR ut, ob DYUR ut) - *adj.* not easily influenced or affected, 2. hard, unfeeling, unyielding.

"'...your inexplicable, obstinate, and almost **obdurate** silence about the source of the money which appeared so suddenly in your hand ... '" –FYODOR DOSTOYEVSKY, *The Brothers Karamazov*, transl. by David Magarshack

phlegmatic (fleg MA tik) - *adj.* not easily excited to action or passion, 2. having a calm, stolid temperament; unemotional.

"Bombing his own men and planes was more than even the most **phlegmatic** observer could stomach." –JOSEPH HELLER, *Catch-22*

po-faced (PO FACED) - *adj.* assuming a solemn, impassive or serious expression or manner; poker-faced; priggish, narrow-minded, or smug.

"They were **po-faced** in ways only the young want to be, and at twenty-four or twenty-five I was just old enough to want to sneer at their earnestness." –NICK HORNBY, *Songbook*

reticent (RET eh sunt) - *adj.* reserved in speech or style; inclined to be silent.

"In a family of passionately expressive people like Father Herzog and Aunt Zipporah Will had developed a quieter, observant, **reticent** style." –SAUL BELLOW, *Herzog*

saturnine (SAH turh NINE) - *adj.* born under or influenced (astrologically) by the planet Saturn, 2. slow to act or change; steady, 3. gloomy, 4. having lead poisoning.

"Convocations of the honor court on the top floor of Durrell Hall were always conducted with an inflexible and **saturnine** efficiency." –PAT CONROY, *The Lords of Discipline*

stolid (STAH lid) - *adj.* unemotional; impassive; insensitive, 2. showing little emotion or sensibility.

"There was neither pity nor passion in his face, but rather the patient, **stolid** look of one who has certain work to do and goes about it methodically." –JACK LONDON, *In a Far Country*

sullen (SUH len) - *adj.* expressing a resentful silence, 2. brooding, gloomy or somber.

"There were only three passengers—dark, unkempt men of **sullen** visage and somewhat youthful cast." –H.P. LOVECRAFT, *The Shadow Over Innsmouth*

wistful (WIST ful) - *adj.* full of a desire or yearning, often melancholy; longing: wistful eyes.

"In accordance with my plan, I attracted his attention by brandishing my newly purchased bottle; and soon realized that he had begun to shuffle **wistfully** after me." –H.P. LOVECRAFT, *The Shadow Over Innsmouth*

DETAIL ORIENTED, DILIGENT, PERSISTENT

assiduous (ah SIJ wus, also ah SIH juh wus) - *adj.* showing careful, persistent attention, 2. hard-working, diligent.

"...he never let her go for an instant out of his sight, and followed her **assiduously** in her course through the stellar spaces." –JULES VERNE, *From the Earth to the Moon*

fastidious (fa STIH dee us, also fuh STIH dee us) - *adj.* meticulous, 2. difficult to please, 3. having extremely high standards.

"...he washed [the pan] fine and finer [looking for gold], with a keen scrutiny and delicate and **fastidious** touch." –JACK LONDON, *All Gold Canyon*

implacable (im PLAH kuh bul, also im PLAY kuh bul) - *adj.* not capable of being pacified, significantly changed, mitigated, or altered: implacable opposition.

"The men murmured, though they did not let their murmurings reach the ears of their **implacable** master, who tramped the poop day and night in gloomy majesty." –ROBERT E. HOWARD, *The Pool of the Black One*

importunate (im POOR chu nuht, also im POOR tyu nuht) - *adj.* stubbornly or unreasonably persistent.

"...as the zeal of the born scientist slowly returned, he again became **importunate** with the college faculty, pleading for the use of the dissecting-room and of fresh human specimens for the work he regarded as so overwhelmingly important." – H.P. LOVECRAFT, *Herbert West—Re-animator*

importune (IM per TOON, also IM per TYOON, im POOR TOON) - *v.* to beset with repeated and insistent requests.

"'Will you let me go away? ... Will you let me, Richard?'

'You distress me, Susanna, by such im-**portunity**!'" –THOMAS HARDY, *Jude the Obscure*

pertinacious (PER tin A shus) - *adj.* adhering resolutely to a purpose, belief or opinion, 2. stubbornly persistent; unyielding.

"Thomas Mugridge, so strangely and **pertinaciously** clinging to life, was soon limping about again and performing his double duties of cook and cabin-boy." –JACK LONDON, *The Sea Wolf*

punctilious (PUNK TIH lee us) - *adj.* very careful about every detail of behavior, convention, etc.: a punctilious host, 2. exact; scrupulous.

9

"[Michael Jackson's] facial reconstruction is a deliberate bid for racial vagueness, and Americans have been, historically, **punctilious** racial taxonomists." —TUNKU VARADARAJAN, *The Asian Wall Street Journal*, 3/18–20/05

sedulous (SEH juh lus) - *adj.* diligent, sincere, careful, industrious.

"Fu-Manchu, who, with all the powers represented by Nayland Smith pitted against him, pursued his dark schemes triumphantly, and lurked in hiding within this very area which was so **sedulously** patrolled." —SAX ROHMER, *The Insidious Dr. Fu-Manchu*

FRIENDLY

affable (A fuh bul) - *adj.* easy to be spoken to or addressed; receiving others kindly and conversing with them in a free and friendly manner; courteous; sociable, 2. gracious; mild; benign.

"Though I had taken no vows of chastity, women responded to me as though I were an **affable** rural curate with no thunder in my pants." —PAT CONROY, *The Lords of Discipline*

amative (A muh tiv) - *adj.* inclined to be loving.

"It has dawned upon me that I have never placed a proper valuation upon womankind. For that matter, though not **amative** to any considerable degree so far as I have discovered, I was never outside the atmosphere of women until now." —JACK LONDON, *The Sea Wolf*

avuncular (a VUN kyu lur) - *adj.* kindly, genial, in the manner of an uncle.

"Minor has an air of **avuncular** kindliness" —SIMON WINCHESTER, *The Professor and the Madman*

blithe (BLIETH) - *adj.* cheerful; sprightly; carefree.

"I was not bothered by their attentions and parried all their questions **blithely** until they at last grew rather personal." —JOHN KENNEDY TOOLE, *A Confederacy of Dunces*

bonhomie (bah nah ME) - *n.* a pleasant nature, a genial disposition.

"...his father must have had the gift of glib **bonhomie**." —TOM WOLFE, *I Am Charlotte Simmons*

clement (KLEH ment) - *adj.* merciful; to be lenient with punishment, 2. mildness of weather.

"Ningauble responded, the piety in his voice now tinged with a certain **clement** disappointment." —FRITZ LEIBER, *Swords Against Death*

complaisance (kum PLAY sents, also kum PLAY zents, kom PLAY sents, kom PLAY zents) - *n.* wanting to please, be obliging and agreeable; affability, 2. an act or instance of this.

"He turned his heavy mouth into a faint smile and bowed his acknowledgement of my **complaisance**." –H.G. WELLS, *The Island of Dr. Moreau*

coquette (ko KET) - *n.* a flirt, 2. one who is playful.

"'I am curious at any business that leads you to turn my landlady into a **coquette**, Uncle.'" —DAVID LISS, *A Conspiracy of Paper*

gregarious (greh GAR e us or greh GER e us) - *adj.* tending to live or move in groups, 2. seeking and enjoying the company of others, sociable.

"I ... listened to the **gregarious** Charles Martin lecture about England with such passion and eloquence that I grew enamored of the country and its people long before I stood on Hadrian's Wall and wrote thank-you notes to Colonel Martin for handing me the country of England as a gift." –PAT CONROY, *My Losing Season*

irenic (eye REH nik, also eye REE nik) - *adj.* conciliatory; preferring peace or moderation.

"In between these extremes of the warlike and the **irenic** are..." –TUNKU VARADARAJAN, *The Wall Street Journal*, 5/17/02

jocose (joh KOS, also juh KOS) - *adj.* merry, humorous, given to joking.

"The **jocose** suggestion of M. Verhaeren about a certain resemblance as connected with the shrivelled face applied with vivid, ghastly and unnatural horror to none other than the sensitive Arthur Jermyn." –H.P. LOVECRAFT, *Facts Concerning the Late Arthur Jermyn and His Family*

jocund (juh KUND, also joh KUND) - *adj.* given to high spirits; cheerful; merry.

"'Ah!' sighed the king—and for a fleeting instant all King Cole **jocundity** was gone." –ABRAHAM MERRITT, *The Ship of Ishtar*

lightsome (LITE suhm) - *adj.* bright, well lighted, 2. lighthearted; free from care; without worry or sorrow, 3. moving lightly; lively, nimble, quick, graceful.

*see other **lightsome** entry for citation, p. 27*

minx (MINKS) - *n.* a pert or flirtatious girl, 2. an insolent girl.

"As the magnificence and originality of my worldview became explicit through conversation, the Minkoff **minx** began attacking me on all levels, even kicking me under the table rather vigorously at one point." –JOHN KENNEDY TOOLE, *A Confederacy of Dunces*

puckish (puh KISH) - *adj.* whimsical, impish, mischievous.

*see **Puck** for citation, p. 167*

risible (RIH zuh bul) - *adj.* capable of or inclined to laughing, 2. causing laughter, 3. associated with laughter.

*see other **risible** entry for citation, p. 99*

sanguine (SAN gwen) - *adj.* having the color of blood; red, 2. ruddy, as the complexion, 2. optimistic; cheerful; anticipating the best.

"The prospects of the newly married couple were certainly not very brilliant even to the most **sanguine** mind." –THOMAS HARDY, *Jude the Obscure*

solicitous (suh LIH suh tus, also suh LIS tus) - *adj.* expressing concern, care or attention: solicitous of her welfare, 2. showing anxious desire; eager: solicitous to make friends, 3. full of anxiety or apprehension; troubled.

"Well, this was his own, his hearth; these were his birches, catalpas, horse chestnuts. His rotten dreams of peace. The patrimony of his children—a sunken corner of Massachusetts for Marco, the little piano for June painted a loving green by her **solicitous** father." –SAUL BELLOW, *Herzog*

solicitude (suh LIH suh TOOD, also suh LIH suh TYOOD) - *n.* the expression of care, concern, 2. the show of excessive care, concern or protectiveness.

"Both Montgomery and Moreau displayed particular **solicitude** to keep the beasts ignorant of the taste of blood." –H.G. WELLS, *The Island of Dr. Moreau*

winsome (WINT sum) - *adj.* pleasing, engaging, charming; winning and cheerful.

"Chad Bradford ... never allowed the television cameras to see his **winsome** smile, even when he sat in the dugout after a successful outing." –MICHAEL LEWIS, *Moneyball*

DIFFICULT

(ALSO SEE THE LOWLY AND CORRUPT— NASTY ABUSIVE TYPES)

asperity (a SPER uh tee, also uh SPER uh tee) - *n.* roughness, harshness, 2. ill temper.

"Murray's notes offer a tolerant and genial-enough response to this kind of complaint, though a faint sense of his Calvinist **asperity** glimmers between the lines." –SIMON WINCHESTER, *The Professor and the Madman*

bantam (BAN tem) - *n.* one of a breed of small domestic fowl, 2. a small but aggressive person, 3. *adj.* like a bantam; small and aggressive (from Bantam, Indonesia).

"**Bantam**, thin-muscled, swift, almost frail, he had an absolutely unreasonable face." –Saul Bellow, *The Adventures of Augie March*

captious (KAP shus) - *adj.* likely to find faults in others, raise objections, quibbling, 2. seeking to confuse or entrap in argument.

"Then the old woman trudged out to get a girl for Hungry Joe, dipping her **captious** head sadly." –JOSEPH HELLER, *Catch-22*

disputatious (DIS pyuh TAY shus) - *adj.* provoking debate, dispute; contentious.

"The surging, **disputatious** throng that milled there was clamorous and bizarre with the sounds and colors of the East." –ROBERT E. HOWARD, *The Spell of Conan*

impertinent (im PER ten ent, also im PERT nent) - *adj.* insolent; impudent; ill-mannered, 2. not pertinent; irrelevant.

"'Don't be **impertinent** with me, cadet,' she said." –PAT CONROY, *The Lords of Discipline*

impudent (IM pyuh dent) - *adj.* contemptuous; acting with brash or bold behavior; showing disrespect.

"Among those who did the honours of the town was a little abbé from Périgord, one of those assiduous people who are always alert, always obliging, **impudent**, fawning, accommodating, always on the look-out for the arrival of foreigners, ready to tell them all the scandals of the town and to procure them pleasures at any price." –FRANCOIS VOLTAIRE, *Candide*, transl. by Richard Aldington

inimical (ih NIH muh kul) - *adj.* hostile, showing malevolence, unfriendly, 2. adverse, in opposition; as an enemy.

"Some iron presence... she felt pressing upon her, stronger and stronger. Some

thing coldly **inimical** to all things human."
–C.L. MOORE, *Jirel of Joiry*

insolent (INT suh lent) - *adj.* insulting in manner or words, arrogant, rude.

"He looked at me **insolently**. 'Your education is only half completed, then.'"
–JACK LONDON, *The Sea Wolf*

invidious (in VIH dee us) - adj. causing discontent, envy, animosity, 2. envious, 3. unpleasant or objectionable, so as to create harm or a slight.

"They are convinced that if she were not in this particular class, their own grades would go up dramatically. She invited **invidious** comparison, and they wish to hell she'd quit it." –RICHARD RUSSO, *Straight Man*

irascible (i RAS a bul) - *adj.* easily angered, short-tempered.

"Pathologically obsessed with his place in history, [John Adams] was envious or **irascible**: He hated Franklin, hated John Jay, hated Hamilton, hated the French and hated the British, once calling London a 'fat, greasy metropolis.'" –JAY WINIK, *The Wall Street Journal*, 3/24/05

misanthrope (MIH sen thrope) - *n.* an individual who hates society and people in general.

"Mel threw a towel that landed between me and Dave Bornhorst, then stormed out into the night like a Tennessee Williams character—Mel Thompson starring as Stanley Kowalski, **misanthropic**, brutish in his exit, in his manner, in his essence." –PAT CONROY, *My Losing Season*

narky (NAR kee) - *adj.* (slang) irritating, annoying, irritable, sarcastic.

*cited in definition of **snarky**, p. 14*

obstreperous (ub STREH puh rus, also ob STREH puh rus) - *adj.* noisily defiant, unruly, clamorous, vociferous.

"...the aimless, riotous celebration continued. It was a raw, violent, guzzling saturnalia that spilled **obstreperously** through the woods to the officers' club." –JOSEPH HELLER, *Catch-22*

pugnacious (pug NAY shus) - *adj.* aggressive, combative, war-like, belligerent.

"He had a brutal, **pugnacious** face."
–JEFFREY EUGENIDES, *Middlesex*

querulous (KWER yuh lus, also KWER uh lus) - *adj.* often complaining, critical; inclined to find fault.

"Yet there was one breach in the wall of security and a note of **querulousness** entered his voice as he said, 'Why did you leave him, Gladia?'" –ISAAC ASIMOV, *The Robots of Dawn*

riley (RYE lee) - *adj.* thick, turbid, muddy, 2. angry, irritable.

"Antoine will ... say something that's a bringdown, something that gets Manx **riley** and griped, and he is already feeling tense enough, with his stomach acting up." –DON DELILLO, *Underworld*

sardonic (sahr DAH nik) - *adj.* scornfully, ironically, or cynically mocking.

"It was his face that held Kenton. **Sardonic** and malicious." –ABRAHAM MERRITT, *The Ship of Ishtar*

snarky (SNAR kee) - *adj.* (slang) irritable or short-tempered; irascible; "narky."

"Radar's cheeky, sometimes **snarky** approach to celebrity and culture attracted news media attention when the magazine was first published, but attempts to line up financing fizzled." –DAVID CARR, *The New York Times*, 10/19/04

snide (SNYD) - *adj.* tricky; deceptive, 2. contemptible, 3. disparaging in a sly or deceptive manner.

"It made me sick to my stomach to watch my father's **snide** face as my team got taken apart." –PAT CONROY, *My Losing Season*

supercilious (soo pur SIH lee us) - *adj.* contemptuously superior, haughty, disdainful.

"She gave Erica a **supercilious** smile." –TOM WOLFE, *I Am Charlotte Simmons*

truculent (TRUH kyuh lunt) - *adj.* fierce; savage; ferocious; barbarous, 2. cruel; destructive; ruthless.

"'You'll, perhaps, batten down your hatches till you're spoke, my friend,' cried Silver **truculently** to this speaker." –ROBERT LOUIS STEVENSON, *Treasure Island*

virulent (VIR uh lunt, also VIR yuh lunt) - *adj.* extremely poisonous or harmful, marked by a severe or rapid ability to overcome the body's defenses. 2. hostile, antagonistic, full of malice.

"A **virulent** woman named Solange, who has coal black hair with an angry streak of white—her mean streak, as I've come to think of it—was in the process of observing that the reason Leo always writes about pussy is that he is one." –RICHARD RUSSO, *Straight Man*

COURAGEOUS AND COWARDLY

(ALSO SEE THE LOWLY AND CORRUPT— COWARDS AND MORAL WEAKLINGS)

chary (CHAR ee, also CHAIR ee) - *adj.* hesitant or cautious; hesitant to grant or expend.

"Borman ... declined an offer ... Anders was not so **chary**; he accepted an appointment as executive secretary of the National Aeronautics and Space Council." –JIM LOVELL AND JEFFREY KLUGER, *Lost Moon: The Perilous Voyage of Apollo 13*

circumspect (SUR kum SPEKT) - *adj.* considerate of all that is pertinent; heedful of consequences.

"A posthumously printed note of Voltaire's on this passage runs as follows: 'Notice the author's extreme discretion; up till now there has never been any Pope called Urban X; he shrank from giving a bastard to a known Pope. What **circumspection**! What conscientious delicacy!'" –FRANCOIS VOLTAIRE, *Candide*, transl. by Richard Aldington

craven (KRAY vuhn) - *adj.* lacking any courage, cowardly, fainthearted.

"He saw... himself waking to find her dead, [then] fleeing the hotel like a **craven** killer." —GREG ILES, *Sleep No More*

diffidence (DIH fuh duhnts, also DIH fuh DENTS) - *n.* a hesitance in acting or asserting oneself due to a lack of self-confidence; shyness.

"Where she had once been softspoken, even **diffident**, now she could hardly keep from interrupting Miro every time he spoke." —ORSON SCOTT CARD, *Children of the Mind*

doughty (DAUGH tee) - *adj.* fearlessly resolute, courageous.

"Like all good histories, it opens a window onto the past—in this case the exotic, pestilential and perilous world of those **doughty** men and women who braved the high seas more than two hundred years ago." —SARA WHEELER, *The New York Times Book Review,* 7/18/04

gallant (guh LANT, also GAH lunt) - *adj.* brave, valliant, honorable, 2. marked by a showy dress or appearance; dashing, 3. chivalrous; self-sacrificing, especially toward women.

"They are now well into their nineties and immensely **gallant**." —KATHARINE GRAHAM, *Personal History*

galliard (GAL yerd) - *adj.* gay, lively, sprightly, 2. *n.* a fashionable man, 3. a courageous, spirited man.

"He was still an old **galliard**, with white Buffalo Bill vandyke, and he swanked around, still healthy and fleshy, in white suits, looking things over with big sex-amused eyes." —SAUL BELLOW, *The Adventures of Augie March*

indefatigable (IN di FAH ti guh bul) - *adj.* extremely persistent and untiring.

"Colonel Cathcart was **indefatigable** that way, an industrious, intense, dedicated military tactician who calculated day and night in the service of himself." —JOSEPH HELLER, *Catch-22*

indomitable (in DAH muh tuh bul) - *adj.* incapable of being subdued or overcome; unconquerable.

"... the almost frighteningly **indomitable** Derek Jeter, who would not even consider leaving the last inning against Arizona, although he was in so much pain from a collision with a base runner that he thought his foot might be broken" —KEVIN BAKER, *The New York Times Book Review,* 10/3/04

ineluctable (ih ni LUK tuh bul) - *adj.* unavoidable, not to be resisted or changed, inevitable.

"This afternoon of love is fascinating, he doesn't want to miss any part of it, not a move, not a word, but the end is drawing near, **ineluctable**, and he must watch the time running out." —MILAN KUNDERA, *Ignorance*

intrepid (in TRE pid) - *adj.* fearless; bold; brave, resolutely courageous.

"... the proud **intrepid** fraternity of Institute men ..." —PAT CONROY, *The Lords of Discipline*

inviolable (in VY uh luh bul) - *adj.* safe from assault or trespass, 2. impregnable.

"The look on his face was her **inviolable** protection against the smirks, the Sarc 3 glances, and the mock ruminations of Nicole and Crissy." —TOM WOLFE, *I Am Charlotte Simmons*

inviolate (in VY uh lut) - *adj.* not violated or profaned; intact; safe.

"She went away terribly indignant, and I shouted after her again that the secret would remain sacred and **inviolate**." —FYODOR DOSTOYEVSKY, *The Brothers Karamazov,* transl. by David Magarshack

milquetoast (MILK TOST) - *n.* an unassertive, timid or meek person (from Caspar Milquetoast, a comic-strip character created by Harold Tucker Webster 1885–1952).

"The jokes would also extend to Cogan's deputy, the **milquetoast** Tom Twetten, who, both decided, bore a striking resemblance to the children's television host Mr. Rogers." —GEORGE CRILE, *Charlie Wilson's War*

moxie (MAHK see) - *n.* (slang) energy, pep, determination; ability to overcome obstacles with spirit (originally the name of a soft drink).

"In 2003, Stephenson published *Quicksilver,* the first volume in a trilogy meant to dwarf, in sheer tonnage if not literary **moxie**, everything Stephenson had previously written." —STEPHEN METCALF, *The New York Times Book Review, 4/18/04*

parlous (PAR lus) - *adj.* perilous; dangerous, risky, 2. shrewd, clever, dangerously mischievous.

"Even without Germany, the pound was already in a **parlous** state." —RON CHERNOW, *The House of Morgan*

preux (PROH) - *adj.* brave, valiant, gallant.

"Ibn Zabul, the Mameluke historian who deplored his caste's downfall, speaks for generations of **preux** chevaliers in the speech by the Mameluke chieftain, Kurtbay." —JOHN KEEGAN, *A History of Warfare*

pusillanimous (PYU suh LAH nuh mus) - *adj.* cowardly; lacking courage or resolution; timid, fainthearted.

"David Dempsey asked in *The New York Times Book Review* if Thidwick's bigheartedness was 'simply a form of moral **pusillanimity**.'" —JUDITH AND NEIL MORGAN, *Dr. Seuss & Mr. Geisel*

recreant (REK ree uhnt) - *adj.* showing disloyalty, cowardly, 2. *n.* a disloyal person, a deserter, a coward.

"'Come hither!' he cried to his servants. 'Come if you are not all **recreant**!'" —J.R.R. TOLKIEN, *The Return of the King*

sportif (SPOR tif) - *adj.* sporty; of or relating to sports, 2. expression of interest in or pursuit of athletic sports, 3. of a garment: suitable for sporting or informal wear, 4. *n.* a sportsman.

"The midget his pal Glaeason is talking about, the three-foot seven-inch **sportif** who came to bat one time for the St. Louis Browns some six weeks ago in a stunt that was also an act, Edgar believes, of political subversion." —DON DELILLO, *Underworld*

stalwart (STOHL wurt) - *adj.* notably strong, sturdy, 2. unwavering, uncompromising, resolute.

"The president was **stalwart** that they absolutely had done the right thing in removing Saddam." —BOB WOODWARD, *Plan of Attack*

timorous (TIH muh rus, also TIM rus) - *adj.* fearful, afraid, timid.

"The fact that no prices are attached only

adds to their **timorousness**, for they fear to ask and discover themselves insufficiently affluent." —MICHEL FABER, *The Crimson Petal and the White*

tremulous (TREM yuh lus) - *adj.* trembling, quivering, 2. timid, fearful.

truckle (TRUH kul) - (among other definitions) *v.* to be submissive, subservient; yield weakly.

"Candide is ... a masterpiece essentially French in its knack of putting big problems in small bottles, popularizing without **truckling** to the popular." —PAUL MORAND, *Introduction, Francois Voltaire's Candide*

AGE AND EXPERIENCE

callow (CAH low) - *adj.* immature, lacking in life experience.

"He was much younger ... His face was just a little **callow** but handsome in a very good-natured way." —MARIO PUZO, *Fools Die*

cat's-paw (KATS PAW) - *n.* one person used as another's tool, dupe.

coot (KOOT) - *n.* a short-billed, water bird, 2. a stupid fellow; a simpleton; as in a silly coot.

dotage (DOH tij) - *n.* a state of senility or mental decline, often at the time of old age.

"Turner never lost a sense of wonder, even in his **dotage**." —TIM HILTON, *The New York Times Book Review,* 9/7/03

dotard (DAH turd) - *n.* a person experiencing senility, often in old age.

"'**Dotard**!'" —J.R.R. TOLKIEN, *The Return of the King*

fatuous (FAH choo us, also FAH tyoo us) - *adj.* imbecilic, obnoxiously stupid, vacantly silly.

"'Let me only get there,' he had said with the **fatuousness** of Crusoe over his big boat, 'and the rest is but a matter of time and energy.'" —THOMAS HARDY, *Jude the Obscure*

feckless (FEK lus) - *adj.* lacking purpose, feeble, ineffective, 2. without skill (feck being Scottish for efficacy).

"'And some in the administration had seen how **feckless** the United Nations had been on this issue and were uncertain as to whether or not the United Nations would be able to get it done.'" —PRESIDENT GEORGE W. BUSH, quoted by Bob Woodward, *Plan of Attack*

fizgig (FIZ GIG) - *n.* a woman considered frivolous or flighty, one who is 'gadding' about.

"... 'late last year we came upon an absolute **fizgig** of a girl, introduced to us by the madam as Lucy Fitzroy, illegitimate daughter of Lord Fitzroy, with horse-riding consequently in her blood.'" —MICHEL FABER, *The Crimson Petal and the White*

fusty (FUS tee) - *adj.* exhibiting a musty or stale odor, 2. old-fashioned; aged; antique.

"And into the interior they all rushed and for several minutes the whole of that dark, horrible, **fusty** old castle echoed with the opening of windows and with everyone's voices crying out at once." —C.S. LEWIS, *The Lion, The Witch and The Wardrobe*

gormless (GORM lus) - *adj.* (of a person) dull; lacking in intelligence, sense or discernment.

"Daisy ... looked just like an ostrich, the same protruding eyes set too widely apart, the receding chin, an expression of **gormless** astonishment." –TAMA JANOWITZ, *A Certain Age*

greenhorn (GREEN HORN) - *n.* a person as yet inexperienced, immature or unsophisticated, 2. a person new (to a country) and not familiar with its customs.

"Nathan Hart, an impoverished **greenhorn** who woos the far more worldly-wise Keni by feeding her installments of his novel-in-progress." –FERNANDA EBERSTADT, *The New York Times Book Review*, 3/20/05

hoary (HOR ee) - *adj.* gray or white as if from age, 2. having white or gray hair due to aging, 3. extremely old, ancient.

"... secrets that were **hoary** when the world was young." –ROBERT E. HOWARD, *The Shadow Kingdom*

incontinent (in KON tuhn unt) - *adj.* lacking in self-restraint or self-contral, 2. lacking the ability to control the body's excretory functions.

"It would have been easy to speak to her there and then, but is seemed scarcely honourable towards his aunt to disregard her request so **incontinently**." –THOMAS HARDY, *Jude the Obscure*

jejune (jih JUNE) - *adj.* without nutritive value, 2. lacking matter; empty; void of substance, 3. childish; juvenile; puerile.

*see **sagacious** entry for citation, p. 105*

Methuselah (meh THOO zuh luh, also meh THYOO zuh luh) - *n.* grandfather of Noah —from the Old Testament (Genesis 5:27) —said to have lived 969 years, 2. extremely old or ancient, 3. a large bottle holding as much as eight ordinary wine bottles (the order of large wine bottles is 'Methuselah, Salmanasar, Balthasar, Nebuchadnezzar'—usually applied respectively to eight, twelve, sixteen, and twenty bottle containers).

"Realizing that my plastic weapon was hardly a match for a long fork wielded by a maddened **Methuselah**, realizing that I was seeing Clyde at his worst, I tried to end our little duel." –JOHN KENNEDY TOOLE, *A Confederacy of Dunces*

naïf (nah EEF) - *adj.* naïve, 2. *n.* one who is naïve.

"The very title of [Sinclair] Lewis's novel ['It Can't Happen Here'] entered long ago into the American language, a sardonic phrase, mocking the sweet **naïfs** who persist in believing that evil dwells anywhere but at home." –PAUL BERMAN, *The New York Times Book Review*, 10/3/04

perspicacity (PUR spuh KAH suh tee) - *n.* acute ability to perceive, discern, understand, or assess.

"'Your father was too **perspicacious** a jobber to believe such a false rumor.'" -DAVID LISS, *A Conspiracy of Paper*

precocious (pri KO shus) - *adj.* exhibiting exceptionally early development or maturity, particularly in mental ability.

"The insight was **precocious**, anticipating as it did the distinction between history as experienced and history as remembered." –JOSEPH J. ELLIS, *Founding Brothers*

priapic (pry AY pik, also pry AH pik) - *adj.* phallic, 2. preoccupied with virility or masculinity.

"[Graham Greene] was relentlessly sexual, ardently **priapic**. 'I think his sexual appetites are voracious, frightening,' one of his close friends remarked, though the man was English and so the word 'frightening' must be taken with a grain of salt." –PAUL THEROUX, *The New York Times Book Review,* 10/17/04

puerile (PYOOR ul, also PYOOR ILE) - *adj.* childish, juvenile, immature.

"Eminem ... veers more toward unmediated hostility and threats of violence, rampant consumerist bragging, casual misogyny, and **puerility**." –NICK HORNBY, *Songbook*

purblind (PUR BLIND) - *adj.* blind or partly blind, 2. lacking vision; slow to understand or discern; dull.

"'I wonder if any other of them are the same **purblind**, simple creatures as I?'" –THOMAS HARDY, *Jude the Obscure*

sagacious (suh GAY shus, also sih GAY shus) - *adj.* of being sage-like; wise; discerning and shrewd.

"It's a good story, marred only by moments of jejune men's-magazine **sagacity**: 'A shipwreck gave a man limitless opportunity to know himself if only he cared to find out.'" –MARK BOWDEN, *The New York Times Book Review,* 7/18/04

senescent (sih NEH sent) - *adj.* becoming old; aging, 2. aging from maturity to death.

"She is almost half-way through her twenties, and the spectre of **senescence** looms." –MICHEL FABER, *The Crimson Petal and the White*

superannuated (SOO pur ANN yuh WAIT ed) - *adj.* too old, discharged or disqualified due to advanced age or infirmity, 2. antiquated; obsolete.

"'Instead of proving him **superannuated**,' Franklin's anti-slavery views showed that 'the qualities of his soul, as well as those of his mind, are yet in their vigor.'" –JOSEPH J. ELLIS, *Founding Brothers*

temerarious (TEH muh RARE ee us, also TEH muh RAR ee us) - *adj.* exhibiting temerity; acting rash or reckless.

"There was a rooster some brakeman's family nearby owned, and he had the instinct or the **temerariousness** to crow in the wet and ashes of the backyard." –SAUL BELLOW, *The Adventures of Augie March*

temerity (teh MER uh tee) - *n.* recklessly bold; stupidly brave; foolhardiness; recklessness.

" ... [this knowledge] lay in the surface of practical anatomy years ago, but no one had the **temerity** to touch it." –H.G. WELLS, *The Island of Dr. Moreau*

tyro (TIE row) - *n.* a beginner to learning; one who is inexperienced; a novice.

> "'We called you an incompetent fool, a **tyro,** a charlatan, a swindler, an egomaniac ...'" —AYN RAND, *The Fountainhead*

tyronic (also tironic) - *adj.* exhibiting inexperience; characteristic of a tyro (tiro); amateurish.

> "'Now how, I wonder, does it happen that you and one servant put into the harbor of Sederado navigating a small merchant ship all by yourselves in most thwart **tyronic** fashion?'" —L. SPRAGUE DE CAMP, *The Tritonian Ring*

verdant (VUHR dunt) - *adj.* green color; green from vegetation, 2. inexperienced in judgement or sophistication.

> *see other* **verdant** *entry for citation, p. 209*

OTHER POSITIVE TRAITS

comity (KAH muh tee, also KOH muh tee) - *n.* courtesy and considerate behaviour towards others, 2. acts of international courtesy, as in the comity of nations.

droll (DROHL) - *adj.* exhibiting a whimsical, comical or amusingly odd quality, 2. *n.* an entertainment exhibited to raise mirth or sport, as a puppet show, a farce, etc.

> "And he had a **droll**, pixie humor which delighted us over the years." —KATHARINE GRAHAM, *Personal History*

epicure (EH pih KYUR) - *n.* one with discriminating and refined tastes, especially in food and wine (after Epicurus [341–270 B.C.], a Greek philosopher).

> "'I like to do things like this.' she said in the delicate voice of an **epicure** in emotions, which left no doubt that she spoke the truth." —THOMAS HARDY, *Jude the Obscure*

estimable (ES tuh muh bul) - *adj.* capable of being estimated, valued, or appraised, 2. valuable, of great worth, 3. (a person) worthy of esteem, 4. (a thing) worthy of consideration or importance.

> "No good comes of any of this, despite Mike Figgis's careful direction of an **estimable** cast that includes Dennis Quaid and Sharon Stone." —JOE MORGENSTERN, *The Wall Street Journal,* 9/19/03

heimisch (HAY mish) - (Yiddish) *adj.* simple; unpretentious, relating to the domestic.

> "A politician in the Cook County Democratic organization who knew the Syndicate, the Juice men, the Policy kings, Cosa Nostra, and all the hoods, still found me good company, **heimisch**, and took me along to the races, the hockey games." —SAUL BELLOW, *Herzog*

inimitable (ih NIH muh tuh bul) - *adj.* defying imitation; matchless; peerless.

> "But Hobbits have never, in fact, studied magic of any kind, and their elusiveness is due solely to a professional skill that heredity and practice, and a close friendship with the earth, have rendered **inimitable** by bigger and clumsier races." —J.R.R. TOLKIEN, *The Fellowship of the Ring*

mensch (MENSH) - (Yiddish) *n.* a person who exhibits honor or integrity; one who is morally just or honorable.

> "... those palmy days when a nebbishy but **menschy** Woody would chew over the bones of Western culture with alluring, unsettled women played by Diane Keaton or Mia Farrow." —JOE MORGENSTERN, *The Wall Street Journal,* 9/19/03

probity (PRO buh tee) - *n.* integrity; honesty.

"'Uniforms ask to be taken seriously, with suggestions of **probity** and virtue.'" –P.J. O'ROURKE quoting Paul Fussell, *The New York Times Book Review,* 12/22/02

vestal (VES tul) - *adj.* virginal; pure and chaste, 2. of or pertaining to Vesta, the Roman virgin goddess of the hearth; hence, pure; chaste.

"It had been no **vestal** who chose that missile for opening her attack on him." –THOMAS HARDY, *Jude the Obscure*

OTHER NEGATIVE TRAITS

execrable (EX si kruh bul) - *adj.* of the poorest quality, 2. hateful; abhorrent; detestable, abominable, atrocious, heinous.

"'No, no, my reputation's **execrable**, I assure you.'" –GUSTAVE FLAUBERT, *Madame Bovary,* transl. by Francis Steegmuller

farshtinkener (far SHTINK en er) - (Yiddish) *n.* a selfish or insecure person; a stinker or a louse, 2. a foul-smelling person or thing.

*see other **farshtinkener** entry for citation*

furshlugginer (fuhr SHLUH ge ner) - (Yiddish) *adj.* a person or thing that has been beaten up or "knocked around."

*see other **furshlugginer** entry for citation*

hapless (HA plus) - *adj.* without luck; unfortunate.

"The apothecary, oppressed by the silence, soon made a few elegiac remarks concerning 'this **hapless** young woman.'" –GUSTAVE FLAUBERT, *Madame Bovary,* transl. by Francis Steegmuller

indecorous (in DEH kuh rus, also IN dih KOR us) - *adj.* in conflict with (accepted standards of) good taste; lack of propriety; unseemly.

"I could not imagine how she had summoned the courage to ask me so improper a thing, and yet she had—and boldly too. She knew she was being **indecorous**, and she cared not a whit." –DAVID LISS, *A Conspiracy of Paper*

meshuggener (me SHOO ge ner) - (Yiddish) *adj.* mad; crazy, 2. *n.* a person who is mad, crazy or stupid.

"Look at the man in the bleachers who's pacing the aisles, a neighborhood crazy, he waves his arms and mumbles, short, chunky, bushy-haired—could be one of the Ritz Brothers or a lost member of the Three Stooges, the Fourth Stooge, called Flippo or Dummy or Shaky or Jakey, and he's distracting the people nearby, they're yelling at him to siddown, goway, **meshuggener**, and he paces and worries, he shakes his head and moans as if he knows something's coming, or came, or went ..." –DON DELILLO, *Underworld*

nebbish (NEB bish) - (Yiddish) *adj.* timid; meek; ineffectual, 2. *n.* an unimportant, insignificant person; a nobody; a nonentity.

"... those palmy days when a **nebbishy** but menschy Woody would chew over the bones of Western culture with alluring, unsettled women played by Diane Keaton or Mia Farrow."–JOE MORGENSTERN, *The Wall Street Journal,* 9/19/03

obsequious (ub SEE kwee us, also ob SEE kwee us) - *adj.* fawning or subservient; excessively eager to please or to obey all instructions.

"... the same bland, polite, **obsequious** seaman of the voyage out." –Robert Louis Stevenson, *Treasure Island*

pharisee (FAR uh see) - *n*. Pharisee —a person belonging to an ancient Jewish sect noted for its strict observance of the rites and ceremonies of the Mosaic law, 2. a hypocritically self-righteous person.

*see other **pharisee** entry for citation, p. 134*

sanctimonious (SANGK tuh mo nee us, also SANGK tuh mo nee yus) - *adj*. affecting piousness or sanctity; hypocritically devout or religious.

schlemiel (shlah MEE el) - (Yiddish) *n*. a chump; a bungler; a "born loser"; one who is clumsy or awkward.

"For he very likely felt that I was the same as before, that my wheels turned too freely, that I was hasty, too enthusiastic, or, in few words, something of a **schlemiel**." –Saul Bellow, *The Adventures of Augie March*

schlepper (SHLEP er) - (Yiddish) *n*. one who moves tediously or awkwardly, 2. a fool; jerk; beggar; one of little value.

"'Has [marriage] saved anybody—the jerks, the fools, the morons, the **schleppers**, the jag-offs, the monkeys, rats, rabbits, or the decent unhappy people, or what you call nice people?'" –Saul Bellow, *The Adventures of Augie March*

schlimazel (shle MAZ el) - (Yiddish) *n*. an accident-prone person, a luckless person, a 'born loser,' 2. hence as *v*. to make a schlimazel of (a person).

"But in truth, let's be honest, it was Marvin who shuffled, Marvin who was the true **schlimazel**, bad-lucked in his own mind." –Don DeLillo, *Underworld*

schmuck (SHMUK) - (Yiddish) *n*. a fool; an incompetent; an idiot, 2. one who is comtemptible or objectionable (originally a taboo-word meaning penis).

"She shut the door, and addressed her companion. '**Schmucks**.'" –Glen David Gold, *Carter Beats the Devil*

schnook (SHNOOK) - (Yiddish) *n*. a stupid, pitifully meek person, easily cheated, easily imposed upon, 2. one who is unimportant.

"'Dear Senator Weicker: You're surprised at what was going on in Tricky Dicky's White House? Don't be a **schnook**.'" –Philip Roth, *American Pastoral*

simpy (SIMP ee) - *adj*. foolish, slow, simple-minded (a simp being a simple or foolish person).

"Eric had a fake stutter he liked to use to texture the conversation, a thing he'd developed to mock himself or his listener, although neither one of them stuttered, or maybe he was imitating some nightclub comic or **simpy** character on TV—it wasn't clear to Matt." –DON DELILLO, *Underworld*

uxorious (uhk SOR ee us, also ug ZOR ee us) - *adj.* excessively fond of one's wife; irrationally doting or submissive to one's wife.

"I regarded my wife a moment. She is a strikingly beautiful woman, if I may be **uxorious** for a moment." –NELSON DE-MILLE, *The Gold Coast*

OTHER PERSONALITY TRAITS

chimerical (kigh MER ih kul, also kuh MER ih kul, kuh MIR ih kul) - *adj.* existing only in fantasy; imaginary; unreal, 2. given to fanciful schemes or plans.

"Similarly, Burgess still seems to be under the apprehension that he has never been taken seriously by that **chimerical** conglomerate, the London Literary World." –MARTIN AMIS, *Visiting Mrs. Nabokov*

contrite (kahn TRITE, also kun TRITE) - *adj.* repentant; penitent; grieving.

"... he said in the **contrite** tone of someone having to pass on to a widow the bills left by her dead husband." –ARTURO PEREZ-REVERTE, *The Flanders Panel*

inscrutable (in SKROO tuh bul) - *adj.* not easily understood or investigated; difficult to fathom; enigmatic.

"It rolled over in bed when he got home before sunrise: a green-eyed monster lying next to his young, **inscrutable** wife, but then Zizmo would blink and the monster would disappear." –JEFFREY EUGENIDES, *Middlesex*

manqué (mahn KAY) - *adj.* unsuccessful or frustrated, as to the fulfillment of one's talent: an artist manqué.

"The barkers were all interesting guys, poets **manqués**, most of them, and spent their time off in City Lights Bookstore, leafing through New Directions paperbacks." –JEFFREY EUGENIDES, *Middlesex*

pixilated (PIK suh LAY ted) - *adj.* mildly unbalanced mentally; bewildered; bemused; confused; intoxicated; tipsy (famously used in the original "Mr. Deeds Goes to Town").

"This powerful but **pixilated** poem was translated into English verse." –LIN CARTER, *Tolkien*

protean (PRO tee un, also pro TEE un) - *adj.* of or pertaining to Proteus; characteristic of Proteus, 2. exceedingly variable; changeable; readily assuming different shapes or forms.

"In cinema, as we all know, there are actors and there are stars. The actors—**protean**, endlessly versatile—are personified by Alec Guinness or, more recently, by women like Cate Blanchett. The stars are always, inexorably, grandly, themselves: John Wayne, Katherine Hepburn, Jack Nicholson." –CLAIRE MESSUD, *The New York Times Book Review*, 10/3/04

scrutable (SKROO tuh bul) - *adj.* not inscrutable; capable of being understood.

"Mirek was willing to do everything for his fate (for its grandeur, lucidity, beauty, style, and **scrutability**)." –MILAN KUNDERA, *The Art of the Novel*

2. PERSONAL ENERGY

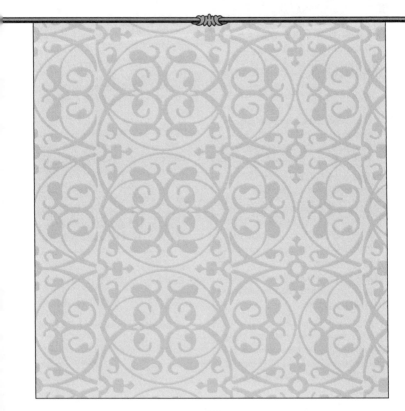

ENERGETIC

actuate (AK choo WAIT, also AK shoo WAIT) - *v.* to set into motion, 2. to move to action, to motivate.

"If I do not interfere, then it may be that you, Dr. Amadiro, and you, Dr. Fastolfe, **actuated** by stubbornness or even vindictiveness, will both marshal your forces and accuse each other of all sorts of things." –ISAAC ASIMOV, *The Robots of Dawn*

alacrity (uh LA kruh tee) - *n.* eagerness, cheerful enthusiasm, sprightliness, liveliness, briskness.

"From the start, Woodward and Bernstein followed the trail of the Watergate burglars with **alacrity** and skill, and a lot of elbow grease." –KATHARINE GRAHAM, *Personal History*

brazen (BRAY zuhn) - *(in addition to the adj.)* v. to brazen it out—to act in a bold or impudent way as if not needing not be ashamed.

"We **brazened** our way into a movie and sat in the back row [with our eagle]." –SAUL BELLOW, *The Adventures of Augie March*

brio (BREE O) - (Italian) *n.* vivacity, liveliness, vigor.

"'Most people who are likely to read this book will already know what they feel about [Bob] Dylan, though they might not always know quite why they feel it or what they think,' is how he opens the book, with typical **brio** and warmth." –JONATHAN LETHEM, *The New York Times Book Review*, 6/13/04

buck (BUHK) - (among other definitions) *n.* a dashing young man, a young man of high spirits, a dandy.

"My words all but slapped him in the face, and he collected himself once again to the posture of an insouciant **buck**." –DAVID LISS, *A Conspiracy of Paper*

caper (KAY pur) - (among other definitions) *n.* a frolicsome leap or spring; a skip; a jump, 2. a prank or escapade, 3. *v.* to jump or frolic about.

"'And even suppose,' he said with a **caper**, 'that the only thing I had to my credit was my perfect record as a volunteer fireman!'" –GUSTAVE FLAUBERT, *Madame Bovary*, transl. by Francis Steegmuller

caprice (KUH PREES) - *n.* a tendency to do things impulsively, 2. sudden or unpredictable changeableness, capriciousness.

"Emma was becoming **capricious**, hard to please." –GUSTAVE FLAUBERT, *Madame Bovary*, transl. by Francis Steegmuller

celerity (suh LEHR uh tee) - *n.* swiftness; speed.

"O Thomas Cook & Son ... unhesitatingly and instantly, with ease and **celerity**, could you send me to Darkest Africa or Innermost Thibet." –JACK LONDON, *The People of the Abyss*

disport (DIH sport) - *v.* to engage oneself in spirited play, to frolic or gambol.

"And yes, it's true, Charlie has practiced this kind of erotic **disport** himself, off and on, with one or another single young woman working in the production department or somesuch level of the mothership." –DON DELILLO, *Underworld*

élan (AY lahn) (e pronounced as a hard a)- *n.* enthusiasm; vivacity, impetuousness; ardor.

"He struck me, in the few minutes we spoke, as a man with a primitive sort of **élan**, somewhat like a conquering soldier from an inferior civilization who has quartered himself in the great villa of a vanquished nobleman." –NELSON DEMILLE, *The Gold Coast*

exigency (EK suh juhnt see, also ig ZI juhnt see) - *n.* the condition or quality of being exigent, 2. conditions that create a situation of urgency or a need for immediate or critical action, 3. the needs, demands or requirements of a particular situation.

"The pressures and exigencies generated by the American Revolution called out and gathered their talents." –JOSEPH J. ELLIS, *Founding Brothers*

exigent (EK suh juhnt) - *adj.* requiring or demanding immediate aid or action, 2. demanding or exacting more than is reasonable.

Gadarene (GA duh REEN) - *adj.* pertaining to Gadara, 2. a headlong rush; a swift and uncontrolled movement (from "the Gadarene swine" [Luke 8:26–39] that ran into the sea after demons possessed them).

"The more visceral Stern's subject, the fancier his writing: A pig escaping the slaughterer is described as scrambling for the stock pond in a '**gadarene** slalom,'" – FERNANDA EBERSTADT, *The New York Times Book Review,* 3/20/05

galvanize (GAL vuh NIZE) - *v.* to stimulate by means of an electric current, 2. to arouse or stimulate as if by shock, 3. to cover metal with a layer of zinc.

hard scrabble (HARD SKRA bul) - *adj.* pertaining to a place barren of fertile soil, 2. working hard to derive a meager living from barren soil, poverty.

*see other **hard scrabble** entry for citation, p. 198*

kundalini (kun duh LEE nee, also KUHN duh LEE nee) - *n.* a life-force or (female) energy held or coiled at the base of the spine (through yoga this energy is said to be sent to the head to bring about enlightenment).

"In those days, chiropractors had a somewhat dubious reputation. People didn't come to Uncle Pete to free up their **kundalini**. He cracked necks, straightened spines, and made custom arch supports out of foam rubber." –JEFFREY EUGENIDES, *Middlesex*

lightsome (LITE suhm) - *adj.* bright, well lighted, 2. lighthearted; free from care; without worry or sorrow, 3. moving lightly; lively, nimble, quick, graceful.

"... the jogger went round the track, alone, thirty stories up, and it was a beautiful thing to see, the woman's **lightsome** stride" –DON DELILLO, *Underworld*

motile (MO tuhl, also MO TILE) - *adj.* exhibiting movement, 2. having the ability to move; mobile.

"Hungry Joe was a throbbing, ragged mass of **motile** irritability." –JOSEPH HELLER, *Catch-22*

panache (puh NASH, also puh NAHSH) - *n.* a plume of feathers, often used for a headdress or helmet, 2. verve, flamboyance; flair.

"The partner, an invective-spewing black dwarf named Marcus, is played with great **panache** by Tony Cox." –JOE MORGENSTERN, *The Wall Street Journal*, 12/5/03

precipitate (pri SIH puh TATE) - *v.* to throw an object or person from a great height, 2. to cause something to happen suddenly, quickly or before required, 3. to come out of a liquid solution into solid form, 4. to have water in the air fall to the ground, for example as rain, snow, sleet, or hail.

"We agreed that the *Post* ought to work its way out of the very supportive editorial position it had taken [re: the Vietnam War], but the we couldn't be **precipitate**; we had to move away gradually from where we had been." –KATHARINE GRAHAM, *Personal History*

raffish (RA fish) - *adj.* suggesting crudeness; vulgar; showy, 2. rakish; jaunty.

"The teams were all folded into each other, basketball players towering over golfers, swimmers looking svelte and **raffish** beside linebackers." –PAT CONROY, *My Losing Season*

recrudesce (REE kroo DES) - *v.* to become active again, to break out again after a period of abatement or inactivity.

"'What can I tell you?' he demanded, with a **recrudescence** of fierceness." –JACK LONDON, *The Sea Wolf*

skylark (SKY LARK) - *n.* a common Old World bird known for its habit of singing while in flight. 2. *v.* to frolic; romp.

"'I can't name the voice: but it's someone **skylarking**—someone that's flesh and blood, and you may lay to that.'" –ROBERT LOUIS STEVENSON, *Treasure Island*

tumultuary (tu MUHL chu WER ee, also tyu MUHL chu WER ee, tuh MUHL chu WER ee) - *adj.* marked by confusion, lawlessness, 2. without order, turbulent; haphazard; random, 3. of troops: gathered hastily and promiscuously, without order or system.

"'Oh, I know you would give me a **tumultuary** time beneath the drugget; but how about the long pull, when teeth decay and skins wrinkle and sag and tempers grow short?'" –L. SPRAGUE DE CAMP, *The Tritonian Ring*

vim (VIM) - *n.* vigor; energy; liveliness; force.

"The sailors must have learned whatever project was on hand, and the **vim** and snap they put into their work attested their enthusiasm." –JACK LONDON, *The Sea Wolf*

vivify (VIH vuh FI) - *v.* to bring to life, 2. to impart vitality.

"During my death-scene, the distracted director, McKendrick, asked me to **vivify** matters with a death-scene death scream." –MARTIN AMIS, *Visiting Mrs. Nabokov*

yare (YAR, also YER) - *adj.* ready; prepared, 2. brisk; alert; active; quick, 3. responding quickly and truly to the helm: said of a ship, *adv.* quickly; promptly.

> "'Back to the ship! And **yare**!'" –L. Sprague de Camp and Lin Carter, *Conan the Buccaneer*

LACKING ENERGY

(ALSO SEE THE LOWLY AND CORRUPT—LAZY SLOBS)

acedia (also **accidie**) (uh SEE DEE uh) - *n.* sloth; torpor; listlessness; apathy.

> "'These experiments with cells, March, will give the clue to the origin of boredom in higher organisms. To what used to be called the sin of **acedia**. The old fellows were right, for it is a sin.'" –Saul Bellow, *The Adventures of Augie March*

dilatory (DIH luh TOR ee) - *adj.* causing or tending to cause delay; intentionally delaying (someone or something), 2. slow or tardy.

> "Questioning him before, she had spoken more quickly, but now she receded again into slowness, raising a mountain of **dilatory** will in his way." –Saul Bellow, *Herzog*

effete (eh FEET, also ih FEET) - *adj.* having lost fertility; spent; sterile, 2. marked by a lack of vigor, stamina; showing a weakness of character; decadent, soft, overrefined, etc.

> "[The Argentine team has] the edge on an England team that is surprisingly **effete** for a land with such a storied soccer history." –Tunku Varadarajan, *The Wall Street Journal*, 6/7/02

enervate (eh nuhr VATE) - *v.* weaken morally and/or mentally (opposite of energize).

> "I have heard more than a little hissing and roaring through the factory door, but my presently somewhat **enervated** condition precludes a descent into that particular inferno at the moment." –John Kennedy Toole, *A Confederacy of Dunces*

ennui (ahn WEE) - *n.* boredom; dissatisfaction; listlessness.

> "Only weeks after exiting the White House, [Theodore Roosevelt] left the United States—partly to give Taft, his hand-picked replacement, the run of the place, partly, as O'Toole puts it, as an 'antidote to … **ennui**.'" –Jeff Shesol, reviewing Patricia O'Toole's 'When Trumpets Call,' *The New York Times Book Review*, 3/20/05

etiolate (EE tee uh LATE) - *v.* to render (a person or plant) unhealthy or pale and colorless by excluding it from sunlight, 2. to deprive of vigor or strength; to weaken.

> "In this (cinema-complex) warren the **etiolated** cineasts grope and blink about their business." –Martin Amis, *Visiting Mrs. Nabokov*

feckless (FEK lus) - *adj.* lacking purpose, feeble, ineffective, 2. without skill (feck being Scottish for efficacy).

"'And some in the administration had seen how **feckless** the United Nations had been on this issue and were uncertain as to whether or not the United Nations would be able to get it done.'" —PRESIDENT GEORGE W. BUSH, quoted by Bob Woodward, *Plan of Attack*

hang fire (HANG FIRE) - *v.* see quotes.

"**hang fire** - v. phr. - To be delayed or stalled; fail to materialize: The whole deal's hanging fire till the jerk decides what to do next." —ROBERT L. CHAPMAN, *American Slang*

"He **hung fire** before their eyes, every muscle in his body cocked against Rosacoke but waiting as if he would give her this last chance to offer what he needed before he called on the church at large." —REYNOLDS PRICE, *A Long and Happy Life*

languid (LANG gwid) - *adj.* lacking in vigor or vitality; drooping; exhausted; weak; faint, 2. lacking interest; dull; spiritless, 3. sluggish; slow.

"... a certain time of day when I used to feel happy. The cries of the newspaper vendors in the already **languid** air, the last few birds in the square, the shouts of the sandwich sellers, the screech of the streetcars turning sharply through the upper town, and that hum in the sky before night engulfs the port." —ALBERT CAMUS, *The Stranger*

languor (LAN guhr) - *n.* without vigor or vitality; weakness; faintness; fatigue; weariness, 2. listlessness; indifference, 3. softness of mood or feeling; lassitude of spirit, 4. a want of activity, lethargy.

"... long after that death yell was still ringing in my brain, silence had re-established its empire, and only the rustle of the redescending birds and the boom of the distant surges disturbed the **languor** of the afternoon." —ROBERT LOUIS STEVENSON, *Treasure Island*

lassitude (LA suh tood, also LA suh tyood) - *n.* weariness; fatigue; languor, a state of listlessness.

"Susan Calvin, except for two hours of resentful **lassitude**, experienced nothing approaching sleep." —ISAAC ASIMOV, *I, Robot*

neurasthenia (NUR ehs THEE nee uh, also NYUR ehs THEE nee uh) - *n.* a disorder marked by fatigue and lassitude, loss of energy, lack of motivation and feelings of inadequacy.

"I had ... even written ... a number of lugubrious short stories in what I thought was the Jocycean manner, mainly devoted to the subject of death and all centered on a **neurasthenic** young hero whom no one truly understood, whose soul was much given to swooning and who went under different names but was always me." —JOHN BANVILLE, *The New York Times Book Review*, 6/13/04

quiescent (kwigh EE suhnt, also KWEE ee suhnt) - *adj.* inactive or still; at rest; dormant.

"... the level land lay **quiescent** beneath the moon" —ROBERT E. HOWARD, *Eons of the Night*

soporific (SAH puh RIH fik) - *adj.* tending to induce sleep or sleepiness.

"He was scarcely conscious of her now, for this utterly soft end of a hard day was as

soporific as the fabled nepenthe and he could feel himself slipping away." —ISAAC ASIMOV, *The Robots of Dawn*

supine (SUH PINE, also SOO PINE) - *adj.* lying on the back with the face upward, 2. exhibiting lethargy, passivity or inertia.

"To sit **supinely** waiting, a helpless decoy." —C.L. MOORE, *Jirel of Joiry*

torpid (TOR pid) - *adj.* sluggish; slow; inactive, 2. without motion or feeling; lethargic; apathetic.

"So he shook off from him the **torpid** sleep that had come upon him in the hot and scented jungle." —LORD DUNSANY, *The Complete Pegana*

torpor (TOR puhr) - *n.* apathy; dullness, 2. mental or physical inactivity; sluggishness; stagnation or cessation of movement or function.

"On the pavement, by the portico of Christ's Church, where the stone pillars rise toward the sky in a stately row, were whole rows of men lying asleep or drowsing, and all too deep sunk in **torpor** to rouse or be made curious by our intrusion." —JACK LONDON, *The People of the Abyss*

vapid (VA pid, also VAY pid) - *adj.* lacking liveliness, animation, or interest; dull, 2. lacking taste, zest, or flavor; flat.

*see other **vapid** entry for citation, p. 107*

wan (WAHN) - *adj.* pale, sickly-looking, 2. dim, faint, feeble or weak, 3. bland, uninterested.

"Langdon gave a **wan** nod and counted himself lucky." —DAN BROWN, *Angels & Demons*

PHYSICAL MOTION

desultory (DE suhl TOR ee) - *adj.* jumping or passing from one thing or subject to another without order of rational connection; without logical sequence; disconnected; aimless.

"The scouts topped the ridges, gazed about; then most of them turned and trotted back down the slopes. Cormac wondered at their **desultory** manner of scouting." —ROBERT E. HOWARD, *Bran Mak Morn*

fossick (FAH sik) - *v.* to search for gold by looking through abandoned mines, 2. to rummage; to search; to ferret out.

"Emmeline leaps off the bed and begins to **fossick** in the dusty, furry piles of books that litter her house, searching for *The Ruined Temple*, an autobiography written by an evangelist with a wasting disease." —MICHEL FABER, *The Crimson Petal and the White*

itinerant (eye TIH nuh rent) - *adj.* habitually traveling from place to place, 2. *n.* one who travels from place to place.

"Between the other [hot dog] vendors—totally beaten and ailing **itinerants** whose names are something like Buddy, Pal, Sport, Top, Buck, and Ace—and my customers, I am apparently trapped in a limbo of lost souls." —JOHN KENNEDY TOOLE, *A Confederacy of Dunces*

jounce (JOWNTS) - *v.* to jolt; to shake, especially by rough riding or by driving over obstructions.

"The rumbling, the rattling, the aluminum clanking, the creaking, the squeaking, the jerking, the **jouncing** of the dollies rico cheted off the walls." —Tom Wolfe, *I Am Charlotte Simmons*

maunder (MON der) - *v.* to move slowly and idly, 2. to speak incoherently or indistinctly.

"... he thought about the penitentes, men in black hoods dragging heavy wooden crosses through the desert, a hundred years ago, or fifty years, and lashing themselves with sisal and hemp, all that Sister Edgarish stuff, and speaking fabricated words—the **maunder** of roaming holy men." —Don DeLillo, *Underworld*

perambulate (puh RAM byu LATE) - *v.* to travel about on foot.

"'I'm gonna put you down in the French Quarter.'

'What?' Ignatius thundered. 'Do you think that I am going to **perambulate** about in that sinkhole of vice?'" —John Kennedy Toole, *A Confederacy of Dunces*

peregrine (PER uh GRUHN, also PER uh GREEN) - *adj.* foreign; alien; belonging to another country; imported, 2. migratory or roaming.

"'Tokyo Doesn't Love Us Anymore' is the story of an unnamed fellow living in the not-so-distant future who roams the globe selling a miracle substance that erases bad memories ... [he] pauses in his **peregrinations** only long enough to deliver tough existential asides" – Sam Lipsyte, *The New York Times Book Review*, 10/17/04

peripatetic (PEHR uh puh TEH tik) - *adj.* Aristotlian, relating to the philosophy of Aristotle, who walked about in the Lyceum while he was teaching, 2. pedestrian; itin-

erant; journeying from place to place, 3. *n.* a follower of Aristotle, 4. a pedestrian; an itinerant; one who walks about.

"This was the third grammar school in my **peripatetic** school career." —Martin Amis, *Visiting Mrs. Nabokov*

retrograde (REH truh GRADE) - *adj.* moving or tending backward, 2. reverting to an inferior condition, 3. counterproductive to a desired outcome.

*see other **retrograde** entry for citation, p. 106*

sidle (SIGH dul) - *v.* to move or turn sideways, to move along with one side forward (from sidelong).

"At last the breeze came; the schooner **sidled** and drew nearer in the dark." —Robert Louis Stevenson, *Treasure Island*

vamoose (vuh MOOS, vah MOOS) - *v.* to leave quickly, to depart in haste (slang, from the Spanish vamos).

vertiginous (vuhr TIH juh nus) - *adj.* revolving or turning, as if on an axis, 2. causing vertigo or dizziness.

"Bursting the bonds of its genre, *Hellboy* fills the screen with gorgeous imagery, **vertiginous** action and a surprising depth of feeling." —Joe Morgenstern, *The Wall Street Journal*, 4/2/04

3. EMOTIONS

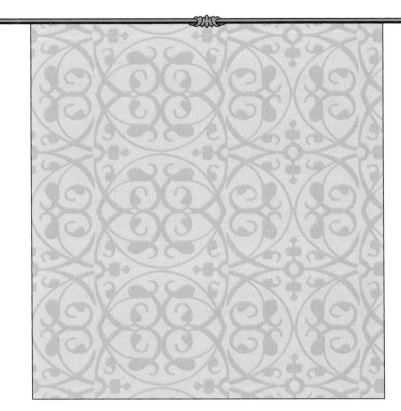

HAPPINESS

beatific (BEE uh TIH fik) - *adj.* expressing or imparting extreme joy or bliss; blissful.

"She took the medal and stared at it. Then a **beatific** smile spread over her face ... 'I'll give it to our priest and he'll say some Masses for me.'" –GUSTAVE FLAUBERT, *Madame Bovary*, transl. by Francis Steegmuller

delectation (DEE LEK TAY shun, also di LEK TAY shun) - *n.* great pleasure, delight.

"... each beauty having been exquisitely prepared for the king's **delectation** by being soaked six months in oil of myrrh and another six in assorted perfumes." –ROBERT ALTER, *The Literary Guide to the Bible*

felicity (fi LI suh tee) - *n.* extreme happiness, 2. apt and pleasing style in writing, speech, etc.

"It was something, indeed, to be able to contemplate this immense Columbiad; but to descend into its depths, this seemed to the Americans the ne plus ultra of earthly **felicity**." –JULES VERNE, *From the Earth to the Moon*

halcyon (HAL see ahn) - *adj.* calm; quiet; peaceful; undisturbed; happy, especially in the phrase *halcyon days,* the peaceful days of an earlier time.

ineffable (i NEH fuh bul) - *adj.* unspeakable, beyond expression in words; inexpressible, 2. not to be uttered; taboo.

"Oh, and as a writer, I don't normally have much patience for the **ineffable**—I ought to think everything's effing effable, otherwise what's the point? But I'm not sure there are words to describe what happens when two voices mesh." –Nick Hornby, *Songbook*

jouisance (also **jouissance**) (JOU IS sans) - (from French) *n.* advantage or enjoyment from the use of something, 2. enjoyment; pleasure; delight; merriment; mirth; festivity.

"Luce was interested in the gender giveaways of my prose, of course. He measured my **jouissance** against my linearity." –JEFFREY EUGENIDES, *Middlesex*

schadenfreude (SHAH den FROI duh) (from German) *n.* pleasure taken from another's misfortune.

"There are few things more satisfying—for fans of the New York Yankees, anyway—than the sensation of **schadenfreude** when the Boston Red Sox fall. Its recurrence diminishes nothing." –STEFAN FATSIS, *The Wall Street Journal,* 10/15/04 (just days before the Red Sox's historic come-from-behind series victory over the Yankees; so much for Mr. Fatsis' **schadenfreude**)

MOURNFUL, DISTRESSED

bathos (BAY thos) - *n.* the sudden transition from an elevated style to the commonplace in writing or speech; anticlimax, 2. overdone or insincere pathos, 3. hackneyed quality; triteness.

*see other **bathos** entry for citation, p. 82*

condole (kuhn DOLE) - *v.* to grieve; to express sorrow or sympathic sorrow.

"'... is this true ... that your wife's going away was on ... a secret elopement with a lover? If so, I **condole** with you.'" –THOMAS HARDY, *Jude the Obscure*

cri de coeur (KREE duh KUHR) - (from French) *n.* (literally "cry of/from the heart") a passionate utterance of appeal or distress.

"'I want,' that objectless, elemental **cri de coeur,** could as easily have been K.'s as Eugene Henderson's." —PHILIP ROTH, *Rereading Saul Bellow*

de profundis (DAY proh FUN dees, also DAY proh FUHN dees) - (from Latin) *n.* the first words of the Latin version of Psalm cxxx (cxxix) = 'Out of the depths (have I cried)'; hence: the name of this psalm, a psalm of penitence, 2. a cry of deep sorrow or misery.

see other de profundis entry for citation, p. 143

doleful (DOLE ful) - *adj.* sad; mournful; cheerless; causing or expressing grief.

"...the [hurdy-gurdy] music, now **doleful** and dragging, now merry and quick, came out of the box through a pink taffeta curtain under a fancy brasswork grill." —GUSTAVE FLAUBERT, *Madame Bovary*, transl. by Francis Steegmuller

dolor (DOH luhr, also DAH luhr) - *n.* mental anguish; suffering; sorrow.

"... through all this thick and interwoven skein of bedlam, the ponderous snoring of the Grey Scrubbers had continued as a recognizable theme of **dolorous** persistence." —MERVYN PEAKE, *Titus Groan*

elegiac (EH luh JIE uk, also EH luh JIE ak, ih LEE gee ak) - *adj.* pertaining to an elegy; written in elegiac couplets, 2. expressing sadness; mournful.

"Maybe the reason 'Thunder Road' has endured for me is that, despite its energy and volume and fast cars and hair, it somehow manages to sound **elegiac**, and the older I get the more I can hear that." —NICK HORNBY, *Songbook*

funereal (fyu NIR EE ul) - *adj.* suggesting or relating to a funeral, 2. mournful; sorrowful.

"His grim tone became **funereal**." —GLEN DAVID GOLD, *Carter Beats the Devil*

Gethsemane (geth SE muh nee) - *n.* the location of the scene of Christ's agony, a garden on the Mount of Olives, (Matt. 26: 36–46), 2. Christ's agony in the garden represented in art, 3. an occasion of deep anguish, mental or physical.

"The atmosphere in the locker room at half-time felt like midnight at **Gethsemane**. I had never seen my teammates closer to despair." –PAT CONROY, *My Losing Season*

harrow (HAR oh) - *n.* a farming tool made up of a heavy frame with sharp teeth or disks, used to break up or level off plowed ground, 2. *v.* - to break up or level off with such a tool, 3. to cause or inflict great distress or torment.

*see other **harrow** entry for citation, p. 198*

lorn (LORN) - *adj.* desolate; forsaken; forlorn.

"Only the soundlessness of the dazed cats—the line of them—the undulating line as blanched as linen, and **lorn** as the long gesture of a hand." –MERVYN PEAKE, *Titus Groan*

maudlin (MAHD lehn) - *adj.* overly sentimental (comes from Mary Magdalen, who was frequently depicted as a tearful penitent).

"Her soliloquies mawkish, her sentiments **maudlin**, malaise dripped like a fever from her pores." –JHUMPA LAHIRI, *Interpreter of Maladies*

pall (PAHL) - *n.* a cloth that covers a coffin, 2. a coffin, 3. something that covers, 4. an element that produces gloominess.

*see other **pall** entry for citation, p. 139*

pathos (PAY THOS, also PAH THOS) - *n.* the aspect of something which gives rise to a sense of pity, sympathy, tenderness, or sorrow in another.

*see other **pathos** entry for citation, p. 85*

plaintive (PLAIN tiv) - *adj.* melancholy; mournful; sorrowful.

"'We will win,' the Polish president said, but sounding like Colin Powell, he added **plaintively**, 'but what are the consequences?'" –BOB WOODWARD, *Plan of Attack*

slough (SLUH, also SLAUGH) - *n.* a mud-filled bog or hollow; a mire, 2. a state or dejection or dispair.

*see other **slough** entry for citation, p.194*

DISCOMFORT, FEAR

abase (uh BASE) - *v.* to humble; to lower or depress; to throw or cast down, 2. to cast down or reduce low or lower, as in rank, office or estimation or worthiness; to degrade.

"... she saw herself **abased** before Pav, her head bowed, her body curving into lines of warm surrender at his feet." –C.L. MOORE, *Jirel of Joiry*

abash (uh BASH) - *v.* to make ashamed and ill at ease; disconcert; put to shame; make self-conscious.

"[Frodo] was both surprised and **abashed** to find that he had a seat at Elrond's table among all these folk so high and fair." –J.R.R. TOLKIEN, *The Fellowship of the Ring*

blench (BLENCH) - *v.* to pull back as in fear; flinch.

"Again it leaped into the air, and then swiftly fell down upon Eowyn, shrieking, striking with beak and claw. Still she did not **blench**." –J.R.R. TOLKIEN, *The Return of the King*

discomfit (dis KUHM fit) - *v.* to thwart; to frustrate; to defeat, 2. to cause confusion, perplexity or embarrassment; disconcert.

"For most Americans, these questions are more than **discomfiting**: They are intolerable." –TUNKU VARADARAJAN, *The Asian Wall Street Journal*, 3/18–20/05

dysphoria (dis FOR ee uh) - *n.* a condition of unease, unhappiness; characterized by feeling unwell.

"'Depression. **Dysphoria**. She's in a very delicate psychological state.'" –JEFFREY EUGENIDES, *Middlesex*

nefandous (neh FAN dous) - *adj.* unmentionable; abominable; horrendous.

"... there were not any real ruins. Only the bricks of the chimney, the stones of the cellar, some mineral and metallic litter here and there, and the rim of that **nefandous** well." –H.P. LOVECRAFT, *The Colour Out of Space*

tenterhook (TEN ter hook) - *n.* a sharp, hooked nail used to attach cloth to a tenter or drying frame, 2. an expression to convey a feeling of uneasiness, anxiety or suspense.

"Charlie glances up from the fridge. 'Yeah,' he says, 'we're all on **tenterhooks**.'" –IAN CALDWELL AND DUSTIN THOMASON, *The Rule of Four*

ANGER, ANTIPATHY

animus (A nuh mus) - *n.* disposition; intention, 2. a malevolent ill will or animosity.

"Her **animus**, her superior airs ... everything intolerable to the Swede in a friend, let alone in a mate." –PHILIP ROTH, *American Pastoral*

choler (KAH ler, also KO ler) - *n.* anger; irritability; the state of being bilious, 2. bile.

"There was a **choler** and **rancor** to his fury that night that none of us had seen before." –PAT CONROY, *My Losing Season*

dudgeon (DUH juhn) -*n.* a wood used to make dagger hilts, 2. anger; resentment; indignation; primarily in the phrase "in high dudgeon"—very angry, offended or resentful, 3. the wooden hilt of a dagger or a dagger.

"Davis was in high **dudgeon** at any insinuation of Morgan dishonesty." –RON CHERNOW, *The House of Morgan*

jaundiced (JON duhst, JAWN duhst) - *adj.* affected with jaundice (yellowish discoloration of tissues and bodily fluids with bile pigment), 2. prejudiced, envious, jealous.

"Cataloging such [interpersonal] games necessarily fosters an ironic, if not outright **jaundiced**, view of human nature." –LAURA MILLER, *The New York Times Book Review*, 6/20/04

livid (LIV ihd) - *adj.* discolored; bruised, 2. pallid or ashen, as from shock or anger, 3. furious, extremely angry.

*see other **livid** entry for citation, p. 212*

nettle (NEH tul) - *n.* an herb covered with stinging hairs, 2. *v.* to pique, irritate, vex or provoke someone.

"'There is always a way, if the desire be coupled with courage,' answered the Cimmerian shortly, **nettled**." –ROBERT E. HOWARD, *The Tower of the Elephant*

pique (PEEK) - *n.* a feeling of hurt, vexation or resentment, awakened by a social slight or injury, 2. a keenly felt desire or longing, 3. *v.* to wound the pride of, to sting; to nettle; to irritate; to fret; to offend; to excite, 4. to excite to action by causing resentment or jealousy; to provoke.

"In a silent rage, Billy called around the league to see who would take Jeremy off his hands ... Paul DePodesta ... tried to talk Billy down from his **pique**." –MICHAEL LEWIS, *Moneyball*

rancor (RAHN kur, also RAHN kor) - *n.* a deep hatred or ill will.

*see **choler** for citation*

roil (ROYL) - *v.* to make muddy or cloudy by stirring up sediment, 2. to irritate; agitate; vex.

*see other **roil** entry for citation, p. 214*

umbrage (UHM brij) - *n.* resentment; offense; a feeling of pique, 2. shade; shadow.

*see other **umbrage** entry for citation, p. 214*

vitriol (VIH tree uhl) - *n.* sulfuric acid, 2. a sulfate of various metals, 3. a caustic quality; wrath; anger.

"... the Special Edition Ann Coulter Barbie-type doll, loaded with recorded sound bites of conservative **vitriol** from the venomous vixen herself." –LIESL SCHILLINGER, *The New York Times Book Review*, 10/31/04

wrath (RATH) - *n.* vengeful or violent anger; rage, 2. an action born of anger, 3. divine punishment.

> "'Then the court waxed **wrath**, and the judge talked a great deal about my duty to the state, and society, and other things I did not understand, and bade me tell where my friend had flown.'" –ROBERT E. HOWARD, *Queen of the Black Coast*

wroth (ROTH, also ROATH) - *adj.* wrathful; angry; incensed, intensely angry.

> "The commanding colonel was **wroth** and shouting at Yossarian that he would not permit his patients to take indecent liberties with his nurses." –JOSEPH HELLER, *Catch-22*

PASSIONATE, AROUSED

concupiscence (kahn KYU pih sunts, also ken KYU pih sunts) - *n.* a strong desire, a strong sexual desire; lust (*adj.* concupiscent).

> "She looked at them with a grin of **concupiscent** mockery and continued to grind her hips." –TOM WOLFE, *A Man in Full*

fervent (FUHR vent) - *adj.* extremely hot, burning, glowing, 2. intensely devoted or earnest, passionate, ardent.

> "Adam's voice rose and rose, and he became more and more **fervent** in his exhortations" –TOM WOLFE, *I Am Charlotte Simmons*

fervid (FUHR vid) - *adj.* extremely hot; burning, 2. exhibiting fervor or passion.

fervor (FUHR ver) - *n.* intensity of emotion, ardor, 2. intense heat.

foment (FOE ment) - *v.* to stir up; arouse, 2. to treat with heat and moisture, 3. to nurse to life or activity; to encourage; to abet; to instigate; used often in a negative sense; as, to foment ill feelings.

> "One rumor maintained that he was a Palestinian Arab who had **fomented** racial unrest in India, South Africa, and London before moving to Detroit." –JEFFREY EUGENIDES, *Middlesex*

frisson (FREE sohn) - *n.* a shudder or shiver, as of excitement, fear, or pleasure, 2. an experience of intense excitement.

> "Both of these presidents [Ronald Reagan and George W. Bush] inspired, and to some extent still inspire, a **frisson** of disbelief: How did this guy get to be president of the mightiest nation on earth?" –BILL KELLER, *The New York Times Magazine*, 1/26/03

incandescent (in can DES ehnt) - *adj.* emitting light as a result of being heated, 2. shining very brightly, 3. showing intense emotion, as of a performance, etc.

> "Because of the **incandescent** joy I take in reading, a secret alchemy worked without my knowledge, and I ceased to be the boy who has just given up thirty-nine points to Johnny Moates" –PAT CONROY, *My Losing Season*

lurid (LUR id) - *adj.* a ghastly pale or wan appearance, 2. glowing through a haze, as flames enveloped by smoke, 3. gruesome; sensational; harsh or shocking, 4. exhibiting violent passions.

> "Ever since the 16th century, when Europeans decided that Paraguay was Arcadia and set about systematically brutalizing it, the country's history has comprised

episodes of **lurid** horror interspersed with periods of mere chaos and grinding hardship." –BEN MACINTYRE, *The New York Times Book Review*, 2/29/04

nympholepsy (NIM fuh LEP see) - *n.* a desire for something unattainable; the passion of men for young girls, 2. a frenzy of desire or emotion.

"David Burkett—scion of a wealthy logging dynasty, narrator of this novel and son of a crooked, **nympholeptic** father ..." –NOT ATTRIBUTED, *The New York Times Book Review*, 6/6/04

paroxysm (PAR ahk SI zem) - *n.* a sudden emotional outburst, 2. a convulsion, spasm or fit.

"But the skies remained unremittingly overcast, which brought public exasperation to a **paroxysm**." –JULES VERNE, *From the Earth to the Moon*

perfervid (pur FUR vid) - *adj.* excessively fervid, expressing overwrought emotions, ardent.

"Crude, untutored, musically unsophisticated, possessed of a primitive, **perfervid** style that most resembled the gospel shouting of the Baptist church, Guitar Slim was the antithesis of all that Ray Charles had sought to become in his musical career to date." –PETER GURALNICK, *Sweet Soul Music*

torrid (TOR id) - *adj.* intense dry heat, 2. passionate; ardent.

*see other **torrid** entry for citation, p. 199*

visceral (VI suh ruhl, also VIS ruhl) - *adj.* having to do with a response of the body as opposed to the intellect, 2. extremely emotional, usually a negative emotion.

"My weeping is so public and **visceral** that I always draw the attention of other visitors, and they put their arms around me to try and console me." –PAT CONROY, *My Losing Season*

EVEN-TEMPERED

athambia (A tham be a) - *n.* imperturbability.

"Lucky: Given the existence as uttered forth in the public works of Puncher and Wattmann of a personal God ... who from the heights of divine apathia divine **athambia** divine aphasia loves us dearly ..." –SAMUEL BECKETT, *Waiting for Godot*

equanimity (EE kwuh NIH muh tee) - *n.* evenness of mind, especially under stress; the state of being balanced, composed; the capacity to remain calm and even-tempered, even in the face of instigation; not easily elated or depressed, 2. impartiality, fairness of judgment.

"She was famous for her **equanimity**; she almost never lost her temper." –MICHAEL CRICHTON, *Prey*

sangfroid (SAHN FRWAH) - (from French) *n.* cool self-possession or composure under strain, equanimity.

"The delicate art of cajoler was a lost skill in modern law enforcement, one that required exceptional poise under pressure. Few men possessed the necessary **sangfroid** for this kind of operation, but Fache seemed born to it." –DAN BROWN, *The Da Vinci Code*

4. FAMILY AND FRIENDS

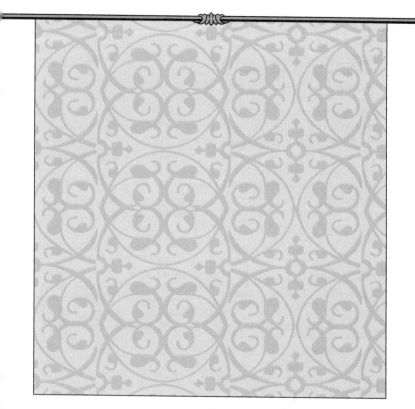

atavism (A tuh viz uhm) - *n.* the appearance of a characteristic or characteristics presumed to have been present in a remote ancestor but not in nearer relatives; reverting back to an earlier biological type, 2. such a characteristic, 3. the individual exhibiting such a characteristic.

"He was a magnificent **atavism**, a man so purely primitive that he was of the type that came into the world before the development of the moral nature." –JACK LONDON, *The Sea Wolf*

avuncular (uh VUN kyu lur) - *adj.* kindly, genial, in the manner of an uncle.

*see other **avuncular** entry for citation, p. 10*

benedict (BEH nuh DIKT) - *adj.* a recently married man, especially one who was formerly a confirmed bachelor, 2. blessed; benign; having a mildly laxative effect.

"... sleek young bulls, living out the loneliness of their bachelorhood and gathering strength against the day when they would fight their way into the ranks of the **benedicts**." –JACK LONDON, *The Sea Wolf*

cognate (KAHG nate) - *adj.* of common ancestry or origin, 2. a word derived from the same roots as another given word.

*see other **cognate** entry for citation, p. 71*

cognomen (kahg NO men) - *n.* a surname; last name; family name, 2. the surname of a male citizen of ancient Rome, 3. a name, a distinguishing nickname.

*see other **cognomen** entry for citation, p. 72*

confrere (KAHN FRER, also KOHN FRER) - *n.* a colleague; a fellow member of one's class or profession.

"... one intense lady [factory worker] asked permission (which, of course, was granted) to gather some of her **confreres** about the cross to occasionally sing spirituals." –JOHN KENNEDY TOOLE, *A Confederacy of Dunces*

connubial (kuh NEW bee ul) - *adj.* of or relating to marriage or the state of being married; conjugal.

"Agnes returns from her brave attempt at a **connubial** breakfast." –MICHEL FABER, *The Crimson Petal and the White*

consanguineous (KAHN SAN GWI nee us) - *adj.* related by blood; descended from the same parent or ancestor.

"'We know now that most birth deformities result from the **consanguinity** of the parents ... Causes all kinds of problems. Imbecility. Hemophilia. Look at the Romanovs. Look at any royal family. Mutants, all of them.'" –JEFFREY EUGENIDES, *Middlesex*

coterie (KO tuh REE) - *n.* a small, exclusive group of persons who associate frequently, often with a common purpose.

"Like a bitch in heat, I seem to attract a **coterie** of policemen and sanitation officials." –JOHN KENNEDY TOOLE, *A Confederacy of Dunces*

distaff (DIS TAF) - *n.* a staff that holds the unspun flax, wool, etc., being used in spinning, 2. work or concerns mainly of importance to women, 3. a woman or women as a group; characteristic of women, 4. *adj.* female; specif., designating the maternal side of a family.

"'Where is our little **distaff** member this morning?'

'I had to send her home. She came to work in her nightgown.'" –JOHN KENNEDY TOOLE, *A Confederacy of Dunces*

dowager (DAU ih jur) - *n.* a widow holding title or property received from her late husband, 2. an older woman of high social station.

" ... 'there could be a small fortune in accrued dividends.'

I nodded. 'My client is vague. You know how some of these old **dowagers** are.'" –NELSON DEMILLE, *The Gold Coast*

filial (FIH lee ul, also FIL yul) - *adj.* of or befitting a son or daughter: filial obedience.

"The other [son], equipped with a greater **filial** sense perhaps, has chosen to live with his mother in Saigon, and to help run her travel agency." –TUNKU VARADARAJAN, *The Wall Street Journal*, 5/17/02

in loco parentis (in LO ko puh REN tus) - (from Latin) *adj.* in the place of position of a parent or parents.

"Squires are boys or young men who serve a knight in exchange for instruction in the arts of combat and the manners of chivalry. This relationship, with the superior at least partly **in loco parentis,** is taken quite seriously by those concerned." –POUL ANDERSON, *The Blade of Conan*

kith (KITH) - *n.* friends, acquantainces, and neighbors.

"... he scampered full of the news he had with which to astonish his **kith**." –LORD DUNSANY, *The King of Elfland's Daughter*

Momism (mohm IZ uhm) - *n.* an excessive adoration or attachment to one's mother, often considered Oedipal in nature; maternal domination.

*see other **Momism** entry for citation, p. 117*

parricide (PAR uh SIDE) - *n.* a person who murders one of his parents or other near relative, 2. one who commits a parricide, 3. the act committed by a parricide.

*see other **parricide** entry for citation, p. 63*

paterfamilias (PAY tur fuh MIH lee us) (from Spanish) - *n.* the male head of a household, family or tribe; the father of a family.

"On the floor nearby, the Lovells' blue merle collie, Christi, completed the domestic scene: He lay dozing at McMurrey's feet, as if accepting this stand-in **paterfamilias** while the real thing was away." —JIM LOVELL AND JEFFREY KLUGER, *Lost Moon: The Perilous Voyage of Apollo 13*

patrimony (PA truh MO nee) - *n.* an inheritance or legacy from an ancestor, esp. from a father.

"Well, this was his own, his hearth; these were his birches, catalpas, horse chestnuts. His rotten dreams of peace. The **patrimony** of his children—a sunken corner of Massachusetts for Marco, the little piano for June painted a loving green by her solicitous father." —SAUL BELLOW, *Herzog*

primogeniture (PRY mo JE neh tur) - *n.* the state of being the eldest child of the same parents, 2. the legal right of the eldest son to inherit the entire estate of his parents.

"In Virginia, however, laws abolishing **primogeniture** and entail had been passed during the Revolution." —JOSEPH J. ELLIS, *Founding Brothers*

progenitor (pro JE nuh tur) - *n.* a direct ancestor, 2. an originator of a line of descent.

"Here at any rate is Ignatius Reilly, without **progenitor** in any literature I know of— slob extraordinary, a mad Oliver Hardy, a fat Don Quixote, a perverse Thomas Aquinas rolled into one." —WALKER PERCY, *Introduction, John Kennedy Toole's A Confederacy of Dunces*

progeny (PRAH juhn ee) - *n.* children, offspring or descendants, esp. when considered as a group.

"... here was Steena Palsson, Iceland and Denmark's American **progeny**, of the bloodline going back to King Canute and beyond." —PHILIP ROTH, *The Human Stain*

propinquity (pruh PIN kwe tee) - *n.* nearness, proximity, 2. kinship; similarity.

"Decent people out there. [Radio announcer] Russ [Hodges] wants to believe they are still assembled in some recognizable manner, the kindred unit at the radio, old lines and ties and **propinquities**." —DON DELILLO, *Underworld*

scion (SIGH en) - *n.* a shoot or bud of a plant, esp. one for planting or grafting, 2. a descendant, offspring.

"Coleman had invited every faculty member in for a talk, including several senior professors who were the **scions** of the old country families who'd founded and originally endowed the place." —PHILIP ROTH, *The Human Stain*

tutelary (TOO tul ER ee, also TYOO tul ER ee) - *adj.* serving or protecting as a guardian, 2. of, pertaining to, or acting as a guardian.

"Yet Greenspan was the **tutelary** spirit behind a partial Glass-Steagall repeal." —RON CHERNOW, *The House of Morgan*

uxorial (UK SOR ee ul) - *adj.* of, pertaining to, or characteristic of a wife.

uxoricide (UK SOR uh SIDE) - *n.* the act of a man killing his wife, 2. a man who kills his wife.

uxorious (UK SOR ee us) - *adj.* excessively fond of one's wife; irrationally doting or submissive to one's wife.

*see other **uxorious** entry for citation, p. 23*

5. THE LOWLY
AND CORRUPT

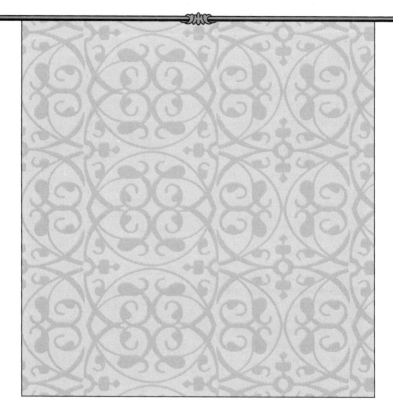

LUSTFUL

bagnio (BAHN YO) - *n.* a brothel; a house or building where prostitutes are available.

"'We shall visit the **bagnio** of your choice and talk probability with the whores.'" —DAVID LISS, *A Conspiracy of Paper*

bawd (BAWD) - *n.* a woman who keeps a brothel; a prostitute.

"Estragon: An Englishman having drunk a little more than usual proceeds to a brothel. The **bawd** asks him if he wants a fair one, a dark one or a red-haired one." —SAMUEL BECKETT, *Waiting for Godot*

catamite (KA tuh MITE) - *n.* a boy kept by a pederast for the purpose of a sexual relationship.

"... perhaps the most arresting first sentence in 20th-century literature is absent ... this from Anthony Burgess's *Earthly Powers*: 'It was the afternoon of my 81st birthday, and I was in bed with my **catamite** when Ali announced that the archbishop had come to see me.'" —BEVIS HILLIER, *The Spectator*, 12/11/04

cocotte (ko kot) - *n.* a prostitute; one of a class of the demi-monde of Paris.

"Prospective house slaves from the shacks got the same kind of going-over, I suppose, or girls brought to an old **cocotte** by their mothers for training." —SAUL BELLOW, *The Adventures of Augie March*

concubine (KAHN kyu BINE) - *n.* a woman who cohabits with a man without being married to him; in some societies, a secondary wife with inferior social and legal status.

"'He even got into the king's zenana, guarded by a three-headed fiend of anthropophagous tastes, who nevertheless could not come near him, and reveled among the king's **concubines** for six days and fled before the king learned of his visit." —L. SPRAGUE DE CAMP, *The Tritonian Ring*

concupiscence (kahn KYU pih sunts, also ken KYU pih sunts) - *n.* a strong desire, a strong sexual desire; lust (*adj.* is concupiscent).

"She looked at them with a grin of **concupiscent** mockery and continued to grind her hips." —TOM WOLFE, *A Man in Full*

courtesan (KOOR teh zen, also KOOR teh zan) - *n.* a female prostitute, one who associates with members or a royal court or men of high social standing, rank, or wealth.

"... the imperial cortege wherein the emperor rode with a **courtesan** in a carriage before the savant." —HAROLD LAMB, *Genghis Khan*

debauch (di BOCH, also dee BOCH) - *v.* to corrupt morally; to deprave, 2. to diminish the value, quality, or excellence of, 3. to indulge in debauchery; dissipation, 4. *n.* the act of debauchery, 5. an orgy (from the French—originally to remove branches from a tree).

"... you turned her against me by means of your vile arts, and then you degraded and **debauched** her, sank her into your own foul slime."—ROBERT E. HOWARD, *Beyond the Borders*

demimonde (DEH mee MAHND) -*n.* a social class (of women) kept by wealthy lovers or protectors, 2. a group of female prostitutes, 3. a group not considered respectable, existing on the fringes of respectable society.

"Herbert Huncke—the man who became a key emissary from the drug **demimonde** for Burroughs, Ginsberg and Kerouac ..." –HAL ESPEN, *The New York Times Book Review*, 6/6/04

doxy (DAHK see) - *n.* a mistress; a female lover; a paramour; a sweetheart, 2. a (sexually) promiscuous woman; a wench; a prostitute (originally the term in Vagabonds' *Cant* for the unmarried mistress of a beggar or rogue).

[In a fight with Amazons] "'Have you reason to think these **doxies** are ready to surrender?'" –L. SPRAGUE DE CAMP, *The Tritonian Ring*

drab (DRAB) - *n.* a slut, 2. a lewd wench; a strumpet; a prostitute.

"'And when the king awakens I will have not only you but that temple **drab** you love!'" –ABRAHAM MERRITT, *The Ship of Ishtar*

gamin (also **gamine**) (GAH mun, also GAH meen) - *n.* a neglected, abandoned child who roams the streets; an urchin, 2. gamine—a girl with impish, saucy appeal.

"And this turned out to be the **gamine** Hispanic actress Salma Hayek." –BILL ZEHME, *Esquire*, 4/02

harlot (HAR luht) - *n.* a female prostitute.

hetaera (also **hetaira**) (hi TIR uh) - *n.* in ancient Greece, a courtesan or concubine; a female companion of a special class, highly cultivated.

"He admitted to himself, when talking about it to some people afterwards, that it was only then that he realized how 'beautiful' that woman was, for though he had seen her several times before, he had always considered her a sort of 'provincial **hetaera**'." –FYODOR DOSTOYEVSKY, *The Brothers Karamazov*, transl. by David Magarshack

hoyden (HOY duhn) -*n.* a high-spirited, boisterous or saucy woman or girl (possibly related to heathen).

"... there minced a painted **hoyden** whose short slit skirt displayed her sleek flank at every step." –ROBERT E. HOWARD, *Eons of the Night*

inamorata (ih NAH muh RAH tuh) - *n.* a female lover or sweetheart; a woman with whom one has an intimate or loving relationship; a mistress.

"'Your new gal, I promise I won't breathe a word,' Hadley said ...

'There is no new **inamorata**.'" –KATHERINE MOSBY, *The Season of Lillian Dawes*

lascivious (luh SIH vee us) - *adj.* characterized by or expressing lust or lewdness; wanton; driven by lust, 2. tending to incite lustful desires.

"William was just thirteen, he later told his doctors, when he first started to enjoy '**lascivious** thoughts' about the young Ceylonese girls on the sands around him." –SIMON WINCHESTER, *The Professor and the Madman*

leman (LE mun, also LEE mun) - *n.* (Archaic) a sweetheart or lover (man or woman); esp. a mistress.

"I whirled to see ... Lord Valerian and his **leman**." —ROBERT E. HOWARD AND L. SPRAGUE DE CAMP, *Conan the Usurper*

libertine (LIH bur TEEN) - *n.* a person who behaves without moral restraint; one who is dissolute, 2. a freethinker; one who defies traditional religious precepts, 3. in ancient Rome, a person who had been freed from slavery, 4. *adj.* morally unrestrained; licentious; dissolute.

"... a prowling middle-aged **libertine** who has sex with a young employee during office hours ..." —WALTER KIRN, *The New York Times Book Review*, 10/31/04

licentious (ly SENT shus) - *adj.* without moral discipline; ignoring accepted rules and standards, 2. morally, esp. sexually, unrestrained; lascivious.

"Cataline was the treacherous and degenerate character whose scheming nearly destroyed the Roman Republic and whose **licentious** ways inspired, by their very profligacy, Cicero's eloquent oration on virtue, which was subsequently memorized by generations of American schoolboys." —JOSEPH J. ELLIS, *Founding Brothers*

Lothario (lo THAR ee O, also lo THER ee O) - *n.* a man who seduces women; an amoral womanizer (from a character in "The Fair Penitent" by Nicholas Rowe [1674–1718]).

"**Lothario**, Casanova, Player: It's no accident that we have as many words for the male operator as Eskimos have for snow." —STEVEN ZEITCHIK, *The Wall Street Journal*, 2/14/03

lubricity (loo BRIH suh tee) - *n.* a slippery or smooth quality, as a lubricant, 2. a tricky or shifty quality, 3. lewdness; wanton or salacious behavior.

"... touching the top of her fly of her jeans with both hands, as if at any moment she was about to unzip them, slip them down off her hips, all with a salacious leer on her lips and a **lubricious** look in her eyes." —TOM WOLFE, *A Man in Full*

malkin (also **mawkin**) (MAHL kin, also MAH kin) - *n.* a chambermaid; a woman of the lower classes, 2. an untidy female; a servant or country wench; a slattern; a slut; a drab; a lewd woman, 3. a mop created by tying a bundle or rags to the end of a stick, used by the kitchen servant to clean the ovens, 4. a scarecrow, 5. a designation for certain animals, such as a cat or hare.

meretricious (MER uh TRIH shus) - *adj.* relating to or characteristic of a prostitute, 2. attractive in a vulgar manner; flashy; tawdry, 3. superficially plausible yet false; insincere; specious.

"He once, to my face, told me that a story of mine was **meretricious**. The word is from a Latin word meaning prostitute and Horace was implying that I was prostituting my talent by writing junk just in order to make money." —ISAAC ASIMOV, *I. Asimov*

moll (MAHL) - *n.* (slang) a female companion of a gangster.

"'Gangster's **moll**. Gang **moll**. That's what they called me in L.A.'" —DON DELILLO, *Underworld*

noceur (NA SIR) - *n.* a reveller; a rake, a libertine; one who stays up late into the night.

"I'll tell you about this du Niveau. He's what the Parisians call a **noceur**, meaning that it's always the wedding night for him or that he plays musical beds." –SAUL BELLOW, *The Adventures of Augie March*

nympholepsy (NIM fuh LEP see) - *n.* a desire for something unattainable; the passion of men for young girls, 2. a frenzy of desire or emotion.

> "David Burkett—scion of a wealthy logging dynasty, narrator of this novel and son of a crooked, **nympholeptic** father ..." –NOT ATTRIBUTED, *The New York Times Book Review*, 6/6/04

odalisque *(OH dul ISK)* - *n.* a concubine or a female slave in a harem.

> "Her eyes alone, even if she were wrapped up like an Arabian **odalisque** with nothing else showing, would be enough to declare her sex ... They are eyes that promise everything." –MICHEL FABER, *The Crimson Petal and the White*

onanism (OH nuh NIH zem) - *n.* masturbation; self-abuse; coitus interruptus (derived from the proper name Onan [Gen. 38: 9]).

> "A nude woman was sitting on the edge of a desk next to a globe of the world. The suggested **onanism** with the piece of chalk intrigued Ignatius." –JOHN KENNEDY TOOLE, *A Confederacy of Dunces*

pederasty (PEH duh RAS tee) - *n.* sexual relations between a man and a boy.

> "Save the World Through Degeneracy ... Our first step will be to elect one of their number to some very high office—the presidency, if Fortuna spins us kindly. Then they will infiltrate the military ... None of the **pederasts** in power, of course, will be practical enough to know about such

devices as bombs." –JOHN KENNEDY TOOLE, *A Confederacy of Dunces*

prurient (PRUR ee unt) - *adj.* having or expressing lustful ideas or desires, 2. characterized by or arousing an interest in sexual matters.

> "She was overweight and sweated profusely in the tent, which itself had become a greenhouse of **prurient** fantasy." –PAT CONROY, *The Lords of Discipline*

quiff (KWIF) - (among other definitions) - *n.* a young woman; specifically a female prostitute; a promiscuous woman; a 'tart,' 2. a lock or tuft of hair, esp. one plastered on the forehead, or one brushed or gelled upward over the forehead.

> "She had so much, gave out so much splendor. A stupendous **quiff**." –SAUL BELLOW, *The Adventures of Augie March*

rake (RAYK) - (among other definitions, contraction of rakehell) *n.* a dissolute, debauched man; roué.

> "His eyes panned around the entire table to show everyone this physical marvel ... and the fact that he was such a high-spirited **rake**." – TOM WOLFE, *I Am Charlotte Simmons*

rakish (RAY kish) - *adj.* having the character of a rake; morally loose; corrupt; dissolute.

> "She appeared to be fashioning a rather colorful but nonetheless **rakish** evening gown." –JOHN KENNEDY TOOLE, *A Confederacy of Dunces*

ribald (RIH buhld, also RIH BOLD, RYE BOLD) - *adj.* coarse; filthy; vulgar; indecent.

> "But that **ribald** wench had been too groggy

from her libations of the previous night to notice the change in her captive's demeanor." —ROBERT E. HOWARD, *The Vale of Lost Women*

roué (roo AY) - *n.* a dissipated, lecherous man; a debauchee; a rake (originally a nickname given to the dissolute companions of the Duc d'Orléans, c. 1720).

"'Do you seriously think that Claude **roué** wants marriage?' Ignatius slobbered." —JOHN KENNEDY TOOLE, *A Confederacy of Dunces*

salacious (suh LAY shus) - *adj.* lecherous; lustful; bawdy, 2. erotically appealing or stimulating; lascivious; pornographic.

"Half of the British population loyally enjoyed the News of the World's **salacious** pages." —RON CHERNOW, *The House of Morgan*

scapegrace (SKAYP GRAYS) - *n.* a reckless man (or boy); an incorrigible scamp; a scoundrel; a rascal, 2. *adj.* showing the characteristics of a scapegrace.

"John Hreggvidsson, a scoundrel, **scapegrace** and candidate for hanging..." —NOT ATTRIBUTED, *The New York Times Book Review, 6/6/04*

slattern (SLA turn) - *n.* a woman who is untidy or dirty in her habits or appearance, 2. a sexually promiscuous woman; a female prostitute; a slut.

"Instantly she regrets this limp gesture of ingratiation, which only makes her seem a **slattern**." —MICHEL FABER, *The Crimson Petal and the White*

strumpet (STRUM puht) - *n.* a harlot, prostitute.

"Another girl, likewise from the Rescue Society's stable of rehabilitated **strumpets**, is supposed to be starting next Wednesday." —MICHEL FABER, *The Crimson Petal and the White*

trollop (TRAH lup) - *n.* a slovenly or untidy woman; a slattern; a strumpet; a trull, 2. a loose woman; a slut; an adulterous woman.

"'I'll show this offensive **trollop**,' Ignatius mumbled." —JOHN KENNEDY TOOLE, *A Confederacy of Dunces*

trull (TRUL) - *n.* a female prostitute; a concubine; a drab; a trollop; a strumpet, 2. a girl; a lass; a wench.

turpitude (TUR puh TOOD, also TUR puh TYOOD) - *n.* depravity; baseness. 2. an act of baseness.

"Another category of restriction [from immigration to the U.S. after the Immigration Act of 1917]: 'persons convicted of a crime or misdemeanor involving moral **turpitude**.' And a subset of this group: 'Incestuous relations.'" —JEFFREY EUGENIDES, *Middlesex*

wanton (WON tun, also WAHN tun) - *adj.* - causing harm or damage for no reason, 2. a sexually "loose" or unrestrained person; undisciplined; spoiled, 3. playful; frolicsome, 4. cruel; merciless, 5. exhibiting unprovoked, gratuitous maliciousness, 6. excessive; luxuriant; abundant; lavish; extravagant.

"'Ironically, the book of Fortuna is itself bad luck. Oh, Fortuna, you degenerate **wanton**!'" —JOHN KENNEDY TOOLE, *A Confederacy of Dunces*

THE MOB

beano (BEE no) - *n.* a form of the game bingo using beans as markers to cover the numbers on a player's card, 2. a festive entertainment frequently ending in rowdyism.

> "By now the knot of gawkers had grown into a real crowd. They were revved up, ready for some action, eager for the **beano**, now that the hapless owner of the automobile had materialized and was acting suitably dismayed, frightened, anguished, and frustrated." –TOM WOLFE, *A Man in Full*

bevy (be VEE) - *n.* a collective term; a group or assemblage.

> "This was the sequence [of pictures] that involved the scramble for the ball, people in **bevies**, Marvin said, scratching and grabbing, and a man in the last photo standing starkly alone." –DON DELILLO, *Underworld*

claque (KLAK) - *n.* a group of people hired to attend a performance and to applaud. 2. a group of people who pre-arrange among themselves to express strong support for an idea, so as to give the false impression of a wider consensus (from the French claquer, to clap).

> "[The speech] competed against the inchoate mob howl and the rhythmic cries of the Fundie **claques** that formed mob-islands within the mob." –ISAAC ASIMOV, *I, Robot*

donnybrook (DON ee brook) - *n.* a free-for-all; a brawl; a rough, rowdy fight (named after the Donnybrook Fair, held near Dublin).

> "They say you're never supposed to get into a public **donnybrook** with news publishers. They can always print more words

about you because they buy ink by the barrel." –BRIAN STEINBERG AND JOSEPH T. HALLINAN, *The Wall Street Journal,* 4/11/05

imbroglio (im BROLE yo) - *n.* a state of confusion, 2. a difficult, embarrassing or intricate situation or misunderstanding.

*see other **imbroglio** entry for ctiation, p. 94*

kerfuffle (also **curfuffle**) (kuhr FUH fuhl) - *n.* a disturbance; disorder; agitation, 2. an annoying noise.

*see other **kerfuffle** entry for citation, p. 94*

lumpen (LUM pun) - *adj.* a class or group of people, often displaced and cut off from their previous socioeconomic class, 2. a low or contemptible segment of society due to their being unproductive, shiftless, 3. vulgar or common; mentally sluggish, 4. *n.* a person or group that is lumpen.

> "Even the **lumpen** simplicity of darts features the loathed 'bounce-outs.'" –MARTIN AMIS, *Visiting Mrs. Nabokov*

roisterer (ROIST er er) - *n.* a particularly noisy, rude, or unrestrained merrymaker, 2. a swaggering bully; one who behaves in a blustering or boisterous manner.

> "... drunken **roisterers** staggered, roaring." —ROBERT E. HOWARD, *The Tower of the Elephant*

rout (RAUT) - (among other definitions) *n.* a disorderly and tumultuous crowd; a mob; hence, the rabble; the herd of common people.

> "These sickening scoundrels had merely intended to keep me back, and presently to fall upon me with a fate more horrible than death, with torture, and after torture the most hideous degradation it was possible to conceive—to send me off, a lost soul, a beast, to the rest of their Comus **rout**." —H.G. WELLS, *The Island of Dr. Moreau*

ruck (RUK) - (among other definitions) *n.* a multitude; a throng, 2. an undistinguished mass, or ordinary run, of people or things.

> "The individuals torn out of the **ruck** became very limp in the seamen's hands." —JOSEPH CONRAD, *Typhoon*

ruction (RUK shun) - *n.* a riotous disturbance or outbreak; a noisy quarrel; a commotion; a ruckus (based on insurrection, orig. with reference to the Irish Insurrection of 1798).

> "'An' didn't they have words or a **ruction** of some kind?'" —JACK LONDON, *The Sea Wolf*

saturnalia (SA tuhr NAYL yuh, also SA tuhr NAY lee uh) - *n.* a celebration characterized by unrestrained merrymaking, revelry, and often licentiousness, 2. Saturnalia—an ancient Roman festival of Saturn lasting for seven days beginning December 17.

> "Everybody drank; the wounded drank; Oofty-Oofty, who helped me, drank ... It was a **saturnalia**." —JACK LONDON, *The Sea Wolf*

DRUNK AND GORGED

absinthe (AB SINTH) - *n.* an alcoholic liqueur flavored with wormwood.

> "This is the part of town near the theatre, full of bars and prostitutes ... There was a smell of **absinthe**, cigars and oysters." —GUSTAVE FLAUBERT, *Madame Bovary*, transl. by Francis Steegmuller

bacchanal (BA kuh nahl, also BA kuh NAL) - *n.* a drunken or riotous celebration, originally in honor of Bacchus (Roman god of wine), 2. a participant in such a celebration, 3. a reveler.

> "In short order, Michael becomes a party-planner nonpareil, turning Limelight, a nightclub backwater, into a **bacchanalian** hotspot." —JOANNE KAUFMAN, *The Wall Street Journal*, 9/5/03

besot (bi SAHT) - *v.* to muddle, make dull or stupefy, esp. with drunkenness.

> "... he wasn't much of a musician at first, either. He was **besotted** by music, though." —JOE KLEIN, *The New York Times Book Review*, 6/13/04

bibulous (BI byuh lus) - *adj.* given to convivial, often excessive drinking.

> "Steve Harvey is funny as a **bibulous** DJ who narrates the action." —JOE MORGENSTERN, *The Wall Street Journal*, 9/19/03

crapulence (KRAP yuh luhns) - *n.* illness caused by excessive drinking or eating, 2.

excessive indulgence; gross intemperance, esp. in eating, drinking, or debauchery (*adj.* crapulent).

> "Curry hailed a cab, ushered Taft into it, and returned to his own apartment where, for the next twelve hours, Taft remained in a deep and **crapulent** stupor." –IAN CALDWELL AND DUSTIN THOMASON, *The Rule of Four*

crapulous (KRA pyuh lus) - *adj.* marked by intemperance, esp. in drinking, 2. illness caused by excessive indulgence or intemperance.

> [after vomiting] "Gleason is on his feet now, **crapulous** Jack all rosy and afloat, ready to lead his buddies up the aisle." –DON DELILLO, *Underworld*

dipsomania (DIP suh MAY nee uh, also DIP suh MAY nee nyuh) - *n.* an insatiable, uncontrollable craving for alcohol, 2. a persistent disire to drink alcohol in excess, 3. also refers to a state of persistent drunkenness.

> "Dwight Carson became a **dipsomaniac**. Two men became drug addicts." –AYN RAND, *The Fountainhead*

eruct (i RUKT) - *v.* to belch; to spew or expel gas from the stomach (also eructate; *n.* eructation).

> "'Move along, you coxcomb,' Ignatius belched, the gassy **eructations** echoing between the walls of the Alley."–JOHN KENNEDY TOOLE, *A Confederacy of Dunces*

Mickey Finn (MIH kee FIN) - *n.* a beverage (alcoholic or other) that has been deliberately and surreptitiously altered (esp. with the sedative chloral hydrate) in order to incapacitate the person who drinks it, 2. the drug used in such a drink.

The Oxford English Dictionary states that "the term derives from the name of 'Mickey' Finn, a Chicago saloon-keeper of the late 19th and early 20th cent. who was alleged to have drugged and robbed his customers: see J. E. Lighter Hist. Dict. Amer. Slang (1997) II. 549 and the following:

1903 Chicago Daily News 16 Dec. 1/7 The complete defense advanced by 'Mickey' Finn, proprietor of the Lone Star saloon … described … as the scene of blood-curdling crimes through the agency of drugged liquor. 1903 Inter-Ocean (Chicago) 17 Dec. 1 (heading), Lone Star Saloon loses its license. 'Mickey' Finn's alleged 'knock-out drops' … put him out of business."

intemperance (in TEM puh runts) - *n.* lack of moderation, esp. the habitual or excessive drinking of alcoholic beverages.

> "If an in-control personality like Pistone finds the temptation to write a sequel irresistible, how can the famously **intemperate** Henry Hill be expected to resist?" –-MARK KAMINE, *The New York Times Book Review*, 10/31/04

laudanum (LOD num, also lo DEN um) - *n.* a tincture of opium.

> "Coleridge ... never lost his kindness and enormous empathy for other people, and consequently his ability to draw forth the same, despite years of drinking **laudanum**." –LAURA MILLER, *The New York Times Book Review, 4/4/04*

lushington (LUSH ing tuhn) - (OED) *n.* (slang). a drunkard.

> "'Lots of loungers and **lushingtons** always coming and going by the horsecar.'" –MATTHEW PEARL, *The Dante Club*

muzzy (muh ZEE) - *adj.* confused mentally, muddled or dazed, esp. due to alcohol, 2. indistinct; vague; blurred, 3. confused or vague, esp. of thinking.

> "He gave me a tight grin and butted me on the forehead and I didn't know if this was an impulsive gesture at the end of a long night when you're **muzzy** with booze and hoarse with talk and smoke, a thing that brings an evening to a formal close, or something a little more deliberate." –DON DELILLO, *Underworld*

raven (RAY vuhn) - (among other definitions) *v.* to seize (food) by force; prey; plunder, 2. to devour greedily, eat voraciously, 3. to prowl hungrily.

> "I also had to accustom myself to the work [the eagle] did with his beak when he **ravened**." –SAUL BELLOW, *The Adventures of Augie March*

replete (ri PLEET) - *adj.* well-filled or plentifully supplied, 2. stuffed with food and drink; gorged; filled to the point of bursting.

> "(After a second helping) He felt **replete**." –ISAAC ASIMOV, *The Robots of Dawn*

schmeck (SHMEK) - *n.* a drug; spec. heroin (from Yiddish - sniff).

> "'The word smack, or heroin? Comes from the Yiddish shmek. You know this, experts? A sniff, a smell, like a pinch of snuff. Dig it, he's got a two hundred dollar **shmek** habit.'" –DON DELILLO, *Underworld*

shicker (SHIK ur) - *(Yiddish) n.* a drunk; drunkard.

> "He drank his pay—a **shicker**." –SAUL BELLOW, *Herzog*

snockered (SNOK urd) - *adj.* intoxicated; affected by alcohol; drunk.

> "At ten minutes past four, the wagons pulled up in front of the Olympic Club's Doric columns, and the police, all in black tie, ran together—or as 'together' as they could, for they were quite **snockered**—into the club." –GLEN DAVID GOLD, *Carter Beats the Devil*

sodden (SAH dehn) - *adj.* saturated; soaked; soggy, 2. heavy or doughy from improper cooking, 3. dull, stupid, esp. from alcohol, 4. *v.* to have been boiled or steeped, 5. to soak; to make sodden.

> "... bleary and **sodden** from their debauch of the night before..." –ROBERT E. HOWARD, *The Vale of Lost Women*

sot (SAHT) - *n.* a drunkard; a chronic drinker.

> "... describing Paine as 'that noted **sot** and infidel, ...'" –JOSEPH J. ELLIS, *Founding Brothers*

surfeit (SUR fuht) - *n.* an overabundance or excess, 2. excessive indulgence, esp. in food or drink.

"She had seen revelers asleep after a night of drunken feasting with not half such **surfeit**, such almost obscene satisfaction upon their faces as Alaric's drugged company wore now." –C.L. Moore, *Jirel of Joiry*

tipple (TIH puhl) - *v.* to drink alcoholic beverages, esp. habitually or to excess (from Middle English tipler, bartender).

"I'm not **tippling**, I'm only 'indulging myself a little,' as that swine of a Rakitin of yours says." –Fyodor Dostoyevsky, *The Brothers Karamazov*, transl. by David Magarshack

toper (TOH puhr) - *n.* a chronic drinker; a drunkard.

"The [bar] room was divided into compartments in the approved manner, between which were screens of ground glass in mahogany framing, to prevent **topers** in one compartment being put to the blush by the recognitions of those in the next." –Thomas Hardy, *Jude the Obscure*

tosspot (TOS PAHT) - *n.* a drunkard; a heavy or chronic drinker.

"Now and then some factory worker straggles into the office to illiterately plead some cause (usually the drunkenness of the foreman, a chronic **tosspot**)." –John Kennedy Toole, *A Confederacy of Dunces*

COWARDS AND MORAL WEAKLINGS

(ALSO SEE PERSONALITY TRAITS—
COURAGEOUS AND COWARDLY)

blackguard (BLA guhrd, also BLA GARD, BLAK GARD) - *n.* a low, unprincipled, vulgar and uncouth person; a scoundrel.

"I see a **blackguard**, a fraud and a mur-

derer." –Arturo Perez-Reverte, *The Flanders Panel*

conclave (KAHN KLAYV) - *n.* a confidential or secret meeting, 2. a meeting in which cardinals of the Catholic Church meet to elect a new pope.

"... a strange **conclave** was taking place in the small velvet-hung taper-lighted chamber of Atalis, whom some called a philosopher and others a rogue." –Robert E. Howard, *The Hand of Nergal*

craven (CRAY vuhn) - *adj.* lacking any courage, cowardly, fainthearted.

see other **craven** *entry for citation, p. 15*

dissipate (DI suh PAYT) - *v.* to disperse; to break up and drive away, 2. to spend intemperately; to waste; to squander, 3. to lose; to vanish; to disappear, 4. to indulge intemperately, esp. in the pursuit of pleasure.

"The dark circles under his still puffy eyes emphasized his habitual air of **dissipation**." –Arturo Perez-Reverte, *The Flanders Panel*

dissolute (DI suh LOOT) - *adj.* lacking moral restraint; dissipated; immoral; debauched; profligate.

"Then, as in every drama in the Flashman series, the charming, **dissolute**, skirt-chasing rogue, having gotten himself by mistake into the thick of a noble challenge, performs with astonishing courage and effectiveness." –George Crile, *Charlie Wilson's War*

effete (eh FEET, ih FEET) - *adj.* having lost fertility; spent; sterile, 2. marked by a lack of vigor, stamina; showing a weakness of character; decadent, soft, overrefined, etc.

"Perhaps, thought Baley, that was how one

ought to define '**effete**': That to which one can become easily accustomed." —ISAAC ASIMOV, *The Robots of Dawn*

furtive (FUHR tiv) - *adj.* marked by stealth, surreptitious, 2. having hidden motives.

"**Furtive** figures slunk from the tall grass." —ROBERT E. HOWARD, *The Hand of Nergal*

ignominious (IG nuh MIH nee us) - *adj.* characterized by shame, disgrace, or dishonor, 2. despicable; disgraceful; shameful, 3. degrading; humiliating; debasing (etymology relates to gnomen, the name).

"'Most unpleasant,' said Alfonso ...

'It was worse than that.' Lola Belmonte had at last found the word she wanted and leaned her bony form forwards in her chair. 'It was **ignominious** ... Anyone would think we were the criminals." —ARTURO PEREZ-REVERTE, *The Flanders Panel*

louche (LOOSH) - *adj.* of questionable taste or morality; decadent; dubious; shifty; disreputable, 2. not straightforward, oblique.

"In Victorian London, even in a place as **louche** and notoriously crime-ridden as Lambeth Marsh, the sound of gunshots was a rare event indeed." —SIMON WINCHESTER, *The Professor and the Madman*

perfidy (PUHR fuh DEE) - *n.* the act of violating faith or allegiance; violation of a promise or vow, or of trust reposed; faithlessness; treachery.

"She wasn't suffering from any sickness or neurosis. She was suffering from the **perfidy** of a man named Charlie Croker." —TOM WOLFE, *A Man in Full*

poltroon (pahl TROON) - *n.* a complete coward, 2. *adj.* cowardly.

"Oh, you're cowards, both of you! **Poltroons**!" —FRITZ LEIBER, *Swords and Deviltry*

profligate (PRAH flih guht, also PRAH flih GAYT) - *adj.* shameless, immoral; vicious; dissolute, 2. recklessly wasteful; extravagant, 3. *n.* a profligate person.

"Cataline was the treacherous and degenerate character whose scheming nearly destroyed the Roman Republic and whose licentious ways inspired, by their very **profligacy**, Cicero's eloquent oration on virtue, which was subsequently memorized by generations of American schoolboys." —JOSEPH J. ELLIS, *Founding Brothers*

putrid (PYOO truhd) - *adj.* decaying; rotting, 2. corrupt; vile; disgusting.

"A great wave of nausea surged through him and his knife felt **putrid** in his hand." —MERVYN PEAKE, *Titus Groan*

recreant (REK ree uhnt) - *adj.* showing disloyalty, cowardly, 2. *n.* a disloyal person, a deserter, a coward.

*see other **recreant** entry for citation, p. 16*

reprobate (REH pruh BAYT) - *n.* a morally unprincipled or shameless person.

"'It is droll, after all,' she said, 'that we two, of all people, with our queer history, should happen to be here painting the Ten Commandments! You a **reprobate**, and I—in my condition.'" –THOMAS HARDY, *Jude the Obscure*

Sardanapalian (SAHR dn uh PAY LUHN, also SAHR dn uh PAY lee uhn) - *adj.* relating to Sardanapalus and his attributes; luxuriously effeminate.

scatology (ska TAH luh jee, also skuh TAH luh jee) - *n.* obscene literature, 2. an interest in obscenity, especially in literature (from the Greek skato, meaning excrement).

"'I saw you riding a horse on my place once or twice. No problem.' I thought he was about to mention the **scatological** side benefits to himself, but he just smiled at me ...This was indeed a horse shit day, I thought." –NELSON DeMILLE, *The Gold Coast*

unregenerate (UN ri JEH nuh rut, also UN re JEN rut) - *adj.* not spiritually or morally renewed; sinful; dissolute, 2. stubborn; obstinate; not reconciled to change.

"'Is he?' teased the **unregenerate** old man, pinching his pointy jaw gravely in a parody of repentance." –JOSEPH HELLER, *Catch-22*

vitiate (VI she ATE) - *v.* to make imperfect, faulty, or impure; spoil; corrupt, 2. to weaken morally; to debase, 3. to make (a contract, etc.) legally ineffective, invalidate.

*see other **vitiate** entry for citation, p. 116*

LAZY SLOBS

(ALSO SEE PERSONAL ENERGY— LACKING LNERGY)

Augean (o JEE uhn) - *adj.* exceedingly filthy, esp. from long neglect (from Augeas, Greek king who did not clean his stables for thir-

ty years; Hercules was said to purify it in a single day by turning the river Alpheus through it).

*see other **Augean** entry for citation, p. 152*

cloacal (klo A kuhl) - *adj.*- relating to or characterized by a cloaca (a sewer or latrine).

*see other **cloacal** entry for citation, p. 273*

Corinthian (kuh RIN thee uhn) - *adj.* pertaining to Corinth, its people, or culture, 2. dissolute and loving luxury, as the people of Corinth were said to be, 3. in the style of the art of Corinth; gracefully elaborate, 4. designating or of the most elaborate of the three orders of Greek architecture (the others being Doric and Ionic), distinguished by a slender, fluted column and bell-shaped capital decorated with a design of acanthus leaves and volutes, 5. *n.* a native of Corinth, 6. a lover of elegantly luxurious living; sybarite.

*see other **Corinthian** entry for citation, p. 274*

fainéant (fay nay AHN) - *adj.* lazy; idle, 2. *n.* one who does nothing; an idler.

"He insisted on kickbacks from plumbing, heating, or painting contractors with whom the Commissioner had always been cronies, and so made enemies. That didn't bother him, to whom the first thing was that the **fainéants** shouldn't be coming after Charlemagne-as long as people understood that." –SAUL BELLOW, *The Adventures of Augie March*

fetid (FE tuhd) - *adj.* foul-smelling, stinking.

"... he makes off as fast as he can from the **fetid** atmosphere of the cottage to the pure air outside." –SAMUEL BUTLER, *The Way of All Flesh*

flâneur (flah NUHR) - *n.* an aimless loafer or lounger; an idler.

"There is a titanic story beneath all this ... Masekela cannot fully tell it. But he lived it, almost as a **flâneur**, and it keeps the story of wastrel somehow emblematic." –ERIC WEISBARD, *The New York Times Book Review,* 6/13/04

frowsy (also **frowzy**) (FRAU zee) - *adj.* neglected appearance; unkempt; slovenly.

"**Frowsy** kitchen scullions and a pair of unwashed girls were carrying in the planks and trestles for the table." –C.L. MOORE, *Jirel of Joiry*

goldbrick (also **goldbricker**) (GOLD BRIK) - *n.* a person, esp. a soldier, who avoids assigned duties or work; a shirker.

indolent (IN duh luhnt) - *adj.* disliking or avoiding work; idle; lazy.

"...as a child he had been violently passionate; now, however, he was reserved and shy, and, I should say, **indolent** in mind and body." –SAMUEL BUTLER, *The Way of All Flesh*

lubber (LUH buhr) - *n.* an awkward, stupid, clumsy person, especially one who is idle, 2. a clod; stubblebum; oaf, 3. an inexperienced or first-time sailor.

"'What a dunce I have been all my days, and what **lubbers** my Children, and Grand Children, were, that none of us have ever thought to make a similar collection.'" –JOHN ADAMS, QUOTED BY JOSEPH J. ELLIS, *Founding Brothers*

otiose (OH she OHS, also OH tee OHS) - *adj.* lazy; indolent, 2. useless; ineffective; futile.

"To speed up the narrative, I condensed it by more than 15% by small cuts of what seemed **otiose** verbiage." –L. SPRAGUE DE CAMP, *The Spell of Conan*

slovenly (SLAH vehn lee, also SLOH vehn lee) - *adj.* untidy or messy in dress or appearance, 2. marked by carelessness, slipshod.

"The trail was red now, and the clean stride of the great beast had grown short and **slovenly**." –JACK LONDON, *The Law of Life*

sordid (SOR duhd) - *adj.* filthy; dirty; foul, 2. depressingly wretched, squalid, 3. unethical; dishonest; morally degraded; vile; base.

"The Maze, a tangle of muddy winding alleys and **sordid** dens, frequented by the boldest thieves in the kingdom." –ROBERT E. HOWARD, *Rogues in the House*

squalid (SKWAH luhd) - *adj.* dirty and wretched in appearance; run-down, 2. morally repulsive; sordid; morally degraded.

"... looked down on the mesquite flat wherein stood Lopez's **squalid** hut." –ROBERT E. HOWARD, *Trails in Darkness*

squalor (SKWHA luhr, also SKWAY luhr, SWKO luhr) - *n.* the state of being squalid.

"... it seemed to him a strange sight, this elegant lady in her nankeen gown here among all this **squalor**." –GUSTAVE FLAUBERT, *Madame Bovary,* transl. by Francis Steegmuller

Sybarite (SIH buh RITE) - *adj.* related to the people of ancient Sybaris, 2. a person fond of luxury and pleasure, 3. one devoted to self-indulgence; a voluptuary.

"On a broad cushion-piled dais reclined the giver of the feast, sensuously stroking the glossy locks of a lithe Arabian who had stretched herself on her supple belly beside him. His appearance of **sybaritic** languor was belied by the subtle sparkling of his dark eyes as he surveyed his guests." —ROBERT E. HOWARD, *Eons of the Night*

voluptuary (vuh LUHPT shuh WER ee) - *n.* one for whom luxury and the sensual pleasures are the chief care; one whose life is given over to physical enjoyment; a sensualist.

"He achieved notoriety as a **voluptuary** and was murdered by his own troops." —S.T. JOSHI, *Explanatory Notes, H.P. Lovecraft's The Call of Cthulhu and Other Weird Stories*

wastrel (WAYS truhl, also WAHS truhl) - *n.* one who wastes time or resources, 2. an idler or loafer.

"'He of all people despised his father for being a **wastrel**. Mr. Balfour-the elder, that is—was once industrious and successful, but as he grew older he felt that he had earned the right to waste all that he had accomplished, and as his son watched his estate disappear, he began to hate his father.'" —DAVID LISS, *A Conspiracy of Paper*

NASTY ABUSIVE TYPES

(ALSO SEE PERSONALITY TRAITS— DIFFICULT)

billingsgate (BIH lingz GAYT) - *n.* coarse, abusive language (after Billingsgate, a fish-market in London).

*see other **billingsgate** entry for citation, p. 79*

bluestocking (BLOO STAH king) - *n.* a woman with strong intellectual or scholarly interests, 2. a pedantic woman (from the Blue Stocking Society, a predominantly female literary club of 18th-century London).

"... she appeared to be a **bluestocking** for whom sex was of decidedly less importance than her academic, scholarly, and intellectual pursuits." —PHILIP ROTH, *The Human Stain*

churl (CHURL) - *n.* one who is rude, surly or boorish, 2. one who is miserly, 3. a medieval English peasant (from the Old English ceorl, peasant).

"... it seems **churlish** to ask this polite, accommodating man, whoever he is, to move out of his own bed." —NICK HORNBY, *How to be Good*

gadfly (GAD fly) - *n.* any of various flies that bite or annoy animals, esp. livestock, 2. a nuisance; a persistent irritation, 3. a person acting as a provocative stimulus; a goad.

"After the theft of the portmaster's diary, Taft vanished from the story of my father's life, only to resurface as the **gadfly** of his career, biting from behind the scholar's veil." —IAN CALDWELL AND DUSTIN THOMASON, *The Rule of Four*

Harpy (HAHR pee) - *n.* a relentless, greedy, or grasping person, 2. a shrewish woman, 3. (Greek Mythology) Harpy—a fabulous winged monster, ravenous and filthy, having the head and trunk of a woman and the tail, legs, and talons of a bird.

"'Please, Mother, I am near the breaking point! ... If you are planning now to be a **harpy**, I shall certainly be pushed over the brink.'" —JOHN KENNEDY TOOLE, *A Confederacy of Dunces*

harridan (HAR uh dun) - *n.* a scolding, vicious woman.

"Well, the Widow Stone, a steely eyed **harridan** of penurious Scottish stock, handed over to me her husband's correspondence of a lifetime." –PAT CONROY, *The Lords of Discipline*

martinet (MAHR tun ET) - *n.* a very strict military disciplinarian, 2. any very strict disciplinarian or stickler for rigid regulations (after Gen. Jean Martinet, 17th-century. Fr. drillmaster).

> "Munisai, a **martinet** who wouldn't have known how to spoil a child in the unlikely event that he had wanted to." –EIJI YOSHIKAWA, *Musashi*, transl. by Charles S. Terry

misanthrope (MIH sen throwp) - *n.* one who hates society and people in general.

*see other **misanthrope** entry for citation, p. 13*

scold (SKOLD) - (among other definitions) *n.* a person, esp. a woman, who persistently nags or criticizes, esp. severely or angrily.

> "The authors suggest Wiener's swings were exacerbated by his oppressive upbringing: home-schooled by a **scold** of a father, Wiener started college at the age of 11 in 1906 ..." –CLIVE THOMPSON, *The New York Times Book Review, 3/20/05*

virago (vuh RAH go, also vuh RAY go, VIR uh GO) - *n.* a a quarrelsome, domineering or shrewish woman; a scold.

> "It met its persecutor with a shriek almost exactly like that of an angry **virago**." –H.G. WELLS, *The Island of Dr. Moreau*

CLOWNS AND DANDIES

baroque (buh ROK, also ba ROK, buh RAHK, buh ROCK) - *adj.* (often Baroque) having an irregular shape, 2. flamboyant; outlandish, 3. an artistic style common in Europe from 1500 to 1700 exhibiting very elaborate and ornate forms, 4. a musical style common in Europe from 1600 to 1750 exhibiting strict forms and elaborate detail.

*see other **baroque** entry for citation, p. 104*

blunderbuss (BLUHN duhr BUHS) - *n.* a short musket with a wide muzzle, formerly used to scatter shot at close range, 2. a stupid or clumsy person.

braggadocio (BRA guh DOE see O, also BRA guh DOE she O, BRA guh DOE chee O) - *n.* a braggart, 2. empty or pretentious boasting, 3. arrogance; cockiness (name derives from the character Braggadocchio, the personification of boasting in *The Faerie Queen* by Edmund Spenser).

*see other **braggadocio** entry for citation, p 78*

coxcomb (also **cockscomb**) (KAHKS com) - *n.* one who is conceited, a dandy; a fop, 2. **cockscomb**—the fleshy red crest on the head of a rooster, 3. a cap worn by a court jester, adorned to resembly the comb of a rooster.

> "'Move along, you **coxcomb**,' Ignatius belched, the gassy eructations echoing between the walls of the Alley." –JOHN KENNEDY TOOLE, *A Confederacy of Dunces*

fop (FAHP) - *n.* a vain, affected man who pays too much attention to his clothes, appearance, etc.; a dandy.

> "His nephew Dondal was a slim, **foppish** youth with keen dark eyes and a pleasant smile." –ROBERT E. HOWARD, *Swords of the Purple Kingdom*

frippery (FRI puh ree) - *n.* pretentious, showy dress, 2. a pretentious display; ostentation, 3. something trivial, nonessential.

> "'But four thousand, my dear young lady, is a bit too much to throw away on such **frippery**, don't you think?'" –FYODOR DOS-

TOYEVSKY, *The Brothers Karamazov*, transl. by David Magarshack

harlequin (HAHR li kwuhn) - *n.* a clown, a buffoon, traditionally presented in mask and many colored costume, 2. having a pattern of parti-colored diamond shapes (the Harlequin being originally a character in Italian comedy).

"He is more than the Italian **Harlequin**."
—PAUL MORAND, *Introduction, Francois Voltaire's Candide*

hauteur (ho TUHR, also o TUHR) - *n.* disdainful pride; haughtiness; snobbery (Note: French haute, high, thus haute couture translates as high sewing [high fashion], and haute cuisine translates as high kitchen [high food]).

"Nevertheless, the **hauteur** of the senior partners could be oppressive." —RON CHERNOW, *The House of Morgan*

jackanapes (JA kuh NAYPS) - *n.* a tame monkey or ape, 2. one who is conceited or impudent; a coxcomb, 3. a playful, pert, or mischievous child, 4. a person whose behavior is compared to an ape or monkey.

"'Anyway I had ceased to love the cowardly **jackanapes**, with his airs and his sneers.'"
—L. SPRAGUE DE CAMP, *The Tritonian Ring*

kowtow (KAU TAU) - *n.* (from Chinese) to kneel and touch the forehead to the ground, (a salutation or expression of deep respect formerly performed in China), 2. an obsequious act to show servile deference or to gain favor through flattery.

"He was there to repair the damage, to **kowtow** to the chairman." —GEORGE CRILE, *Charlie Wilson's War*

ostentation (AHS tuhn TAY shun) - *n.* pretentious display or boastful showiness meant to impress others.

"The cook borrowed a stone from Johansen and proceeded to sharpen the knife. He did it with great **ostentation**, glancing significantly at me the while." —JACK LONDON, *The Sea Wolf*

popinjay (PAH puhn JAY) - *n.* one who is vain, conceited, talkative, or supercilious (from the Arabic, babagha for parrot).

"Nevertheless, I was none of your sprightly **popinjays** who wore the latest bright colors and frills; a man of my trade always prefers simple fashions that draw to himself no particular attention." —DAVID LISS, *A Conspiracy of Paper*

raffish (RA fish) - *adj.* cheaply showy or vulgar, esp. in appearance, 2. expressing a carefree unconventionality; rakish; jaunty.

*see other **raffish** entry for citation, p. 27*

scaramouch (SKAR uh MOOSH, also SKAR uh MOOCH, also SKAR uh MAUCH) - *n.* a stock character in old Italian farce, a cowardly and foolish boaster of his own prowess, who is constantly being cudgelled by Harlequin, 2. a boastful coward or rascal.

> "'Stand still, **scaramouch**!' she cries."
> —MICHEL FABER, *The Crimson Petal and the White*

simper (SIM puhr) - *v.* to smile in a silly, coy or self-conscious way.

> "The real hall of mirrors in Crowe's flabby maze is the competing agendas; he's hoping to win points for edginess even as he vitiates the material with his own **simpering** urge to make nice." —TOM CARSON, *Esquire*, 4/02

tawdry (TO dree, also TAH dree) - *adj.* gaudy or cheap in nature or appearance, 2. indecent; shameful.

> "... rascals gathered in every stage of rags and tatters—furtive cut-purses, leering kidnappers, quick-fingered thieves, swaggering bravoes with their wenches, strident-voiced women clad in **tawdry** finery." —ROBERT E. HOWARD, *The Tower of the Elephant*

twee (TWEE) - *adj.* excessively sweet, dainty or cute; precious; over-refined; mawkish.

vainglory (VAYN GLOR ee) - *n.* boastful, unwarranted self-pride; outspoken conceit, 2. a vain or ostentatious display.

> "... one of the untold zillions who move to New York, looking to make good on their **vainglory**, only to end up stuck in the menial labor force." —STEPHEN METCALF, *The New York Times Book Review*, 6/20/04

SINNERS, EVILDOERS

anathema (uh NA thuh muh) - *n.* a thing or person accursed, damned, or intensely disliked, 2. a formal ecclesiastical ban, curse, or excommunication.

> "So she sat on her companion's—or captor's—knee with a docility that would have amazed Zarallo, who had **anathematized** her as a she-devil out of Hell's seraglio." —ROBERT E. HOWARD, *Conan the Warrior*

bohunk (BO HUNGK) - *n.* a disparaging term for a Hungarian or a person from east-central Europe, esp. a laborer (combination of Bohemian and Hungarian).

> "... there were going to be some remarkable results begotten out of the mass. I knew ... **Bohunk** wizards at the Greeks ..." —SAUL BELLOW, *The Adventures of Augie March*

bravo (BRAH VO) - (among other definitions) *n.* a villain; a hired killer; assassin; desperado.

> "... three reliable and lethal **bravos** hired for the evening from the Slayers' Brotherhood." —FRITZ LEIBER, *Swords and Deviltry*

bucket-shop (BUH kuht SHAHP) - *n.* a small office originally used for gambling transactions in grain; now use extends to other forms of gambling, betting on the market, stocks, etc., 2. a gin-mill, a low-end liquor store, 3. a cut-price retailer (originally derives from a practice at the Chicago Board of Trade of gathering small orders from speculators outside in a bucket).

> "Tommy sent us to his **bucket-shop** stockbroker on Lake Street, back of the panels of a cigar-store front." —SAUL BELLOW, *The Adventures of Augie March*

buffer (BUH fuhr) - (among other definitions, obscure, slang) *n.* horse thief.

> "... a gang of a half-dozen **buffers**—thieves that steal horses, slaughter them, and sell their skins." –DAVID LISS, *A Conspiracy of Paper*

cabal (kuh BAHL, also kuh BAL) - *n.* a conspiratorial group formed of plotters or intriguers, 2. a secret plot or scheme, 3. *v.* to form a cabal; to conspire.

> "... a ring engraved in the floor with curious, **cabalistic** symbols." –C.L. MOORE, *Jirel of Joiry*

cardsharp (KARD SHARP) - *n.* one who is expert in cheating at cards.

> "... the many lives depicted—from those of aging dancers and hustlers to New York's last trapper—are rendered with respect and the style of a **cardsharp**." –TYLER D. JOHNSON, *The New York Times Book Review, 3/28/04*

crimp (KRIMP) - (among other definitions) *n.* an agent who tricks, seduces, decoys, entraps, coerces, or impresses others into service as sailors or soldiers.

> "**Crimps** were paid a seaman's first two months wages for every man they delivered. This spawned the nefarious shanghaiing trade, the practice of kidnapping men to serve on ships." –DANIEL BACON, *The Official Guide to San Francisco's Barbary Coast Trail*

dacoit (duh KOIT) - *n.* one of a gang or band of robbers in India or Myanmar (Burma); also applied to pirates who formerly infested the Ganges between Calcutta and Burhampore, 2. *v.* to plunder as a dacoit.

> "You remember the cry in the back lane? ... It was the cry of a **dacoit**. Oh, dacoity, though quiescent, is by no means extinct. Fu-Manchu has dacoits in his train, and probably it is one who operates the Zayat Kiss, since it was a dacoit who watched the win-dow of the study this evening. To such a man an ivy-covered wall is a grand staircase." –SAX ROHMER, *The Insidious Dr. Fu-Manchu*

footpad (FUT PAD) - *n.* a thief who robs on foot.

> "I could only assume that the scurrying we heard around us bespoke **footpads** and prigs who knew Kate." –DAVID LISS, *A Conspiracy of Paper*

goniff (also **ganef, ganof**) (GAH nuhf) - (Yiddish) *n.* a thief; a bandit.

> "'And now, with your still? You had to escape from the Czar's police. And now the Revenue? And you have to have a partner, a **goniff**.'" –SAUL BELLOW, *Herzog*

gullion (GUHL yuhn) - *n.* a mean and worthless wretch, 2. also a drunkard.

> "'You bastardly **gullion**,' she breathed." –DAVID LISS, *A Conspiracy of Paper*

guttersnipe (GUH tuhr SNYP) - *n.* a street urchin, 2. one from the lowest class.

> "'That's enough from you, you **guttersnipe**.'" –JOHN KENNEDY TOOLE, *A Confederacy of Dunces*

jade (JAYD) (among other definitions)- *n.* a woman of ill repute.

> "'Interrogate the Trixie **jade**. The senility is a guise.'" –JOHN KENNEDY TOOLE, *A Confederacy of Dunces*

knave (NAYV) - *n.* a serving boy or male servant, 2. a dishonest person; tricky rascal; a rogue, 3. a playing card marked with the figure of a page, servant, or soldier; a jack.

> "Help me down, then, you hell-spawned **knaves**." –C.L. MOORE, *Jirel of Joiry*

macher (MOKH er) - *(Yiddish) n.* an important or influential person; a fixer; a braggart.

> "'... that **macher**, Alexander. Always some scandal about him. Now he's connected with the Juice racket, and next with Jimmy Hoffa.'" –SAUL BELLOW, *Herzog*

malefactor (MA luh FAK tuhr) - *n.* a felon; a criminal, 2. an evildoer, one who behaves wickedly toward others.

> "Bis ... lived in a state of constant rebellion. 'My whole life was **malefaction**,' Bis later told me." –KATHARINE GRAHAM, *Personal History*

mamzer (MAHM zer) - (Yiddish) *n.* one who was conceived outside the rabbical traditions, in a forbidden sexual union, (extended definitions include use as a term of abuse or familiarity).

> "'[Your father] can't sleep ... because of that **mamzer** [President Nixon]. He's up in the middle of the night writing him letters.'" –PHILIP ROTH, *American Pastoral*

miscreant (MIS kree uhnt) - *n.* an evildoer; a villain; a scoundrel.

> "'For vanquishing and dismaying the arrogant, For sustaining and counselling worthy men, And vanquishing and dismaying **miscreants**, In no land is there a finer knight.'" –*The Song of Roland*, transl. by Glyn Burgess

mountebank (MAUN ti BANGK) - *n.* a person who would mount a bench or platform from which to sell quack medicines, attracting customers by tricks, stories, jokes, etc., 2. a charlatan, a flamboyant quack, 3. *v.* to act as a mountebank.

> "... it seems to me ridiculous to suppose that there are no charlatans, posers, and **mountebanks** in the ranks of art; or that even a sincere artist can not have objectionable characteristics." –ROBERT E. HOWARD, *Selected Letters 1931–1936*.

parricide (PAR uh SIDE) - *n.* a person who murders one of his parents or other near relative, 2. one who commits a parricide, 3. the act committed by a parricide.

> "'Yours isn't the most important case of the session. Right after you, there's a **parricide** coming up.'" –ALBERT CAMUS, *The Stranger*

pettifogger (PE tee FO guhr, also PE tee FAH guhr) - *n.* a person, esp. a lawyer, who is petty, quibbling, or unscrupulous.

> "'He'd have employed a whole regiment of **pettifogging** lawyers,'" –FYODOR DOSTOYEVSKY, *The Brothers Karamazov*, transl. by David Magarshack

scalawag (SKA li WAG) - *n.* a scoundrel; a reprobate; a rascal.

> "'I know that, **scalawag**,' Gene said." –PAT CONROY, *My Losing Season*

scut (SKUHT) - *n.* a stubby, stumpy tail as that of a hare, rabbit or deer, 2. one who is contemptible.

"'Aye, there's heroes and there's **scuts** in every folk and nation.'" –L. SPRAGUE DE CAMP AND LIN CARTER, *Conan the Buccaneer*

tenderloin (TEN dehr LOIN) - *n.* the most tender part of a cut of meat, ex: beef or pork, cut from below the short ribs and made up of the psoas muscle, 2. (usually T-) a city district known for corruption and vice, so called because it is regarded as a choice assignment for police seeking graft, 3. the district of New York City below 42nd Street and west of Broadway.

tout (TAUT, also TOOT) - *v.* to obtain and deal in information regarding horse races, 2. to publicize as being of great worth, 3. *n.* one who touts.

"'You can't run a business. You're a failure, a playboy, a racetrack **tout**.'" –JOHN KENNEDY TOOLE, *A Confederacy of Dunces*

uxoricide (UK SOR uh SIGHD) - *n.* the act of a man killing his wife, 2. a man who kills his wife.

varlet (VAHR luht) - *n.* an attendant; a servant, 2. a rascal; a knave.

"Make haste, you **varlets**! Bring me Giraud!" –C.L. MOORE, *Jirel of Joiry*

EVIL ACTS AND INTENTIONS

anomy (A nuh mee) - *n.* disregard for the law, 2. absence of social standards and values leading to social instability, 3. alienation, unrest, or purposelessness due to a lack of purpose or ideals.

"Sourmelina was bad with babies but terrific with teenagers. She was there for your first crushes and heartbreaks, your party dresses and spins at sophisticated states like **anomie**." –JEFFREY EUGENIDES, *Middlesex*

arrogate (AHR uh GAYT) - *v.* to claim or seize for oneself without right; to appropriate arrogantly, 2. to ascribe or attribute in an unwarranted manner.

"'I'm saying the structure of the entire culture is flawed,' Chip said. 'I'm saying the bureaucracy has **arrogated** the right to define certain states of mind as 'diseased.'" –JONATHAN FRANZEN, *The Corrections*

bale (BAYL) - (among other definitions) *n.* evil, 2. mental suffering; anguish; misery; sorrow; grief, 3. a great consuming fire, a conflagration, a bonfire, a funeral pyre.

"His sword was naked in his hand, and his eyes blazed like **bale**-fire, whether with anger, suspicion or surprize she could not judge." –ROBERT E. HOWARD, *The Vale of Lost Women*

baleful (BAYL fuhl) - *adj.* sinister or malignant in intent or effect, 2. portending evil, ominous; sinister.

"I saw … an awful torrent of blackness, with scores of **baleful** eyes glowing in it." –H.P. LOVECRAFT, *He*

boodle (BOO duhl) - (slang) *n.* informal term for money; counterfeit money, 2. money used in a bribe, 3. stolen goods.

"Before setting off for the fifteen-minute drive down to the Hill, Avrakotos was familiarized with the sins of Congressman Wilson: a **boodling**, boozing, indiscriminate skirt chaser who was giving the

Agency no end of trouble." —GEORGE CRILE, *Charlie Wilson's War*

cozen (KUH zuhn) *v.* to deceive; to cheat, 2. to persuade or mislead by using a petty trick or fraud (possibly from the Italian cozzone, horse trader).

> "... for he echoed the lies of Melkor, that the Valar had **cozened** them and would hold them captive so that Men might rule in Middle-Earth." —J.R.R. TOLKIEN, *The Silmarillion*

depredation (DE pruh DAY shun) - *n.* an act or instance of destruction, plunder, or ravaging; a raid; a predatory attack, 2. damage; loss.

> "... the four dwarves sat round the table, and talked about mines and gold and troubles with the goblins, and the **depredations** of dragons, and lots of other things." —J.R.R. TOLKIEN, *The Hobbit*

despoil (DI spoil) - *v.* to deprive of possessions or valuables by force; to sack; to plunder (noun is despoliation).

> "'Look!' a muscular black arm stabbed toward the Tigress, and Bêlit wheeled, her crimson lips a-snarl, as if she expected to see a rival corsair sweeping in to **despoil** her of her plunder." —ROBERT E. HOWARD, *The Conan Chronicles*

dissimulate (DI sim yuh LAYT) - *v.* to conceal or disguise under a feigned or false appearance; to dissemble.

> "We have not the strength with which to fight this man; we must **dissimulate**, and win, if win we can, by craft." —JACK LONDON, *The Sea Wolf*

fell (FEL) - (among other definitions) *adj.* fierce, terrible, cruel, 2. *n.* a rocky or barren hill or ridge, 3. a moor; down; wild field.

> "[The Riders'] cold eyes glittered, and they called to him with **fell** voices." —J.R.R. TOLKIEN, *The Fellowship of the Ring*

fob (FAHB) - *v.* to deceive or cheat another, 2. to dispose of goods through deception or fraud, 3. *n.* a short chain or ribbon attached to a pocket watch, often seen hanging in front of a vest or waist.

> "Karamazov ... would **fob** him off with small sums of money, which he sent him from time to time." —FYODOR DOSTOYEVSKY, *The Brothers Karamazov*, transl. by David Magarshack

hob (HAHB) - *n.* a goblin (hobgoblin); a sprite; an elf, 2. mischievous behavior, 3. *v.* to act mischievously, especially in the phrase to raise hob (with).

> "Padilla raised **hob** with me about the Merz because it took so long to finish and a man in the History department was after him for it." —SAUL BELLOW, *The Adventures of Augie March*

hugger-mugger (HUH guhr MUH guhr) - *n.* disorder; confusion; a muddle, 2. a person who keeps things secret or concealed, 3. *adj.* secrecy; concealment; clandestine; disorderly, 4. *v.* to act in a secretive or clandestine manner.

> "... a rough-hewn, rollicking, **hugger-mugger**, devil-may-care, peculiarly London type of good cheer." —SIMON WINCHESTER, *The Professor and the Madman*

iniquity (i NIK wi tee) - *n.* wickedness; sinfulness; gross immorality or injustice, 2. a wicked or grossly immoral act; a sin.

> "'You put so much stock in winning wars,' the grubby **iniquitous** old man scoffed." —JOSEPH HELLER, *Catch-22*

insidious (in SI dee us) - *adj.* working or spreading in a hidden or subtle manner, 2. meant to entrap; treacherous, 3. alluring or beguiling but harmful, seductive.

> "In fact, [the movie industry's studio system] was about to topple, thanks to antitrust litigation and to an **insidious** little invention called television." —NEIL GENZLINGER, *The New York Times Book Review, 3/20/05*

jape (JAYP) - *v.* to joke or quip; to trick, 2. to make fun of; to jest, 3. *n.* a joke, a quip, a trick.

> "One loaf and one fish to be shared among five thousand wretches—that's His jolliest **jape**." —MICHEL FABER, *The Crimson Petal and the White*

malefic (muh LE fik) - *adj.* evil; baleful, 2. malicious; having a malignant influence.

> "[Our coach's] dark eyes smoldered with **malefic** competitiveness as he screamed, 'The SEC. The SEC. Let's see if we can play with the big boys.'" —PAT CONROY, *My Losing Season*

maleficence (muh LE fuh suhnts) - *n.* the act of doing evil or harm; mischief, 2. the nature or condition of being evil or harmful (there is an evil fairy in Disney's *Sleeping Beauty* named Maleficent).

nefarious (ne FAIR ee us) - *adj.* evil, villainous, wicked.

> "Crimps were paid a seaman's first two months' wages for every man they delivered. This spawned the **nefarious** shanghaiing trade, the practice of kidnapping men to serve on ships." —DANIEL BACON, *The Official Guide to San Francisco's Barbary Coast Trail*

purloin (puhr LOIN) - *v.* to steal; to commit a theft; to filch, 2. to steal in a violation of trust.

> "Camerlengo Carlo Ventresca had **purloined** the key and ventured inside." —DAN BROWN, *Angels & Demons*

rapine (RA puhn, also RA PINE) - *n.* the seizure of another's property by force or plunder.

> "For my part, the mystic phase of the East has always interested me less than the material side-the red and royal panorama of war, **rapine**, and conquest." —ROBERT E. HOWARD, *Selected Letters 1923-1930*

raven (RAY vuhn) - (among other definitions) *v.* to seize (food) by force; prey; plunder, 2. to devour greedily, eat voraciously, 3. to prowl hungrily.

> "With sweep and thrust he cleared away the priests **ravening** at him." —ABRAHAM MERRITT, *The Ship of Ishtar*

reave (REEV) - *v.* to take away by violence; seize; rob; plunder, 2. to break apart.

> "'This day I have seen four score men fall, and I alone have survived the field where Wulfhere's **reavers** met the wolves of Bragi." —ROBERT E. HOWARD, *The Frost Giant's Daughter*

recidivism (ri SI duh VI zuhm) - *n.* a tendency to lapse into a former pattern of behavior, esp. a return to a pattern of criminal habits.

> "A three page letter from the camp director, heavy with correctional, parole-style adjectives, ranked me among the worst Boy Scout **recidivists** of greater central Ohio." —IAN CALDWELL AND DUSTIN THOMASON, *The Rule of Four*

sanguinary (SANG gwuh NER ee) - *adj.* bloody, 2. bloodthirsty; eager for bloodshed.

> "From the moment this word [afraid] was used the state of things became intolerable. A **sanguinary** encounter seemed daily imminent between the two parties in the streets of Baltimore." –JULES VERNE, *From the Earth to the Moon*

skulk (SKUHLK) - *v.* to hide or lurk in a sneaking manner, 2. to move about stealthily or furtively.

> "All I want is the **skulker** here, whom I have sworn to kill." –C.L. MOORE, *Jirel of Joiry*

suborn (suh BORN) - *v.* to induce another to commit an unlawful act, 2. to induce or obtain perjured or false testimony from a witness.

venal (VEE nuhl) - *adj.* that can readily be bribed or corrupted: a venal judge, 2. corrupt; crooked, 3. available for a price, willing to take bribes, 4. characterized by corruption and bribery (a venal bargain).

> "By then we had been fighting this battle against **venality** for two years in the case of two of the challenges [to the *Post's* television license renewals] ..." –KATHARINE GRAHAM, *Personal History*

DEVICES OF PUNISHMENT

bilbo (BIL BO) - *n.* an iron bar fitted with sliding shackles or fetters used to shackle the ankles of prisoners.

> "The light coming from the windows showed him he'd been clapped into the **bilboes**. There was a pole attached to the wall and soldered to the pole was a pair of foot-cuffs, from which he dangled, upside-down, so that the blood was rushing to his head." –GLEN DAVID GOLD, *Carter Beats the Devil*

branks (BRANKS) - *n.* a device consisting of a metal frame to enclose the head and a gag or bit to restrain the tongue used to punish, primarily scolds (referred to as a scold's bridle).

> "The **brank**, 'the crown of the curste,' was a set of iron bands that made up a slatted cage into which the head was placed. A strong adult needed two hands to carry it. Beneath the space for the nose was 'the Devil's bit,' a spiked plate of adjustable length that was inserted, spikes down, into the victim's mouth. A second set of spikes fit just under the chin. The penitent, as long as his jaw remained still, would be uninjured, but a single attempt at speech would puncture his mouth in a dozen places. It was used on women who scolded, or men who spoke blasphemy, or debtors who claimed to be wealthy." –GLEN DAVID GOLD, *Carter Beats the Devil*

cucking stool (KUH king STOOL) - *n.* an instrument of punishment, a chair in which the offender, usu. a disorderly woman, scold, or cheat was tied and exposed to public derision or ducked in water (from the ME coking-stole, lit., toilet seat: the instrument was orig. made like a toilet seat to heighten the indignity).

fetter (FE tehr) - *n.* a chain or shackle attached to the ankles or feet, 2. something that restricts, esp. freedom; a restraint, 3. *v.* to restrain, 4. to restrict freedom.

> "They put an iron collar round his neck And place him in **fetters** like a bear." –*The Song of Roland,* transl. by Glyn Burgess

gantlet (GONT leht, also GAHNT leht) - (variation of gauntlet, among other definitions) *n.* a military punishment in which two rows of men facing each other swing clubs at the offender who must run between them, 2. an ordeal, a trial, severe difficulties; 3. *v.* run the gantlet—to suffer the punishment of the gantlet, 4. to advance despite attack from both sides.

> "Mr. Lieberman's cast will be recognizable to anyone who has had experience of private schools and thus run the admissions **gantlet** for himself or his children." —NED CRABB, *The Wall Street Journal,* 9/14/04

garrote (or **garrotte**) (guh RAHT, also guh ROAT, GAR uht) - *n.* execution using an iron collar to strangle or break the neck of a condemned person, 2. the iron collar used in such an execution, 3. strangulation, esp. in order to rob.

> "I waited for the **garrote** to encircle my neck and the sound of cackling as it drew tight, but instead she replied, 'Perhaps I'll write to Mr. Stanhope and ask his permission.' Touché." —NELSON DEMILLE, *The Gold Coast*

gibbet (JI beht) - *n.* a gallows, 2. a structure from which a person is hanged (by the neck) until dead, 3. *v.* to execute by hanging on a gibbet, 4. to hang (a person) on a gibbet, 5. to expose to public ridicule.

> "'... where the road to Fenworth branches off, and the handpost stands. A **gibbet** once stood there not unconnected with our history. But let that be.'" —THOMAS HARDY, *Jude the Obscure*

Lubyanka (also **Lubianka**) (LOO byahng kuh) - *n.* a street in Moscow, 2. related to the former headquarters of the Soviet secret police located on this street in Moscow and the detention center within used to hold political dissidents.

> "Sandor himself used police methods, clever psychology, the same as in the **Lubianka**, the same the world over." —SAUL BELLOW, *Herzog*

pillory (PIH luh ree, also PIL ree) - *n.* a device of punishment in which offenders were locked with head and hands in holes while exposed to public ridicule or scorn, 2. *v.* to expose to public ribicule, contempt, scorn, or abuse.

> "There's an old **pillory** on the wall above his head, mounted with its jaws open." —IAN CALDWELL AND DUSTIN THOMASON, *The Rule of Four*

pizzle (PIH zuhl) - *n.* the penis of an animal, esp. that of a bull, formerly used as a flogging instrument.

> "Among the galley-slaves were two convicts who rowed very badly and from time to time the Levantine captain applied several strokes of a bull's **pizzle** to their naked shoulders." —FRANCOIS VOLTAIRE, *Candide*, transl. by Richard Aldington

6. KNOWLEDGE, LANGUAGE, AND PHILOSOPHY

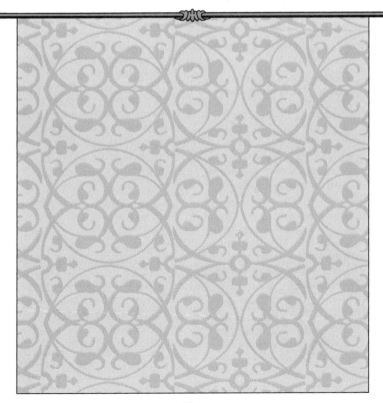

FIGURES OF SPEECH, WRITING, LOGIC, AND KNOWLEDGE—NOUNS

FIGURES OF SPEECH
PITHY SAYINGS AND RULES

aphorism (A fuhr RIH zuhm) - *n.* a short phrase conveying some principal or concept of thought; maxim; adage.

> "... the narrator [of John Edgar Wideman's 'God's Gym'], mid-reverie, blurts out a truth so raw and clear it sounds like an **aphorism**. 'You can go a little insane,' he says, 'trying to find something new about yourself.'" —TERRENCE RAFFERTY, *The New York Times Book Review*, 3/20/05

apothegm (A puh THEM) - *n.* a maxim; a proverb; an adage.

> "In reading the above sentence, a curious **apothegm** of an old weatherbeaten Dutch navigator comes full upon my recollection. 'It is as sure,' he was wont to say, when any doubt was entertained of his veracity, 'as sure as there is a sea where the ship itself will grow in bulk like the living body of the seaman.'" —EDGAR ALLAN POE, *The Fall of the House of Usher*

bromide (BRO MYD) - *n.* a binary compound of bromine and some other element or radical, 2. a dose of bromide taken as a sedative, 3. a dull person with conventional thoughts, 4. a trite remark or idea (the adjective is bromidic).

> "May I name another vicious **bromide** you've never felt? ... You've never felt how small you were when looking at the ocean.'" —AYN RAND, *The Fountainhead*

epigram (EH puh GRAM) - *n.* a brief and witty or satirical poem, 2. a brief, witty saying, often antithetical (Eex.: "Experience is the name everyone gives his mistakes").

> "... the cruel **epigrams** and occasional harsh witticisms of the fellows at the Bibelot." —JACK LONDON, *The Sea Wolf*

gnome (NOME) - *n.* an imaginary being, supposed by the Rosicrucians to inhabit the inner parts of the earth, and to be the guardian of mines, quarries, etc., 2. a dwarf; a goblin; a person of small stature or misshapen features, or of strange appearance, 3. a brief reflection or maxim.

gnomic (NO mik) - *adj.* containing aphorisms; wise; pithy, 2. relating to a writer of aphorisms.

> "... an itinerant philosopher was supposed to be **gnomic** in her speech and mantic in her thought." —ORSON SCOTT CARD, *Children of the Mind*

maxim (MAK suhm) - *n.* a fundamental principle or general truth presented within a concise formula.

> "'May I venture to ask you, sir,' said Candide, 'if you do not take great pleasure in reading Horace?'
>
> 'He has some **maxims**,' said Pococuratne, 'which might be useful to a man of the world, and which, being compressed in energetic verses, are more easily impressed upon the memory.'" —FRANCOIS VOLTAIRE, *Candide,* transl. by Richard Aldington

precept (PRE SEPT) - *n.* a command or principal intended to impose a standard of action or conduct.

> "According to the **precepts** of his education, particularly his study of St. Thomas Aquinas and St. Augustine, two leading philosophers on the concept of 'just war,'

the U.S. could strike militarily on what he called a 'proportional response based upon the evidence available at the time.'" —BOB WOODWARD, *Plan of Attack*

OTHER FIGURES OF SPEECH

anthropomorphism (ANT thruh puh MOR FIH zuhm) - *n.* the ascription of human characteristics to that which is not human, be they non-living objects, animals, or even a deity.

"Jehovah was **anthropomorphic** because he could address himself to the Jews only in terms of their understanding; so he was conceived as in their own image, as a cloud, a pillar of fire, a tangible, physical something which the mind of the Israelites could grasp." —JACK LONDON, *The Sea Wolf*

antonomasia (AN tuh no MAY zhe uh, also AN TAH nuh MAY zhe uh) - *n.* the use of a title or epithet for a name, as His Honor for mayor, 2. the use of the name of an individual instead of a common noun, as Romeo for lover.

apocrypha (uh PAH kruh fuh) - *n.* writing or anecdotes of dubious authenticity, 2. Apocrypha—fourteen books of the Sep-

tuagint accepted by the Roman Catholics though excluded from the Jewish and Protestant cannons of the Old Testament, 3. writings omitted from the New Testament and not accepted as resulting from revelation.

*see **apocryphal** entry for citation, p. 135*

apotheosis (uh PAH thee OH suhs, also a PUH thee uh suhs) - *n.* glorification, sometimes to a divine lever; deification, 2. a glorified example or ideal (*v.* is apotheosize).

"Printers and designers and bookbinders worldwide see [the Oxford English Dictionary] as an **apotheosis** of their art." —SIMON WINCHESTER, *The Professor and the Madman*

canard (KUH nahrd, also KUH nahr) - *n.* a fabricated or false report, an unfounded story.

"The NCAA needs to shelve this **canard** that they are all amateur student-athletes." —ALBERT R. HUNT, *The Wall Street Journal*, 3/28/02

cavil (KA vuhl) - *v.* to criticize for petty reasons, 2. to quibble, to make a trivial objection.

"A tangential **cavil**: to me, an acronym is a pronounceable word created out of the initials or major parts of a compound term, like NATO, radar, or TriBeCa ... I say that makes G.O.P. an intialism or abbreviation." —WILLIAM SAFIRE, *The New York Times Magazine*, 12/15/02

cognate (KAHG NAYT) - *adj.* of common ancestry or origin, 2. a word derived from the same roots as another given word.

"The trilogy is most obviously **cognate** with epic poetry." —LIN CARTER, *Tolkien*

cognomen (kahg NOH muhn, also KAHG nuh muhn) - *n.* a surname; last name; family name, 2. the surname of a male citizen of ancient Rome, 3. a name, a distinguishing nickname.

> "Reagan is said to hate the **cognomen** 'Star Wars'; he thinks it trivializes his proud dream.' —MARTIN AMIS, *Visiting Mrs. Nabokov*

crotchet (KRAH chuht) - *n.* a small hook or hook-like instrument, 2. an unusual whim, trick or notion.

> "Though Ted was occasionally a victim of Capra's **crotchets**, he revered the man as an editor." —JUDITH AND NEIL MORGAN, *Dr. Seuss & Mr. Geisel*

epithet (EH puh THET, also EH puh thut) - *n.* a word or phrase characterizing a person and used in place of a proper name, often negative or disparanging.

> "The term American, like the term democrat, began as an **epithet**, the former referring to an inferior, provincial creature, the latter to one who panders to the crude and mindless whims of the masses." —JOSEPH J. ELLIS, *Founding Brothers*

eponym (EH puh NIM) - *n.* a word formed from a person's name, e.g., stentorian after the Greek herald Stentor, 2. a person whose name has become identified with some period, movement, theory, etc. (eponymous, eponymic are the adjective forms).

> "Henry Bech, the **eponym** of *Bech: A Book* (1970) and *Bech Is Back* (1983)." —MARTIN AMIS, *Visiting Mrs. Nabokov*

exemplum (ig ZEM pluhm, also eg ZEM pluhm) - *n.* an example, 2. a story demonstrating a moral point.

> "The little-known 1902 version of 'To Build a Fire' is another **exemplum**." —EARLE LABOR, *Note on the Text and Selections, The Portable Jack London*

idiom (IH dee uhm) - *n.* an expression having a special meaning not obtainable or not clear from the usual meaning of the words in the expression, as fly off the handle (lose one's temper), 2. the specific grammatical, syntactic, and structural character of a given language, 3. a regional speech or dialect, 4. a specialized vocabulary: legal idiom.

> "Another nod to Poe, this time to his tale 'The Imp of the Perverse,' which introduced this **idiom** into the language." —S.T. JOSHI, *Explanatory Notes, H.P. Lovecraft's The Call of Cthulhu and Other Weird Stories*

metonymy (muh TAH nuh ME) - *n.* the use of a single characteristic to identify a more complex entity.

> "Spencer had taught me the trope of **metonymy**, by which one part represents the whole, and I had found that its application in this circumstance rendered a nearly poetic understanding of the poignant hopes and vainglorious suffering reflected in the choices of heel height, color, and toe box." —KATHERINE MOSBY, *The Season of Lillian Dawes*

neologism (nee AH luh JIH zuhm) - *n.* a word or phrase which has recently been coined; a new word or phrase.

> "... that's why the verb 'to Google' is now a familiar **neologism**." —RANDY COHEN, *The New York Times Magazine*, 12/15/02

periphrasis (puh RI fruh sus) - *n.* using many words when fewer words would suffice, an inexact manner of speaking; circumlocution, 2. a periphrastic statement, also periphrase.

> "'But now,' Vance continued, 'it is time for me to propose a toast to you.' He paused. The ensuing silence, in a roomful of drunks in an advanced stage of wreckage, was a tribute to the **periphrastic** performance he was putting on. Charlotte wondered if anybody in the room other than herself knew the adjective '**periphrastic**.'" –TOM WOLFE, *I Am Charlotte Simmons*

prolepsis (pro LEP suhs) - *n.* the assumption of something in the future as if already done or existing; anticipation, 2. an example in which an issue or point is first summarized and then explained in detail, 3. the anticipation of an objection or argument in order to disqualify their use or address them in advance, 4. to use an adjective and noun combination in an anticipatory manner.

> "The **proleptic** quality of the text. Coleman doesn't have to ask what all this means. He knows ..."–PHILIP ROTH, *The Human Stain*

rebus (REE buhs) - *n.* a riddle or puzzle made up of pictures of objects or symbols, the series of which indicates a word or phrase (a picture of an eye followed by an L followed by an ampersand is a rebus for "island"—remember the *Concentration* game show).

> "... [the meaning of a dream is] a **rebus** to be decoded." –MILAN KUNDERA, *The Art of the Novel*

rubric (ROO brik, also ROO BRIK) - *n.* a title, heading or first letter often printed in red ink, 2. the title or heading of a statute or chapter in a code of law, 3. something under which a thing is classed or categorized, 4. a rule for conduct of a liturgical service (from the Latin ruber—red).

> "Watergate—that is, all of the many illegal and improper acts that were included under that **rubric**—was a political scandal unlike any other." –KATHARINE GRAHAM, *Personal History*

shibboleth (SHI buh luhth, also SHI buh LETH) - *n.* a word which was made the criterion by which to distinguish the Ephraimites from the Gileadites—the Ephraimites, not being able to pronounce sh, called the word sibboleth (see Judges xii), 2. the criterion, test or watchword of a party; a party cry or pet phrase.

> "... both the dogma of sin and the practice of proselytizing have been slain by the **shibboleth** of 'nonjudgmentalism.'" –STEPHEN PROTHERO, *The Wall Street Journal,* 9/3/03

sobriquet (SO bri KAY, also SO bri KET) - *n.* a nickname, 2. a familiar name for a person, typically a shortened version of a person's given name.

> "Among the astronauts, many of whom were approaching forty, the Saturn 5 had already earned the **sobriquet** 'the old man's rocket.'" –JIM LOVELL AND JEFFREY KLUGER, *Lost Moon: The Perilous Voyage of Apollo 13*

trope (TROHP) - *n.* a figure of speech, 2. use of a word or expression in a different sense from that which properly belongs to it; the use of a word or expression as changed from the original signification to another, for the sake of giving life or emphasis to an idea.

> "It's a classic **trope** of American family life: the high-powered executive with a Type A personality who has no problem juggling billion-dollar deals and conference calls in his corner office, but finds himself at a loss

when faced with an unhappy spouse or a troubled child at home." –PAUL TOUGH, *The New York Times Magazine*, 12/15/02

SPEAKING AND DEBATING

DISCUSSION, DEBATE, PUBLIC SPEAKING

ad hominem (ad HAH meh NEM) (from Latin) - *adj.* an attempt to argue against an opponent's idea by discrediting the opponent himself, 2. a personal attack, 3. a logical fallacy, arguing that an idea or concept is wrong because its proponent is flawed.

"It was understood that the abuse and indignities, even **ad hominem** attacks, were fair weapons in arguing for your position" –KATHARINE GRAHAM, *Personal History*

apostrophe (uh PAHS truh FEE) - (besides the ' mark) *n.* a style of speech, a rhetorical device consisting of speech directed in an abstract direction, to a person not present, or to a thing, such as an aside to an audience in a play.

"Wonderfully does he convey the rapture with which Jude walks on that rainy evening among the dimly seen colleges, **apostrophizing** them with the learning and the zeal which he has picked up for himself." –JOHN BAYLEY, *Introduction to Thomas Hardy's Jude the Obscure*

casuistry (KAZH wuh STREE, also KA zhuh wuh STREE) - *n.* an attempt to determine the correct response to a moral problem, often a moral dilemma, by drawing conclusions based on general principles of ethics, 2. subtle but misleading or false reasoning, especially about moral issues; sophistry.

"… 'you're talking through your hat, **casuist**!'" –FYODOR DOSTOYEVSKY, *The Brothers Karamazov*, transl. by David Magarshack

colloquy (KAH luh kwee) - *n.* a formal conversation or conference.

"As this **colloquy** had taken no small attention away from him, Mysterioso shouted, 'Carter, come now!'" –GLEN DAVID GOLD, *Carter Beats the Devil*

disquisition (DIS kwuh ZIH shun) - *n.* a formal discussion of a subject; a formal inquiry; discourse.

"Three years ago, Michael Hardt and Antonio Negri became the toast of the international left with the publication of 'Empire,' a ramshackle, theory-stuffed **disquisition** on globalization and its discontents." –GARY ROSEN, *The Wall Street Journal*, 8/3/04

harangue (huh RANG) - *n.* a rant; a tirade; a lengthy, pompous speech.

"Cheney **harangued** about the United Nations. Going to the U.N. would invite a never-ending process of debate, compromise and delay. Words not action." –BOB WOODWARD, *Plan of Attack*

homily (HAH muh lee) - *n.* a lecture or a lengthy discourse on or of a moral theme, 2. a sermon.

"Each new volume of advice [from self-help books] promises life-changing lessons; each delivers more or less the same fistful of **homilies**." –LAURA MILLER, *The New York Times Book Review*, 6/20/04

palaver (puh LA vuhr, also puh LAH vuhr) - *n.* talk, unnecessary talk, fuss, idle chatter, 2. a meeting at which there is much talk 3. *v.* to discuss with much talk, to talk idly or flatteringly.

"People said it was the den in which the thieves of Lankhmar gathered to plot and **palaver** and settle their private bickerings." –FRITZ LEIBER, *Swords Against Death*

parley (PAHR lee) - *n.* a conference, often between opponents.

"'But do not command many men to go with you, Theoden. We go to a **parley**, not to a fight.'" –J.R.R. TOLKIEN, *The Two Towers*

periphrasis (puh RI fruh sus) - *n.* using many words when fewer words would suffice, an inexact manner of speaking; circumlocution, 2. a periphrastic statement, also periphrase.

*see other **periphrasis** entry for citation, p 73*

peroration (PER uh RAY shun, also PUHR uh RAY shun) - *n.* the concluding portion of a speech or oration, 2. a highly rhetorical or bombastic speech.

"The public prosecutor passed to his **peroration**." –FYODOR DOSTOYEVSKY, *The Brothers Karamazov*, transl. by David Magarshack

polemic (puh LE mik) - *n.* a controversy or aggressive argument, an attack or refutation of another's opinions or principles, 2. polemics (used with a singular or plural verb)—the practice of argumentation or controversy.

"[Jefferson] had sponsored Callender's **polemics** against the Adams administration even though he knew them to be gross misrepresentations." –JOSEPH J. ELLIS, *Founding Brothers*

riposte (also **ripost**) (ri POST) - *n.* a fencer's swift return thrust after an opponent's parry, 2. a retort; a verbal retaliation, 3. *v.* to make a riposte.

"'Behave yourself!' barked Vakar, and cuffed the animal's nose, jerking his hand away in time to avoid a **riposte** with equine incisors." –L. SPRAGUE DE CAMP, *The Tritonian Ring*

sedition (si DI shun) - *n.* any conduct that tends toward insurrection but does not amount treason, 2. inciting others to insurrection.

"... [in 1798, Napoleon] arrived in Egypt, and for the first time subjected one of the heartlands of Islam to the rule of a Western power and the direct impact of Western attitudes and ideas. Interestingly, this aspect of French occupation was seen immediately in Istanbul, where the sultan, the suzerain of Egypt, was much concerned about the **seditious** effect of these ideas on his subjects." –BERNARD LEWIS, *What Went Wrong?*

sophism (SA FI zuhm) - *n.* a subtly deceptive argument, apparently plausible, though actually invalid.

sophist (SOHF ist) - *n.* a group or class of teachers of philosophy, rhetoric, etc., in ancient Greece known for their adroit subtle yet often fallacious reasoning (often Sophist), 2. an individual known for fallacious yet plausible reasoning.

syllogism (SIH luh JIH zuhm) - *n.* an inference in which one proposition (the conclusion) follows of necessity from two others (known as premises), 2. deductive logic, 3. specious or tricky reasoning.

"Hamming it up before the camera—as two bemused guards from the Khyber Rifles posed behind him—he gave us his spiel, and this vulgar **syllogism**: Here's Geraldo; Geraldo is in a dangerous place; so Geraldo has cojones." –TUNKU VARADARA-JAN, *The Wall Street Journal*, 12/10/01

trepverter (TREP vuhr tuhr) - *n.* defined in quote.

"... in the Yiddish of his long-dead mother, **Trepverter**—retorts that came too late, when you were already on your way down the stairs." –SAUL BELLOW, *Herzog*

valedictory (VAHL ih DIK tuh ree) - *n.* a farewell address or statement, esp. at a graduation ceremony, 2. expressing a farewell.

"*Jude* is Hardy's last novel and in some ways his most interesting one. It is both exploratory and **valedictory**: In it Hardy moves with intention into a new subject and a new kind of characterization; but he also seems to be saying goodbye to the world of his imagination as a novelist." –JOHN BAYLEY, *Introduction, Thomas Hardy's Jude the Obscure*

SPEECH, LANGUAGE

aorist (A uh ruhst) - *n.* a verb tense indicating the simple occurrence of an action without limitation or reference to its completeness, duration, etc. (used in Greek).

"With the same concentration he trained on the **aorist** tense of ancient Greek verbs—a tense so full of weariness it specified actions that might never be completed—Lefty now cleaned the huge picture windows." –JEFFREY EUGENIDES, *Middlesex*

aposiopesis (a puh SIGH uh PEE suhs) - *n.* a sudden breaking off in speech, leaving the statement or thought incomplete, as if the speaker were disinclined to continue.

argot (AHR GO) - *n.* a secret language or conventional slang peculiar to a particular group, esp. the underworld of thieves, tramps and vagabonds.

"... the coarse **argot** of real estate development" –TOM WOLFE, *A Man in Full*

brogue (BROG) - *n.* a stout, heavy oxford shoe, 2. an Irish accent of a particular dialect or region.

*see other **brogue** for citation, p. 227*

dragoman (DRA guh muhn) - *n.* an interpreter, esp. for the Arabic and Turkish languages.

"... **dragomans** who, initially employed as translators or interpreters, became far more than that, serving as intermediaries and sometimes as principals in major negotiations." –BERNARD LEWIS, *What Went Wrong?*

elide (ih LIED) - *v.* to omit or slur over (a vowel or syllable) in pronunciation, usually the final one, 2. to eliminate or leave out, 3. to break or dash in pieces, to demolish (the noun is elision).

> "... it was the exhausting habit of many letter writers of the time to prepare a fair copy of all of their outgoing mail, and in so doing occasionally to edit and **elide** some passages." —SIMON WINCHESTER, *The Professor and the Madman*

fricative (FRI kuh tiv) - *adj.* a sound produced by air flowing through a constriction in the oral cavity, a fricative consonant, e.g. the English "F" and "S."

> "... roughly corresponding to the light, aspirated **fricative** j of New World Spanish." —ROBERT ALTER AND FRANK KERMODE, *The Literary Guide to the Bible*

idiom (IH dee uhm) - *n.* an expression having a special meaning not obtainable or not clear from the usual meaning of the words in the expression, as fly off the handle (lose one's temper), 2. the specific grammatical, syntactic, and structural character of a given language, 3. a regional speech or dialect, 4. a specialized vocabulary: legal idiom.

*see other **idiom** entry for citation, p. 72*

lingua franca (LING gwuh FRANG kuh) - (from Italian - "Frankish tongue) *n.* a language used by people of diverse speech to communicate with one another, often a basic form of speech with simplified grammar, 2. a mixed language made up of mostly Italian words spoken without their inflections.

> "And the master sidemen [Howlin' Wolf] hired, notably Willie Johnson and Hubert Sumlin, overdrove their amplifiers to achieve those burry, distorted textures that are still the **lingua franca** of rock guitar." —DAVID GATES, *The New York Times Book Review,* 6/13/04

patois (PA TWAH, also PAH TWAH) - *n.* a nonstandard form of some language; dialect.

> "This academic **patois**, with its recycled bits of Foucault and other Continental Theorists, has its uses." —GARY ROSEN, *The Wall Street Journal,* 8/3/04

phoneme (FO NEEM) - *n.* an indivisible unit of sound in a language necessary to distinguish one word from another.

> "In Gustaf's company ... all addressed him in English, so Czech was no more than an impersonal murmur, a background of sound against which only Anglo-American **phonemes** stood forth as human words." —MILAN KUNDERA, *Ignorance*

plosive (PLO siv) - *n.* a consonantal sound produced from opening a previously closed oral passage; for example, when pronouncing the letter "P" in "pug."

> "The huddled men nod and rock, sending **plosive** noises from their moon jowls." —DON DELILLO, *Underworld*

vulgate (VUHL GAYT) - *n.* speech of the common people, colloquial speech.

> "... the voices took him back to earliest memory, the same slurred words, the dropped vowels, the **vulgate**." —DON DELILLO, *Underworld*

APPROVAL, BRAGGING

approbation (AHP ruh BAY shun) - *n.* the act of approving; a formal approval, sanction or commendation.

> "Obviously accustomed to these curtain calls of **approbation**, she beamed at Charlie and his guests." —TOM WOLFE, *A Man in Full*

ballyhoo (BA lee HOO) - *n.* flamboyant or sensational advertising, 2. a clamorous, attention-getting demonstration, 3. *v.* to advertise in a flamboyant, sensational or loud manner.

> "When they set up in a new town, acts from the program would give a free demonstration, a **ballyhoo**, in the largest public square." –GLEN DAVID GOLD, *Carter Beats the Devil*

braggadocio (BRA guh DOE see O, also BRA guh DOE she O, BRA guh DOE chee O) - *n.* a braggart, 2. empty or pretentious boasting, 3. arrogance; cockiness (name derives from the character Braggadocchio, the personification of boasting in *The Faerie Queen* by Edmund Spenser).

> "'I was a lot better than you, Conroy.' It was a statement of fact in the world of athletics, not **braggadocio**." –PAT CONROY, *My Losing Season*

encomium (en KO mee uhm) (pl. -ums or -mia) - *n.* high praise, an expression of enthusiastic praise.

> "... the proud son, introducing his father in the longest, most laudatory of the evening's jocular **encomiums**." –PHILIP ROTH, *American Pastoral*

panegyric (PA nuh JIR ik, also PA nuh JY rik) - *n.* formal or elaborate praise, in speech or writing, of a person or even, 2. laudation; eulogistic oration.

> "William launches into a **panegyric** on perfume: the miracle of its mysterious mechanisms." –MICHEL FABER, *The Crimson Petal and the White*

plaudit (PLAU diht) - *n.* a mark or expression of applause; praise bestowed (from the Latin plaudere —to applaud).

> "Throughout it all, under the rains of slings, arrows, **plaudits**, and encomiums, Samuel Johnson remained calmly modest." –SIMON WINCHESTER, *The Professor and the Madman*

rodomontade (ROD uh mon TAYD, also ROD uh mon TAHD) - *n.* arrogant boasting or bluster, a vain and bragging speech; rant, 2. *adj.* arrogantly boastful, 3. *v.* to boast; to bluster; to rant (from the Italian character Rodomonte, a boastful Saracen leader in Ariosto's "Orlando Furioso").

> "Straight simple answer now—no **rodomontades**." –FRITZ LEIBER, *Swords and Deviltry*

BANTER

badinage (BA duhn AHZH) - *n.* playful raillery, banter, 2. *v.* to tease with playful repartee.

> "I had entered Underwriter (a pub) to a blizzard of **badinage** and dirty jokes (nymphomaniacs, vibrators) and there was more fierce cajolery when me and my mate Bob emerged from behind the heavy drapes." –MARTIN AMIS, *Visiting Mrs. Nabokov*

persiflage (PUHR sih FLAZH, also PER sih FLAZH) - *n.* light teasing; gentle raillery; frivolous, teasing talk.

> "The issue most alive was whether he would have married her without money. It was much too troubling not to be spoken of, so it was spoken of in a kind of fun and terrible **persiflage**." –SAUL BELLOW, *The Adventures of Augie March*

raillery (RAY luh ree) - *n.* playful teasing; good-natured banter.

> "I listened to them singing in their rich Fife accents, ... listened to their laughter and **raillery**, to the sounds of golfers stomping grass from their cleats, then a cheer from

the eighteenth green." —MICHAEL MUR-PHY, *Golf in the Kingdom*

repartee (REH puh TEE, also REH pahr TAY) - *n.* a swift and clever reply, 2. an interchange of witty retorts.

"Born in 1925, [William F.] Buckley grew up at Great Elm, a huge house in Sharon, Conn., learned **repartee** at the family dinner table, was educated privately, went to Yale ..." —JON MEACHAM, *The New York Times Book Review,* 10/17/04

DISAPPROVAL

asperity (a SPER uh tee, also uh SPER uh tee) - *n.* roughness, harshness, 2. ill temper.

*see other **asperity** entry for citation, p. 12*

billingsgate (BIH lingz GAYT) - *n.* coarse, abusive language (after Billingsgate, a fish-market in London).

"In fact, the characters become too garrulous at times; the story stands still while they shout picturesque **billingsgate** for a page at a time." —L. SPRAGUE DE CAMP, *The Spell of Conan*

calumny (KA luhm nee, also KAL yuhm nee) - *n.* a misrepresentation intended to slander another, 2. the act of uttering maliciously calculated misrepresentations to harm another's reputation.

"'They go the length of declaring that this honest creature would do anything for money, that the Hispaniola belonged to him, and that he sold it to me absurdly high—the most transparent **calumnies**.'" —ROBERT LOUIS STEVENSON, *Treasure Island*

contumely (kahn TOO muh lee, also kuhn TOO muh lee, kahn TYOO muh lee, kahn TOO MEE lee) - *n.* harsh and insulting language or treatment brought about from haughti-

ness and contempt, 2. an instance of such language or treatment; scornful insult.

"He told them so, and was met by general **contumely**." —JOSEPH CONRAD, *Typhoon*

diatribe (DY uh TRYB) - *n.* a verbal or written bitter and abusive attack on a person.

"The book concludes with a passionate and vainglorious **diatribe** about the pre-eminence of military history and the need to apply the insights he has ostensibly just offered us to the post-Sept. 11 situation." —LAURA MILLER, *The New York Times Book Review,* 3/21/04

disapprobation (dih SA pruh BAY shun) - *n.* disapproval; condemnation; the act of disapproving.

"'You don't want to live down there!' everybody said, with **disapprobation** writ large upon their faces." —JACK LONDON, *The People of the Abyss*

gantlet (GONT leht, also GAHNT leht) - (NWD, among other definitions) *n.* a military punishment in which two rows of men facing each other swing clubs at the offender who must run between them, 2. an ordeal, a trial, severe difficulties, 3. *v.* run the gantlet—to suffer the punishment of the gantlet, 4. to advance despite attack from both sides.

"Mr. Lieberman's cast will be recognizable to anyone who has had experience of private schools and thus run the admissions **gantlet** for himself or his children." —NED CRABB, *The Wall Street Journal,* 9/14/04

invective (in VEK tiv) - *n.* a severe or violent censure or reproach; something uttered or written to cast opprobrium, censure or reproach on another; violent denunciation.

"The partner, an **invective**-spewing black dwarf named Marcus, is played with great panache by Tony Cox." —JOE MORGENSTERN, *The Wall Street Journal*, 12/5/03

obloquy (AH bluh kwee) - *n.* condemnatory or abusive language, 2. the state of one who is disgraced; ill repute.

"Yes, the presidency was a thankless job, 'a most unpleasant seat, full of thorns, briars, thistles, murmuring, fault-finding, calumny, **obloquy**.'" —JOSEPH J. ELLIS, *Founding Brothers*

opprobrium (uh PROH bree uhm) - *n.* disgrace arising from exceedingly shameful conduct; ignominy, 2. scornful reproach or contempt, 3. a cause of shame or disgrace.

"'The only thing wrong with that old cliché [two's company, three's a crowd],' said Toohey, 'is the erroneous implication that 'a crowd' is a term of **opprobrium**.'" —AYN RAND, *The Fountainhead*

NONSENSE

bosh (BAHSH) - *(slang) n.* nonsense, foolish talk.

"Oliver Wendell Holmes and his shy younger brother, John, had been reared with that awful **bosh** that still buzzed in the doctor's ears: 'In Adam's fall, we sinned all.'" —MATTHEW PEARL, *The Dante Club*

bunk (BUHNGK) - (besides the type of bed) *(slang) n.* senseless talk, nonsense (also bunkum, from Buncombe County, North Carolina).

"'**Bunkum**!' snorted Brill. 'I'm sick of listening to your pipe dreams.'" —ROBERT E. HOWARD, *Beyond the Borders*

flummery (FLUHM ree, also FLUH muh ree) - *n.* a kind of soft food, made of wheatflour or oatmeal, 2. various sweets made from milk, flour, eggs, etc., 3. empty flattery; meaningless compliment; trifling.

"And why this **flummery** with the danger flag and signal drum that were only used on ceremonial occasions?" —IAN FLEMING, *The Living Daylights*

folderol (FAHL duh RAHL) - *n.* nonsense; trifle, 2. a useless trinket or bauble.

gammon (GA muhn) - (among other definitions) (Informal) *n.* Chiefly Brit. . deceptive, misleading or nonsensical talk; blather.

"'No, by thunder!' he cried, 'it's us must break the treaty when the time comes; and till then I'll **gammon** that doctor.'" —ROBERT LOUIS STEVENSON, *Treasure Island*

meshugas (meh SHU guhs) - (Yiddish, many possible spellings) *n.* foolishness; craziness; nonsense; madness; a foolish idea, an indiosyncrasy or weakness.

"For 'fun' pulling a trigger and shooting with a gun. They're **meshugeh**." —PHILIP ROTH, *American Pastoral*

mullock (MUL lok) - (among other definitions) *n.* nonsense; information of no value; rubbish.

"'Christ Jesus, Christ Jesus ... what **mullock** you talk.'" —MICHEL FABER, *The Crimson Petal and the White*

rigmarole (RIH guh muh ROLL, also RIG muh ROLL) - *n.* nonsense, meaningless talk,

2. a complex procedure (from the Middle English rageman rolle, a scroll used in a game of chance).

> "'Do you understand anything of all this **rigmarole**, Alyosha, or don't you?'" —FYODOR DOSTOYEVSKY, *The Brothers Karamazov*, transl. by David Magarshack

twaddle (TWAH duhl) - *n.* empty or silly talk or writing; trivial or idle talk.

> "'Let us be modest in the vast pride of this realization. Everything else is **twaddle**.'" —AYN RAND, *The Fountainhead*

OTHER SPEAKING AND
DEBATING TERMS

cadge (KAJ) - *v.* to beg, sponge or mooch in order to acquire.

> "Beckwith rang the bell about two hours later, clearly hoping to **cadge** dinner." —KATHERINE MOSBY, *The Season of Lillian Dawes*

cant (KANT) - (different definition in sailing) *n.* empty, hypocritical talk, 2. a private or secret language used by a religious sect, gang, or other group; jargon, 3. hypocritical use of pious language, 4. whining or sing-song speech, 5. *v.* to speak so to moralize.

> "A favorite column-writing strategy [for A.J. Liebling] was for him simply to compare the way all the big papers of the day (he was blessed in having so many to work from) played a certain story—the last days of Stalin, say, or the obituary of William Randolph Hearst—and where there was **cant**, posturing, bloviation, jingoism, false piety, or what he called "on-the-one-hand-this" writing (Walter Lippmann was a prime culprit), he would unerringly and delightedly point it out." —CHARLES MCGRATH, *The New York Times Book Review*, 9/26/04

kibitz (KI buhtz, also kuh BITS) - (Yiddish) *v.* to give advice when it is not wanted, especially to someone playing a card game.

> "A thousand feet below lay the old Ottoman capital of Bursa, like a backgammon board spread out across the valley's green felt ... Desdemona Stephanides, however, **kibitzing** from afar, gazed down on the board and saw what the players had missed." —JEFFREY EUGENIDES, *Middlesex*

KNOWLEDGE AND WRITING

WRITING

bathos (BAY thahs) - *n.* the sudden transition from an elevated style to the commonplace in writing or speech; anticlimax, 2. overdone or insincere pathos, 3. hackneyed quality; triteness.

"Fuck all that dewy-eyed sentimental bull-shit about people who are sick. And that includes any athlete whose father died a week before the game who says, 'This one's for Pop.' American **bathos**. Keep it to yourself. Play ball!" —GEORGE CARLIN, *Brain Droppings*

bildungsroman (BIL dungks row MAHN, also BIL dungz row MAN) - *n.* a type of novel in which the main theme focuses on the formative years or spiritual education of one individual, 2. a traditional novel in German literature (from German: bildung education + roman novel).

"'Me and Shakespeare' is a lively hybrid of memoir, **Bildungsroman** and literary criticism, and has the conversational ease, raconteur's charm and digressive storytelling of a one-man show." —SHERIE POSESORSKI, *The New York Times Book Review,* 6/9/02

billet-doux (BI lee DOO, also BIL LAY DOO) - *n.* a love letter(from the French, "sweet note").

"He had, in fact, pioneered a new epistolary form: the trade ad as **billet-doux**." —ADAM STERNBERGH, *The New York Times Magazine,* 12/15/02

chef-d'oeuvre (sha DUHRV) - *n.* (from the French, "chief [piece] of work") a masterpiece.

"He regarded this speech as his chef d'oeuvre, as the **chef d'oeuvre** of his whole life, as his swan-song." —FYODOR DOSTOYEVSKY, *The Brothers Karamazov,* transl. by David Magarshack

coda (KOH duh) - *n.* the final section of a musical or written composition, usually distinct from the rest of the piece.

"'But one afternoon a storm came up and gust of wind hit the henhouse and lifted the roof right off, and hens came flying out, sucked after it, I suppose, and also just acting like hens.' (How deceptively easy that little **coda** is—'and also just acting like hens'—but how much it conveys.)" —JAMES WOOD (reviewing Marilynne Robinson's *Gilead,* from which the first part of the quotation is taken), *The New York Times Book Review,* 11/28/04

deus ex machina (DAY uhs EKS MAH ki nuh, also DAY uhs EKS MAH kin NAH, DAYS uhs EKS muh SHE nuh) - *n.* (from Latin—"god from a machine"—referring to the device by which gods were suspended above the stage in the Greek theater) any resolution to a story that does not pay due regard to the story's internal logic and that is so unlikely that it challenges suspension of disbelief, and presumably allows the author, director, or developer to end the story in the way that he or she desired.

*see other **deus ex machina** entry for citation, p. 120*

discursion (DIS KUR shun) - (among other definitions) *n.* rambling; passing from one topic to another without order, 2. digression (*adj.* is discursive).

"After Eliza and Shaftoe's stories briefly converge—in a wonderfully cinematic frenzy—the narrative goes slack, as we're treated to endless levées, epistles, political economical—metaphysical **discursions** and Stephenson's favorite, conspiracies." —STEPHEN METCALF, *The New York Times Book Review,* 4/18/04

ellipsis (ih LIP suhs, also eh LIP suhs) - *n.* the omission of word(s) not required to comprehend a sentence but needed to make that sentence grammatically correct or complete, 2. a mark or marks that indicate such an omission (typically "…").

"When she just grins at me, I roll my window up and get out, ashamed to have been caught in a reverie, something that seems to happen to me more and more. I check my watch, try to gauge how long I've been there, how much time has elapsed during this particular **ellipsis**." —RICHARD RUSSO, *Straight Man*

epistle (ih PIH suhl) - *n.* a formal communication in writing; a letter, 2. a literary work in letter form, 3. Epistle—letters in the New Testament written by an Apostle; a selection from the apostolical Epistle used in the Communion Service.

"He accordingly addressed a carefully considered **epistle** to Sue, and, knowing her emotional temperament, threw a Rhadamanthine strictness into the lines here and there." —THOMAS HARDY, *Jude the Obscure*

epistolary (ih PIS tuh LAR ee, also EH pih STO leh ree) - *adj.* relating to letters or letter writing, 2. conducted, communicated or carried by letter, 3. a style of writing, esp. in 18th century novels, composed as a series of letters.

"In the middle of the 18th century, Richardson discovers the form of the **epistolary** novel in which the characters confess their thoughts and their feelings." —MILAN KUNDERA, *The Art of the Novel*

graphomania (GRAF oh MAY nee uh, also GRAF oh MAY nyuh) - *n.* a mania or passion for writing.

"**Graphomania**—'Not a mania to write letters, diaries or family chronicles (to write for oneself or one's immediate family)' but 'a mania to write books (to have a public of unknown readers)' (*The Book of Laughter and Forgetting*). The mania not to create a form but to impose one's self on others. The most grotesque version of the will to power." —MILAN KUNDERA, *The Art of the Novel*

hagiography (ha gee AH grah fee, also ha jee AH grah fee) - *n.* the biography of a saint, 2. a biography which expresses extreme reverence and respect for its subject, 3. associated with iconography, or worship of an icon or person (related terms: hagiographer, hagiographic, hagiology, all stem from Hagiographa—the third and final part of the Jewish Scriptures, those books not in the Law or the Prophets).

"In truth, Lee Iacocca is not the genius portrayed a decade ago in his autobiography and in business-magazine **hagiography**." —JAMES GLASSMAN, *The Wall Street Journal*, 7/19/95

hamartia (HA MAHR TEE uh) - *n.* a tragic flaw or error; an error resulting in the ruin of the tragic hero (with particular reference to Aristotle's Poetics).

"Shivas … asked me if I knew the word '**hamartia**.' …"It originally meant bein' off the taraget, in archery or in some such,' he said, 'and then in came to mean bein' off the taraget in general in all yer life—it got to mean a flaw in the character." —MICHAEL MURPHY, *Golf in the Kingdom*

historiography (hih STOR ee OG ruh fee) - *n.* the writing of history, 2. study of the principles and theories of historical research and writing, 3. a collection of historical writing or literature.

"**Historiography** writes the history of society, not of man." —MILAN KUNDERA, *The Art of the Novel*

in media res (in MAY dee ah RAYS) - *adv.* (from Latin) - in the midst of a narrative or plot rather than at the beginning, as in commencing an epic.

> "[Virgil], like Homer, opens his epic **in media res,** 'in the middle of the story'."
> —Lin Carter, *Tolkien*

jeremiad (JER uh MY uhd, also JER uh my AD) - *n.* a lengthy lament, a prolonged tale of woe: in allusion to the Lamentations of Jeremiah.

> "American intellectuals have been lamenting the decline of religious vitality in their land at least since 1670, when Samuel Danforth railed against New Englanders for losing their way on their 'errand into the wilderness.' The classic genre for this lament is the **jeremiad**, which typically concludes with an impassioned plea for God's chosen people to repent (or else)." —Stephen Prothero, *The Wall Street Journal*, 9/3/03

kitsch (KICH) - *n.* art, decorative objects and other forms of representation of questionable artistic or aesthetic value; a representation that is excessively sentimental, overdone or vulgar.

> "Back in the teens, when the immigration was still going on, back in the twenties, the thirties, the forties, even into the fifties, none of the [Jewish] American-raised boys whose parents or grandparents had spoken Yiddish had the slightest interest in writing shtetl **kitsch** such as came along in the sixties with Fiddler on the Roof."
> —Philip Roth, *Rereading Saul Bellow*

leitmotif (also **leitmotiv**) (LIGHT mo TEEF) - *n.* a dominant, recurring theme or underlying pattern found in novels or other works of art.

> "... many slave narrators, like Frederick Douglass, explicitly make their own literacy training a **leitmotif** in their tales."
> —Henry Louis Gates Jr., *The New York Times Book Review*, 6/2/02

longueur (LONE guer) - *n.* a tedious, dull or lengthy passage as from a book, work of music, etc.

> "Few figures in literary history frustrate the modern sensibility the way the female Victorian poets do, with their maidenly **longueurs**, coquettish letters deflecting would-be visitors and long hours in darkened rooms that resulted in inexplicably fiery, sexy, sharp-witted verse." —Judith Shulevitz, *The New York Times Book Review*, 9/22/02

madeleine (MA duh luhn, also MA duh LAYN) - *n.* a small gateau or sponge cake, usually shaped like an elongated scallop shell, 2. with reference or allusion to Proust's use as a type of something that strongly evokes memories or nostalgia (used in Proust's *A la recherche du temps perdu* [*Remembrance of Things Past*]).

> "I once studied Proust and the theories of time and duration that he had absorbed during his infatuation with the works of Henre Louis Bergson ... My life is chock full of **madeleines** that send me reeling back on tides of pure consciousness to moments in my life lit up with consequence." —Pat Conroy, *My Losing Season*

monograph (MAH nuh GRAF) - *n.* a written account of a single, specific subject; a scholarly book on a limited area of learning.

> "You've written a fine **monograph**. I hope I made that clear in my review." —SAUL BELLOW, *Herzog*

nostrum (NAHS truhm) - *n.* a quack medicine with overinflated claims of efficacy, 2. a scheme for solving some political or social malady; a panacea.

> "But when it comes to politics, the Forum reflects a 'Davos Consensus'—that is, clichés, **nostrums**, banalities, elisions, evasions, upstanding sentiments and lowest common denominators generated when people of differing views are at their most polite." —BRET STEPHENS, *The Wall Street Journal*, 1/31/05

nota bene (frequently abbreviated "N.B.") (NOH tuh BEHN ee) - (from the Latin - note well) *v.* used to highlight something of particular importance.

> "... 'you were very closely acquainted with Miss Svetlov [**Nota bene:** Grushenka's surname was Svetlov. This I learnt for the first time that day in the course of the trial], didn't you?'" —FYODOR DOSTOYEVSKY, *The Brothers Karamazov*, transl. by David Magarshack

paean (PEE un) - *n.* a song of joyful praise, triumph or exultation.

> "[Tim] Russert is a phenomenally busy man who probably did not have time to write a heartwarming **paean** to his lovable father all by himself." —JOE QUEENAN, *The New York Times Book Review*, 3/20/05

pastiche (pas TEESH, pahs TEESH) - *n.* a stylistic imitation made up of selections from previous artistic, musical or architectural works.

> "The first literary translation, or rather adaptation, was based on a work by a French orientalist called Pétis de la Croix. His book, *Les mille et un jours (A Thousand and One Days)*, first published in 1710–1712, is a collection of pseudo-oriental tales, a **pastiche** of *The Thousand and One Nights*." —BERNARD LEWIS, *What Went Wrong?*

pathos (PAY THAHS, also PAY THOS, PA THOS) - *n.* the aspect of something which gives rise to a sense of pity, sympathy, tenderness, or sorrow in another.

> "'And think of it, a criminal vagabond and he can't even get his own sweetheart.'
>
> 'I was struck by the **pathos**, too, Mr. Yardley.'" —GLEN DAVID GOLD, *Carter Beats the Devil*

roman a clef (row MAHN AH KLAY) - *n.* a novel in which real persons are represented under fictitious names (from French, "novel with a key").

> "One of these stories was a **roman a clef** in which a number of science fiction authors, notably Heinlein, appeared in recognizable guises." —ISAAC ASIMOV, *I. Asimov*

solecism (SAH luh sih ZUHM, also SOW luh sih ZUHM) - *n.* a combination of words that construct a grammatically incorrect sentence, 2. a departure from the proper or accepted order, 3. a violation of decorum.

> "...but the very name of my enterprise would suggest to him only capitulations of sincerity and **solecisms** of style." —ROBERT LOUIS STEVENSON, *Introduction, Treasure Island*

thanatopsis (than UH TOP sihs) - *n.* a contemplation or consideration of death.

"... he only played the **Thanatopsis** stoic but always maneuvered to beat this other—Death!—who had already gained so much on him." —SAUL BELLOW, *The Adventures of Augie March*

topos (TOW PAHS, also TAH PAHS) - *n.* a conventional theme in a literary composition; a traditional rhetorical theme, convention or formula.

"It is for example a **topos** of Islamic biography of men of religion in the Middle Ages that the pious hero of the narrative was offered an appointment by the ruler and refused it." —BERNARD LEWIS, *What Went Wrong?*

DOCUMENTS AND PAPER

brevet (bri VET) - *n.* an official, written message; esp. a Papal Indulgence, 2. an official document granting specific privileges from a sovereign or government, 3. a commission granting a military officer higher rank without increase in pay.

"By the end of the year, though still nominally a lieutenant, he was **breveted** with the rank of captain as reward for his services ... In the official view of the army, Brevet Capt. Asst. William C. Minor was now wholly 'incapacitated by causes arising in the line of duty.'" —SIMON WINCHESTER, *The Professor and the Madman*

codex (KO DEKS) - *n.* a manuscript volume of, classics, ancient annals or of the Scriptures.

"'**Codex**' ... means, as a snooty scholar tells Edward, 'what someone like you would call a book.'" —POLLY SHULMAN. *The New York Times Book Review*, 3/21/04

colophon (KAH luh fuhn, also KAH luh FAHN) - *n.* an inscription found at the back of a book giving the facts relating to its publication or production, 2. the distinctive emblem of the publisher.

"However, looking for an index—there was none—Charles found a page in the back of the book that changed his life ... At the top, written in tiny cloister text, was a **colophon**: If you have diligently worked through this humble tome, perhaps you have the disposition to be indoctrinated into the mystery. Here are the rules ..." —GLEN DAVID GOLD, *Carter Beats the Devil*

crib (KRIB) - (among other definitions) *n.* notes or aids used to cheat during a school exam, 2. a translation of writing from another language.

"I flung aside a **crib** of Horace." —H.G. WELLS, *The Island of Dr. Moreau*

festschrift (also **F-**) (FEST SHRIFT) - *n.* a tribute or memorial volume filled with essays and articles by admirers of a scholar or savant upon his attaining a certain age or period in his career or in memory of a dead colleague.

"It's almost certain that had he retired, without incident, in his own good time, there would have been the **festschrift**, there would have been the institution of the Coleman Silk Lecture Series, there would have been a classical studies chair established in his name ..." —PHILIP ROTH, *The Human Stain*

foolscap (FUHL SKAP) - *n.* a writing paper made in sheets 16 x 13 inches and folded to make a page of 13 x 8 inches.

"Before the court, at that instant, 25 years almost to the week after he seized power in Baghdad, stood Saddam Hussein al-Majid al-Tikriti, the man who awarded himself titles of honor and glory to fill a **foolscap** page." —JOHN BURNS, *The New York Times*, 7/4/04

glassine (gla SEEN) - *n.* a dense, transparent and glossy paper.

"As an adult, she traveled around with her own teas, her own salad dressings, her own vitamins neatly arranged in little **glassine** packs." —MICHAEL CRICHTON, *Prey*

incunabulum (in KYUH NA byuh luhm, also ing KYUH NA byuh luhm) (pl. -la) - *n.* a book printed before 1501 using movable type, 2. a work of art from an early period.

"He passed [a glass] to Phoebe, who had pulled out the oldest book on the shelf— **incunabula**—spells the Inquisition suspected were used to conjure up demons." —GLEN DAVID GOLD, *Carter Beats the Devil*

octavo (ahk TAY VO, also ahk TAH VO) - *n.* the size of a page created by cutting a sheet of paper into eighths (from 5 x 8 to 6 x 9.5 inches), 2. a book or a piece of paper of this size.

"I could see that anything I might say to him should be vastly less interesting than watching the young lady leaf through an **octavo**." —DAVID LISS, *A Conspiracy of Paper*

palimpsest (pa LUHMP SEST, also puh LIMP SEST) - *n.* a document that has been erased or scraped clean in order to reuse the parchment or vellum, often with remnants of earlier, imperfectly erased writing still visible.

"'Lazy B' [focused on the childhood of Sandra Day O'Connor and her brother] provides a **palimpsest** of the adult author." —LINDA GREENHOUSE, *The New York Times Book Review*, 2/3/02

précis (pray SEE) - *n.* a concise or abridged statement or view; an abstract; a summary.

"Now the one-page **précis** had become a 124-page script called 'The Academy Purple ...'" —JONATHAN FRANZEN, *The Corrections*

ukase (yoo KAYS, also yoo KAYZ, oo KAHZ) (from Russian) - *n.* an authoritative decree or order by a government carrying the weight of law; edict.

"The Journal's editors issued a new **ukase** to the writers: 'Beginning in December, use it only in direct quotations and then be sure to explain what GOP means ...'" —WILLIAM SAFIRE, *The New York Times Magazine*, 12/15/02

variorum (VER ee OR uhm, also VAR ee OR uhm) - *n.* a text including notes from various scholars; often includes various versions of the text.

"During the whole bygone week he had been resolving to set this afternoon apart for a special purpose—the rereading of his Greek Testament—his new one, with better type than his old copy, following Griesbach's text as amended by numerous correctors, and with **variorum** readings in the margin." —THOMAS HARDY, *Jude the Obscure*

SCHOLARLY WORK, INTELLIGENCE

autodidact (o TOW dy DAKT) - *n.* a self-taught person.

"'In that town,' he says, 'you've got more intellectuals than anyone knows what to do with. Geniuses. Polymaths. Thinkers who are gunning for the big answers to the big questions. **Autodidacts** who have taught themselves ancient languages no one else knows ...'"

—Ian Caldwell and Dustin Thomason, *The Rule of Four*

bailiwick (BAY la WIK) - *n.* the precincts within which a bailiff has jurisdiction, 2. the limits or field of one's authority or interest.

> "'[The Washington Post] has become a ... force for good in its **bailiwick**.'" —Katharine Graham, *Personal History*

deconstruct (DEE kuhn STRUHKT) - *v.* to take apart, to reverse the construction of, 2. to discuss and interpret (a text) using the methods of criticism that rely only on the language contained within the text and not incorporating an extratextual reality (a strategy associated with Jacques Derrida).

> "But even if deconstruction cannot be defined, it can be described. For one thing, deconstruction comes with a lifetime guarantee to render discussion of any subject completely unintelligible. It does this by linguistic subterfuge ... **deconstruction** is an updated version of nominalism, the view that the meanings of words are completely arbitrary and that, at bottom, reality is unknowable." —Roger Kimball, *The Wall Street Journal*, 10/12/04

diegesis (di uh JEE sis) - *n.* a narrative or history, esp. the fictional world of a film or a written work.

> "The critic's voice is as legitimate as the voice of Herodotus. Narratology. The **diegetic**. The difference between diegesis and mimesis." —Philip Roth, *The Human Stain*

epigraphy (e puh GRA FEE) - *n.* epigraphs; inscriptions, 2. the study of inscriptions, especially ancient inscriptions.

> "Bellow's Herzog, whose thoughts on what it is 'to be a man. In a city. In a century. In transition. In a mass,' provide this book's **epigraph**." —Zoe Heller, referring to Ian McEwan's 'Saturday,' *The New York Times Book Review*, 3/20/05

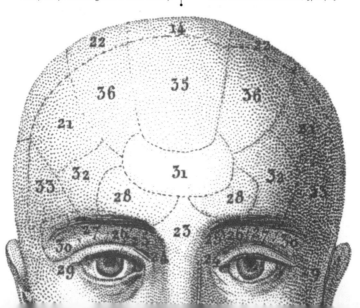

epiphenomenon (E puh fi NAH muh NAHN) - *n.* a secondary phenomenon that appears in conjunction with the first and is often caused by it, 2. relates to consciousness as a sympton of the physical interaction of the brain and nervous system.

> "He passed me the joint again and I took it. I inhaled and held the smoke in ... 'Everything looks really blue,' I said. 'Did you notice that?'
>
> 'Oh yeah,' said Jerome. 'All kinds of strange **epiphenomena**.'" —JEFFREY EUGENIDES, *Middlesex*

exegesis (EK suh JEE suhs) - *n.* a formal written exposition or explanatory essay analyzing a text or religious scripture.

> "Wexford's public library was voluminously stocked with critical studies of Joyce, and I devoured them all, understanding little of their import but enthralled by their aura of arcane, priestly **exegesis** and grateful for the extended extracts quoted from the sacred text." —JOHN BANVILLE, *The New York Times Book Review*, 6/13/04

exegete (EK suh JEET) - *n.* a practitioner of exegesis, 2. a person skilled in the science of interpretation.

> "Probably everybody knows how the Sherlock Holmes stories are studied by the Baker Street Irregulars; in the last decade the same sort of thing has happened with the works of J.R.R. Tolkien—who set his **exegetes** the example by adding a series of fanzine articles to *The Lord of the Rings*." —RICHARD H. ENEY, *The Blade of Conan*

ken (KEN) - *n.* knowledge; understanding, 2. range of sight or view.

> "And fresh and fair though it came from beyond the bourn of geography, and out of an age long lost and beyond history's **ken**, a dawn glowed upon Elfland that had known no dawn before." —LORD DUNSANY, *The King of Elfland's Daughter*

mimesis (mih MEE suhs) - *n.* imitation; mimicry of another (according to the Oxford English Dictionary, Plato in Republic "contrasts two types of speech: the author's own narrative voice [diegesis] and the 'imitated' voice of a character [mimesis]).

> "The critic's voice is as legitimate as the voice of Herodotus. Narratology. The diegetic. The difference between diegesis and **mimesis**." —PHILIP ROTH, *The Human Stain*

misomusist (MEE soh MYOO sist) - *n.* one who hates learning (Greek: miso = hater of).

> "The [**misomusist**] feels humiliated by the existence of something that is beyond him, and he hates it ... But there is an intellectual, sophisticated misomusy as well: it takes revenge on art by forcing it to a purpose beyond the aesthetic." —MILAN KUNDERA, *The Art of the Novel*

morphology (mor FAH luh jee) - *n.* a scientific study of form and structure without regard to function, 2. the study of word formation, including the origin and function of inflections and derivations.

numismatics (noo MIZ mah tiks) - *n.* the collection or study of money, coins, medals, etc.

pansophism (PAN soh FIZ uhm) - *n.* the assertation of universal wisdom, universal knowledge.

philology (FUH lah luh jee, also FY la luh jee) - *n.* the study of linguistics in its broadest sense, 2. the study of historical linguistics.

"I am fairly familiar with all hieroglyphics known to researchers and **philologists**." —ROBERT E. HOWARD, *Cthulhu*

pleiad (PLEE uhd, also PLAY uhd) - *n.* a small group, usually seven, of illustrious persons, 2. a group of seven 16th-century French poets who favored the use of classical forms, 3. any of the Pleiades (see also Pleiades).

"The **pleiad** of great Central European novelists: Kafka, Hasek, Musil, Broch, Gombrowicz." —MILAN KUNDERA, *The Art of the Novel*

polyglot (PAH lee GLAHT) - *adj.* containing, or made up of, several languages, 2. versed in, or speaking, many languages, 3. *n.* one who speaks several languages, 4. a book containing the same subject matter in several different languages.

"Sir John Stevens, the inveterate traveler and former **polyglot** Bank of England executive ..." —RON CHERNOW, *The House of Morgan*

polymath (PAH lee MATH) - *n.* a person with extraordinarily broad and comprehensive knowledge.

"'In that town,' he says, 'you've got more intellectuals than anyone knows what to do with. Geniuses. **Polymaths**. Thinkers who are gunning for the big answers to the big questions. Autodidacts who have taught themselves ancient languages no one else knows ...'" —IAN CALDWELL AND DUSTIN THOMASON, *The Rule of Four*

savant (sa VAHNT, also suh VAHNT, suh VANT) - *n.* a person of learning, 2. one who is versed in literature or sciences (from the French savoir—to know).

"The **savant** Astreas, traveling in the East

in his never-tiring search for knowledge, wrote a letter to his friend and fellow-philosopher Alcemides." —ROBERT E. HOWARD, *A Witch Shall Be Born*

semiotics (SEE mee OT iks, also SEHM ee OT iks) - *n.* the study of communication through interpretation of messages or signs, 2. the area of medical science focusing on interpretation of physical symptoms.

"... smarty-pants digressions on arcane topics like earthquake detection, Quebecois exceptionalism and the **semiotics** of hot-dog stands ..." —DANIEL ZALEWSKI, *The New York Times Magazine*, 12/15/02

structuralism (STRUHK chu ruh LI zuhm) - (among other definitions) *n.* the field of psychological study focusing on the structural elements of the mind, 2. the field of anthropology or sociology focusing on the structure or form of human society and social relationships within an abstract relational structure (based on the work of Claude Lévi-Strauss [b. 1908]).

"Her bookshelves were full of anthropology texts and works by French **structuralists** and deconstructionists." —JEFFREY EUGENIDES, *Middlesex*

symbolist (SIM buh list) - *n.* one skilled in the use or interpretation of symbols; one skilled in symbolism, 2. one highly skilled in the use of metaphor, 3. a movement of the late 19th century, started by French poets and later incorporating the arts and theater, that sought to express individual emotional experience through the subtle and suggestive use of highly metaphorical language.

"Finally the miserable silence is punctuated by the ringing of scouting director Eric Kubota's cell phone—only instead of ringing it plays, absurdly, Pachelbel's Canon. Eric snatches it quickly off the table. 'Oh, is that what it is?' he says into the phone, in a clipped tone, and hangs up. The draft room has become a **symbolist** play." —MICHAEL LEWIS, *Moneyball*

teleology (te lee AH luh jee) - *n.* the study of the design or purpose of natural occurrences, 2. the use of a non-natural purpose to explain an occurrence.

"Like Darwin, with whom he declares his allegiance, Eldredge pursues a quasi-**teleological** investigation of the main objective of life." —ROBERT J. RICHARDS, *The New York Times Book Review*, 6/20/04

BELIEF AND HERESY

apostasy (uh PAHS tuh SEE) - *n.* the renunciation of one's faith, religion or principles, 2. the renunciation of a belief or set of beliefs (an apostate is the person who apostatizes).

"During this false honeymoon, the House of Morgan committed a famous act of **apostasy**: it applauded Roosevelt for taking America off the gold standard." —RON CHERNOW, *The House of Morgan*

heretic (HER uh TIK) - *n.* a person holding unorthodox views or beliefs, esp. religious beliefs, 2. *adj.* of or pertaining to unorthodox views or beliefs.

"... gave rise in him to a new sensation, this interest in phenomena beyond ritual and obedience—something which he hoped was not **heretical** in him." —MERVYN PEAKE, *Titus Groan*

idolatry (eye DOL uh tree) - *n.* the worship of idols, 2. blind admiration or devotion.

"Not only had I mythologized him, but others shared the same **idolatrous** view, which

added to my confusion." —KATHARINE GRAHAM, *Personal History*

orthopraxy (also **orthopraxis**) (OR thuh PRAK see) - *n.* rightness of action; practical righteousness; correct practice; freq. opposed to orthodoxy, meaning rightness of belief.

"One may even say that there is no orthodoxy and heresy [in Islam], if one understands those terms in the Christian sense, as correct and incorrect belief defined as such by duly constituted religious authority. There has never been any such authority in Islam, and consequently no such definition. Where there are differences, they are between the mainstream and the fringes, between **orthopraxy** and deviation." —BERNARD LEWIS, *What Went Wrong?*

testament (TES tuh muhnt) - *n.* a solemn, authentic document in writing, by which a person declares his will as to disposal of his estate and effects after his death, 2. one of the two distinct revelations of God's purposes toward man; also, one of the two general divisions of the canonical books of the sacred Scriptures, in which the covenants are respectively revealed; as, the Old Testament; the New Testament; 3. tangible evidence, 4. a statement of conviction; credo.

OTHER "KNOWLEDGE" TERMS

anagram (A nuh GRAM) - *n.* a word or phrase that is created by rearranging the letters of another word.

"'But Rodge Epp Lang also happens to be an **anagram.** A rearrangement of the letters in 'doppelganger.'" —IAN CALDWELL AND DUSTIN THOMASON, *The Rule of Four*

antipode (AN tuh POHD) - *n.* an exact opposite; 2. something that is diametrically opposed.

> "My life has almost been **antipodal**, in its associations, to yours." −ROBERT E. HOWARD, *Selected Letters 1931–1936*

aperçu (A puhr SOO) - *n.* an immediate impression, 2. a brief outline, 3. an intuitive insight.

> "Five of the seven stories … originally appeared in *The New Yorker,* and there are certain ways in which they might be said to exemplify that magazine's polished [and often parodied] literary sensibility, composed as they are of discriminating **aperçus** and minutely observed social transactions." −DAPHNE MERKIN, *The New York Times Book Review,* 3/31/02

avatar (A vuh TAHR) - (from Hindu mythology) *n.* - the earthly incarnation of a deity or soul in a body, 2. a representation; exemplar, archetype.

> "Mr. Kapasi walked ahead, to admire, as he always did, the three life-sized bronze **avatars** of Surya, the sun god, each emerging from its own niche on the temple facade to greet the sun at dawn, noon, and evening." −JHUMPA LAHIRI, *Interpreter of Maladies*

bagatelle (BA guh TEL) - *n.* a trifle, 2. a type of game played by rolling a ball into a scoring zone.

> "'A mere matter of detail, a **bagatelle**,' said J.T. Maston." −JULES VERNE, *From the Earth to the Moon*

concordance (kuhn KOR dunce, also kahn KOR dunce) - *n.* an agreement; accordance, 2. an alphabetical verbal index showing the places in the text of a book where each principal word may be found, with its immediate context in each place, 3. a topical index or orderly analysis of the contents of a book.

> "But Taft, who by then was pursuing the Hypnerotomachia from his own angles, assembling huge catalogs of textual references into a **concordance**, so that every word of Colonna's could be traced to its origins, failed to see any possible relevance to the chicken-scratch notes the portmaster claimed to see Colonna keeping." −IAN CALDWELL AND DUSTIN THOMASON, *The Rule of Four*

consonance (KAHNT suh nuhnts) - *n.* harmony; agreement; concord, 2. a recurrence of consonant sounds at the end of words (e.g. plank and wink).

> "Even in his anguish, the unity of the moment was intoxicating … the world prayed as one. Like synapses of a giant heart all firing in tandem, the people reached for God, in dozens of languages, in hundreds of countries … The **consonance** felt eternal." −DAN BROWN, *Angels & Demons*

cynosure (SY nuh SHUR, also SI nuh SHUR) - *n.* the center of attention, 2. something that guides; something used as a guide, (e.g., the North Star).

> "Lately, the 25-year-old Mr. Kutcher has been the **cynosure** of tabloids and celebrity magazines, thanks to his April-July romance with actress Demi Moore." −JOANNE KAUFMAN, *The Wall Street Journal,* 8/29/03

divertissement (dee vuhr tees MAHN) - (French) *n.* a diversion; an entertainment, 2. a brief dance, often performed between longer pieces.

"'God Is in the House,' a small-town satire that Randy Newman might have caught himself whistling, is the closest [Nick] Cave comes to being merely amusing, but it still contains more savagery than your typical **divertissement**." —NICK HORNBY, *Songbook*

dystopia *(dis TOW pee uh)* - *n.* a vision of the future or an imaginary place that is as corrupted and bad as possible (the opposite of utopia).

"In the draft Major League Baseball has brought to life Bill James's **dystopic** vision of closing the stadium to the fans and playing the game in private." —MICHAEL LEWIS, *Moneyball*

felicity (fi LI suh tee) - *n.* extreme happiness, 2. apt and pleasing style in writing, speech, etc.

"To say, then, that [Alan Hollinghurst's] latest novel, the Booker Prize-winning 'Line of Beauty,' is also his finest should give some idea of its accomplishment, not just in the breadth of its ambition but in its **felicities** of observation and expression." — ANTHONY QUINN, *The New York Times Book Review*, 10/31/04

fount (FAUNT) - *n.* something from which water flows; a fountain; a source; a wellspring.

"The creators were not selfless. It is the whole secret of their power—this it was self-sufficient, self-motivated, self-generated. A first cause, a **fount** of energy, a life force, a Prime Mover.'" —AYN RAND, *The Fountainhead*

fustian (FUHS chuhn) - *n.* a kind of coarse twilled cloth, 2. pompous or pretentious speech or writing, 3. *adj.* relating to language that is pompous, bombastic or overly inflated.

"...since she had seen her brother tear at the leaves that encased him, she had known that there was another being in the room for whom the whole **fustian** of Gormenghast was a thing to flee from." —MERVYN PEAKE, *Titus Groan*

harbinger (HAHR buhn juhr) - *n.* a forerunner, 2. a sign that foreshadows some occurrence.

"Like **harbingers** of Fate a wavering line of herons flapped slowly away toward the reed-grown banks of the river." —ROBERT E. HOWARD, *The Hand of Nergal*

idée fixe (E DAY FEEKS) - *n.* an obsession, a thought or idea that takes over one's mind (French = fixed idea).

"If we had a hotel room [the eagle] shared it. I'd hear his step; he crackled his feathers or hissed as if snow was sliding. He was right away her absorption and **idée fixe**, almost child, and he made her out of breath. She turned to him continually in her seat as we rode, or when we ate, and I wondered at other times whether he was on her mind." —SAUL BELLOW, *The Adventures of Augie March*

imbroglio (im BROLE yo) - *n.* a state of confusion, 2. a difficult, embarrassing or intricate situation or misunderstanding.

"As a book reviewer, I find that the current ghostwriting **imbroglio** puts me in a hopelessly difficult situation." –JOE QUEENAN, *The New York Times Book Review*, 3/20/05

kerfuffle (also **curfuffle**) (kuhr FUH fuhl) - *n*. a disturbance; disorder; agitation, 2. an annoying noise.

"For the last year, the literary world has been in a mild uproar over the supposedly vexed question of harsh reviewing. The ruckus started when the novelist Dale Peck tried to bury his fellow novelist Rick Moody's memoir ... The ensuing **kerfuffle** culminated in a long essay by Heidi Julavits ..." –CLIVE JAMES, *The New York Times*, 9/7/03

lacuna (luh KOO nuh, also luh KYOO nuh) (pl. -nas, -nae) -*n*. a vacancy, where something once was, 2. a small opening, a small pit or depression, 3. a blank space; gap; hiatus.

"... the humor was more effective when the ribaldry was merely hinted at. The listener fills in the **lacunae** in his mind according to his own tastes." –ISAAC ASIMOV, *I. Asimov*

Lethe (LEE THEE) -*n*. forgetfulness, oblivion (from Greek mythology: the river in Hades the waters of which cause forgetfulness).

"'First, you descend into your emotional life with a doctor as your guide, and then the repressed memories are washed away in the **Lethe**.'" –GLEN DAVID GOLD, *Carter Beats the Devil*

pablum (PA bluhm) - *n*. the proprietary (brand) name of cereal for infants made from wheat, oat and corn meal, 2. overly bland or simplistic speech or writing.

"If the Key Judgments used words such as 'maybe' or 'probably' or 'likely,' the [National Intelligence Estimate] would be '**pablum**,' he said." –BOB WOODWARD, *Plan of Attack*

pith (PITH) - *n*. the soft, spongy substance in the center of the stems of many plants and trees, 2. the essential or vital part of an idea or theory, 3. strength; vigor.

*see other **pith** entry for citation, p. 182*

portent (POR TENT) - *n*. a foreshadowing, the sign of a coming event, an omen, 2. something of great significance; marvel; prodigy.

rede (REED) - *n*. counsel; advice, 2. counsel given to one or more persons, used to create a plan or scheme.

"'Strange **rede** the demon gave me.'" –POUL ANDERSON, *Three Hearts and Three Lions*

touchstone (TUHCH STON) - *n*. a stone once used to test the purity of gold and silver, 2. a test, criterion or standard used to determine authenticity or genuiness.

"It was to be a story for boys; no need of psychology or fine writing; and I had a boy at hand to be a **touchstone**." –ROBERT LOUIS STEVENSON, *Introduction, Treasure Island*

Urheimat (ur HY maht) - *n*. a place, the location where a people or language originated.

"Ancient Ireland and analogues of it— Conan's own Cimmeria is the **urheimat** of the Gaels in Howard's mythos—were among Howard's favorite settings." –S.M. STIRLING in Robert E. Howard's *Eons of the Night*

verisimilitude (VER uh suh MI luh TOOD, also VER uh suh MI luh TYOOD) - *n.* the appearance of being true or real, 2. something that appears to be true or real.

> "Several other citations of real events or persons augment the **verisimilitude** of the tale." –S.T. JOSHI, *Explanatory Notes, H.P. Lovecraft's The Call of Cthulhu and Other Weird Stories*

volte-face (VOLT FAHS, also VOL tuh FAHS) - *n.* a reversal of attitude, opinion or policy, 2. an about-face; physically turning to face the opposite direction.

> "The man whom Sue, in her mental **volte-face**, was now regarding as her inseparable husband, lived still at Marygreen." –THOMAS HARDY, *Jude the Obscure*

Weltanschauung (VELT AHN shau UHNG) - *n.* worldview (from German "world perception"), 2. a philosophy or perception of the world held by an individual or group.

> "'You must realize the fear and hatred which my **weltanschauung** instills in people.' Ignatius belched." –JOHN KENNEDY TOOLE, *A Confederacy of Dunces*

POETRY

acrostic (uh KROS tik, also uh KRAHS tik) - *n.* a poem or composition in which sets of a letter, such as the first letter in a line, form a word when taken in order.

> "When the first letters of every chapter in the Hypnerotomachia are strung together, they form an **acrostic** in Latin: Poliam Frater Franciscus Columna Peramavit, which means 'Brother Francesco Colonna loved Polia tremendously.'" –IAN CALDWELL AND DUSTIN THOMASON, *The Rule of Four*

anapest (A NUH PEST) - *n.* a metrical foot made up of two short syllables preceeding one long syllable.

> "... my grandfather preferred to spend his mornings working on a modern Greek translation of the 'restored' poems of Sappho. For the next seven years, despite repeated strokes, my grandfather worked at a small desk, piecing together the legendary fragments into a larger mosaic, adding a stanza here, a coda there, soldering an **anapest** or an iamb." –JEFFREY EUGENIDES, *Middlesex*

assonance (A suh nuhnts) - *n.* the repetition of similar vowel sounds without the repetition of consonant sounds, found in verse.

> "One of Flaubert's great concerns during the years of writing *Madame Bovary* was for the rhythm and **assonance** of his prose." –FRANCIS STEEGMULLER, *Introduction, Gustave Flaubert's Madame Bovary*

ballade (buh LAHD, also ba LAHD) - *n.* a form of verse or poem made up of three stanzas of equal length with a recurrent line or refrain at the end of each stanzas.

> "'Perchance you know a **ballade**, villanelle, or sirvente which would fall sweetly on ears too long accustomed to howling wolves and rainy winds.'" –POUL ANDERSON, *Three Hearts and Three Lions*

caesura (si ZYUR uh, also si ZHUR uh) - *n.* a break or pause in the flow of a metrical line; break; interruption.

> "'Longitudes and Attitudes' is a collection of columns, from December 2000 to this past July, broken by September's great **caesura**, and including material from his diary, notes made but not used as he traveled to the Persian Gulf, Pakistan,

Afghanistan, Indonesia, India, Saudi Arabia, London, Brussels." —GEOFFREY WHEATCROFT, *The New York Times Book Review*, 9/8/02

Calliope (kuh LIE uh PEE) - *n.* (Greek mythology) the muse of eloquence and epic poetry; one of nine muses and the mother of Orpheus by Apollo.

"'**Calliope** was one of the Muses, right?'

'Right.'

'In charge of what?'

'Epic poetry.'" —JEFFREY EUGENIDES, *Middlesex*

dactyl (DAK tuhl, also DAK til) - *n.* a poetical foot of three syllables, one long followed by two short or one accented followed by two unaccented.

"By March of 1930, only half as many patrons gave the secret **dactylic**-spondaic knock on the basement door." —JEFFREY EUGENIDES, *Middlesex*

dithyramb (di thi RAM) - *n.* a Greek choir hymn, 2. a Bacchanalian song, 3. a poem or metrical composition written in this form, 4. a speech or composition written in an inflated, enthusiastic or exalted style.

"When he came to the distribution of the prizes, he depicted the joy of the winners in **dithyrambic** terms." —GUSTAVE FLAUBERT, *Madame Bovary*, transl. by Francis Steegmuller

doggerel (DO guh ruhl, also DO guh rahl) - *n.* a loosely styled verse in an irregular rhythm, often for comic effect (from the Middle English word for worthless).

"I at once showed Mr. Perkhotin the poem ... Mr. Perkhotin immediately burst out laughing and began criticizing it: what awful **doggerel**! he said." —FYODOR DOSTOYEVSKY, *The Brothers Karamazov*, transl. by David Magarshack.

eclogue (EK LOG, also EK LAHG) - *n.* a pastoral poem; one of shepherds conversing.

"A long explanation followed, about Virgil's tenth **eclogue**." —IAN CALDWELL AND DUSTIN THOMASON, *The Rule of Four*

elegy (E luh jee) - *n.* a mournful or plaintive poem; a funereal song; a poem of lamentation.

epithalamium (E puh thuh LAY mee uhm) - *n.* a wedding song or poem to honor and praise the bride and bridegroom.

"But why, if somewhere there existed a strong and handsome being—a man of valor, sublime in passion and refinement, with a poet's heart and an angel's shape, a man like a lyre with strings of bronze, intoning elegiac **epithalamiums** to the heavens—why mightn't she have the luck to meet him?" —GUSTAVE FLAUBERT, *Madame Bovary,* transl. by Francis Steegmuller

iamb (EYE amb) - *n.* a poetical or metrical foot of two syllables, one long followed by one short or one accented followed by one unaccented.

*see **anapest** for citation, p. 95*

idyll (EYE duhl, also i DIL) - *n.* a carefree episode or experience, esp. in a rustic setting, 2. a short poem about a carefree episode or experience or rustic life, 3. a romantic episode.

*see other **idyll** entry for citation, p. 198*

monody (MAH nuh dee) - *n.* an ode; an elegy or dirge.

"He was not listening to Barquentine, who was rattling off the catechismic **monody** as fast as he could, for he was suffering the first twinges of rheumatism." —MERVYN PEAKE, *Titus Groan*

prosody (PRAH suh dee, also PRAH zuh dee) - *n.* the study of versification, of metrical structures.

"Lack of access to traditional education meant that women so inclined were comparatively free to come up with original readings of the classics and to flout **prosodic** convention." —JUDITH SHULEVITZ, *The New York Times Book Review,* 9/22/02

sestina (se STEE nuh) - *n.* a form of poem of six six-line stanzas in which the end words of the first stanza recur in the following five stanzas in a rotating order.

"'I joy in the company of gentlefolk who can turn a **sestina** as well as break a lance.'" —POUL ANDERSON, *Three Hearts and Three Lions*

sirvente (sir VAHNT) - *n.* a poem or song, usually religious or moral, that satirizes social vices, employed by the troubadours of the Middle Ages.

*see **ballade** for citation, p. 95*

spondee (SPAHN DEE) - *n.* a poetical or metrical foot of two long or accented syllables.

*see **dactyl** for citation, p. 96*

stave (STAYV) - *n.* one of a number of narrow strips of wood, or narrow iron plates, placed edge to edge to form the sides, covering, or lining of a vessel or structure, 2. one of the cylindrical bars of a lantern wheel; one of the bars or rounds of a rack, a ladder, etc., 3. a metrical portion; a stanza; a staff, 4. the five horizontal and parallel lines on and between which musical notes are written or pointed; the staff.

"'Now, Barbecue, tip us a **stave**,' cried one voice ... 'Ay, ay, mates,' said Long John, who was standing by, with his crutch under his arm, and at once broke out in the air and words I knew so well—'Fifteen men on The Dead Man's Chest—' And then the whole crew bore chorus: 'Yo-ho-ho, and a bottle of rum!'" —ROBERT LOUIS STEVENSON, *Treasure Island*

strophe (STROW FEE) - *n.* a stanza of a poem or verse.

"Because now they pranced onstage: the chorus girls. Dressed in silver halters, robed in see-through shifts, they danced, reciting **strophes** that didn't scan to the eerie piping of flutes." —JEFFREY EUGENIDES, *Middlesex*

villanelle (VI luh NE lee) - *n.* a form of poem usually consisting of five three-line stanzas and one quatrain containing only two rhymes. Line one and three of the first stanza are alternately repeating in the following stanzas as a refrain and appear as a final couplet in the quatrain.

see **ballade** *for citation*

MIXTURES

admixture (ad MIKS chuhr) - *n.* a mixture or blend, 2. something added in mixing.

"Very close around the stockade—too close for defence, they said—the wood still flourished high and dense, all of fir on the land side, but towards the sea with a large **admixture** of live-oaks." —ROBERT LOUIS STEVENSON, *Treasure Island*

agglomerate (uh GLAH muh RAYT) - *v.* to collect into a ball, heap or rounded mass, 2. *n.* a jumbled collection or mass, 3. a mass of angular volcanic fragments united by heat.

"He cited a great number of words, sayings, and gestures, all confirmed by witnesses, and the picture he drew had a telling effect on his listeners. It was the **agglomeration** of facts that made itself felt in the end." —FYODOR DOSTOYEVSKY, *The Brothers Karamazov,* transl. by David Magarshack

congeries (KAHN juh REES) - *n.* a collection or aggregation of things massed or heaped together, as in a pile.

"... odd low hills topped by **congeries** of black rock appeared." —FRITZ LEIBER, *Swords Against Death*

farrago (fuh RAH go, also fuh RAY go) - *n.* a collection containing a variety of miscellaneous things; a medly; a jumble; a hodgepodge.

"... many will choose to believe the whole **farrago**, against their own better sense, because of their dislike of Earth and Earth-people." —ISAAC ASIMOV, *The Robots of Dawn*

gallimaufry (GA luh MO free) - *n.* a hash of various kinds of meats, a ragout, 2. any absurd medly; a hodgepodge or hotchpotch; a jumble.

"The whole point of such an elaborate and highly complicated **gallimaufry** of symbolism adds up to a total waste of time on the author's part if the reader is unable to get the point." —LIN CARTER, *Tolkien*

mélange (also **melange**) (may LAHNZH, also may LAHNJ) - *n.* a mixture.

"He then painted a verbal portrait of the **mélange** of weapons he was urging Gust to deploy to bring down the Hind." —GEORGE CRILE, *Charlie Wilson's War*

shambles (SHAM bulz) - (uses a singular verb) *n.* a condition of complete disorder or destruction, 2. a scene of great clutter, a jumble.

see other **shambles** *entry for citation, p. 199*

WRITING, LOGIC, AND KNOWLEDGE—ADJECTIVES

POSITIVE ADJECTIVES

apposite (A puh zuht) - *adj.* appropriate; well-suite; relevant; apt.

"People start to realize their potential [for once the cliché is **apposite**]." —GORDON CHANG, *The Wall Street Journal,* 3/12/01

fecund (FE kuhnd, also FEE kuhnd) - *adj.* prolific; fruitful; fertile; productive.

"'I am very busy with my work at the moment, and I feel that I am entering a very **fecund** stage.'" –JOHN KENNEDY TOOLE, *A Confederacy of Dunces*

lapidary (LA puh DER ee) - *n.* a person who cuts and polishes stones or gems, 2. the art of cutting and polishing stones or gems, 3. *adj.* worthy of engraving in stone: lapidary prose.

"The sixth novel in 40 years of careful, **lapidary** production by this elegant Irish writer [John McGahern]." –NOT ATTRIBUTED, *The New York Times Book Review*, 6/2/02

limpid (LIM pid) - *adj.* transparent; clear; serene, 2. clear or simple in style.

"He had meant the remark to stand on its own—a **limpid** statement of fact—something that he imagined Fuchsia might often turn over in her mind and cogitate upon." –MERVYN PEAKE, *Titus Groan*

lucid (LOO sid) - *adj.* easily understood, clear, 2. clear-headed; rational, 3. transparent.

"Krist Novoselic's memoir turned civics manual, 'Of Grunge and Government,' is **lucid**, unpretentious and, as the architect Louis Sullivan once described the ideal of democracy, 'thrillingly sane.'" –SARAH VOWELL, *The New York Times Book Review*, 10/17/04

pellucid (puh LOO sid) - *adj.* transparent; translucent; clear; allowing for maximum passage of light, 2. clearly understood; of a clear or simple style.

[the documentary] "'Faith and Doubt at Ground Zero' is an outstanding document, sensitive, careful and **pellucidly** intelligent." –TUNKU VARADARAJAN, *The Wall Street Journal*, 8/30/02

piquant (PEE kuhnt, also PEE kahnt, PI kwuhnt) - *adj.* pleasantly stimulating to the palate; of an agreeable taste; pungent; spicy, 2. exhibiting a lively charm; provocative.

"... a fleeting glance of a pair of dark, daring eyes in a face of **piquant** beauty." –ROBERT E. HOWARD, *Kull*

risible (RI zuh buhl) - *adj.* capable of or inclined to laughing, 2. causing laughter, 3. associated with laughter.

"'Team America' is all of the above, though with strings attached—the whole thing's done with marionettes. (The strings remain **risibly** visible)." –JOE MORGENSTERN, *The Wall Street Journal*, 10/15/04

salient (SAY lyuhnt, also SAY lee uhnt) - *adj.* worthy of note, 2. standing out or projecting beyond a line or surface, 3. prominent; striking; conspicuous.

*see other **salient** entry for citation, p. 276*

seminal (SE muh nuhl) - *adj.* consisting of or relating to seed or semen, 2. creative; original; stimulating growth.

"Over a longer stretch of time, [Washington's] Farewell Address achieved transcendental status, ranking alongside the Declaration of Independence and the Gettysburg Address as a **seminal** statement of America's abiding principles." –JOSEPH J. ELLIS, *Founding Brothers*

trenchant (TREN chunt) - *adj.* keen; incisive, 2. forceful, effective (from the old French, trenchier, to cut).

"I expected tirades of righteousness, howls of orthodox wrath, scathing rebukes and **trenchant** remarks about the general absence of merit of my slop, but his criticism was as follows ..." —ROBERT E. HOWARD, *Selected Letters 1923-1930*

NEUTRAL, DESCRIPTIVE ADJECTIVES

à la mode (AH luh MOWD) - *adj.* fashionable (from the French, "in the manner or fashion"), 2. served with ice cream.

"He fell into a black melancholy and took no part in the opera **à la mode** or in the other carnival amusements." —FRANCOIS VOLTAIRE, *Candide*, transl. by Richard Aldington

abstruse (uhb STROOS, also ab STROOS) - *adj.* difficult to comprehend or understand; unclear.

"As the founder, honorary CEO and chief publicist for an **abstruse** philosophical doctrine he called 'deconstruction,' Mr. Derrida was celebrated and vilified in about equal measure." —ROGER KIMBALL, *The Wall Street Journal*, 10/12/04

antithetical (AN tuh THE ti kuhl) - *adj.* pertaining to antithesis or opposition of words and sentiments, 2. containing, or of the nature of, antithesis; contrasted; contradictory; exactly opposite.

"'It is not a temple, but its perfect **antithesis**, an insolent mockery of all religion.'" —AYN RAND, *The Fountainhead*

apodictic (A puh DIK tik) - *adj.* that can clearly be shown or proved; absolutely certain or necessarily true.

"... the new art of specifically novelistic essay (which does not claim to bear an **apodictic** message but remains hypothetical, playful or ironic)." —MILAN KUNDERA, *The Art of the Novel*

arch (AHRCH) - *adj.* of high rank; chief; principal; the primary among many, 2. mischievous; saucy; 3. exhibiting a forced brashness or irony.

"The writers imitated James's prose style but, lacking anything interesting to say, they wound up sounding empty and **arch**." —MICHAEL LEWIS, *Moneyball*

autotelic (O tow TEH lik, also O tow TEE lik) - *adj.* having an end in itself; engaged in for its own sake.

"In her mind, the [carved] squirrels were probably **autotelic**, each a study in the discrepancy within mass repetition." —ROBERT MAILER ANDERSON, *Boonville*

capacious (kuh PAY shus) - *adj.* able to hold or contain a great deal; spacious; roomy.

"... what the author Rosemary Haughton once called 'The Catholic Thing'—the **capacious**, sacramental religious imagination that operates by analogy rather than linear logic and perceives virtually everything human (including the body and sexual love) as occasion for a graced encounter with the divine mystery." —R. SCOTT APPLEBY, *The New York Times Book Review*, 9/7/03

didactic (DY dak tick, also DUH dak tik) - *adj.* intended to teach, 2. designed to be morally informative or instructive.

> "'Could you drop the anger, the self-right-eousness, and that irritating **didacti-cism**?'" –PAT CONROY, *My Losing Season*

elegiac (EH luh JIE uk, also EH luh JIE ak, ih LEE gee ak) - *adj.* pertaining to an elegy; written in elegiac couplets, 2. expressing sadness; mournful.

> "One might say that Lively's book is itself a product of another era, a time when novelists and poets wrote reminiscences, not memoirs, and offered **elegiac** tours of a lost social landscape rather than deeply revelatory excavations of self or family." –JOHN VERNON, *The New York Times Book Review*, 5/19/02

extant (EK stuhnt, also ek STANT) - *adj.* still in existence; not having disappeared; not lost or destroyed.

> "It originally contained 7,000 verses, but only one line from it is **extant** today." –LIN CARTER, *Tolkien*

gnostic (NAHS tik) - *adj.* of or having knowledge; cognitive, 2. *n.* one skilled or learned in a subject, 3. Gnostic: a believer in Gnosticism—a system of belief combining elements of Greek philosophy, Oriental mysticism and Christianity and stressing salvation through a positive, intuitive knowledge of spiritual matters (referred to as gnosis).

> *see other **gnostic** entry for citation, p. 146*

gravid (GRA vuhd) - *adj.* pregnant; with child; fruitful; heavy with young.

> "... there were kids walking along and babies in backpacks and slings, and the marchers chanted a sort of hummed syl-lable, a thing with a twang, it sounded to me like Bomb, a vibe with the **gravid** tone of prayer, repeated, repeated, but they would-n't be chanting an ominous word, would they, with infants strapped to their chests and backs." –DON DELILLO, *Underworld*

hermeneutic (HUHR muh NOO tik, also HUHR muh NYOO tik) - *adj.* interpretive; of or relating to interpretation, esp. as distinguished from exegesis or practical exposition.

> "Long before deconstruction, we were fond of a **hermeneutics** of suspicion. We had partisanship even before we had parties." –ALAN WOLFE, *The New York Times Book Review*, 7/11/04

heterodox (HE tuh ruh DAHKS) - *adj.* of or pertaining to creeds, beliefs or teachings, esp. religious ones that depart from the norm, 2. unorthodox but not to the extent of being heretical.

> "... the 1922 brochures proclaimed that 'the University of California is committed to excellent thought, even the **heterodox**.'" –GLEN DAVID GOLD, *Carter Beats the Devil*

heuristic (hyu RIS tik) - *adj.* a process or method of education or computer programming in which rules of thumb are used to find solutions, emphasizing discovery and observation, 2. information used in a heuristic process.

> "Energy that's pumped [in] ... will turn into extra mass: The shuttle example is only **heuristic**; we'll see as the book goes on that energy is mass: the unified thing called 'mass-energy' just happens to take on different aspects, depending on how we're viewing it." –DAVID BODANIS, *E=MC Squared*

innominate (i NAH muh nuht) - *adj.* unnamed; anonymous; having no name.

> "And though it was but an image and without even the semblance of life, she felt unmistakably the presence of something alive in the temple, something so alien and **innominate** that instinctively she drew away." –C.L. MOORE, *Jirel of Joiry*

mordant (MOR dent) - *adj.* biting; caustic; sarcastic; keen; severe, 2. incisive; trenchant.

> "'Kid Charlemagne' is a typically clever, **mordant** look at the death of the sixties, but the solo that closes it is the sound of pure, untethered joy" –NICK HORNBY, *Songbook*

mythopoeic (MI thu PEE ik) - *adj.* of or relating to the making of myths; productive in myth-making.

> "... marking London as a **mythopoeic** genius who often wrote better than he knew." –EARLE LABOR, *Introduction, The Portable Jack London*

neoteric (NEE uh TER ik) - *adj.* a person with a modern sensibility; espousing a modern outlook; new; recent.

normative (NOR muh tiv) - *adj.* of or pertaining to a standard or norm.

passim (PA suhm, also PA SIM, PAH suhm, PAH SIM) - (Latin) *adv.* here and there; throughout, as in a book or text.

> "And gradually we begin to get hard, in-depth interviews with actual players [David Remnick on Reggie Jackson, George Plimpton on all the parties to Henry Aaron's record home run, etc.], leading both to a deeper understanding of the game as played [Roger Angell, Keith Her-

nandez] and to a much more grown-up sense of its history [Lawrence S. Ritter and Donald Honig **passim**]." –WILFRED SHEED, *The New York Times Book Review,* 3/31/02

peremptory (puh REMP tuh ree) - *adj.* precluding debate or expostulation, 2. not admitting of question or appeal; positive; absolute; decisive; conclusive; final, 3. positive in opinion or judgement; decided; dictatorial, 4. firmly determined; unawed.

> "Musicians and whole bands have left [James Brown] over his **peremptory** ways." –PETER GURALNICK, *Sweet Soul Music*

picaresque (PI kuh resk, also PEE kuh resk) - *adj.* of or relating to rogues or rascals, 2. a type of fiction, of Spanish origin, dealing with rogues and vagabonds.

> "Clinton's [autobiography] is a galloping, reckless, political **picaresque**, a sort of pilgrim's progress, lowercase." –LARRY MCMURTRY, *The New York Times Book Review,* 7/4/04

portentous (por TEN tuhs) - *adj.* pertaining to a portent, 2. eliciting wonder and awe, 3. a serious matter, grave, 4. pretentiously weighty; pompous.

> "'Harken, fellow,' he said, turning **portentously** to the other, 'I suppose you are some sort of a northern barbarian.'" –ROBERT E. HOWARD, *The Tower of the Elephant*

putative (PYOO tuh tiv) - *adj.* commonly believed to be true on inconclusive grounds; generally regarded as truth; supposed.

> "The problem with Hamilton's distinction, however, was that the **putative** barrier between personal and political criticism, or private and public behavior, kept getting

overwhelmed by real choices." —JOSEPH
J. ELLIS, *Founding Brothers*

recondite (RE kuhn DYT, also ri KAHN
DYT) - *adj.* beyond the grasp of the ordinary mind or understanding; profound;
abstruse, 2. dealing with abstruse or difficult subjects, 3. obscure or concealed.

"He clung to his intellectual ambitions,
reading Bryce and Thucydides and writing essays, studded with **recondite** references, in favor of the League of Nations."
—RON CHERNOW, *The House of Morgan*

ruminant (ROO muh nuhnt) - *n.* any of a
variety of hoofed, cud-chewing mammals,
e.g. cow or deer, 2. *adj.* relating to chewing
cud, 3. meditative; contemplative.

semantic (si MAN tik) - *adj.* pertaining to
meaning, especially in language, 2. the study
of meanings, esp. in language, 3. the historical or psychological significance of words as
factors in the development of linguistics.

"In each language these words have a different **semantic** nuance." —MILAN KUN-
DERA, *Ignorance*

sesquipedalian (SESS kwuh puh DAL yun)
- *adj.* given to using long words, 2. characterized by overly long words.

"Shea, glancing up, suppressed an impulse
to tweak the **sesquipedalian** nose that the
troll had thrust through the bars." —L.
SPRAGUE DE CAMP and FLETCHER PRATT,
The Complete Compleat Enchanter

stochastic (stow KAS tik) - *adj.* arising from
chance; involving probability; random.

tendentious (ten DENT shus) - *adj.* marked
by a tendency in favor of a particular point
of view; biased.

"Mr. Shapiro is frustrated by his fellow students' acceptance of the **tendentious** curriculum and of their professors' outspoken
(liberal) beliefs." —RUSS SMITH, *The Wall
Street Journal*, 6/4/04

NEGATIVE ADJECTIVES

acrid (AK rid) - *adj.* sharp and harsh or bitter to the taste or smell; pungent, 2. caustic; bitter; bitterly irritating as in temper,
mind or writing.

antic (AN tik) - (often antics) *n.* a ludicrous
act or gesture; caper, 2. *adj.* odd; ludicrous.

"Readers may indeed be disconcerted by
Ricks's sheer goofiness. But this is hardly
confined to his writing on this new, pop-
culture subject [i.e., Bob Dylan]: Ricks's
'Beckett's Dying Words' (1993), taken as
a more or less random sample, is equally
antic, even as it worries at Beckett's
deathly gravity." —JONATHAN LETHEM, *The
New York Times Book Review*, 6/13/04

apocryphal (uh PAH kruh fuhl) - *adj.* of
dubious authenticity; of doubtful veracity,
2. not genuine; counterfeit, 3. of or like the
Apocrypha.

"There also exists the **apocryphal** story of
the German sniper who disemboweled a
felled horse and fired from within the remains of the carcass, the muzzle protruding through the mouth of the corpse,
the sniper acquiring his targets through
the dead animal's eyeholes." —ANTHONY
SWOFFORD, *Jarhead*

banal (buh NAL, also bah NAL, bay NAL,
bay NAHL) - *adj.* common in a boring way,
to the point of being predictable; trite; commonplace; ordinary.

"Adultery, Emma was discovering, could be as **banal** as marriage." —GUSTAVE FLAUBERT, *Madame Bovary*, transl. by Francis Steegmuller

baroque (buh ROK, also ba ROK, buh RAHK, buh ROCK) - (often Baroque) *adj.* having an irregular shape, 2. flamboyant; outlandish, 3. an artistic style common in Europe from 1500 to 1700 exhibiting very elaborate and ornate forms, 4. a musical style common in Europe from 1600 to 1750 exhibiting strict forms and elaborate detail.

"By accident, or perhaps by some unknown design, I found a house where Tennessee Williams had lived as a young playwright turned loose in the city and wondered if it was the house where Blanche and Stanley were born in his tortured and **baroque** imagination." —PAT CONROY, *My Losing Season*

bromidic (brow MI dik) - *adj.* lacking originality; trite; commonplace.

"When Felix's prose occasionally turned elaborate, purple, or **bromidic**, Phil, disapproving, simply stopped typing." —KATHARINE GRAHAM, *Personal History*

captious (KAP shus) - *adj.* likely to find faults in others, raise objections, quibbling. 2. seeking to confuse or entrap in argument.

"Warren concluded with a scathing diagnosis of the Adams correspondence with her as a scattered series of verbal impulses and 'the most **captious**, malignant, irrelevant compositions that have ever been seen.'" —JOSEPH J. ELLIS, *Founding Brothers*

cloying (KLOY ing) - *adj.* excessively sweet; distasteful in excess: cloying praise.

"Roth shows us how swiftly the rights and democratic customs of American life are lost, under the authoritarian guidance of President Lindbergh and his **cloyingly** named 'Just Folks' program, which sets out to break up Jewish families and neighborhoods by scattering Jewish children into the Christian heartland." — PAUL BERMAN, *The New York Times Book Review*, 10/3/04

deprecatory (DEP reh keh TOR ee) - *adj.* expressing deprecation or disapproval; belittling; disparaging.

"Colonel Cathcart uttered a **deprecatory** laugh." —JOSEPH HELLER, *Catch-22*

ersatz (ER SAHTS, also ER ZAHTS, er SAHTS, er ZAHTS, UHR SATS) - (German) *adj.* something made in imitation; an effigy or substitute.

"I don't want any **ersatz** soldiers, dragging their tails and ducking out when the party gets rough." —ROBERT HEINLEIN, *Starship Troopers*

factitious (fak TI shus) - *adj.* produced by man; man-made; artificial; false; sham.

"Roman strategy centered on the protection of the internal territories whose integrity the fortified frontiers defined. That being so, it is not **factitious** to argue that, even if in diluted strength, the outline of the frontiers ... exerted throughout (the first century B.C. through the beginning of the fifth A.D.) a determining influence on the Roman military outlook." —JOHN KEEGAN, *A History of Warfare*

florid (FLOR uhd, also FLAHR uhd) - *adj.* flowery in style; ornate; embellished, 2. tinted red; flushed; ruddy.

"Down obscure alleys, apparently never trodden now by the foot of man, and whose very existence seemed to be forgotten, there would jut into the path porticoes, oriels, doorways of enriched and **florid** middle-age design, their extinct air being accentuated by the rottenness of the stones." —THOMAS HARDY, *Jude the Obscure*

fulsome (FUL suhm) - *adj.* exhibiting abundance; offensively excessive; copious; overdone; effusive; insincere.

"Algren's **fulsome** description of Katsumoto's followers as 'an intriguing people—from the moment they wake, they devote themselves to perfection of whatever they do.'" —JOE MORGENSTERN, *The Wall Street Journal*, 12/5/03

inapposite (I NA puh zuht) - *adj.* not apposite; not appropriate; irrelevant; poorly suited.

"'When's the next train to Cockfosters?' cracked a Director, not **inappositely**." —MARTIN AMIS, *Visiting Mrs. Nabokov*

innocuous (i NAH kyuh wuhs) - *adj.* harmless; producing no ill effect (from Latin, not nocuus, not harmful), 2. not controversial or offensive; innocent, 3. not stimulating; dull and uninspiring.

"But it transpires that St. Lucia, for now, is both beautiful and **innocuous**, like its people." —MARTIN AMIS, *Visiting Mrs. Nabokov*

insipid (in SI pid) - *adj.* utterly lacking in intelligence, depth or excitement; foolish; dull, 2. lacking flavor or taste, tasteless.

"Steerpike was looking at himself in a mirror and examining an **insipid** moustache." —MERVYN PEAKE, *Titus Groan*

jejune (jih JUNE) - *adj.* without nutritive value, 2. lacking matter; empty; void of substance, 3. childish; juvenile; puerile.

"It's a good story, marred only by moments of **jejune** men's-magazine sagacity: 'A shipwreck gave a man limitless opportunity to know himself if only he cared to find out.'" —MARK BOWDEN, *The New York Times Book Review*, 7/18/04

maudlin (MAHD lehn) - *adj.* overly sentimental (comes from Mary Magdalen, who was frequently depicted as a tearful penitent).

"Her soliloquies mawkish, her sentiments **maudlin**, malaise dripped like a fever from her pores." —JHUMPA LAHIRI, *Interpreter of Maladies*

mawkish (MO kish) - *adj.* having an insipid, sweet, or sickening taste; nauseating, 2. sickly or insipidly sentimental.

"Nor do I wanna know about some athlete's crippled little brother or his hemophiliac big sister. The Olympics specialize in this kind of **mawkish** bullshit." —GEORGE CARLIN, *Brain Droppings*

mendacious (men DAY shus) - *adj.* untruthful; laying; dishonest, 2. false; untrue.

"The past is as irrelevant as the future: speculative and warped, fictionalized by a thousand distorting forces, and filtered through the **mendacious** scrim of emotion." —KATHERINE MOSBY, *The Season of Lillian Dawes*

nugatory (NEW guh TOR ee, also NYOO guh TOR ee) - *adj.* trivial or of little importance, 2. ineffective; futile; without force; invalid.

Ollendorffian (ah LUHN DORF ee uhn) - *adj.* in the stilted, artificial, overly formal language of foreign phrase-books (from Heinrich Gottfried Ollendorff, German educator and grammarian [1803–65]).

"'Yesterday he bled and wept,' said the Satyr. 'You never bleed nor weep. The Master does not bleed nor weep.' '**Ollendorffian** beggar!' said Montgomery. 'You'll bleed and weep if you don't look out.'" –H.G. WELLS, *The Island of Dr. Moreau*

orotund (OR uh TUND, also AHR uh TUND) - *adj.* full in sound, sonorous, 2. pompous and bombastic.

"The event that in Hayden Church's **orotund** phrase 'was the most striking feature in the American's history' struck without any warning that was heeded, on a cold morning at the beginning of December 1902." –SIMON WINCHESTER, *The Professor and the Madman*

prolix (PRO liks) - *adj.* overly wordy; verbose; tedious (seems to be used to describe writing more than speaking).

"... his seven-year-old daughter, who has been through *The Hobbit* countless times ... and whose interest has been held by its more **prolix** successors." –EDMUND WILSON, *The QPB Companion to The Lord of the Rings*

retrograde (REH truh GRADE) - *adj.* moving or tending backward, 2. reverting to an inferior condition, 3. counterproductive to a desired outcome.

"In that letter Jefferson had mentioned Adams in passing as a **retrograde** thinker opposed to all forms of progress, one of the 'ancients' rather than 'moderns.'" –JOSEPH J. ELLIS, *Founding Brothers*

scabrous (SKA bruhs, also SKAY bruhs) - *adj.* rough to the touch; harsh.

"I'm conflicted about the picture ['Bad Santa'], which is **scabrously** funny in fits and starts—an over-the-counter (and over-

the-top) antidote for Yuletide treacle— but sometimes clumsy enough to give misanthropy a bad name." –JOE MORGENSTERN, *The Wall Street Journal*, 12/5/03

snarky (SNAR kee) - (slang) *adj.* irritable or short-tempered; irascible; 'narky.'

"Radar's cheeky, sometimes **snarky** approach to celebrity and culture attracted news media attention when the magazine was first published, but attempts to line up financing fizzled." –DAVID CARR, *The New York Times*, 10/19/04

snide (SNYD) - *adj.* tricky; deceptive; 2. contemptible, 3. disparaging in a sly or deceptive manner.

*see other **snide** entry for citation, p. 14*

specious (SPEE shus) - *adj.* seeming to be good, sound, correct, logical, etc., without really being so; plausible but not genuine: specious logic.

"'I know his kind. They spend the morning combing their beards to present a **specious** appearance of wisdom, and in the afternoon they haul in gold with hoes by lecturing on the worthlessness of wealth." –L. SPRAGUE DE CAMP, *The Tritonian Ring*

spurious (SPYUR ee uhs) - *adj.* false; fake; counterfeit, lacking authenticity.

"The charge of racism is **spurious**. It is preposterous." –PHILIP ROTH, *The Human Stain*

tumid (TOO mid, also TYOO mid) - *adj.* swollen; enlarged; exhibiting swelling, 2. bombastic; overblown; turgid.

turbid (TUHR bid) - *adj.* having the sediment disturbed or roiled; muddy; thick not clear, 2. disturbed; confused; disordered;

perplexed; muddled, 3. thick or opaque as with clouds or smoke.

*see other **turbid** entry for citation, p. 189*

turgid (TUHR JID) - *adj.* distended beyond the natural state; swollen; bloated, 2. bombastic; pompous; inflated or embellished in style or language.

> "That blossom business comes back to blight the movie's climax, which would have been silly enough without the added burden of **turgid** dialogue." —JOE MORGENSTERN, *The Wall Street Journal,* 12/5/03

twee (TWEE) - *adj.* excessively sweet, dainty or cute; precious; over-refined; mawkish.

unctuous (UHNGK chu whus, also UHNGK chus) - *adj.* oily; greasy, 2. profusely and unpleasantly flattering, 3. overly suave or oily in speech or manner.

> "Courteously, perhaps cravenly, ingratiating himself with the Feddens and their friends, Nick nevertheless makes you wonder whether, behind the show of slightly **unctuous** civility, he actually likes these people." —ANTHONY QUINN, *The New York Times Book Review,* 10/31/04

vapid (VA pid, also VAY pid) - *adj.* lacking liveliness, animation, or interest; dull, 2. lacking taste, zest, or flavor; flat.

> "[Madonna] 'couldn't believe how **vapid** and vacant and empty all of the [children's] stories were.'" —MADONNA, QUOTED BY MEGHAN COX GURDON, *The Wall Street Journal,* 9/16/03

WRITING, LOGIC, AND KNOWLEDGE—VERBS

VERBS OF CRITICISM

abnegate (AB ni GAYT) - *v.* to deny; to reject; to abjure; to refuse.

> "'Our life has been a vain attempt at self-delight. But self-**abnegation** is the higher road. We should mortify the flesh—the terrible flesh—the curse of Adam!'" —THOMAS HARDY, *Jude the Obscure*

abjure (ab JUR) - *v.* to renounce upon oath; to forswear; to disavow, 2. to renounce or reject with solemnity; to recant to abandon forever; to reject; repudiate.

> "As a philosopher Singer must **abjure** the cynicism with which, he tells us, many of his friends greeted his intention seriously to study [President Bush's] ethics." —PAUL MATTICK, *The New York Times Book Review,* 4/25/04

admonish (AD mah NISH) - *v.* to warn or notify; to reprove gently or kindly but seriously, 2. to counsel against wrong pratices; to caution or advise; to warn against danger or offense.

> "He would have had a chance to win the city half-mile if he hadn't hurt his wind with cigars and—he bragged about it—what the health manuals called self-abuse and depletion of manhood. He jeered at his wickedness and at all the things that make the **admonitory** world groan." —SAUL BELLOW, *The Adventures of Augie March*

animadvert (ahn UH mahd VURT) - *v.* to make a critical, usually disapproving, comment.

"'You see how the little bird pulls the worm? The little worm wants to stay in the ground. The little worm doesn't want to come out...' And she'd sharply push his forehead off with her old prim hand, having fired off for Simon and me, mindful always of her duty to wise us up, one more **animadversion** on the trustful, loving, and simple surrounded by the cunning-hearted and tough, a fighting nature of birds and worms, and a desperate mankind without feelings." —SAUL BELLOW, *The Adventures of Augie March*

beard (BEERD) - (besides the noun) *v.* to confront or oppose with boldness.

"They were struck speechless at hearing the all-powerful police thus **bearded** and expected a command to seize the barbarian." —ROBERT E. HOWARD, *The God in the Bowl*

decry (di KRY) - *v.* to denouce as harmful; to censure; to belittle.

"... dinner-table outbursts **decrying** her selfish mother and father and their bourgeois life." —PHILIP ROTH, *American Pastoral*

demur (di MUHR) - *v.* to take exception; object.

"Candide **demurred** a little, but discreetly. Martin entirely agreed with the Senator." —FRANCOIS VOLTAIRE, *Candide*, transl. by Richard Aldington

deprecate (de pri KAYT) - *v.* to express disapproval of; deplore, 2. to belittle; depreciate.

"He wished to obtain a fly to take her back in, but economy being so imperative she **deprecated** his doing so, and they walked along slowly." —THOMAS HARDY, *Jude the Obscure*

deride (di RIYD, also dee RIYD) - *v.* to subject to ridicule, 2. to approach or treat with scorn; scoff at.

"It was a smile that had in it something both of pain and weakness—a haggard, old man's smile; but there was, besides that, a grain of **derision**, a shadow of treachery, in his expression as he craftily watched, and watched, and watched me at my work." —ROBERT LOUIS STEVENSON, *Treasure Island*

derogate (DER uh GAYT) - *v.* to detract, 2. to cause to appear inferior; disparage; belittle.

"I have the right to praise Einhorn [along with Caesar, Machiavelli, and Ulysses] and not care about smiles of **derogation** from those who think the race no longer has in any important degrees the traits we honor in those fabulous names." —SAUL BELLOW, *The Adventures of Augie March*

excoriate (ek SKOR ee AYT) - *v.* to abrade the skin; to flay; to chafe, 2. to censure harshly.

"The ripest moment of Polish culture: Gombrowicz joyously **excoriating** 'Polishness.'" —MILAN KUNDERA, *The Art of the Novel*

execrate (EK suh KRAYT) - *v.* to declare as evil; to curse, 2. to denounce harshly, 3. to detest; to loathe; to abhor.

execration (EK suh KRAY shun) - *n.* an instance of execrating, the act of cursing; a curse dictated by violent feelings of hatred; imprecation; expression of utter detestation, 2. that which is execrated; a detested thing.

> "... an American man of letters ... read on and on, wondering when the harmfulness was going to begin, and at last flung it across the room with **execrations** at having been induced by the rascally reviewers to waste a dollar-and-a-half on what he was pleased to call 'a religious and ethical treatise.'"
> —THOMAS HARDY, *Jude the Obscure*

fulminate (FUL muh NAYT) - *v.* to make a verbal attack; to denounce harshly; to criticize or condemn, 2. to explode (from the Latin fulminare, to strike with lightning).

> "But my crew that night was one of those inefficients against whom the capitalist is wont to **fulminate**, because, forsooth, such inefficients increase expenses and reduce dividends." —JACK LONDON, *What Life Means to Me*

gibber (JI buhr) - *v.* to talk unintelligibly, to speak in gibberish.

> [after a snake had escaped in the zoo] "Piers and Dudley could only **gibber**." —J.K. ROWLING, *Harry Potter and the Sorcerer's Stone*

hector (HEK tuhr) - *v.* to intimidate or dominate in a blustering way, 2. to behave like a bully; swagger (derived from the Greek hero Hector).

> "On top of everything else, Mr. Jerome Quat lectured and **hectored** them in a highly scholarly, lofty manner" —TOM WOLFE, *I Am Charlotte Simmons*

inveigh (in VAY) - *v.* to declaim or rail (against a person or thing); to attack with harsh criticism or reproach, either spoken or written.

> "Then, after declaring flatly that he would have to amputate, he visited the pharma-

cist and **inveighed** against the jackasses capable of reducing an unfortunate man to such a plight." —GUSTAVE FLAUBERT, *Madame Bovary*, transl. by Francis Steegmuller

maunder (MON duhr, also MAHN duhr) - *v.* to move slowly and idly, 2. to speak incoherently or indistinctly.

> "... he thought about the penitentes, men in black hoods dragging heavy wooden crosses through the desert, a hundred years ago, or fifty years, and lashing themselves with sisal and hemp, all that Sister Edgarish stuff, and speaking fabricated words—the **maunder** of roaming holy men." —DON DELILLO, *Underworld*

objurgate (AHB juhr GAYT) - *v.* to sharply rebuke; to berate harshly; to chide with vehemence.

> "Growling an **objurgation** in her ear, he snatched her up under his free arm."
> —ROBERT E. HOWARD, *Conan the Warrior*

pillory (PI luh ree, also PIL REE) - *n.* a device of punishment in which offenders were locked with head and hands in holes while exposed to public ridicule or scorn, 2. *v.* to expose to public ridicule, contempt, scorn or abuse.

> "'We have had this discussion many times, Mr. Conroy, and you **pilloried** me in the last issue of *The Shako* because of it.'"
> —PAT CONROY, *My Losing Season*

prate (PRAYT) - *v.* to talk with little purpose; trifling or idle talk or chatter.

remonstrate (RE muhn STRAYT, also ri MAHN STRAYT) - *v.* to plead in opposition; to present or urge in objection or protest.

"Machines are more powerful than servants and more obedient and less rebellious, but machines have no judgment and will not **remonstrate** with us when our will is foolish, and will not disobey us when our will is evil." —ORSON SCOTT CARD, *Children of the Mind*

reprove (ri PROOV) - *v.* to scold, to correct, to rebuke, 2. to express disapproval of; to find fault with.

"'Oh, he was a wild one,' she said in that fondly **reproving** way I remembered all his friends doing." —MICHAEL MURPHY, *Golf in the Kingdom*

stultify (STUHL tuh FY) - *v.* to stifle: stultify free thought, 2. to cause to appear stupid, inconsistent or foolish.

"'You threw off old husks of prejudices, and taught me to do it; and now you go back upon yourself. I confess I am utterly **stultified** in my estimate of you.'" —THOMAS HARDY, *Jude the Obscure*

tergiversate (TUHR juhr vuhr SAYT, also TUHR JI vuhr SAYT) - *v.* to engage in tergiversation; to desert a cause, faith or party; to turn renegade; to use subterfuge or evasion.

"Pedant that he proves to be, Dobel like to use big, obscure words-tergiversate, for

one, instead of waffle or waver. I won't **tergiversate** her. 'Anything Else' is awful." —JOE MORGENSTERN, *The Wall Street Journal,* 9/19/03

traduce (truh DOOS, also truh DYOOS) - *v.* to slander or betray; to violate; to defame.

"'... he is wrong in regard to the Marquis of Avonshire, who, as you know, killed his wife's **traducer** years ago, and went to Australia where he did not long survive his wife.'" —ROBERT W. CHAMBERS, *The King in Yellow*

vilify (VI luh FY) - *v.* to say defamatory things about someone; to speak evil of someone.

"'This is an outrage,' Ignatius was shouting. 'I have not only been ignored and **vilified** at this gathering. I have been viciously attacked within the walls of your cobweb of a home.'" —JOHN KENNEDY TOOLE, *A Confederacy of Dunces*

vituperate (vy TOO puh RAYT, also vuh TOO puh RAYT) - *v.* to verbally abuse; to censure harshly; berate; revile.

"... he presents a thoroughly researched, richly detailed and lively book on the 'bone hunters' who traversed the badlands of the world searching for the fossils of mammals and on the **vituperative** intellectual battles that some of these paleontologists waged with one another." —HELEN E. FISHER, *The New York Times Book Review,* 6/13/04

VERBS OF SUPPORT

asseverate (uh SE vuh RAYT) - *v.* to aver; to affirm; to declare positively and earnestly.

"The more I laughed at such theories, the more these stubborn friends **asseverated** them." –H.P. LOVECRAFT, *The Whisperer in Darkness*

aver (uh VUIIR) - *v.* to assert, or prove, the truth of, 2. to avouch or verify; to prove of justify, 3. to affirm with confidence; to declare in a positive manner.

> "... the finding of a stuffed goddess. It was, the Belgian **averred**, a most extraordinary object; an object quite beyond the power of a layman to classify." –H.P. LOVECRAFT, *Facts Concerning the Late Arthur Jermyn and His Family*

blandish (BLAN DISH) - *v.* to cajole; to coax with flattery.

> "He couldn't have held out against her **blandishments** much longer." –POUL ANDERSON, *Three Hearts and Three Lions*

lionize (LY uh NIYZ) - *v.* to treat with great interest or importance, as with a celebrity.

> "And Osano walked away to a group of women who were waiting to **lionize** him." –MARIO PUZO, *Fools Die*

mirate (MY rate) - *v.* to show wonder, admiration or awe; to marvel at.

> "That paper-doll mother was still **mirating** at her own flesh and blood having lice." –REYNOLDS PRICE, *A Long and Happy Life*

palliate (PA lee AYT) - *v.* to reduce the violence, pain or severity, esp. of a disease, without curing; to alleviate; to ease, 2. to moderate the severity of.

propitiate (pro PI shee AYT) - *v.* to cause to become favorably inclined; to gain or regain another's good will or favor; to conciliate; to appease; sacrifices made to propitiate the gods.

> "Within 18 months, Obeidi had created what he calls 'very likely the most efficient covert enrichment program in history.' But nothing could **propitiate** his masters." –JACOB HEILBRUNN, *The New York Times Book Review,* 10/31/04

OTHER "SPEAKING" VERBS

bloviate (BLOW vee AYT) - *v.* to deliver a verbose speech; to speak, pompously or boastfully, at length.

> "As with the Reagan farewell, pundits obsessively ask of the Clinton rollout: how will it affect the election? This is a recipe for infinite **bloviation**, since there is no answer." –FRANK RICH, *The New York Times,* 7/4/04

bruit (BROOT) - *n.* a noise; a clamor, 2. a rumor or report, 3. *v.* to spread a rumor (often with about).

> "... the manner of the author's demise was **bruited** about." –ROBERT E. HOWARD, *Cthulhu*

chaffer (CHA fuhr) - *v.* to bargain over price; to haggle.

> "In the squares the black folk **chaffered** and bargained over plantains, beer and hammered brass ornaments." –ROBERT E. HOWARD, *The Snout in the Dark*

declaim (di KLAYM, also dee KLAYM) - *v.* to speak rhetorically; to speak bombastically or loudly; harangue (declamation is noun, declamatory is adjective).

> "The contemporary scenes are predictably ridiculous ... Rick, who calls himself the 'Auteur of the Future,' **declaims** on film theory in an intellectualized Valleyspeak." –DAVID L. ULIN, *The New York Times Book Review,* 6/13/04

descant (DES kant) - *v.* to discourse or comment on a topic at length, 2. to sing or play part music.

> "... he could already hear Enid's invidious **descants** on the topic of Denise's wonderfulness." –JONATHAN FRANZEN, *The Corrections*

dilate (DY LAYT) - *v.* to enlarge; distend; widen; expand, 2. to discuss at length, 3. to describe in great detail.

> "'There is no need to **dilate** on the tragic significance of this fact.'" –FYODOR DOSTOYEVSKY, quoted by David Magarshack, *Introduction, Dostoyevsky's The Brothers Karamazov*

épater (ay PA tay) - (French) *v.* to startle or shock the common man, as if from complacency, conventionality, etc.

> "By now readers will be aware of Madonna's latest sizzling, bourgeoisie-**épatering** incarnation [as a children's-book author]." –MEGHAN COX GURDON, *The Wall Street Journal*, 9/16/03

expatiate (ek SPAY shee ayt) - *v.* to speak or write at length; elaborate.

> "... the public prosecutor **expatiated** particularly about Grushenka's 'former' and 'rightful' lover and gave expression to a number of highly diverting thoughts on this subject." –FYODOR DOSTOYEVSKY, *The Brothers Karamazov*, transl. by David Magarshack

inveigle (in VAY guhl) - *v.* to allure or seduce in a deceitful manner, 2. to gain or obtain through deceit or flattery; to entice; to seduce.

> "... he thought that when Merry got to be a schoolgirl he'd **inveigle** Orcutt into taking her along on this very same trip so she could learn firsthand the history of the county where she was growing up." –PHILIP ROTH, *American Pastoral*

obtrude (uhb TROOD, also ab TROOD) - *v.* to thrust out; eject; extrude, 2. to impose or force (oneself, one's opinions or ideas) without request, 3. to obtrude oneself (on or upon).

> "I do not wish, Mr. Chairman, to **obtrude**, unasked, any observations." –ISAAC ASIMOV, *The Robots of Dawn*

redound (ri DAUND) - (among other definitions) *v.* to have an effect or result in; to have a consequence, 2. to add, contribute or accrue.

> "'If my thoughts are the same as yours, then it only **redounds** to my honour,' the gentleman declared with delicacy and dignity." –FYODOR DOSTOYEVSKY, *The Brothers Karamazov*, transl. by David Magarshack

rejoin (ri JOIN) - *v.* to reply; to respond; to answer.

> "After lunch on March 5, Bush met with a personal envoy who had been sent by Pope John Paul II to argue against war ... It would not be a just war, it would be illegal and it would not make things better. 'Absolutely,' the president **rejoined**, 'it will make things better.'" –BOB WOODWARD, *Plan of Attack*

supplicate (SUH pluh KAYT) - *v.* to ask for earnestly or humbly; to beseech; to beg, 2. to pray, as if to God.

temporize (TEM puh RYZ) - *v.* to act in a way to suit the time or occasion, without reference to principle, 2. to yield to the current opinion, 3. to comply temporarily, so as to gain time, 4. to compromise or negotiate.

"The Chairman must **temporize** by hearing both sides and by giving at least the appearance of deliberation before coming to a decision." —ISAAC ASIMOV, *The Robots of Dawn*

THINKING, KNOWLEDGE, AND WRITING

adduce (uh DOOS, also uh DYOOS) - *v.* to offer as reason or proof (in discussion); to cite in example.

"In retrospect, Braine **adduces** two main causes of his disaffection from the Left— a liking for capitalism as it was revealed to him by a tour of the U.S., and the 'we are all guilty' response to the Moors Murders." —MARTIN AMIS, *Visiting Mrs. Nabokov*

adumbrate (A duhm BRAYT, also a DUHM BRAYT) - *v.* to give a sketchy outline, 2. to foreshadow vaguely, 3. to obscure, overshadow, 4. *adj.* in a shadow or shadows.

"... the uncertain aftermath embodies the other part of his complaint against fiction: its brazen inexactitude, its failure to ever fully resolve the complexities it **adumbrates**." —ZOE HELLER, *The New York Times Book Review*, 3/20/05

anatomize (uh NAHT uh MYZ) - *v.* to cut into pieces in order to study the structure (of a plant or animal); to dissect, 2. to analyze.

belie (bi LY) - *v.* to falsely represent; to disguise, 2. to show as false or wrong; to contradict, 3. to frustrate, disappoint.

"The sentinel glared back, his colorful costume **belying** his decidedly ominous air." —DAN BROWN, *Angels & Demons*

bowdlerize (BOWD luh RYZ, also BAUD luh RYZ) - *v.* to edit (a book) prudishly, 2.

to modify, shorten or simplify by skewing or remove content—often that which might be considered indecent (derived from Thomas Bowdler, 1754–1825, who produced a bowdlerized version of Shakespeare's works).

"Here's a cheerful, **bowdlerized** version of the story [of the song 'Frankie Teardrop']: Frankie works two jobs, but even then he can't make ends meet, so one night, in despair, he goes back home, murders his wife and children, shoots himself and ends up in Hell." —NICK HORNBY, *Songbook*

conflate (kuhn FLAYT) - *v.* to bring together; to meld; to fuse; to bring together from a variety of sources or various elements; to put together, 2. to fuse or meld metals, 3. to combine (as in two separate texts) into one.

"As Bill James had shown, baseball data **conflated** luck and skill, and simply ignored a lot of what happened during a baseball game." —MICHAEL LEWIS, *Moneyball*

deconstruct (DEE kuhn STRUHKT) - *v.* to take apart, to reverse the construction of, 2. to discuss and interpret (a text) using the methods of criticism that rely only on the language contained within the text and not incorporating an extratextual reality (a strategy associated with Jacques Derrida).

descry (di SKRY) - *v.* to see; to catch sight of, 2. to notice carefully; detect.

"Steerpike had learned to **descry** from the almost imperceptible movements which they made with their limp fingers, roughly what was happening in their minds." —MERVYN PEAKE, *Titus Groan*

dissemble (di SEM buhl) - *v.* to conceal behind a false appearance; disguise, 2. to conceal or disguise one's true nature or state; to feign, 3. to hide the truth, or one's true motives or feelings by pretense; to behave hypocritically.

> "'Yes, I fear you,' she replied, too distracted to **dissemble**." –ROBERT E. HOWARD, *Shadows in the Moonlight*

educe (i DOOS, also i DYOOS) - *v.* to draw out; to evoke; to elicit, 2. to work out or determine from given facts; deduce.

> "Bronzini couldn't help seeing a challenge here. He liked to **educe** comment from the untalkative man, draw him forth." –DON DELILLO, *Underworld*

embrangle (also **imbrangle**) (im BRANG guhl) - *v.* to entangle; embroil; confuse; perplex.

> [describing a baseball umpire] "This is the small dogged conscience of the game. Even in repose he shows a history thick with **embranglement**, dust-stomping men turning figures in the steep sun." –DON DELILLO, *Underworld*

emend (ee MEND) - *v.* to improve, or correct, (a text) through critical editing or alteration.

> "In one or two instances of a different kind, however, the translator had presumed to **emend**." –FRANCIS STEEGMULLER, *Introduction, Gustave Flaubert's Madame Bovary*

ideate (EYE dee AYT) - *v.* to form an idea (of); imagine; conceive.

> "... he was majoring in anthropology. As part of an assignment for one of his courses, Chapter Eleven conducted what he called 'fieldwork' during most of that vacation. He carried a tape recorder around with him, recording everything we said. He took notes on our '**ideation** systems' and 'rituals of kin bonding.'" –JEFFREY EUGENIDES, *Middlesex*

impute (im PYOOT) - *v.* to attribute fault or responsibility to another; to charge, 2. to ascribe to a particular cause or source; to attribute.

> "All the legends of the past, and all the stupefying **imputations** of Henry Akeley's letters and exhibits, welled up in my memory to heighten the atmosphere of tension and growing menace." –H.P. LOVECRAFT, *The Whisperer in Darkness*

inculcate (in KUHL KAYT, also IN KUHL KAYT) - *v.* to teach or impress by repeated instruction; instill.

> "A very special sort of lunatic expects to **inculcate** his principles." –SAUL BELLOW, *Herzog*

lucubrate (LOO kyoo BRAYT) - *v.* to study laboriously or intensively, especially late at night.

> "'More than fifty years has [the issue of slavery] attracted my thoughts and given me much anxiety,' Adams confessed in 1817. 'A Folio Volume would not contain my **Lucubrations** on this Subject.'" –JOSEPH J. ELLIS, *Founding Brothers*

nonplus (NAHN PLUHS) - *v.* to bewilder; perplex (from Latin non plus, no more).

> "I sat there somewhat **nonplussed** as the president discussed the issues of freedom and security, which were very much beside the points Powell had made." –BOB WOODWARD, *Plan of Attack*

prescribe *(pri SKRYB) - v.* to set down as a rule, guide or required procedure, 2. to order or recommend the use of a remedy or treatment.

"The Irish Code Duello: In 1777 ... the Gentlemen delegates of Tipperary, Galway, Mayo, Sligo, and Roscommon **prescribed** a series of rules governing the practice of dueling and settling points of honor." —BEN SCHOTT, *Schott's Original Miscellany*

ratiocinate (RA tee OH suhn AYT, also RA shee OH suhn AYT) - *v.* to reason; esp. to reason methodically and logically.

"I always liked mysteries that involve a limited number of suspects and that are solved by **ratiocination** rather than by shooting." —ISAAC ASIMOV, *I, Asimov*

ruminate (ROO muh NAYT) - *v.* to turn over in the mind; to reflect on over and again; to meditate; to muse, 2. to chew cud.

"The day over, he would sit at the door of his cabin, his knees beneath his chin, his bony hands clasping his elbows, and stare **ruminatively** (a stranger would have thought sullenly) before him as the shadows lengthened inch by inch." —MERVYN PEAKE, *Titus Groan*

vide (VY dee, also VEE day) - *v.* see—used to direct a reader's attention to another item or location, for example: vide page 64 (from Latin, videre, to see).

"But [soul music] will evolve in ways that are never entirely predictable, make its mark in the oddest of manners (**vide** the Blues Brothers phenomenon), become an object of eclectic delight instead of a style-setter on its own." —PETER GURALNICK, *Sweet Soul Music*

OTHER KNOWLEDGE VERBS

deign (DAYN) - *v.* to condescend to offer or give.

"'You're actually **deigning** to pay him a visit?'" —RICHARD RUSSO, *Straight Man*

expiate (EK spee AYT) - *v.* to atone; to make amends or reparations for.

"Permitted to **expiate** his crime by exile, [Voltaire] went to England in 1726." —*Publisher's Preface, Easton Press edition Francois Voltaire's Candide*

obviate (AHB vee AYT) - *v.* to prevent by anticipating and making unnecessary.

"Why not **obviate** the subject of dispute?" —URSULA K. LE GUIN, *The Left Hand of Darkness*

precipitate (pri SIH puh TATE) - *v.* to throw an object or person from a great height, 2. to cause something to happen suddenly, quickly or before required, 3. to come out of a liquid solution into solid form, 4. to have water in the air fall to the ground, for example as rain, snow, sleet, or hail.

*see other **precipitate** entry for citation, p. 27*

reify (RAY uh FY, also REE uh FY) - *v.* to convert mentally into a thing; to materialize, 2. to treat an abstract concept as existing physically; having material form.

"I was baptized into the Orthodox faith; a faith that had existed long before Protestantism had anything to protest and before Catholicism called itself catholic; a faith that stretched back to the beginnings of Christianity, when it was Greek and not Latin, and which, without an Aquinas to **reify** it, had remained shrouded in the smoke of tradition and mystery whence it began." –JEFFREY EUGENIDES, *Middlesex*

sublimate (SUH bluh MAYT) - *v.* Chem. to change from a solid to a gas or from a gas to a solid without becoming a liquid, 2. to express potentially violent or socially unacceptable impulses in a modified, socially acceptable manner.

"'His unfulfilled physical desires therefore sought **sublimation** in food.'" –JOHN KENNEDY TOOLE, *A Confederacy of Dunces*

vitiate (VI she ATE) - *v.* to make imperfect, faulty, or impure; spoil; corrupt, 2. to weaken morally; to debase, 3. to make (a contract, etc.) legally ineffective, invalidate.

"Still, our satisfaction was to a large extent **vitiated** by dismay at the extent of what really was going on in the Nixon White House." –KATHARINE GRAHAM, *Personal History*

vouchsafe (vauch SAYF) - *v.* to grant or bestow (a privilege); deign.

"She asked no further questions, and I **vouchsafed** no remarks, devoting myself to Wolf Larsen's command, which was to make her comfortable." –JACK LONDON, *The Sea Wolf*

ACADEMICS, SCHOLARSHIP, AND PHILOSOPHY

a priori (AH pree OR ee, also AY pri OR AYE) - *adj.* from a known or assumed cause to a necessarily related effect; deductive (from Latin, "from the former"), 2. based on theory rather than experience (as opposed to a posteriori—"from the subsequent"—denoting reason from observed facts).

"He tried to throw himself after him into the sea; he was prevented by the philosopher Pangloss, who proved to him that the Lisbon roads had been expressly created for the Anabaptist to be drowned in them. While he was proving this **a priori**, the vessel sank, and every one perished except Pangloss, Candide and the brutal sailor who had drowned the virtuous Anabaptist." –FRANCOIS VOLTAIRE, *Candide*, transl. by Richard Aldington

afflatus (uh FLAY tuhs, also a FLAY tuhs) - *n.* a sudden rush of creative impulse, inspiration (from Latin afflare, to breath on).

"He endeavored to trap and nourish the impression in order to predict, and perhaps even control, what incident would occur next, but the **afflatus** melted away unproductively, as he had known beforehand it would. Déjà vu." –JOSEPH HELLER, *Catch-22*

cosmology (kahs MAH luh jee) - *n.* the metaphysical study of the history, structure and nature of the universe, 2. the study of the origin, structure and dynamics of the universe.

"He had invented the prophecies and the **cosmologies** 'to get all the money he could.'" –JEFFREY EUGENIDES, *Middlesex*

egoism (EE guh WI zuhm, also E guh WI zuhm) - *n.* the belief that self-interest is the just and proper motive force, 2. egotism (note: egotism, though, is defined as: the tendency to speak or write excessively about oneself, 2. an exaggerated sense of self-importance; conceit).

"Are there any substantial changes I would want to make in *The Fountainhead*? ... there is one minor error ... The error is semantic: the use of the word '**egotist**' in Roark's courtroom speech, while actually the word should have been 'egoist.'" –AYN RAND, *The Fountainhead*

epistemology (i PIS teh MAH luh jee) - *n.* the study of the method or grounds of knowledge.

"Most of [the philosophical questions] fall broadly under the rubric of **epistemology**: the nature and scope of knowledge." –STEPHEN MILLER, *The Wall Street Journal*, 5/21/02

eschatology (ES kuh TAH luh jee) - *n.* the branch of theology, or doctrines, dealing with death, resurrection, judgment, immortality, and the time preceeding the end of the world when the world will be judged.

"Why did God not fight Evil that day [September 11]? By what grand design, what **eschatology**, were innocent people required to die? And why should we respect that design?" –TUNKU VARADARAJAN, *The Wall Street Journal*, 8/30/02

etiology (EE tee AH luh jee) - *n.* the study of causes, origins, or reasons, 2. the cause of pathological conditions as determined by medical diagnosis.

"The generic variety of this anthology [the Hebrew Bible] is altogether remarkable, encompassing as it does historiography, fictional narratives, and much that is a mixture of the two, lists of laws, prophecy in both poetry and prose, aphoristic and reflective works, cultic and devotional poems, laments and victory hymns, love poems, genealogical tables, **etiological**

tales, and much more." –ROBERT ALTER, *The Literary Guide to the Bible*

koan (KOII AIIN) - *n.* from Zen Buddhism, a puzzling or paradoxical statement or story often used to aid meditation and gain spiritual awakening.

*see other **koan** entry for citation, p. 165*

metaphysics (ME tuh FI ziks) - *n.* pl. the branch of philosophy that deals with first principles and seeks to explain the nature of being or reality (ontology) and of the origin and structure of the world (cosmology): it is closely associated with the study of the nature of knowledge (epistemology).

"Philosophically, Nietzsche is a mystic and an irrationalist. His **metaphysics** consists of a somewhat 'Byronic' and mystically 'malevolent' universe; his epistemology subordinates reason to 'will,' or feeling or instinct or blood or innate virtues of character." –AYN RAND, *The Fountainhead*

Momism (mohm IZ uhm) - *n.* an excessive adoration or attachment to one's mother, often considered Oedipal in nature; maternal domination.

"The tyranny of propriety. It was hard, halfway through 1998, for even him to believe in American propriety's enduring power, and he was the one who considered himself tyrannized: the bridle is still on public rhetoric, the inspiration it provides for personal posturing, the persistence just about everywhere of this de-virilizing pulpit virtue-mongering that H.L. Mencken identified with boobism, that Philip Wylie thought of as **Momism**, that the Europeans unhistorically call American puritanism, that the likes of a Ronald Reagan call America's core values." –PHILIP ROTH, *The Human Stain*

monism (MOH NI zuhm, also MAH NI zuhm) - *n.* the doctrine of the oneness and unity of reality, despite the appearance of diversity in the world.

"... professing throughout his life that he was a 'materialistic **monist**,' his art betrays him, time and again revealing him to be, in fact, a philosophical dualist whose approach to truth was ultimately hermeneutical rather than epistemological." –EARLE LABOR, *Introduction, The Portable Jack London*

ontological argument (AHN tuhl AH ji kuhl AHR gyu muhnt) - *n.* Metaphysics, an a priori argument for the existence of God, asserting that the conception of a perfect being implies that being's existence outside man's mind.

ontology (ahn TAH luh jee) - *n.* the branch of metaphysics dealing with the nature of being, reality, or ultimate substance: as opposed to phenomenology.

"What are the possibilities for man in the trap the world has become? To answer this, one must have a certain idea of what the world is. One must have an **ontological** hypothesis about it." –MILAN KUN-DERA, *The Art of the Novel*

phenomenology (fi NAH muh NAH luh jee) - *n.* the philosophical study of phenomena, as distinct from that of being (ontology), 2. the branch of science that describes and classifies phenomena as they are perceived in human consciousness without any metaphysical explanation.

"The novel dealt with the unconscious before Freud, the class struggle before Marx, it practiced **phenomenology** (the investigation of the essence of human situations) before the **phenomenologists**.

What superb '**phenomenological** descriptions' in Proust, who never even knew a **phenomenologist**!" –MILAN KUNDERA, *The Art of the Novel*

Pyrrhonism (PIR uh NI zuhm) - *n.* a system of sceptic philosophy founded by Pyrrho of Elis (c. 300 B.C.), 2. the doctrine of the impossibility of attaining certainty of knowledge, 3. skepticism; incredulity; philosophic doubt; universal doubt.

"I have often been reproached with the aridity of my genius; a deficiency of imagination has been imputed to me as a crime; and the **Pyrrhonism** of my opinions has at all times rendered me notorious." –EDGAR ALLAN POE, *Ms. Found in a Bottle*

satori (suh TOR ee, also sah TOR ee) - *n.* from Zen Buddhism, a spiritual awakening or indescribable inner experience of enlightenment, often coming on suddenly.

*see other **satori** entry for citation, p. 165*

solipsism (SOH luhp SI zuhm, also SAH luhp SI zuhm) - *n.* the philosophical theory that the self is the only reality that can be proven to exist.

"She got here, I conclude **solipsistically**, in the usual way, by my opening my eyes." –RICHARD RUSSO, *Straight Man*

theosophy (THEE ah SAH fee) - *n.* religious speculation based on mystical insight into the nature of God.

7. DRAMA

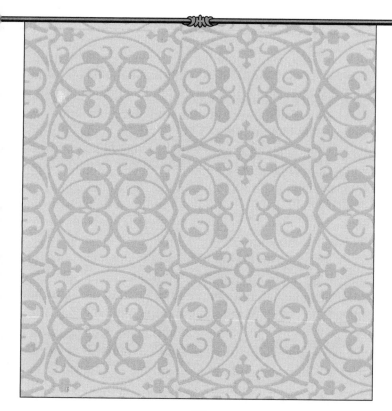

apostrophe (uh PAHS truh FEE) - (besides the mark) *n.* a style of speech, a rhetorical device consisting of speech directed in an abstract direction, to a person not present, or to a thing, such as an aside to an audience in a play.

> "Jude found himself speaking out loud, holding conversations with them as it were, like an actor in a melodrama who **apostrophizes** the audience on the other side of the footlights." —THOMAS HARDY, *Jude the Obscure*

busker (BUHS KUHR) - *n.* one who "busks"; an itinerant entertainer or musician who works for tips.

> "And over by the Library Mall members of the San Francisco Mime Troupe, if that's who they were, kept turning up among the police, more or less suicidally, wearing whiteface and carrying panpipes and dressed in **busker** costume, quaint and ill-fitting mid-Victorian drag, with cricket caps." —DON DELILLO, *Underworld*

buskin (BUS kin) - *n.* a thick-soled, laced half boot or high shoe that reaches halfway up to the knee, worn in Greek and Roman tragedies, 2. a tragic drama.

> *see other **buskin** entry for citation, 227*

claque (KLAK) - *n.* a group of people hired to attend a performance and to applaud, 2. a group of people who pre-arrange among themselves to express strong support for an idea, so as to give the false impression of a wider consensus (the word derives from the French claquer, to clap).

> *see other **claque** entry for citation, p. 50*

deus ex machina (DAY uhs EKS MAH ki nuh, also DAY uhs EKS MAH kin NAH) - *n.* any resolution to a story that does not pay due regard to the story's internal logic and that is so unlikely that it challenges suspension of disbelief, and presumably allows the author, director, or developer to end the story in the way that he or she desired (from Latin, "god from a machine," referring to the device by which gods were suspended above the stage in the Greek theater).

> "Knives are brandished. Noses are punched. Terrifying violations are threatened. And then, at the very moment of crisis, the recitation of a poem effects a miraculous transformation. Disaster is averted by the unlikely **deus ex machina** of a Victorian poet." —ZOE HELLER, *The New York Times Book Review, 3/20/05*

droll (DROHL) - *adj.* exhibiting a whimsical, comical or amusingly odd quality, 2. *n.* an entertainment exhibited to raise mirth or sport, as a puppet show, a farce, etc.

> "He looked much like a puppet at a Smithfield **droll**—his mouth opened and closed without making a sound and his eyes grew absurdly large." —DAVID LISS, *A Conspiracy of Paper*

extempore (ik STEM poh REE) - *adj.* extemporaneous (not rehearsed or prepared in advance; impromptu), 2. *adv.* extemporaneously.

> "In the era of the conquests the problem of how [the warriors] were to be maintained did not arise, and in unsettled times they lived by **extempore** means." —JOHN KEEGAN, *A History of Warfare*

guignol (gee NYOL) - *n.* Grand Guignol—a type of theater with sensational dramatic intent; a Punch and Judy show (a characatured type of theater).

"Those of us who love movies, as opposed to thrill rides, demolition derbies or grossout **guignols**, should thank our lucky stars, and writers and directors, that every year comes equipped with 12 months." –JOE MORGENSTERN, *The Wall Street Journal*, 1/4/02

histrionic (HIS tree AH nik) - *adj.* relating or pertaining to actors or acting, 2. excessively dramatic or theatrical; affected.

"'Help me, sir,' Ignatius slobbered, grabbing **histrionically** at the lapels of Mr. Levy's sports jacket." –JOHN KENNEDY TOOLE, *A Confederacy of Dunces*

masque (MASK) - *n.* a masquerade; masked ball, 2. a form of dramatic entertainment performed by masked actors representing mythological or allegorical figures, popular in England during the 16th and 17th centuries and having lavish costumes, scenery, music and dancing, originally performed without dialogue.

McGuffin (muh GUF in) - *n.* in a film, or other narrative fiction, an event or other plot device initially seeming to be of great significance to the story, but often having little actual importance for the plot as it develops (the term is generally ascribed to Alfred Hitchcock).

mummer (MUH muhr) - *n.* a masked or costumed actor or merrymaker, esp. at a festival.

"... a performance by a belly dancer or a troupe of **mummers**." –POUL ANDERSON, *The Blade of Conan*

proscenium (proh SEE NEE uhm) - *n.* the part of a stage located between the curtain and the orchestra.

"At an unhoped-for speed Prague forgot the Russian language ... and now, eager for applause on the world's **proscenium**, displayed to the visitors its new attire of English-language signs and labels." –MILAN KUNDERA, *Ignorance*

scrim (SKRIM) - (among other definitions) *n.* a transparent or gauze cloth used as a screen in a theater or to generate a lighting effect, 2. a screen of such a fabric.

"The past is as irrelevant as the future: speculative and warped, fictionalized by a thousand distorting forces, and filtered through the mendacious **scrim** of emotion." –KATHERINE MOSBY, *The Season of Lillian Dawes*

soubrette (soo BRET) - *n.* in a play or light opera, a minor female role, esp. a pert, flirtatious lady's maid, often involved in intrigue, 2. a pert, flirtatious or frivolous young woman.

"From her constant yearning look, one might have thought the actress a silly homesick **soubrette**, already regretting this freezing Northern tour." –FRITZ LEIBER, *Swords and Deviltry*

supernumerary (SOO puhr NOO muh RER ee) - *adj.* exceeding the normal or prescribed number; extra, 2. *n.* a minor performer or actor without a speaking part who appears in crowd scenes.

tableau (TA BLOH, also ta BLOH) - *n.* a vivid or graphic depiction, 2. a scene or interlude during a theatrical performance in which all performers remain silent and motionless as if in a picture.

"'Hurry-up! We don't have time to stage a **tableau**-vivant here before the house.'" –JOHN KENNEDY TOOLE, *A Confederacy of Dunces*

8. RELIGION, MYTH, AND MYSTICISM

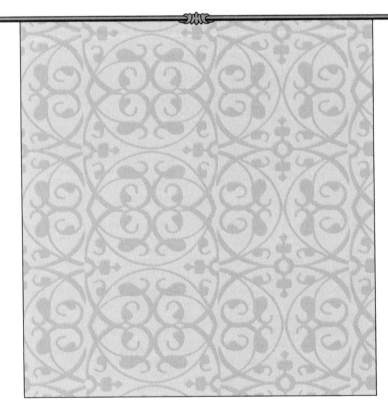

MYTHICAL CREATURES

afrite (also **afreet** or **afrit**) (af REET) - *n.* from Muslim mythology, a powerful evil demon or jinnee; a monster; a monstrous giant.

"'It is unlawful for one of our religion to initiate other than true Muslims in the magical rites; were I to do so, you would instantly be torn in pieces by an **ifrit** stronger than a lion and with tusks three feet in length.'" –L. SPRAGUE DE CAMP AND FLETCHER PRATT, *The Complete Compleat Enchanter*

Apollyon (uh PAHL yuhn, also uh PAH LEE uhn) - (Greek translation of the Hebrew "Abaddon") *n.* the destroyer; the angel of the bottomless pit; the Devil, 2. a subject of follower of Apollyon.

"He anxiously descended the ladder, and started homewards at a run, trying not to think of giants, Herne the Hunter, **Apollyon** lying in wait for Christian, or of the captain with the bleeding hole in his forehead and the corpses round him that remutinied every night on board that bewitched ship." –THOMAS HARDY, *Jude the Obscure*

apparition (A puh RI shuhn) - *n.* a ghost; a spectre; a phantom, 2. an unexpected, sudden or unusual sight.

bandersnatch (BAND uhr SNACH) - *n.* a dangerous creature; a fleet, furious, fuming, fabulous yet dangerous creature; a creature that cannot be outrun or bribed (from Lewis Carroll's *Through the Looking Glass*).

"No one ever influenced Tolkien—you might as well try to influence a **bandersnatch**." –C.S. LEWIS, CITED BY LIN CARTER IN *Tolkien*

banshee (BAN SHEE, also ban SHEE) - (from Gaelic folklore) *n.* a female spirit who warns of impending death, esp. in the family, by wailing.

"When Zora spoke you were aware of the skin stretching over these cheekbones and hollowing out between her jaws, the tight mask it made, **banshee**-like, with her blue eyes piercing through above." –JEFFREY EUGENIDES, *Middlesex*

basilisk (BA suh LISK, also BA zuh LISK) - *n.* a mythical serpent, a dragon or lizard-like monster with lethal breath and glance, fabled to have hatched from a cock's egg; see also **cockatrice**, 2. an ancient, now obsolete, brass cannon, 3. a type of small, crested lizard.

"She crouched, watching her captors with eyes baleful as those of a **basilisk**." –ROBERT E. HOWARD, *Conan the Warrior*

bogle (BOH guhl) - *n.* a goblin; a hobgoblin; a bogy (bogey).

"'From your account, I'm thinking it was a **bogle**.'" –H.G. WELLS, *The Island of Dr. Moreau*

bogy (BU gee, also BOH gee, BOO gee) - *n.* an evil or mischievous being or spirit; a goblin; a hobgoblin, 2. a bugbear; something that is often needlessly feared, 3. something that annoys or harasses.

brownie (BRAU nee) - *n.* a small, helpful sprite, thought to perform helpful tasks at night.

"Giants, trolls, kelpies, **brownies**, goblins, imps; wood, tree, mound and water spirits; heath-people, hill-watchers, treasure-guards, good people, little people, pishogues, leprechauns, night-riders, pixies, nixies, gnomes and the rest—gone, all gone!" –RUDYARD KIPLING, *Puck of Pook's Hill*

bugaboo (BUH guh BOO) - *n.* the object of excessive or exaggerated fear or anxiety, 2. a bugbear.

bugbear (BUHG BAR, also BUHG BER) - *n.* an imaginary cerature evoked to frighten children into good conduct, 2. anything causing apparently needless or excessive fear or anxiety, 3. a bugaboo.

"He had taken a great deal of pains with his sermon, which was on the subject of geology-then coming to the fore as a theological—**bugbear**." –SAMUEL BUTLER, *The Way of All Flesh*

centaur (SEN TOR) - (from Greek mythology) *n.* one of a race of monsters having a man's head, arms and trunk and a horse's legs and body.

"... like Greece in the mythological age before history began, men still share their world with beings that are not men, as the characters in Greek myths move through landscapes still inhabited by dryads and nymphs, tritons, fauns, satyrs, **centaurs,** and unearthly hybrid monsters." –LIN CARTER, *Tolkien*

Cerberus (SUHR buh ruhs) - (from Greek mythology) *n.* the three-headed dog guarding the gate to Hades.

"... the Cerberus slaver-choke turmoil was at the full when I came in from the last pick-up." –SAUL BELLOW, *The Adventures of Augie March*

cherub (CHER uhb) - (pl. cherubim) *n.* one of the second (of nine) order of angels, 2. a small angel, portrayed as a winged child with a chubby, rosy face.

"'I heard the joyful cries of the **cherubim**, singing and shouting: 'hosannah', and the thunderous shouts of the rapture of the seraphim which shook heaven and all creation.'" –FYODOR DOSTOYEVSKY, *The Brothers Karamazov*, transl. by David Magarshack

Chimera (ky MER uh, also kuh MER uh) - (from Greek mythology) *n.* a fire-breathing monster represented as a composite of a lion's head, a goat's body, and a serpent's tail, 2. any similar monster made up of grotesquely disparate parts, 3. an impossible or foolish fancy, 4. (in biology) a living structure, organism or organ consisting of tissues from diverse genetic constitution, sometimes as the result of transplant or grafting.

"The foreground of the scene had grown funereally dark, and near objects put on the hues and shapes of **chimaeras**." –THOMAS HARDY, *Jude the Obscure*

chimerical (kigh MER ih kul, also kuh MER ih kul, kuh MIR ih kul) *adj.* existing only in fantasy; imaginary; unreal, 2. given to fanciful schemes or plans.

*see other **chimerical** entry for citation, p. 23*

cockatrice (KAH kuh truhs, also KAH kuh TRYS) - *n.* a serpent hatched from a cock's egg and able to kill with a look or a glance, 2. (from the Bible) a deadly, unidentified serpent.

"... should any of Gloriana's people essay to enter, the **cockatrice** looks on them and they turn to stone." –L. SPRAGUE DE CAMP AND FLETCHER PRATT, *The Complete Compleat Enchanter*

Dagon (DAY GON) - *n.* the chief god of the ancient Philistines, represented with the head, chest, and arms of a man and the tail of a fish.

> "You enter your native water like a fish. And there sits the great fish god or **Dagon**. You then bear your soul like a minnow before **Dagon**, in your familiar water." –SAUL BELLOW, *The Adventures of Augie March*

dryad (DRY uhd, also DRY AD) - *n.* a divinity living in the forest; a wood nymph.

> "Fafhrd and the Mouser stood as stockstill as if she were a doe or a **dryad**" –FRITZ LEIBER, *Swords Against Death*

eidolon (eye DO luhn) - *n.* a phantom; an apparition; an unsubstantial image; a spectre.

> "'I was reading Whitman, and thinking of the whole country as holy: every unfurled prairie and oil-stained filling station and filthy city, every mountain range and strip-malled nowhere had its **eidolon**; but when we gathered for shows it seemed to focus this quality, and the stadiums shimmered like mirages in the rising excitement." –MAX LUDINGTON, QUOTED BY BRUCE BARCOTT, *The New York Times Book Review, 9/14/03*

faerie (also **faery**) (FAY ree, also FAR ee, FER ee) - *n.* a fairy, 2. the land of the fairies.

> "Trooping down upon this court like a forest of **faëry**, halting in a wide semicircle around it, were hosts of slender pillars, elfin shafts all gleaming red and black whose tapering tops were crowned with carven, lace-tipped fronds glistening like gigantic ferns wet with dew of diamonds and sapphires." –ABRAHAM MERRITT, *The Ship of Ishtar*

fairy (FAR ee, also FER ee) - *n.* an imaginary being in human form supposed to have magical powers and depicted as clever and mischievous.

faun (FON, also FAHN) - *n.* a group of minor deities shown having the body of a man and the horns, ears, tail, and hind legs of a goat (see also **satyr**).

*see **centaur** for citation, p. 124*

fay (FAY) - *n.* a fairy, 2. an elf.

> "'Yours is not a passionate heart—your heart does not burn in a flame! You are, upon the whole, a sort of **fay**, or sprite—not a woman!'" –THOMAS HARDY, *Jude the Obscure*

fetch (FECH) - (among other definitions) *n.* a ghost; an apparition; a wraith, 2. a doppelganger, 3. an apparition of a living person.

> "He slowed down a little and some sense came back into his head, so that he peered for living late-walkers as well as for demons and **fetches**." –FRITZ LEIBER, *Swords and Deviltry*

firedrake (FYR DRAYK) - (from Germanic mythology) *n.* a fire-breathing dragon.

> "'A dragon flying hither!' ... 'A **firedrake**, och, och, 'tis been sent by Alfric and noo we're done!'" –POUL ANDERSON, *Three Hearts and Three Lions*

gnome (NOHM) - *n.* an imaginary being, supposed by the Rosicrucians to inhabit the inner parts of the earth, and to be the guardian of mines, quarries, etc., 2. a dwarf; a goblin; a person of small stature or misshapen features, or of strange appearance, 3. a brief reflection or maxim.

*see **brownie** for citation, p. 124*

goblin (GAHB luhn) - (from folklore) *n.* an ugly or grotesque elfin creature, thought to be mischievous or evil.

*see **brownie** for citation, p. 124*

griffin (also **gryphon**) (GRI fuhn) - *n.* a mythical beast with the head and wings of an eagle and the body and hind legs of a lion.

"'There in Mirkwood do the Pharisee lairds hunt **griffin** and manticore,' whispered Hugi." —POUL ANDERSON, *Three Hearts and Three Lions*

Harpy (HAHR pee) - *n.* a relentless, greedy, or grasping person, 2. a shrewish woman, 3. (Greek Mythology) Harpy—a fabulous winged monster, ravenous and filthy, having the head and trunk of a woman and the tail, legs, and talons of a bird.

"Senapus, King of Ethiopia ... has his daily rations intercepted by a band of **harpies**." —LIN CARTER, *Tolkien*

hippocampus (HI puh KAM puhs) - (from Greek mythology) *n.* a sea monster with a horse's forelegs and a dolphin's tail, 2. the complex structure or ridge along each lateral ventrical of the brain.

hippogriff (HI POH GRIF) - *n.* a mythical monster with the wings, claws, and head of a griffin and the body and hindquarters of a horse.

"Or the hybrids, such as the gryphon, made up of left-over parts of eagle, lion, and serpent; and the wyvern, the firedrake, the hydra, the **hippogriff**, the sphinx, and the basilisk ... and other creatures of similar kidney, nowadays met with most frequently on coats-of-arms." —LIN CARTER, *Tolkien*

hob (HAHB) - *n.* a goblin (hobgoblin); a sprite; an elf, 2. mischievous behavior, 3. *v.* to act mischievously, especially in the phrase to raise hob (with).

hobgoblin (HAHB GAHB luhn) - *n.* a mischievous, ugly elf or goblin, 2. an imaginary source of fear, anxiety or dread; a bugbear.

Hydra (HY druh) - (from Greek mythology) *n.* the nine-headed serpent slain by Hercules: when any of its heads was cut off, it was replaced by two others, 2. any persistent or ever-increasing evil with many sources and causes.

*see **basilisk** for citation, p. 123*

imp (IMP) - *n.* a supernatural creature similar to a demon but smaller and less powerful; a devil's offspring; a young demon, 2. a mischievous child.

*see **brownie** for citation, p. 124*

incubus (ING kyuh buhs, also IN kyuh buhs) - *n.* an evil spirit thought to descend upon women while they sleep for the purpose of sexual intercourse (see also **succubus**), 2. a nightmare, 3. a nightmarish, oppressive burden.

"She moved under me as a sleeping girl might while being ravished by an **incubus**." —JEFFREY EUGENIDES, *Middlesex*

kelpie (KEL pee) - (from Gaelic folklore) *n.* a malevolent water spirit, thought to take the form of a horse and cause drownings.

*see **brownie** for citation, p. 124*

kobold (KOH BOLD) - (from German folklore) *n.* a haunting spirit of the household, often mischievous, thought to render services to the inmantes; a brownie, 2. a spirit that haunts the underground, mines or caves; a goblin or gnome.

> "'I only ken a few o' the lesser folk in the Middle World, some **kobolds** and nisser, a toadstool fay or two, and the like.'" –POUL ANDERSON, *Three Hearts and Three Lions*

kraken (KRAH kuhn) - *n.* an enormous sea-monster of Norwegian legend.

> " ... at times [we] became dizzy with the velocity of our descent into some watery hell, where the air grew stagnant, and no sound disturbed the slumbers of the **kraken**." –EDGAR ALLAN POE, *A Descent Into the Maelström*

leprechaun (LEP ruh KAHN, also LEP ruh KON) - (from Irish folklore) *n.* a fairy, in the form of a little old man who can reveal hidden treasure to those who catch them.

> *see **brownie** for citation, p. 124*

leviathan (li VY uh thuhn) - (from Hebrew) *n.* a monstrous sea creature, 2. something unusually large, esp. a ship, 3. an unusually large animal, esp. a whale.

> "The fog seemed to break away as though split by a wedge, and the bow of a steamboat emerged, trailing fog-wreaths on either side like seaweed on the snout of **Leviathan**." –JACK LONDON, *The Sea Wolf*

Lorelei (LOHR uh LY) - *n.* in German literature and legend, a siren who sings on a rock in the Rhine and lures sailors to shipwreck on the reefs.

> "The desert was beautiful beneath the moon, with the beauty of a cold marble **lorelei** to

lure men to destruction." –ROBERT E. HOWARD, *Beyond the Borders*

malkin (also **mawkin**) (MOL kuhn, also MAL kuhn) - *n.* a chambermaid; a woman of the lower classes, 2. an untidy female; a servant or country wench; a slattern; a slut; a drab; a lewd woman, 3. a mop created by tying a bundle or rags to the end of a stick, used by the kitchen servant to clean the ovens, 4. a scarecrow, 5. a designation for certain animals, such as a cat or hare.

mandrake (MAN DRAYK) - *n.* a poisonous plant native to southern Europe having greenish-yellow flowers, very short stems, thick, fleshy, often forked, roots, and fetid lance-shaped leaves, 2. the forked root of the plant, which resembles the human body and was formerly thought to have magical powers and was said to utter a deadly shriek when pulled from the ground.

> "Estragon: (highly excited). An erection!
>
> Vladimir: With all that follows. Where it falls **mandrakes** grow. That's why they shriek when you pull them up. Did you know that?" –SAMUEL BECKETT, *Waiting for Godot*

manticore (MAN ti KOR) - *n.* a fabulous monster having the head of a man, the body of a lion, and the tail of a dragon or scorpion.

> *see **griffin** for citation, p. 126*

Minotaur (MI nuh TOR, also MY nuh TOR) - (from Greek mythology) *n.* a monster, half bull and half man, offspring of a bull sent by Neptune (Poseidon) and Pasiphaë, the wife of King Minos of Crete. Young Athenians were sacrificed to this monster in King Minos' labyrinth (built by

Daedalus). Theseus, one of the Athenian victims, killed the monster with the help of Ariadne, Minos' daughter.

> "My grandfather ... had splurged on four tickets to *The **Minotaur*** ... When the curtain rose at the Family Theater, my relatives expected to get the whole story. How Minos, King of Crete, failed to sacrifice a white bull to Poseidon. How Poseidon, enraged, caused Minos's wife Pasiphaë to be smitten with love for a bull. How the child of that union, Asterius, came out with a bull's head attached to a human body. And then Daedalus, the maze, etc."
> —JEFFREY EUGENIDES, *Middlesex*

naiad (NAY uhd, also NI uhd, NAY ad, NI ad) - *n.* one of the nymphs who preside over fresh water, springs, brooks, fountains and rivers.

> "There were Tree-Women there and Well-Women (Dryads and **Naiads** as they used to be called in our world)" —C.S. LEWIS, *The Lion, The Witch and The Wardrobe*

nereid (NIR ee uhd) - (from Greek mythology) *n.* a sea-nymph

*see **Nereid** for citation, p. 158*

nixie (NIK see) - *n.* a female water-elf; a water nymph.

*see **brownie** for citation, p. 124*

nymph (NIMPF) - (from Greek and Roman mythology) *n.* any of a group of minor goddesses or deities represented as beautiful maidens inhabiting and sometimes personifying nature (rivers, mountains, trees, etc.), 2. a lovely girl, a beautiful maiden.

*see **centaur** for citation, p. 124*

orc (ORK) - *n.* a ferocious sea creature, 2. a large cetacean, esp. the killer whale, 3.

creatures described in the works of J.R.R. Tolkien (1892–1973) as having the combined characteristics of humans and ogres.

> "But most of the **Orcs** of the Misty Mountains were scattered or destroyed in the Battle of Five Armies." –J.R.R. TOLKIEN, *The Fellowship of the Ring*

pixie (PIK see) - *n.* a fairy or sprite, esp. one that is puckish.

*see **brownie** for citation, p. 124*

pooka (POO kuh) - (from Irish folklore) *n.* a mischievous sprite; a hobgoblin.

> "These faeries are not leprechauns or **pookas**, but the heroic, kingly, and godlike race." –LIN CARTER, *Tolkien*

revenant (RE vuh NAHN, also RE vuh nuhnt) - *n.* one who returns from death; a ghost, 2. returning to a place after a lengthy absence.

> "... a wondrous soufflé that includes such standard ingredients as slime, glop, glowerings, slashings and skeletal **revenants**." –JOE MORGENSTERN, *The Wall Street Journal, 4/2/04*

roc (RAHK) - *n.* an enormous mythical bird.

> "She knew, however, that I could no more stay here and let her go than I could put out my eyes. Even if it was African vultures, condors, **rocs**, or phoenixes. She had the initiative and carried me." –SAUL BELLOW, *The Adventures of Augie March*

satyr (SAY tuhr) - *n.* a woodland creature depicted as having pointed ears, short horns, the head and body of a man and the legs of a goat and with a fondness for unrestrained revelry, 2. a licentious or lecherous man.

*see **centaur** for citation, p. 124*

seraph (SER uhf) - *n.* the highest choir or order of angels in Christian angelology, ranked above cherubim and below only God Himself (certain citations refer to them having burning wings).

> "Even the type of angel Bernini had selected seemed significant. It's a **seraphim**, Langdon realized. **Seraphim** literally means 'the fiery one.'" –DAN BROWN, *Angels & Demons*

sphinx (SFINGKS) - *n.* an ancient Egyptian figure from mythology having the body of a lion and the head or a man, ram or hawk, esp. the figure at Giza, near Cairo, 2. (from Greek mythology) a winged monster with the head and breasts of a woman and the body of a lion, known to kill those who could not answer its riddle, 3. a mysterious person; one who is hard to know or understand.

*see **hippogriff** for citation, p. 126*

sprite (SPRYT) - *n.* an elf, pixie, fairy, or goblin, 2. an elflike person.

> "... daintily walking to her room like a wood **sprite** ..." –PHILIP ROTH, *American Pastoral*

succubus (SUK yuh buhs) - *n.* a female demon thought to descend upon and have sexual intercourse with a sleeping man.

sylph (SILF) - *n.* an imaginary being that has air as its element, 2. a graceful, slim woman or girl.

> [referring to his headless servants] "'When you speak to one, your thoughts are perceived directly by the **sylph** animating it.'" –L. SPRAGUE DE CAMP, *The Tritonian Ring*

troll (TROHL) - (among other definitions, from Scandinavian folklore) *n.* a super-natural creature variously portrayed as a giant or a friendly or mischievous dwarf, living in caves, underground or under bridges.

*see **brownie** for citation, p. 124*

warg (WARG) - (from the tales of J.R.R. Tolkien) *n.* a particularly evil kind of wolf.

> "'It is howling with wolf-voices. The **Wargs** have come west of the Mountains!'" –J.R.R. TOLKIEN, *The Fellowship of the Ring*

wight (WYT) - *n.* a living being; a living creature, 2. supernatural or unearthly beings.

> "And some said: 'They are Elvish **wights**. Let them go where they belong, into the dark places, and never return.'" –J.R.R. TOLKIEN, *The Two Towers*

will-o'-the-wisp (WIL uh thuh WISP) - *n.* a pale or phosphorescent light seen at night over swampy ground, 2. a delusive goal, a misleading hope.

> "Why should he toil to regain the rule of a people which had already forgotten him?—why chase a **will-o'-the-wisp**, why pursue a crown that was lost for ever?" –ROBERT E. HOWARD, *Conan the Conqueror*

wraith (RAYTH) - *n.* a ghost, 2. an apparition of a living person appearing as a premonition just before his own death.

> "After several minutes Rodolphe stopped; and when he saw her in her white dress gradually vanishing into the shadows like a **wraith**, his heart began to pound so violently that he leaned against a tree to keep from falling." –GUSTAVE FLAUBERT, *Madame Bovary*, transl. by Francis Steegmuller

wyvern (WY vuhrn) - *n.* Heraldry a fire-breathing dragon having two legs, wings, and a barbed tail.

*see **hippogriff** for citation*

MAGIC AND MAGICIANS

archimage (AR chi mage) - *n.* a great magician, a chief wizard or enchanter.

"... 'prudent men do not disturb the great **archimage** without good cause.'" –L. SPRAGUE DE CAMP, *The Tritonian Ring*

augur (O guhr) - *n.* in ancient Rome, one of a group of officials who foretold events by observing signs and interpreting omens, 2. a prophet; a seer; a fortureteller; a soothsayer, 3. *v.* to predict or prophesy from omens.

"... a black bird on a telephone line **augured** that somebody was about to die." –JEFFREY EUGENIDES, *Middlesex*

augury (O gyuh ree, also O guh ree) - *n.* the art or practice of divination from omens, 2. an omen; a sign; an event indicating something important to come, 3. the ceremony conducted by an augur.

"I tried to draw some **augury** of assistance from my memory." –H.G. WELLS, *The Island of Dr. Moreau*

cantrip (KAN truhp) - *n.* a witch's spell, a magic spell, 2. a prank; a sham; a deception.

"His lips moved rapidly as he murmured two or three prayers and **cantrips**." –FRITZ LEIBER, *Swords Against Death*

coven (KUH vuhn, also KOH vuhn) - *n.* an assembly of witches (usually 13 in number).

"'A **coven** was met.' ... 'it must have been a coven. Thirteen men stood about the balefire that was kindled before a great altar stone where a crucifix big as life lay broken.'" –POUL ANDERSON, *Three Hearts and Three Lions*

demerlayk (also **dweomerlayk**) - *n.* the practice of the occult arts; magic; jugglery.

"'Begone, foul **dwimmerlaik**, lord of carrion! Leave the dead in peace!'" –J.R.R. TOLKIEN, *The Return of the King*

domdaniel (DAHM DA nyuhl) - *n.* defined below

"Domdaniel - n. a fabled submarine hall where a magician or sorcerer met with his disciples: placed by Cazotte 'under the sea near Tunis', by Southey 'under the roots of the ocean'; used by Carlyle in the sense of 'infernal cave', 'den of iniquity.'" –*The Oxford English Dictionary*

"I saw this vista, I say, and heard as with the mind's ear the blasphemous **domdaniel** of cacophony which companioned it." –H.P. LOVECRAFT, *He*

dweomercraft (DWEE mer KRAFT) - *n.* jugglery, magic.

"...'he is a wizard both cunning and **dwim-mer-crafty**, having many guises.'" –J.R.R. TOLKIEN, *The Two Towers*

ensorcell (IN sor suhl) - *v.* to enchant; to bewitch; to fascinate.

"The **ensorcelled** ship of which the toy ship was the symbol." –ABRAHAM MERRITT, *The Ship of Ishtar*

epiphany (i PI fuh nee) - *n.* a divine manifestation or the appearance of a superhuman being, 2. a sudden comprehension of reality by means of an intuitive realization.

fey (FAY) - *adj.* exhibiting an enchanted, magical or otherworldly quality, 2. clairvoyant, having visionary power, 3. slightly insane; affected; appearing as if crazy.

"And before all the host rode King Brian Boru on a white steed, his white locks blown about his ancient face and his eyes strange and **fey**, so that the wild kerns gazed on him with superstitious awe." –ROBERT E. HOWARD, *Eons of the Night*

glamour (also **glamor**) (GLA muhr) - *n.* an enchantment, a magic spell, esp. to cast the glamour over one, 2. a compelling charm, a magical or fictitious beauty, esp. when delusively alluring, 3. physical allure, esp. feminine beauty.

"The wizard has thrown a **glamor** over them so that, so long as they remained still, the watch would simply not notice them; they were for practical purposes invisible." –L. SPRAGUE DE CAMP, *The Tritonian Ring*

goety (GOH uh tee) - *n.* witchcraft, the invocation of evil spirits; necromancy.

"For no clear reason, this quality in an artist can fascinate readers as hypnotically as

Thoth-Amon's most baneful and **goetic** spell." –RICHARD ENEY, *The Blade of Conan*

grimoire (GRIM WAR) - *n.* a magician's manual of black magic, used for invoking demons and spirits.

"'Old books,' he said. '**Grimoires**. Treatises on magic.'" –POUL ANDERSON, *Three Hearts and Three Lions*

imprecate (IM pri KAYT) - *v.* to invoke harm or evil upon; to curse, 2. to pray for evil.

imprecation (IM pri KAY shun) - *n.* the act of imprecating evil, etc., on someone, 2. a curse.

"Growling the foulest **imprecations**, he crawled along the sand till he got hold of the porch and could hoist himself again upon his crutch." –ROBERT LOUIS STEVENSON, *Treasure Island*

juju (JOO JOO) - *n.* an object used as a magic charm or fetish by some West African tribes, 2. the power held by such an object, 3. the taboo connected with use of such a object.

"'[The Stinger] became a force multiplier, a **juju** amulet, a Saint Christopher medallion—you name it ...'" –MILT BEARDEN, QUOTED BY GEORGE CRILE IN *Charlie Wilson's War.*

legerdemain (LE juhr duh MAYN) - *n.* sleight of hand; a magician's tricks performed with the hand, 2. an illusion; a deception, a trickery (from the French, leger de main, light of hand).

"... many of the pamphlets decried stock-jobbers as villainous Jews and foreigners who made Englishmen effeminate with their financial **legerdemains**." –DAVID LISS, *A Conspiracy of Paper*

lycanthropy (ly KANT thruh pee) - *n*. a delusional state or form of insanity in which one assumes the characteristics of a wolf, or other animal, 2. (from folklore) the ability to assume the form and nature of a wolf using magic.

> "... **lycanthropy** was probably inherited as a set of recessive genes." –POUL ANDERSON, *Three Hearts and Three Lions*

magus (MAY guhs) - *n*. a member of the priesthood of the ancient Persians, said to have originally been a Median tribe, 2. (Irish) heathen sorcerers who opposed St. Patrick, 3. the (three) Magi: the three wise men from the East, bearing offerings to the infant Christ, 4. a sorcerer, a magician.

> "Long before 'Frodo Lives!' began to appear in the New York subways, J.R.R. Tolkien was the **magus** of my secret knowledge." –PETER BEAGLE, INTRODUCTION, J.R.R. TOLKIEN'S *The Two Towers*

mantic (MAN tik) - *adj*. relating to having the power of divination; prophetic.

> "... an itinerant philosopher was supposed to be gnomic in her speech and **mantic** in her thought." –ORSON SCOTT CARD, *Children of the Mind*

necromancy (NE kruh MANT see) - *n*. the supposed art of predicting the future by communicating with the dead, 2. sorcery; black magic.

> "The wizards of Acheron practiced foul **necromancy**, thaumaturgy of the most evil kind, grisly magic taught them by devils." –ROBERT E. HOWARD, *Conan the Conqueror*

oneiromancy (OH ny ruh MANT see) - *n*. the practice of telling the future through dream interpretation.

philtre (also **philter**) (FIL tuhr) - *n*. a love potion, 2. a magic potion; a magic charm.

> "Her swelling womb, the pleasures of the fourth month, the time alone with her handsome boys, the envy of her neighbors all were colorful **philtres** over which she'd waved the wand of her imagination." –JONATHAN FRANZEN, *The Corrections*

pishogue (pih SHOHG) - *n*. black magic; sorcery; witchcraft, 2. an evil spell; an incantation, 3. a fairy, a witch.

> "Giants, trolls, kelpies, brownies, goblins, imps; wood, tree, mound and water spirits; heath-people, hill-watchers, treasureguards, good people, little people, **pishogues**, leprechauns, night-riders, pixies, nixies, gnomes and the rest—gone, all gone!" –RUDYARD KIPLING, *Puck of Pook's Hill*

prestidigitation (PRES tuh DI juh TAY shuhn) - *n*. sleight of hand; manual dexterity in performing magic tricks, 2. a show of skill; deceitful cleverness (from French).

> "'Real mint-julep in the latest style!' cried out these adroit manipulators, as—like **prestidigitators** handling their accessories—they kept switching from glass to glass the sugar, lemon, green mint, crushed ice, water, cognac, and fresh pineapple that compose this refreshing drink." –JULES VERNE, *From the Earth to the Moon*

scapulimancy (SKAP yuh luh MANS ee) - *n*. the practice of using a shoulder-blade bone, that has been heated in a fire to a cracked or burned state, in divination.

> "The Huns ... may have used shamans ... and are certainly known to have practised **scapulimancy**, the telling of omens from

patterns on sheeps' shoulder-blades."
—JOHN KEEGAN, *A History of Warfare*

sibyl (SI buhl) - *n.* any of certain women consulted as prophetesses or oracles by the ancient Greeks and Romans, 2. a witch; sorceress; fortuneteller.

"His gray hairs are records of the past, and his grayer eyes are **sibyls** of the future."
—EDGAR ALLAN POE, *The Fall of the House of Usher*

sigil (SI jil) - *n.* a seal; a signet, 2. a sign or image considered to have magical powers or a mysterious power in astrology.

"He had dimly heard of this sacred talisman of the serpent-men of Valusia—the most potent sorcerous **sigil** the earth had ever borne—the all-commanding crown of the serpent-kings." —L. SPRAGUE DE CAMP AND LIN CARTER, *Conan the Buccaneer*

spaeman (SPAY man) - *n.* a prophet; a diviner; a soothsayer; a fortuneteller; a wizard.

"... 'they'll need a **spaewoman** to raise his ghost.'" —ROBERT E. HOWARD AND L. SPRAGUE DE CAMP, *Conan the Usurper*

thaumaturge (THO muh TUHRJ) - *n.* a magician; one who performs miracles or magical feats.

*see **necromancy** for citation, p. 132*

Wicca (WI kuh) - *n.* a name used to describe the modern practices and religion of witchcraft.

"If she got lost, she pretended she was a **wiccan** and asked directions from animals and birds, the moon and stars."
—ROBERT MAILER ANDERSON, *Boonville*

THE JUDEO-CHRISTIAN TRADITION AND RELIGIONS

JUDAISM

cabbala (also **cabala, caballa, kabbala**) (kuh BAH luh, also KA buh luh) - *n.* an occult philosophy of rabinical origin based on a mystical interpretation of the Hebrew Scriptures, 2. any esoteric, secret or occult doctrine.

"The mystical teachings of the **Kabbala** drew heavily on anagrams—rearranging the letters of Hebrew words to derive new meanings." —DAN BROWN, *The Da Vinci Code*

diaspora (dy AS puh ruh, also dee AS puh ruh) - *n.* The Dispersion; the dispersal of Jews outside of Isreal from the 6th century B.C. to the present, 2. a dispersal of people from their original homeland.

"'Will the **Diaspora** head back?' Bush asked, referring to the Iraqis living out of the country." —BOB WOODWARD, *Plan of Attack*

Hadassah (ha DAS sah) - *n.* a women's organization, founded in 1912 by the American Zionists, that contributes to welfare works in Isreal.

"Gersbach the public figure, Gersbach the poet, the television-intellectual, lecturing at the **Hadassah** on Martin Buber." —SAUL BELLOW, *Herzog*

Haggada (also **Haggadah**) - *n.* traditional Jewish literature, esp. the anecdotes and parables found in the Talmud to illustrate a point of law, 2. the narrative portion of the Talmud containing the story of Exodus, read during a Passover Seder, 3. the book containing this story and read at the Seder ritual.

"I took a list of the traits of paranoia from a psychiatrist recently—I asked him to jot them down for me ... I put the scribbled paper in my wallet and studied it like the plagues of Egypt. Just like 'DOM, SFARDEYA, KINNIM' in the **Haggadah**. It read 'Pride, Anger, Excessive "Rationality," Homosexual Inclinations, Competitiveness, Hostile Projections, Delusions.' It's all there—all!" –SAUL BELLOW, *Herzog*

Halakha (also Halacha) (HAH lah KAH) - *n.* from the Talmud, an interpretation of the laws of the Scriptures, 2. that portion of the Talmud devoted to laws and ordinances.

Kaddish (KAH dish) - *n.* the prayer recited by mourners after the death of a close relative during daily synagogue services.

"I heard the **Kaddish** begin before I realized that somebody there was chanting it." –PHILIP ROTH, *The Human Stain*

Megillah (muh GI luh) - *n.* the scroll containing the narrative of the Book of Esther traditionally read at the festival of Purim, 2. a long, tediously detailed or embroidered account; a complicated story, frequently in the phrase the whole megillah.

"But I'm making a whole big **megillah** out of this." –DON DELILLO, *Underworld*

mezuza (also **mezuzah**) (muh ZU zuh) - *n.* a small piece of parchment inscribed with the Shema from Deuteronomy (6:4–9, 11:13–21), rolled up and contained in a small case which is attached to the doorframe of a Jewish household, in accordance with Jewish law.

"Visiting us ... she mounted the stairs ... Quickly and nervously she kissed her fingertips and touched the **mezuzah**. En-

tering, she inspected Mama's house keeping." –SAUL BELLOW, *Herzog*

Mishnah (also **Mishna**) (MISH nuh) - *n.* the first section, and basis of, the Talmud, a collection of early oral interpretations of the scriptures, 2. a paragraph from this section.

Passover (PAS OH vuhr) - *n.* a Jewish festival commemorating the Exodus of the Hebrews from Egypt, celebrated for eight days each spring.

pharisee (FAR uh see) - *n.* a person belonging to an ancient Jewish sect noted for its strict observance of the rites and ceremonies of the Mosaic law, 2. a hypocritically self-righteous person.

"'Whoso prefers either Matrimony or other Ordinance before the Good of Man and the plain Exigence of Charity, let him profess Papist, or Protestant, or what he will, he is no better than a **Pharisee**.'" –J. MILTON, QUOTED BY THOMAS HARDY, *Jude the Obscure*

sanctum sanctorum (SANGK tuhm SANGK TOHR uhm) - *n.* the innermost shrine, the Holy of Holies, of a Jewish temple and tabernacle, 2. one inviolably private place or retreat.

*see **sanctum sanctorum** entry for citation, p. 259*

Seder (SAY duhr) - *n.* the Jewish feast commemorating the exodus of the Israelites from Egypt, usually celebrated on the first evening of Passover.

Shema (sheh MAH) - *n.* a liturgical prayer, a declaration of the basic principle of Jewish belief, it proclaims the absolute unity of God and is recited twice daily by adult Jewish males to affirm their faith (see **mezuza**).

Shiva (also **Siva**) (SHI vuh, also SHEE vuh) - *n.* the third of the principal Hindu deities, worshipped for his powers of reproduction and dissolution, 2. a representation of this deity, 3. Judaism—[shiva]—the seven-day mourning period following the death of a loved one, freq. in the phrase "sit shiva."

> "Sitting **shiva** at ninety for her beloved Seymour." –PHILIP ROTH, *American Pastoral*

tabernacle (TA buhr NA kuhl) - *n.* the portable sanctuary used by the Jews to carry the ark of the covenant through the desert, 2. a case or box on a church alter containing the consecrated elements of the Eucharist, 3. a large temple or place of worship.

Talmud (TAHL MUD, also TAL muhd) - *n.* a collection of ancient Rabbinical writings that collectively constitute the basis of religious authority for Orthodox Judaism.

Tudesco - *n.* a term used by Sephardic Jews for an Ashkenazic Jew.

> "The division between the Iberians and the **Tudescos**—or the Sephardim and Ashkenazim, as we would say today—is a longstanding one. The two traditions are in many ways very different, and in this period the differences were only becoming more pronounced with the rise of the ecstatic movements among Eastern European Jews." –DAVID LISS, *A Conspiracy of Paper*

yahrzeit (YAHR tsit, also YAHR zit) - *n.* the anniversary of a relative's death, esp. a parent, observed by the Jews with mourning and the recitation of religious texts.

> "... the minutest gradations of social position conveyed by linoleum and oilcloth, by **yahrzeit** candles and cooking smells ..." –PHILIP ROTH, *American Pastoral*

Yahudi (YA hoo dee) - *n.* a Jew; Jews; Jewish (a term used primarily in Arabic-speaking or Muslim countries, in some Jewish use—mainly in the US as a slang term).

> "... she had a scheme for writing to Julius Resenwald whenever she read that he was making a new endowment. It was always to Negroes, never to Jews, the he gave his money, she said, and it angered her enormously, and she cried, 'That German **Yehuda**!'" –SAUL BELLOW, *The Adventures of Augie March*

yeshiva (yuh SHEE vuh) - *n.* an Orthodox Jewish college or seminary for talmudic studies, 2. a Jewish school with a curriculum that includes religious and cultural study as well as general education.

> "... the dangling earlocks of a **yeshiva** student gawking at the famous Yiddish writers sipping tea and quarreling in a cafe on Division Street." –FERNANDA EBERSTADT, *The New York Times Book Review, 3/20/05*

Yom Kippur (YOM ki PUR, also YAHM ki PUR) - *n.* the holiest Jewish holiday, observed in September or October, marked by fasting, prayer and atonement.

THE OLD TESTAMENT

apocrypha (uh PAH kruh fuh) - *n.* writing or anecdotes of dubious authenticity, 2. Apocrypha—fourteen books of the Septuagint accepted by the Roman Catholics though excluded from the Jewish and Protestant cannons of the Old Testament, 3. writings omitted from the New Testament and not accepted as resulting from revelation.

Babel (BAY buhl, also BA buhl) - *n.* in the Old Testament, the city and tower in the land of Shinar, where construction was interrupted by God who caused a confusion of tongues, 2. babel—a place or scene of noise and confusion; a confused mixture of sounds, as of voices or languages.

"He wrote many clever things about the Tower of **Babel** that could not reach heaven and about Icarus who flopped on his wax wings." —AYN RAND, *The Fountainhead*

manna (MA nuh) - *n.* spiritual nourishment from a divine source, 2. in the Old Testament, a food-substance miraculously provided for the Israelites in the wilderness after their departure from Egypt, 3. something of value received unexpectedly.

"'You gotta love academe,' Jacob says. 'Rumors are the **manna** of our particular desert.'" —RICHARD RUSSO, *Straight Man*

Pentateuch (PEN tuh TOOK, also PEN tuh TYOOK) - *n.* the first five books of the Old Testament (Genesis, Exodus, Leviticus, Numbers, Deuteronomy); together they are attributed to Moses and often called the "Books of Moses."

"If you've never heard of the Five Books of Moses (not actually composed by Moses; people who believe in divine revelation see

him as more secretary than author), you've heard of the Torah and the **Pentateuch**, the Hebrew and Greek names, respectively, for the first five books of the Hebrew Bible: Genesis, Exodus, Leviticus, Numbers and Deuteronomy." —JUDITH SHULEVITZ, *The New York Times Book Review, 10/17/04*

prelapsarian (PREE LAP SER ee uhn) - *adj.* pertaining to the period before the Fall of Adam and Eve.

"... from the blood-soaked bullrings of South America to the **prelapsarian** pastures of the Valley of the Moon ..." —EARLE LABOR, INTRODUCTION, *The Portable Jack London*

Septuagint (sep TOO uh juhnt, also sep TYOO uh juhnt) - *n.* a pre-Christian Greek translation of the Old Testament made several centuries B.C.

shibboleth (SHI buh luhth, also SHI buh LETH) - *n.* a word which was made the criterion by which to distinguish the Ephraimites from the Gileadites. The Ephraimites, not being able to pronounce sh, called the word sibboleth (see Judges 12), 2. the criterion, test or watchword of a party; a party cry or pet phrase.

*see other **shibboleth** entry for citation, p. 73*

testament (TES tuh muhnt) - *n.* a solemn, authentic document in writing, by which a person declares his will as to disposal of his estate and effects after his death, 2. one of the two distinct revelations of God's purposes toward man; also, one of the two general divisions of the canonical books of the sacred Scriptures, in which the covenants are respectively revealed; as, the Old Testament; the New Testament; 3. tangible evidence, 4. a statement of conviction; credo.

BIBLICAL PLACES

Calvary (KAL vuh ree) - *n.* the place where Christ was crucified outside Jerusalem.

"The model of the ancient city stood in the middle of the apartment ... Mount Moriah, the Valley of Jehoshaphat, the City of Zion, the walls and the gates, outside one of which there was a large mound like a tumulus, and on the mound a little white cross. The spot ... was **Calvary**." –THOMAS HARDY, *Jude the Obscure*

Gehenna (gi HE nuh) - *n.* the valley of the sons of Hinnom; a valley near Jerusalem where refuse and filth was cast and consumed by a fire kept always burning in Biblical times, 2. a place of everlasting torment or destruction, 3. a place of suffering.

"... convinced me that I had but jumped from purgatory into **gehenna**." –EDGAR RICE BURROUGHS, *A Princess of Mars*

golgotha (GAHL guh thuh, also gahl GAH thuh) - *n.* a place or time of great suffering, 2. a graveyard; a place of interment; a charnel-house, 3. another name for Calvary, the location where Christ was crucified outside Jerusalem.

*see other **golgotha** entry for citation, p. 253*

Pisgah (PIZ guh) - *n.* a mountain summit east of Jordan from which Moses viewed the Promised Land.

"Going back to the yards, I climbed down a steep path, like a cliff of **Pisgah**." –SAUL BELLOW, *The Adventures of Augie March*

Zion (ZY uhn) - *n.* the historic land of Israel and a symbol of the Jewish people, 2. one of the hills of Jerusalem where the city of David was built, ultimately becoming the center of life and worship for Jews, 3. used allusively for God's house or household.

*see **Calvary** for citation, opposite page*

CHRISTIANITY

anathema (uh NA thuh muh) - *n.* a thing or person accursed, damned or intensely disliked, 2. a formal ecclesiastical ban, curse, or excommunication.

*see other **anathema** entry for citation, p. 61*

conclave (KAHN KLAYV) - *n.* a confidential or secret meeting, 2. a meeting in which cardinals of the Catholic Church meet to elect a new pope.

"**Conclave**. Even the name was secretive. 'Con clave' literally meant 'locked with a key.' The cardinals were permitted no contact whatsoever with the outside world." –DAN BROWN, *Angels & Demons*

ecclesiastical (ih KLEE zee AHS tih kuhl) - *adj.* relating to a church, esp. the church as an organized institution.

"For though it had seemed to have an **ecclesiastical** basis during the service, and he had persuaded himself that such was the case, he could not altogether be blind to the real nature of the magnetism." –THOMAS HARDY, *Jude the Obscure*

ecumenical (E kyuh MEH ni kuhl) - *adj.* worldwide in scope or applicability, universal, 2. relating to the universal Christian Church, 3. relating to the promotion of accord among churches and religions.

"... the vicars in Lambeth banded together to make collections, **ecumenically**." –SIMON WINCHESTER, *The Professor and the Madman*

ecumenism (also **ecumenicism**) (e KYOO meh NI zuhm) - *n.* a movement seeking to achieve unity among Christian churches or denominations, 2. a movement seeking accord among religions through cooperation and understanding.

"The competition among true believers of all faiths (in Jerusalem) creates tension, not **ecumenicism**." –STEVEN ERLANGER, *The New York Times, 10/19/04*

hallow (HA loh) - (among other definitions) *n.* a saint; a holy one, 2. *v.* to define as holy, 3. hallows, 4. *n.* often applied to relics or shrines of saints; often applied to the gods of the heathen and their shrines.

"Two of them had already fallen to his sword, staining the **hallows** with their blood." –J.R.R. TOLKIEN, *The Return of the King*

homily (HAH muh lee) - *n.* a lecture or a lengthy discourse on or of a moral theme, 2. a sermon.

*see other **homily** entry for citation, p. 75*

hossana (hoh ZAN uh) -*n.* interjection; an expression used to praise or adore God.

"Four Saints in black tie, they sang **hossanas** to winners, dirges to losers." –MARIO PUZO, *Fools Die*

Mahound (ma HOUND) - *n.* the "false prophet," a term of contempt used by Christians to describe Muhammed in the Middle Ages, 2. the prophet Muhammed, 3. a false god; an idol; an evil spirit; a devil.

"'Though even were I still a follower of **Mahound**, I would not be so discourteous as not to drink to your most beautiful lady's health.'" –POUL ANDERSON, *Three Hearts and Three Lions*

Mammon (MA muhn) - *n.* from the New Testament, the qualities of wealth, avarice and worldly gain personified as a false god, 2. an evil influence brought on by material wealth.

"... unfrocked preachers too wide in their Christianity for any congregation of **Mammon**-worshippers ..." –JACK LONDON, *What Life Means to Me*

Nicene Council (NY SEEN KAUNT suhl) - *n.* an ecclesiastical Council held at Nicea in 325 A.D. for the purpose of settling the Arian controversy; Arius proposing that if the Father begat the Son, there must have been a time before the Son was in existence; a position that was widely disputed in the Church.

"'During this fusion of religions, Constantine needed to strengthen the new Christian tradition, and held a famous ecumenical gathering known as the **Council of Nicaea**.' Sophie had heard of it only insofar as its being the birthplace of the **Nicene Creed**. 'At this gathering,' Teabing said, 'many aspects of Christianity were debated and voted upon—the date of Easter, the role of bishops, the administration of sacraments, and of course, the divinity of Jesus.'" –DAN BROWN, *The Da Vinci Code*

Nicene Creed (NY SEEN KREED) - *n.* a formal statement of Christian belief expounded by the Nicene Council holding that the Son was one with the Father, in opposition to the belief held by Arias that the Son had been created by the Father like the rest of creation (the "Arian controversy"). This formulation was later expanded by the Council of Constantinople in 381 A.D., and is in regular use as part of the Eucharist.

*see **Nicene Council** for citation*

pall (PAHL) - *n.* a cloth that covers a coffin, 2. a coffin, 3. something that covers, 4. an element that produces gloominess.

> "The black **pall**, embroidered with white tears, flapped up now and again, exposing the coffin beneath." —GUSTAVE FLAUBERT, *Madame Bovary*, transl. by Francis Steegmuller

paynim (PAY nuhm) - (Archaic) *n.* pagan or non-Christian lands collectively; pagandom, heathendom, 2. a pagan, a non-Christian, esp. a Muslim, 3. a heathen.

> "'I am a Christian like yourself. Once, true, I fought for the **paynim**, but the gentle and chivalrous knight who overcame me also won me to the True Faith.'" —POUL ANDERSON, *Three Hearts and Three Lions*

perdition (pehr DI shuhn) - *n.* eternal damnation, hell.

> "I felt that the most desirable thing in the world was complete deafness, to be like that blank-eyed mute who neither heard nor felt the **perdition** of sound he was creating." —ROBERT E. HOWARD, *Beyond the Borders*

popery (POH puh ree) - *n.* the doctrines, practices and rituals associated with the Roman Catholic Church and the pope, 2. often considered as a term of opprobrium for the rituals of the Roman Catholic Church.

> "Talbot had argued vigorously ... that **popery**, the great foreign menace controlling all aspects of the Catholic operation, threatened the independence of all American religions with its proselytizing and its goal of overrunning the country." —MATTHEW PEARL, *The Dante Club*

sacerdotal (SA suhr DOH tuhl, also SA kuhr DOH tuhl) - *adj.* relating to priests, the priesthood; priestly, 2. marked by a strong belief in the devine authority of the priesthood.

> "As the magical influence of the Church gradually faded, the (occupational) uniform replaced the **sacerdotal** habit and rose to the level of the absolute." —MILAN KUNDERA, *The Art of the Novel*

simony (SY muh nee, also SI muh nee) - *n.* the traffic, buying or selling, of ecclesiastical offices, pardons or emoluments (the word derives from Simon Magus, who tried to buy spiritual powers from the Apostle Peter).

> "'We must question the sexton some more. We still do not know Talbot's **simony,** and this could be an indication!' They had found nothing to suggest Talbot was anything but a good shepherd to his flock." —MATTHEW PEARL, *The Dante Club*

stigmata (stig MAH tuh) - *n.* marks or sores resembling the wounds on the crucified body of Christ.

> "'... when God points to the **stigmata** on the hands and feet of her Son and asks her: 'How am I to forgive his torturers?'— she bids all the saints, all the martyrs, all the angels and archangels to kneel with her and pray for a free pardon for all without distinction.'" —FYODOR DOSTOYEVSKY, *The Brothers Karamazov*, transl. by David Magarshack

synod (SI nuhd) - *n.* an assembly of church officials or churches, 2. a council; an assembly.

> "In classical Islam there are no lords spiritual—no bishops, cardinals, popes, no councils, **synods**, or ecclesiastical courts." —BERNARD LEWIS, *What Went Wrong?*

ultramontane (UHL truh MAHN TAYN) - *adj.* relating to the people or regions beyond the mountains, esp. the Alps, 2. supporting the supreme authority of the papal court.

"'But I maintained that, on the contrary, the Church ought to contain the whole State and not occupy only a corner in it ...'

'The purest **Ultramontanism**!' cried Miusov." —FYODOR DOSTOYEVSKY, *The Brothers Karamazov,* transl. by David Magarshack

venial (VEE nee uhl, also VEE nee yuhl) - *adj.* excusable; forgiveable; pardonable (venial sins being forgiveable, unlike mortal sins).

"'While I have known you, Harold, to commit **venial** sins of rhetorical exaggeration incompatible with true scientific accuracy, I have never known you to engage in deliberate fabrication.'" —L. SPRAGUE DE CAMP AND FLETCHER PRATT, *The Complete Compleat Enchanter*

CHRISTIAN RITES AND CEREMONIES

absolution (AB suh LOO shuhn) - *n.* the act of absolving, a formal release from sin, 2. the formal remission of sin pronounced by a priest as part of the sacrament of penance, 3. forgiveness.

"I could see his face begin to change from the hollow countenance of shame to the hopeful expression of a man who believes he is on the verge of **absolution**." —DAVID LISS, *A Conspiracy of Paper*

absolve (uhb ZAHLV, also uhb SAHLV, uhb ZOLV) - *v.* to declare as free of guilt or blame, 2. to free from obligation or requirement, 3. to grant remission from sin.

"... the archbishop **absolved** them with the cross ..." —*The Song of Roland,* trans. by Glyn Burgess

banns (also **bans**) (BANZ) - *n.* announcement in a church of an intended marriage.

"... 'as this is Saturday I mean to call about the **banns** at once, so as to get the first publishing done tomorrow, or we shall lose a week.'" —THOMAS HARDY, *Jude the Obscure*

benedict (BEH nuh DIKT) - *adj.* a recently married man, especially one who was formerly a confirmed bachelor, 2. blessed; benign; having a mildly laxative effect.

*see other **benedict** entry for citation, p. 41*

benediction (BEH nuh DIK shuhn) - *n.* a blessing, 2. the invocation of a divine blessing, esp. following a church service, 3. an expression of good will.

"'But,' [William F.] Buckley writes, 'all is not lost; all is never lost'—a warm **benediction** from a man who has long found joy in the journey." —JON MEACHAM, *The New York Times Book Review, 10/17/04*

benison (BE nuh suhn, also BE nuh zuhn) - *n.* a blessing; a benediction; a spoken blessing.

"'God's **benison** on you, my lords' came the voice." —ROBERT E. HOWARD, *Cormac Mac Art*

chalice (CHA luhs) - *n.* a cup, a goblet, 2. a drinking vessel, esp. for the consecrated wine of the Eucharist.

"On his head he put a cowl with an octagonal cross. The cowl was left open, but the face of the deceased was covered with the black cloth used to cover the **chalice**." —FYODOR DOSTOYEVSKY, *The Brothers Karamazov,* transl. by David Magarshack

chrism (KRI zuhm) - *n.* a consecrated mixture of oil and balsam used in church sacraments for anointing, especially in baptism and confirmation.

> "During the [baptism] rite itself, Father Stylianopoulos clipped a lock of Milton's hair and dropped it into the water. He **chrismed** the sign of the cross on the baby's forehead." –JEFFREY EUGENIDES, *Middlesex*

communicant (KUH MYOO ni kuhnt) - *n.* a person who receives Communion, 2. a person who communicates, an informant.

> "A daily **communicant** in the Roman Catholic Church and the mayor of Mount Pleasant." –PAT CONROY, *My Losing Season*

Communion (kuh MYOO nyuhn) - *n.* a spiritual fellowship, 2. Christians sharing a common faith, practices and rites; a denomination, 3. the consecrated elements of the Eucharist received by a congregation.

> "And virtually all the elements of the Catholic ritual—the miter, the altar, the doxology, and **communion**, the act of 'God-eating'—were taken directly from earlier pagan mystery religions." –DAN BROWN, *The Da Vinci Code*

consecrate (KAHNT suh KRAYT) - *v.* to declare or otherwise make something holy, 2. to render holy through a religious ritual, 3. to dedicate to some service or goal, 4. in Christian theology, the ritual tranformation of (bread and wine) into the body and blood of Jesus.

> "... this terrible discipline is accepted voluntarily by the man who **consecrates** himself to this life in the hope that after a long novitiate he will attain to such a degree of self-mastery and self-conquest that at last he will, after a life of obedience, achieve complete freedom, that is to say, freedom from himself." –FYODOR DOSTOYEVSKY, *The Brothers Karamazov*, transl. by David Magarshack

Eucharist (YOO kuh rihst) - *n.* the Christian sacrament commemorating Christ's Last Supper; Holy Communion, 2. the ceremonial consecration and consumption of bread and wine in remembrance of Jesus's death.

font (FAHNT) - (among other definitions) *n.* a basin holding baptismal or holy water in a church, 2. a source of abundance.

> "A pagan Valdabrun is also there; ... He once captured Jerusalem by treachery And violated the Temple of Solomon, Slaying the patriarch before the **fonts**." –*The Song of Roland*, trans. by Glyn Burgess

pyx (also **pix**) (PIKS) - *n.* a container holding the supply of wafers for the Eucharist, 2. a container used to carry the Eucharist to the sick.

> "The sheets of her bed were sprinkled with holy water; the priest drew the white host from the sacred **pyx**; and she was all but swooning with celestial bliss as she advanced her lips to receive the body of the

Saviour." –GUSTAVE FLAUBERT, *Madame Bovary*, transl. by Francis Steegmuller

sacrament (SA kruh muhnt) - *n.* a sacred act in Christianity that is done to consecrate oneself to God, 2. any of the rites of the Christian church considered to have been instituted by Christ, such as the Eucharist or baptism, 3. (with capital "S") the consecrated elements of the Eucharist.

> "... what the author Rosemary Haughton once called 'The Catholic Thing'—the capacious, **sacramental** religious imagination that operates by analogy rather than linear logic and perceives virtually everything human (including the body and sexual love) as occasion for a graced encounter with the divine mystery." –R. SCOTT APPLEBY, *The New York Times Book Review, 9/7/03*

shrive (SHRYV) - *v.* to confess and give absolution to (a penitent), 2. to confess and receive absolution.

> "True, Guillaume had died **unshriven**, with all his sins upon him, and because of this she had supposed that his soul plunged straight downward to the gates of hell." –C.L. MOORE, *Jirel of Joiry*

tabernacle (TA buhr NA kuhl) - *n.* the portable sanctuary used by the Jews to carry the ark of the covenant through the desert, 2. a case or box on a church alter containing the consecrated elements of the Eucharist, 3. a large temple or place of worship.

> *see other **tabernacle** entry for citation, p. 251*

tonsure (TAHNT shuhr) - *n.* the act of shaving one's head prior to becoming a monk or a priest, 2. the shaved portion of a monk's or priest's head, 3. *v.* to shave the head.

> "There are many bishops and abbots there (at the charnel-house), Monks, canons and **tonsured** priests, And they absolved and signed them in God's name." –*The Song of Roland,* transl. by Glyn Burgess

unction (UHNGK shuhn) - *n.* the act of anointing during a religious, ceremonial or healing ritual, 2. an ointment; a salve; an oil, 3. something applied to soothe or restore, 4. excessive earnestness, superficial compliments, 5. Extreme Unction—a rite practiced by a Catholic priest in which a sick, injured or dying person is anointed with oil and prayed over for salvation. In 1972 the name was changed to the "Anointing of the Sick."

> "'As you can see, Tradd,' I said, 'sex is a sacrament to our Italian roommates.'
>
> 'It has Extreme **Unction** beat all to hell,'' Mark said." –PAT CONROY, *The Lords of Discipline*

CHRISTIAN SONGS AND PRAYERS

angelus (AN juh luhs) - *n.* a devotional prayer recited at morning, noon and night commemorating the Incarnation, 2. a bell rung to announce the time for reciting this prayer.

> "He asked Madame Lefrançois to have it brought to him at the rectory during the evening, and then left for the church, where the bell was tolling the **Angelus**." –GUSTAVE FLAUBERT, *Madame Bovary,* transl. by Francis Steegmuller

breviary (BREE vuh ree, also BREE vyuh ree) - *n.* a book of prayers, hymns and offices to be recited daily by certain priests and members of religious orders.

"At the far end, under some spruces, a plaster priest stood reading his **breviary**." —GUSTAVE FLAUBFRT, *Madame Bovary*, transl. by Francis Steegmuller

canticle (KAN ti kuhl) - *n.* a song or chant, 2. a hymn from the Bible.

"'Tomorrow they will chant 'Our Helper and Defender' over him—a glorious anthem—and over me, when I kick the bucket, they'll only chant 'What earthly joy'—a little **canticle**.'" —FYODOR DOSTOYEVSKY, *The Brothers Karamazov*, transl. by David Magarshack

chantry (CHAN tree) - *n.* singing or chanting of the Mass, 2. an endowment to cover the expenses for the singing of the Mass, 3. a chapel or alter endowed for the singing of the Mass and prayers.

*see other **chantry** entry for citation, p. 256*

confiteor (kuhn FEE tee OR) - *n.* a form of prayer, as at the beginning of the Mass, in which a confession of sin is made.

"Anyway, I became the ship's confidant. Though not all the confidences gave hope to the soul ... on the fifteenth day out ... we were ... sent down by a torpedo. It happened while I was hearing one of these unofficial **confiteors**, in fact." —SAUL BELLOW, *The Adventures of Augie March*

de profundis (DAY proh FUN dees) - *n.* the first words of the Latin version of Psalm 130 (129): 'Out of the depths (have I cried)'; hence: the name of this psalm, a psalm of penitence, 2. a cry of deep sorrow or misery.

"The priests, the cantors and the two choirboys recited **De profundis;** and their voices carried over the fields, rising and falling in waves." —GUSTAVE FLAUBERT, *Madame Bovary*, transl. by Francis Steegmuller

lauds (LODZ) - *n.* praise, glorification, 2. a song or hymn of praise, 3. a morning church service.

"He was as serious as calculus and played basketball with the same devotion that monks often display at **lauds** or matins." —PAT CONROY, *My Losing Season*

litany (Li tuhn ee, also LIT nee) - *n.* a liturgical prayer comprising phrases recited by a leader alternating with responses from the congregation, 2. a repetitive or long and tedious recital.

"A voice behind me began a softer, more menacing chant, strangely rhythmic, like a **litany**." —PAT CONROY, *The Lords of Discipline*

matins (often **Matins**) (MA tihnz) - *n.* the morning prayer, 2. the service of morning worship in the Anglican Church.

*see **lauds** for citation*

missal (MI suhl) - *n.* from the Roman Catholic Church, a book containing all the prayers and responses necessary for celebrating Mass throughout the year, 2. a prayer book.

"The shop ... contained Anglican books, stationery, texts, and fancy goods: little plaster angels on brackets, Gothic-framed pictures of saints, ebony crosses that were almost crucifixes, prayer-books that were almost **missals**." —THOMAS HARDY, *Jude the Obscure*

missalette (mih suh LET) - *n.* a sheet or pamphlet including all the prayers, readings and responses necessary for the Mass on a specific day.

[in church] "My mother was peering over a **missalette**, eyes huge." —CHRIS FUHRMAN, *The Dangerous Lives of Altar Boys*

novena (noh VEE nuh) - *n.* a Roman Catholic devotion comprising prayers on nine consecutive days.

> "That was the story people told, I don't know, nuns, old ladies on **novena** nights, maybe well-heeled parishioners too, pink and fit, officers of the Knights of Columbus." –DON DELILLO, *Underworld*

prie-dieu (PREE DYUHR) - *n.* a narrow desklike kneeling bench with a ledge to hold a book, used by a person at prayer.

> "... the nuns bowed over their **prie-dieus**." –GUSTAVE FLAUBERT, *Madame Bovary*, transl. by Francis Steegmuller

Psalter (also **psalter**) (SAHL tuhr) - *n.* the Book of Psalms, 2. a collection of Psalms, or a particular version of, musical setting for, or selection from, for use in religious services.

> "As the deceased was, according to his rank, a priest and a monk, leading a life of the strictest monastic rules, the Gospel, and not the **Psalter**, had to be read over him by monks who were ordained priests or deacons." –FYODOR DOSTOYEVSKY, *The Brothers Karamazov*, transl. by David Magarshack

rosary (ROH zuh ree, also ROHZ ree) - *n.* a series of prayers said in devotion to the Virgin Mary, 2. a string of beads on which to count the series of prayers.

> *see other **rosary** entry for citation, p. 233*

rubric (ROO brik) - *n.* a title, heading or first letter often printed in red ink, 2. the title or heading of a statute or chapter in a code of law, 3. something under which a thing is classed or categorized, 4. a rule for conduct of a liturgical service (from Latin ruber, red).

> "... they could hear her through the ceiling below, honestly saying the Lord's Prayer in a loud voice, as the **Rubric** directed." –THOMAS HARDY, *Jude the Obscure*

versicle (VEHR si kuhl) - *n.* a short verse or short sentence spoken or chanted by a priest or minister in public worship followed by a response from the congregation.

Vespers (also **vesper**) (VES puhrz) - *n.* a religious service held in the late afternoon or evening, 2. a bell used to summon the congregation to the service.

> "... it is even the hour of **vespers** ..." –L. SPRAGUE DE CAMP AND FLETCHER PRATT, *The Complete Compleat Enchanter*

CHRISTIAN HOLIDAYS

Ascension (uh SENT shuhn) - *n.* the act of ascent, 2. the bodily rising of Jesus into heaven, celebrated on the 40th day after Easter (which in turn commemorates the Resurrection of Christ), 3. a feast celebrating the ascension.

> "'Time's so short I always keep [the students] an extra hour on Wednesdays after **Ascension**.'" –GUSTAVE FLAUBERT, *Madame Bovary*, transl. by Francis Steegmuller

Epiphany (i PI fuh NEE) - *n.* the festival commemorating the manifestation of Christ to the Gentiles in the persons of the Magi; observed on Jan. 6th, the 12th day after Christmas.

maundy (MAUN dee) - *adj.* the ceremonial washing of the feet of the poor on Maundy Thursday (the Thursday before Easter), to commemorate Jesus' washing the feet of the disciples, 2. the alms distributed during the ceremonial washing of the feet or on Maundy Thursday, 3. the Last Supper.

> "The remainder of the week, which was Holy Week before Easter, passed in predictable fashion. On Thursday evening, **Maundy** Thursday, we went to St. Mark's with the Allards, who were well again." —NELSON DEMILLE, *The Gold Coast*

Michaelmas (MI kuhl muhs) - *n.* a feast honoring St. Michael, celebrated on September 29th.

> "**Michaelmas** came and passed, and Jude and his wife ..." —THOMAS HARDY, *Jude the Obscure*

Pentecost (PEN ti KOST, also PEN ti KAHST) - *n.* the seventh Sunday after Easter, commemorating the descent of the Holy Ghost upon the disciples; Whitsunday.

> "But at **Pentecost** she left Yonville without warning, eloping with Théodore and stealing everything that was left of the wardrobe." —GUSTAVE FLAUBERT, *Madame Bovary*, transl. by Francis Steegmuller

Sexagesima (SEK suh JEHS uh muh) - *adj.* in full Sexagesima Sunday: the second Sunday before Lent.

> "'In the year 1645, early in the morning of **Sexagesima** Sunday, it raged with such noise and impetuosity that the very stones of the houses on the coast fell to the ground.'" —EDGAR ALLAN POE, *The Fall of the House of Usher*

CHRISTIAN SECTS

anabaptist (A nuh BAP tist) - *n.* literally one who baptizes again; generally refers to a radical Protestant movement of the 16th century that arose in Germany and neighboring regions that rejected childhood baptism, holding that baptism should be administered to believers only (hence the need to "re-baptize" after childhood).

> "A man who had not been baptized, an honest **Anabaptist** named Jacques, saw the cruel and ignominious treatment of one of his brothers, a featherless two-legged creature with a soul." —FRANCOIS VOLTAIRE, *Candide*, transl. by Richard Aldington

Copt (KAHPT) - *n.* a native of Egypt descended from the ancient inhabitants of that country, 2. a member of the Coptic church, an Egyptian Christian belonging to the Jacobite sect of Monophysites.

> [in Egypt] "'... we eat dates with aphrodisiacs in them and beautiful **Coptic** girls come rowing up [the Nile] to the music of the lateen sails'" —SAUL BELLOW, *The Adventures of Augie March*

episcopal (i PIS kuh puhl, also i PIS kuh buhl) - *adj.* relating to a bishop or bishops, 2. relating to the church government by bishops, 3. of or pertaining to the Anglican Church or the Protestant Episcopal Church.

> "He is also a seriously committed Catholic intellectual, for whom the late Cardinal Joseph Bernardin, Archbishop of Chicago, stands as a model of consensus-building, moderately liberal **episcopal** leadership." —R. SCOTT APPLEBY, *The New York Times Book Review, 9/7/03*

gnostic (NAHS tik) - *adj.* of or having knowledge; cognitive, 2. *n.* one skilled or learned in a subject, 3. Gnostic—a believer in Gnosticism—a system of belief combining elements of Greek philosophy, Oriental mysticism and Christianity and stressing salvation through a positive, intuitive knowledge of spiritual matters (referred to as gnosis).

> "... 'people like you who don't fish—' and here he looked up to take in again, to divine, **gnostically**, my unpardonable they-ness. 'I'm guessin' you don't fish.'"
> –PHILIP ROTH, *The Human Stain*

Jansenist (JANT suh nist) - *n.* the theological principles of Cornelius Jansen, bishop of Ypres in Flanders (d. 1638), emphasizing predestination, denying free will and maintaining that human nature is not capable of good; condemned by the Roman Catholic Church as heretical and strongly opposed by the Molinists and other Jesuits.

> "'I think everything goes awry with us, that nobody knows his rank or office ... the rest of their time is spent in senseless quarrels: **Jansenists** with Molinists, lawyers with churchmen, men of letters with men of letters, courtiers with courtiers, financiers with the people, wives with husbands, relatives with relatives—'tis an eternal war.'" –FRANCOIS VOLTAIRE, *Candide*, transl. by Richard Aldington

Jesuit (JE zu uht, also JE zhu uht) - *n.* a member of the Society of Jesus, an order founded by St. Ignatius Loyola in 1534, 2. *adj.* having qualities or characteristics of a Jesuit or Jesuitism.

> "I often wondered why no one pointed out that [President Clinton] was educated by Jesuits, for whom the meaning of 'is' is a matter not lightly resolved." –LARRY MC-

MURTRY, *The New York Times Book Review, 7/4/04*

Molinism (MOH lin ism) - *n.* the doctrine, put forward in 1588 by Luis de Molina linking the efficacy of divine grace with the free cooperation of mankind, thus safeguarding free will by divine grace.

*see **Jansenist** for citation*

Monophysite (muh NAH fuh SYT) - *n.* one who adheres to the doctrine that within the person of Jesus there was but a single divine nature, or a composite inseparable nature, partly divine, and partly (subordinately) human; a tenet held by members of the Eastern Orthodox Churches (Ethiopian, Armenian, Syrian and, especially, Coptic).

Nestorianism (ne STOHR ee uh NI zuhm) - *n.* a theological doctrine (named after Nestorius, patriarch of Constantinople, appointed in 428 A.D.) asserting that Christ is both the son of God and the man Jesus as opposed to the Roman Catholic doctrine that Christ is fully God; declared heretical in 431 A.D.

> "Yet moral authority in post-Roman Europe did not altogether lose a home; it migrated to the institutions of the Christian church, firmly established in its Roman rather than **Nestorian** form thanks to the conversion of the Franks in 496." –JOHN KEEGAN, *A History of Warfare*

Pentecostal (PEN ti KAHS tuhl, also PEN ti KOS tuhl) - *adj.* of or relating to the Pentecost, 2. relating to any of the various Christian religions whose congregants seek to be filled with the Holy Spirit, as in emulation of the Apostles at Pentecost and in glossolalia.

"Trinity, Texas ... lies in the very heart of the Bible Belt ... Just down the road are the huge **Pentecostal** summer revival camps. A kind of fundamentalism flourishes in the religious practices of its citizens." —GEORGE CRILE, *Charlie Wilson's War*

Socinian (suh SI nee uhn, also soh SI nee uhn) - *n.* a 16th-century Italian sect (founded by Laelius and Faustus Socinus) that rejected the divinity of Christ, the Trinity, and original sin, 2. of or pertaining to Socinians or their doctrines.

"This man of letters ... had just been deprived of a small post on which he depended and the preachers of Surinam were persecuting him because they thought he was a **Socinian**." —FRANCOIS VOLTAIRE, *Candide,* transl. by Richard Aldington

MONASTIC ORDERS

Baphomet (BAF o met) - *n.* a form of the name Mahomet or Mohammed, the Arabian prophet, 2. a symbolic figure or idol which the Templars were accused of worshipping in their mysterious rites.

"... 'the Church accused the Templars of secretly performing rituals in which they prayed to a carved stone head ... the pagan god—**Baphomet**!' Teabing blurted ... **Baphomet** was a pagan fertility god associated with the creative force of reproduction. **Baphomet's** head was represented as that of a ram or goat, a common symbol of procreation and fecundity ... The modern belief in a horned devil known as Satan could be traced back to **Baphomet** and the Church's attempts to recast the horned fertility god as a symbol of evil." —DAN BROWN, *The Da Vinci Code*

Benedictine (BE nuh DIK tuhn, also BE nuh DIK TEEN) - *n., adj.* a monk or nun of the order founded by St. Benedict, c. 529 A.D., also known as the 'Black Monks' due to the color of their attire, 2. relating or belonging to the religious order founded by St. Benedict.

"In the same hotel was a **Benedictine** prior." —FRANCOIS VOLTAIRE, *Candide,* transl. by Richard Aldington

Carmelite (KAHR muh LYT) - *n.* and adj. a member of an order of mendicant friars belonging to the order of Our Lady of Mount Carmel. The order was founded in 1155. The members of the order were also called "White Friars" due to the white cloak that was part of their dress, 2. one of the order of Carmelite nuns, founded in 1452.

"I humanized him and sanctified my mother by making Lillian Meecham an emporium of human virtue with a saintliness that would become even **Carmelite** nuns." —PAT CONROY, *My Losing Season*

Dominican (duh MI ni kuhn) - *n., adj.* of or relating to the an order of preaching friars (and nuns) established in 1216 by St. Dominic, 2. *n.* a friar of the Dominican order, also called a "Black Friar."

"'In all Italy, we only write what we do not think; those who inhabit the country of the Caesars and the Antonines dare not have an idea without the permission of a **Dominican** monk.'" —FRANCOIS VOLTAIRE, *Candide,* transl. by Richard Aldington

Franciscan (fran SIS kuhn) - *n.* and *adj.* of or pertaining to the order of St. Francis of Assisi (founded in 1209), pertaining to the Franciscans, 2. a friar of the Franciscan order.

"'I was very innocent when you knew me. A **Franciscan** friar who was my confessor easily seduced me.'" –Francois Voltaire, *Candide*, transl. by Richard Aldington

hospitaller (also **hospitaler**) (HAHS PI tuhl uhr) - n. a member of a religious order, brotherhood or sisterhood founded among European crusaders to care for the sick and infirm in hospitals and for needy pilgrims. Founded in the 12th century in Jerusalem. More fully, Knights Hospitallers, the order followed chiefly the rule of St. Augustine and took on a military aspect and organization. The order grew to be a wealthy fraternity and became one of the primary bulwarks of Christendom in the East. The organization subsequently operated under many names including Brothers of the Hospital of St. John the Baptist, Knights of the Hospital of St. John of Jerusalem, Knights of Rhodes, Knights of Malta, etc. The order was suppressed in most European countries in or after 1799.

"To his enormous surprise, in 1984 this work came to the attention of a group of Catholics, who invited him to join the ancient order of the **Knights of Malta**." –George Crile, *Charlie Wilson's War*

Knights of Columbus (NYTZ uhv kuh LUHM buhs) - n. a benevolent and fraternal society of Roman Catholic men founded in 1882.

"That was the story people told, I don't know, nuns, old ladies on novena nights, maybe well-heeled parishioners too, pink and fit, officers of the **Knights of Columbus**." –Don DeLillo, *Underworld*

monastic (or **monastical**) (muh NAS tik) - *adj.* relating to or characteristic of life within a monastery or the communal life (of monks) sequestered from all others under religious vows.

"The Citadel in winter was a refuge of cold, **monastic** beauty to me ... Most of the time, the barracks were boisterous, noisy places, but always turned monastery—like when our trial by examinations began in earnest." –Pat Conroy, *My Losing Season*

Templar (TEM pluhr) - *n.* a knight of a religious military order founded c. 1118 for the protection of pilgrims visiting the Holy Land and the Holy Sepulcher. The name is derived from their occupation of a building on or contiguous to the site of the Temple of Solomon at Jerusalem. They were suppressed in 1312.

*see **Baphomet** for citation, page 147*

Theatine - *n., adj.* a member of an order of Italian monks (they bore various names, among them were: "Regular Clerks," "Pauline Monks," "Apostic Clerks") founded in 1524 by St. Cajetan along with John Peter Caraffa (at that time the Archbishop of Chieti and later Pope Paul IV). A corresponding order of nuns was founded c. 1600.

"While arguing about this important subject and waiting for Cunegonde, Candide noticed a young **Theatine** in the Piazza San Marco, with a girl on his arm. The Theatine looked fresh, plump and vigorous" –Francois Voltaire, *Candide*, transl. by Richard Aldington

Ursuline (UHR suh luhn, also UHR suh LYN) - *n., adj.* a member of an order of nuns established under the rule of St. Augustine in 1572 and devoted to the education of girls.

"... she learned that Mademoiselle Rouault had had her schooling in a convent, with the **Ursuline** nuns—had received, as the saying went, a 'fine education,' in the course of which she had been taught dancing, geography, drawing, needlework and a little piano." —GUSTAVE FLAUBERT, *Madame Bovary,* transl. by Francis Steegmuller

RELIGIOUS ART

Gethsemane (geth SE muh nee) - *n.* the location of the scene of Christ's agony, a garden on the Mount of Olives (Matt. 26:36–46), 2. Christ's agony in the garden represented in art, 3. an occasion of deep anguish, mental or physical.

"The atmosphere in the locker room at halftime felt like midnight at **Gethsemane.** I had never seen my teammates closer to despair." —PAT CONROY, *My Losing Season*

Panagia (also **Panaghia**) (PAHN uh GEE ah) - *n.* a name or title of the Virgin Mary from the Orthodox Eastern Church; the All-Holy, 2. a likeness or image of the Virgin Mary.

"And then she called on the **Panaghia,** using every one of her names. 'All-Holy, immaculate, most blessed and glorified Lady, Mother of God and Ever-Virgin, do you hear what my son Milton is saying?'" —JEFFREY EUGENIDES, *Middlesex*

Pantocrator (pan TAHK ruh tuhr) - *n.* a reference to God or Christ, 2. an artistic representation of the figure or form of Christ, esp. such a form in Byzantine art.

"Tessie and company advanced down the central aisle [of the church] ... Above, as big as a float in the Macy's Thanksgiving Day Parade, was the Christ **Pantocrator**. He curved across the dome like space itself. Unlike the suffering, earthbound Christs depicted at eye level of the church walls,

our Christ Pantocrator was clearly transcendent, all-powerful, heaven-bestriding." —JEFFREY EUGENIDES, *Middlesex*

Pietà (PEE ay TAH, also PYAY TAH) - *n.* an artistic representation, a painting or sculpture, of the Virgin Mary shown mourning the dead body of Christ she holds in her lap.

"Tatyana Nazarenko's *The Partisans Have Arrived,* an ironic **pietà** of help brought too late to a scene of German atrocity." —JOHN KEEGAN, *A History of Warfare*

shekinah (also **shechinah**) (shu KEE nuh, also shu KY nuh) - *n.* a visible manifestation of the Divine Majesty as described in Jewish theology; a refulgent light symbolizing the divine presence.

"Early Jews believed that the Holy of Holies in Solomon's Temple housed not only God but also His powerful female equal, **Shekinah**." —DAN BROWN, *The Da Vinci Code*

GREEK AND ROMAN MYTHS

Acheron (A kuh RAHN, also A kuh RUHN) - *n.* the river of woe in Hades; a fabulous river of the Lower World.

"I argued back to myself that it was just the Rio Grande I had to cross, not the **Acheron**, but anyway it oppressed me from somewhere." —SAUL BELLOW, *The Adventures of Augie March*

Acherontic (ach EH RON tik) - *adj.* relating to Acheron, infernal; dismal, gloomy, dark or moribund, 2. in wait to cross the river of death, tottering on the brink of the grave.

"Jude was too much affected to go on talking at first; she, too, was now such a mere cluster of nerves that all initiatory power seemed to have left her, and they proceeded through the fog like **Acherontic** shades for a long while, without sound or gesture." —THOMAS HARDY, *Jude the Obscure*

Achilles (uh KI leez) - *n.* the hero of Homer's Iliad, the son of Peleus and the Nereid Thetis, King of the Thessalian tribe of the Myrmidon, a fabled warrior for the Greeks at the siege of Troy and the slayer of Hector. When he was a baby, his mother bathed him in the magical River Styx making him invulnerable except in the heel by which his mother held him. He was fatally wounded in the heel by an arrow shot by Paris, Hector's younger brother.

"He knew the wrath of **Achilles**, the rage of Philoctetes, the fulminations of Medea, the madness of Ajax, the despair of Electra, and the suffering of Prometheus the many horrors that can ensue when the highest degree of indignation is achieved and, in the name of justice, retribution is exacted and a cycle of retaliation begins." —PHILIP ROTH, *The Human Stain*

Aeneas (i NEE uhs) - *n.* the Trojan hero of Virgil's epic poem the Aeneid. He is the son of Anchises and Venus. He escaped the sack of Troy and is revered as the ancestral hero of the Romans.

"In the ancient myths, gods favoring mortals often hid them away. Aphrodite blotted out Paris once, saving him from certain death at the hands of Menelaus. She wrapped **Aeneas** in a coat to sneak him off the battlefield." —JEFFREY EUGENIDES, *Middlesex*

Aeolus (EE uh luhs) - (from Greek mythology) *n.* the god of the winds, 2. King of Thessaly and the Aeolian Islands, ancestor of the Aeolians.

"What did I wish for at seven? I don't remember. In the film I lean forward and, **Aeolian**, blow the candles out." —JEFFREY EUGENIDES, *Middlesex*

Ajax (AY JAKS) - *n.* the son of Telamon and Salamis. A Greek hero in the Trojan War, second only to Achilles, a warrior of great stature and prowess.

"I remember I used to look, in those days, upon every three-volume novel with a sort of veneration, as a feat—not possibly of literature—but at least of physical and moral endurance and the courage of **Ajax**." —ROBERT LOUIS STEVENSON, INTRODUCTION, *Treasure Island*

Andromache (an DRAH muh KEE) - *n.* the wife of Hector and mother of Astyanax, captured by the Greeks at the fall of Troy, eventually becoming the wife of Hector's brother Helenus.

"Jude's Arabella and Sue, by contrast, are very different figures, sisters not of **Andromache** and Desdemona but of Molly Bloom and Hedda Gabler." —JOHN BAYLEY, *Introduction to Thomas Hardy's Jude the Obscure*

Antaeus (ahn TEE uhs) - *n.* a giant wrestler (son of Earth and Sea, Ge and Poseidon) invicible as long as he remained in contact with his mother, the earth; killed by Hercules who lifted him from the earth and squeezed him to death.

"Street-smart Hercules! When he wrestled with **Antaeus**, the Libyan giant whose mother was the Earth itself, he hoisted him in the air. Why? Because he knew that the giant's strength depended entirely on contact with his mother; when no part of his body touched her, he was helpless. And so Hercules was able to crush the monster, known for killing everyone else he had wrestled with." –GRACE GLUECK, *The New York Times, 10/15/04*

Antigone (an TI guh NEE) - *n.* the daughter of Oedipus and Jocasta, she was the Greek ideal of filial and sisterly fidelity. She defies her Uncle Creon by performing funeral rites over her brother's body. A series of family tragedies follows this act, including the suicides of Antigone, Haemon (Creon's son), and Eurydice (Creon's wife). Also a drama by Sophocles, based on these events, possibly performed in 442 or 441 B.C.

"'As **Antigone** said, I am neither a dweller among men nor ghosts.'" –THOMAS HARDY, *Jude the Obscure*

Aphrodite (A fruh DY tee) - *n.* the Greek goddess of love and beauty, daughter of Zeus. The most important of Aphrodite's mortal lovers were the Trojan shepherd Anchises, by whom she bore Aeneas, and the handsome youth Adonis. Aphrodite was identified by the Romans with Venus.

*see **Aeneas** for citation*

Apollonian (A puh LOH nee uhn) - *adj.* relating to or having the characteristics of Apollo, the Greek and Roman sun god, the patron of music and poetry, 2. noble; high-minded.

"Benedict proposed the existence of two main cultural forms, **Apollonian** and Dionysian, the former authoritarian, the latter permissive." –JOHN KEEGAN, *A History of Warfare*

argonaut (AHR guh NOT, also AHR guh NAHT) - *n.* one of the legendary heroes who sailed with Jason on the Argo in search of the Golden Fleece, 2. a person embarking on a dangerous but rewarding quest.

"Percy Cuthfert's evil star must have been in the ascendant, for he, too, joined this company of **argonauts** [in the quest for Klondike gold]." –JACK LONDON, *In a Far Country*

Asclepius (uh SKLEE pee uhs) - *n.* the Greek god of medicine, son of Apollo. He was typically represented standing, dressed in a long cloak, with bare breast, holding a staff with a serpent coiled around it (a "caduceus"). The staff became a symbol of medicine.

"Some wanted diagnosis, as if I were a professional head-feeler and not the humble understudy's understudy of the cult of **Asclepius** the Maritime Commission had made me." –SAUL BELLOW, *The Adventures of Augie March*

Athene (uh THEE NEE) - *n.* the Greek goddess of wisdom, the useful arts, and warfare; guardian of Athens, which was named after her. Daughter of Zeus, she sprang full-armored from his head. Athene corresponded to the Roman Minerva.

"There were ... busts of Pericles and Cicero and **Athena**, and who-else-not." –SAUL BELLOW, *The Adventures of Augie March*

Atreus (AY TROOS, also AY tree uhs) - *n.* King of Mycenae, brother of Thyestes, father of Agamemnon and Menelaus.

"The chief importance of the story of **Atreus** and his descendants is that the fifth-century [B.C.] tragic poet Aeschylus took it for the subject of his greatest drama, the Oresteia, which is made up of three plays, the Agamemnon, the Libation Bearers, the Eumenides. It has no rival in Greek tragedy except for the four plays of Sophocles about Oedipus and his children." –EDITH HAMILTON, *Mythology*

Attis (AT ihs) - *n.* the mythical consort of Cybele—the Great Mother of the Gods. The Goddess drove him mad from jealousy whereupon he castrated himself and died.

"One of that old sister-society whose pins and barrettes and little jars and combs from Assyria or Crete lie so curious with the wavy prongs and stained gold and green—gnawed bronze in museum cases—those sacred girls laid in the bed by the priests to wait for the secret night visit of **Attis** or whoever, the maidens who took part in the hot annual battles of gardens, amorous ditty singers, Syrians, Amorites, Moabites, and so on." –SAUL BELLOW, *The Adventures of Augie March*

Augean (o JEE uhn) - *adj.* exceedingly filthy, esp. from long neglect (from Augeas, Greek king who did not clean his stables for thirty years; Hercules was said to purify it in a single day by turning the river Alpheus through it).

"In the latter days of his **Augean** labors to purge England of the unclean thing which had fastened upon her, my friend was more lean and nervous-looking than I had ever known him." –SAX ROHMER, *The Insidious Dr. Fu-Manchu*

bacchanal (BA kuh nahl, also BA kuh NAL) - *n.* a drunken or riotous celebration, originally in honor of Bacchus (Roman god of wine), 2. a participant in such a celebration, 3. a reveler.

see other **bacchanal** *entry for citation, p. 51*

Cadmus (KAD muhs) - *n.* King of Phoenicia and Telephassa, reputed to have introduced the Greek alphabet. He killed a dragon and sowed its teeth into the ground from which sprang up armed men who fought each other until only five remained. These five helped him to found the city of Thebes.

"The slow progress of beauty into decay and into beauty continued, and like the serpent's teeth that **Cadmus** sowed, the blood of evil watered Roman earth and brought about rebirth." –IAN CALDWELL AND DUSTIN THOMASON, *The Rule of Four*

Calliope (kuh LIE uh PEE) - n. the muse of eloquence and epic poetry; one of nine muses and the mother of Orpheus by Apollo.

"'**Calliope** was one of the Muses, right?'

'Right.'

'In charge of what?'

'Epic poetry.'" –JEFFREY EUGENIDES, *Middlesex*

Calypso (kuh LIP soh) - *n.* a sea nymph, queen of the island of Ogygia upon which Ulysses wrecked. Calypso kept Ulysses for seven years promising him perpetual youth and immortality if he were to stay with her forever.

"After leaving **Calypso**, during his return journey, [Odysseus] was shipwrecked in Phaeacia, whose king welcomed him to his court. There he was a foreigner, a mysterious stranger. A stranger gets asked 'Who are you? Where do you come from? Tell us!' and he had told. For four long books of the Odyssey he had retraced in detail his adventures before the dazzled Phaeacians. But in Ithaca he was not a stranger, he was one of their own, so it never occurred to anyone to say, 'Tell us!'" —MILAN KUNDERA, *Ignorance*

Cassandra (kuh SAN druh, also kuh SAHN druh) - *n.* daughter of Priam, King of Troy, and Hecuba. Cassandra had the power of prophecy but was fated by Apollo, whose advances she had refused, never to be believed, although her predictions were invariably correct.

"He wondered whether his pyloric valve might be trying, **Cassandra**like, to tell him something." —JOHN KENNEDY TOOLE, *A Confederacy of Dunces*

Ceres (SIR EEZ) - *n.* the Roman name of Mother Earth, the goddess or protectress of agriculture.

"From the Olympian heights has flown Mother **Ceres** swift to find Her dear lost Proserpine, her own." —FYODOR DOSTOYEVSKY, *The Brothers Karamazov*, transl. by David Magarshack (possibly quoting Schiller)

Circe (SUHR SEE) - *n.* a goddess; a sorceress who turned Ulysses' men into swine temporarily and later directed them home. Ulysses resisted the change by virtue of the herb moly, given to him by Mercury.

"Well, it was hard to take this from wild nature, that there should be humanity mixed with it; such as there was in the beasts that embraced Odysseus and his men and wept on them in **Circe**'s yard." —SAUL BELLOW, *The Adventures of Augie March*

Clytemnestra (KLY tuhm NES truh) - *n.* wife of Agamemnon who, with help from her paramour Aegisthus, murdered Agamemnon upon his return from the Trojan War, she was later killed by her son, Orestes.

"There was nothing to be gained by her going any further than the break-in story, and much to be lost if '**clytemnestra @houseofatreus.com**' were somehow discovered to be her brainchild." —PHILIP ROTH, *The Human Stain*

Comus (KOH muhs) - *n.* the god of festivity and revelry.

"These sickening scoundrels had merely intended to keep me back, and presently to fall upon me with a fate more horrible than death, with torture, and after torture the most hideous degradation it was possible to conceive—to send me off, a lost soul, a beast, to the rest of their **Comus** rout." —H.G. WELLS, *The Island of Dr. Moreau*

Cressida (KRE suh duh) - (from Greek mythlogy) *n.* a Trojan woman first in love with Troilus, but later forsaking him and defecting to the Greek side to love Diomedes.

"'... **Cressida** going over to the Greek camp ...'" —SAUL BELLOW, *The Adventures of Augie March*

Daedalus (DE duhl uhs, also DEE duhl uhs) - (from Greek mythology) *n.* an Athenian inventor and architect, who built the Labyrinth of Minos for King Minos of Crete, imprisoning himself in it. To escape the labyrinth he fashioned wings for himself and his son, Icarus. Icarus flew too close to the sun and fell to the sea, Daedalus reached Sicily safely.

> "My grandfather ... had splurged on four tickets to The Minotaur ... When the curtain rose at the Family Theater, my relatives expected to get the whole story. How Minos, King of Crete, failed to sacrifice a white bull to Poseidon. How Poseidon, enraged, caused Minos's wife Pasiphaë to be smitten with love for a bull. How the child of that union, Asterius, came out with a bull's head attached to a human body. And then **Daedalus**, the maze, etc." —JEFFREY EUGENIDES, *Middlesex*

Damocles, sword of (DA muh KLEEZ) - *n.* an object of Greek legend: Damocles, a servile courtier to King Dionysius, gave the king frequent and obsequious flattery. The king grew weary of this flattery and held a banquet, seating Damocles under a sword hung by a single hair, thus pointing out to Damocles the precariousness of the king's position and to demonstrate that kingship brought fears and worries as well as pleasures, 2. an impending disaster.

> "She was dangling the butcher knife over Annelise's head like a miniature **sword of Damocles**." —GREG ILES, *Sleep No More*

Danaë (DA nuh EE) - (from Greek mythology) *n.* the daughter of Eurydice and King Acrisius of Argos, she was imprisoned by her father who had been told that one day his daughter's son would kill him. She was saved by Jupiter, who came to her in the disguise of a shower of gold, and bore his son Perseus.

> "The ring, an eighteenth-century copy of a Roman signet ring, was a man-sized ring formerly worn by a man. On the oval agate, set horizontally which was what

made the ring so masculinely chunky— was a carving of **Danaë** receiving Zeus as a shower of gold." —PHILIP ROTH, *The Human Stain*

Demeter (di MEE tuhr) - (from Greek mythology) *n.* the goddess of the harvest and the protectress of marriage. One of the great Olympian deities, she is the daughter of Rhea and mother of Persephone (Proserpine; see Thesmophoria).

Dionysian (DY uh NI zhee uhn, also Dy uh NEE zhee uhn) - *adj.* of or relating to Dionysus or the Dionysia, festivals held in honor of Dionysus, 2. devoted to the worship of Dionysus.

> "Benedict proposed the existence of two main cultural forms, Apollonian and **Dionysian**, the former authoritarian, the latter permissive." —JOHN KEEGAN, *A History of Warfare*

Dionysus (DY uh NI shee uhs, also DY uh NI shus) - (from Greek mythology) *n.* the god of wine and fertility.

> "Surely, as the outnumbered Greek hoplites crashed into their lines, the Persians must have at last understood that these men worshipped not only the god Apollo, but the wild, irrational **Dionysus** as well." —V. HANSON, QUOTED BY JOHN KEEGAN, *A History of Warfare*

Electra (i LEK truh) - (from Greek mythology) *n.* daughter of Clytemnestra and Agamemnon who avenged her father's murder with her brother Orestes by slaying their mother and her lover, Aegisthus, 2. one of the Pleiades, wife of Darbanus, she disappeared before the Trojan War to be saved from witnessing the ruin of her beloved city (known at "the Lost Pleiad").

*see **Achilles** for citation, p. 150*

Fortuna (for TOO NAH) - (from Roman mythology) *n.* the goddess of fortune and good luck; the goddess of chance.

"**Fortuna's** wheel has turned on humanity, crushing its collarbone, smashing its skull, twisting its torso, puncturing its pelvis, sorrowing its soul." —JOHN KENNEDY TOOLE, *A Confederacy of Dunces*

Galatea (GA luh TEE uh) - (from Greek mythology) *n.* a sea-nymph, in love with Acis but beloved by Polypheme. Polypheme, a jealous giant, crushed Acis and Galatea threw herself into the sea, 2. a statue created by Pygmalian and brought to life by Aphrodite in answer to Pygmalian's pleas. She caused great mischief and ultimately returned to her original state.

"He's a **Galatea** in the market for a Pygmalion—more to the point, a Paula Abdul searching for a Janet Jackson." —JOANNE KAUFMAN, *The Wall Street Journal, 9/5/03*

Hector (HEK tuhr) - (from Greek mythology) *n.* noblest of all the Trojan chieftains, eldest son of Priam and Hecuba, he was killed by Achilles, as told in Homer's Iliad.

"Clinton's [autobiography] is about being a president at the end of the 20th century. Grant's is an Iliad, with the gracious Robert E. Lee as **Hector** and Grant himself the murderous Achilles." —LARRY MC-MURTRY, *The New York Times Book Review, 7/4/04*

Hecuba (HE kyoo buh) - (from Greek mythology) *n.* wife of Priam, mother of Hector, Paris and Cassandra, she was taken prisoner when Troy was captured by the Greeks.

"It's supposed to be easier to suffer for hypothetical people too, for **Hecubas**. It ought to be easier than for the ones you yourself hurt, for you see their enemies or persecutors better than you can see yourself balking someone of life or doing him wrong." —SAUL BELLOW, *The Adventures of Augie March*

Helios (HEE lee uhs, also HEE lee OHS) - (from Greek mythology) *n.* the sun god, son of the Titan Hyperion. Helios was said to drive the chariot of the sun across the sky from east to west each day.

"'The rising and setting of the sun was once attributed to **Helios** and a flaming chariot.'" —DAN BROWN, *Angels & Demons*

Hermaphroditus (HUHR MAH fruh DY tuhs) - (from Greek mythology) *n.* the son of Hermes and Aphrodite, he spurned the nymph Salmacis and she punished him with an embrace in which their bodies became united, creating a new body with both male and female characteristics.

"'Once upon a time in ancient Greece, there was an enchanted pool. This pool was sacred to Salmacis, the water nymph. And one day **Hermaphroditus**, a beautiful boy, went swimming there ... Ladies

and Gentlemen, behold the god Hermaphroditus! Half woman, half man!'"
—JEFFREY EUGENIDES, *Middlesex*

Hermes (HUHR MEEZ) - (from Greek mythology) *n.* the god of commerce, invention, cunning, and theft. Also known as the messenger of the gods and the conductor of the dead to Hades. Because he was considered to be a dream god, Greeks often offered him the last libation before sleep. Hermes was the son of Zeus and Maia; often identified with the Roman god Mercury.

"Hermaphroditus's parents were **Hermes** and Aphrodite. Ovid doesn't tell us how they felt after their child went missing."
—JEFFREY EUGENIDES, *Middlesex*

Hesperides (he SPER uh DEEZ) - (from Greek mythology) *n.* a group of three to seven nymphs, daughters of Hesperus, who, along with a watchful dragon, guarded over a garden in which golden apples grew on the Isles of the Blest, 2. the garden guarded by the nymphs, 3. a fabled garden at the western end of the earth, beyond the Pillars of Hercules, where golden apples grow.

"I might have confessed even worse, if I'd cared to, since Simon had decided on the roughest treatment for me and sent me on errands not exactly for **Hesperides** apples." —SAUL BELLOW, *The Adventures of Augie March*

Hyperion (hy PIR ee uhn) - (from Greek mythology) *n.* a Titan, the son of Uranus and Gaea, the father of Helios, Selene and Eos, he owned the island of Thrinakia and there Lampetia and Phaethusa tended to his cattle.

"... when she argued against my sympathy with these gilded **Hyperion's** kids [re-

ferring to Mexican lizards] made me laugh and also squirm." —SAUL BELLOW, *The Adventures of Augie March*

ichor (EYE KOR, also EYE kuhr) - (from Greek mythology) *n.* the rarified, ethereal fluid flowing through the veins of the gods, 2. a watery, acrid fluid from a wound, sore or ulcer.

"What a monster he's caressing! What terrifying **ichor** flows through her veins."
—MICHEL FABER, *The Crimson Petal and the White*

Janus (JAY nuhs) - (from Roman mythology) *n.* the god of doorways, passages and gates, patron of beginnings and endings. Depicted as having two faces looking in opposite directions. The name of the month of January comes from Janus.

"**Janus**, the killer thought. A code name, obviously. Was it a reference, he wondered, to the Roman two-faced god ... or to the moon of Saturn?" —DAN BROWN, *Angels & Demons*

Jove (JOHV) - (from Roman mythology) an alternate name for Jupiter (Zeus in Greek mythology). The supreme god of the Romans, the supreme deity of classical antiquity, father of gods and men.

"I had originally thought to borrow Elias's costume—with an appropriate sense of self, my friend had planned on attending dressed as **Jove**, and we traveled to his lodgings, where I found that the Olympian's robes fit too snug upon me."
—DAVID LISS, *A Conspiracy of Paper*

Jupiter (JOO puh tuhr) - (from Roman mythology) *n.* an alternate name for Jove (Zeus in Greek mythology). The supreme god of the Romans, the supreme deity of classical antiquity, father of gods and men. In his flirtations he often appeared in the shape of an animal.

> "'He merely again touched lightly and ironically upon 'fictitious tales' and 'psychology' and interpolated at the appropriate place, '**Jupiter,** thou art angry, therefore thou art wrong', which provoked a burst of approving laughter in the audience, for our public prosecutor certainly bore no resemblance to **Jupiter**." –FYODOR DOSTOYEVSKY, *The Brothers Karamazov*, transl. by David Magarshack

Laocoön (lay AH kuh WAHN) - (from Greek mythology) *n.* the Trojan priest of Apollo who was crushed to death, along with his two sons, by two sea serpents as revenge for having warned the Trojans to beware of Greeks bearing gifts when they were presented with the Trojan horse, described by Virgil in the Aenid, 2. often depicted in statues representing he and his sons in their death-struggle.

> "But that relief [of screaming] being denied to his virility, he clenched his teeth in misery, bringing lines about his mouth like those in the **Laocoön**, and corrugations between his brows." –THOMAS HARDY, *Jude the Obscure*

Leda (LEE duh) - (from Greek mythology) *n.* Queen of Sparta, wife of Tyndareus, mother of Castor and Clytemnestra by her husband, and mother of Helen of Troy and Pollux by Zeus, who came to her in the form of a swan.

> "... the mythological queen **Leda** is caught in the heat of passion with Zeus, who is shown lodged between her thighs in the shape of a swan." –IAN CALDWELL AND DUSTIN THOMASON, *The Rule of Four*

Lethe (LEE thee) - (from Greek mythology: the river in Hades the waters of which cause forgetfulness) *n.* - forgetfulness, oblivion.

> "'First, you descend into your emotional life with a doctor as your guide, and then the repressed memories are washed away in the **Lethe**.'" –GLEN DAVID GOLD, *Carter Beats the Devil*

Medea (muh DEE uh) - (from Greek mythology) *n.* a sorceress and the princess of Colchis, daughter of Aeetes and wife of Jason. Through her sorcery she helped Jason obtain the Golden Fleece from her father. After Jason left her to marry Creusa, Medea killed her own and Jason's children as revenge.

*see **Achilles** for citation, p. 150*

Melpomene (mel PAH muh NEE) - (from Greek mythology) *n.* the Muse of tragedy, one of the nine Muses.

> "Him they found to be in the habit of sitting silent, his quaint and weird face set, and his eyes resting on things they did not see in the substantial world. 'His face is like the tragic mask of **Melpomene**,' said Sue." –THOMAS HARDY, *Jude the Obscure*

Menelaus (ME nuhl AY uhs) - (from Greek mythology) *n.* the king of Sparta during the Trojan War, husband of Helen of Troy.

*see **Aeneas** for citation, p. 150*

Minos (MY nuhs) - (from Greek mythology) *n.* a king of Crete, son of Zeus and Europa. He ordered Daedalus to build the labyrinth. After his death he was made one of three judges in the underworld.

*see **Daedalus** for citation, p. 154*

Nemea (NEE mee uh) - *n.* a valley in ancient Greece, where the Nemean games were held, c. 573 B.C. (Nemean—of or pertaining to Nemea), 2. from Greek mythology—designating a fierce lion said to have terrorized the Nemean region until killed by Hercules as the first of his twelve labors.

> "The only way my father could think to instill in me a sense of my heritage was to take me to dubbed Italian versions of the ancient Greek myths. And so, every week, we saw Hercules slaying the **Nemean** lion, or stealing the girdle of the Amazons ..." –JEFFREY EUGENIDES, *Middlesex*

Nemesis (NE muh suhs) - (from Greek mythology) *n.* the goddess of divine retribution, retributive justice and vengeance, 2. a cause of misery, of death; a bane, 3. the cause of just punishment; just retribution; avenger, 4. an invincible rival.

> "The better class of men, even if caught by airy affectations of dodging and parrying, is not retained by them. A **Nemesis** attends the woman who plays the game of elusiveness too often, in the utter contempt for her that, sooner or later, her old admirers feel; under which they allow her to go unlamented to her grave." –THOMAS HARDY, *Jude the Obscure*

Nereid (NIR ee uhd) - (from Greek mythology) *n.* any one of the fifty to one hundred sea nymphs, the beautiful daughters of the sea god Nereus and Doris; they played, danced and were wooed by the Tritons. The three best known were Amphitrite, Thetis and Galatea.

> "Dawdling infants are being tugged away from sandcastles by their parents; promenading dandies are heading for cover; oddly costumed **nereids** are emerging from the sea and disappearing into bathing-machines." –MICHEL FABER, *The Crimson Petal and the White*

Orpheus (OR FYOOS, also OR fee uhs) - (from Greek mythology) *n.* an ancient Greek poet and musician of superhuman skills. His music is said to have the power to move animals, trees, and rocks to dance. When his wife, Euridice, died he went to Hades to bring her back but failed.

> "The source of the music was none other than a Brylcreemed **Orpheus** who lived directly behind her. Milton Stephanides, a twenty-year-old college student, stood at his own bedroom window, dexterously fingering his clarinet." –JEFFREY EUGENIDES, *Middlesex*

pantheon (PANT thee AHN, also PANT thee uhn) - *n.* all the gods of a people, 2. a temple dedicated to all the gods, 3. a monument or public building memorializing the dead, esp. the famous dead, heroes or heroines of a country, 4. Pantheon—a circular temple in Rome dedicated to all the gods, completed in 27 B.C.

Paris (PAR uhs) - (among other definitions, from Greek mythology) *n.* the son of Priam, King of Troy and Hecuba; his abduction of Helen provoked the Trojan War. He killed Achilles with a poisoned arrow.

*see **Aeneas** for citation, p. 150*

Pasiphae (puh SI fuh EE) - (from Greek mythology) *n.* wife of Minos and mother of the Minotaur (by a white bull), a half-man, half-bull monster.

*see **Daedalus** for citation, p. 154*

Phaeacians (FEE AY shunz) - *n.* a seafaring, god-like people fond of food, music and dance, they received Ulysses hospitably.

*see **Calypso** for citation, p. 152*

Phaedra (FAY druh) - (from Greek mythology) *n.* the daughter of Pasiphae, half-sister of the Minotaur, wife of Theseus. She killed herself after falsely accusing Hippolytus, her stepson, of rape after he had rejected her advances. Hippolytus was killed but his innocence was ultimately revealed.

> "The deep consideration women give, as seen privately in their thoughtful eye, to demands for the most part outlawed out of fear for everything that has been done to make a reasonable, continuous life, the burden that made **Phedra** cry she wanted to throw off her harmful clothes, you could find that in Lucy too." –SAUL BELLOW, *The Adventures of Augie March*

Phaëthon (FAY uh tuhn) - (from Greek mythology) *n.* son of Helios (Phoebus), killed by Zeus with a thunderbolt while attempting to drive his father's chariot of the sun across the sky and losing control of the vehicle.

> "He was, in short, a Bohemian from the Land of Many Marvels, adventurous, but not an adventurer, a daredevil, a **Phaëthon** driving the chariot of the sun at top speed, an Icarus with extra set of wings." –JULES VERNE, *From the Earth to the Moon*

Philoctetes (fi LAHK tuh TEEZ, also FI lahk TEE TEEZ) - (from Greek mythology) *n.* an archer with the Greeks against Troy. Upon his death, Hercules gave Philoctetes his arrows. Philoctetes used these arrows to slay Paris at Troy.

*see **Achilles** for citation, p. 150*

Phlegethon (FLE guh THAHN) - (from Greek mythology) *n.* the river of fire, one of the five rivers of Hades.

> "Looking down from this pinnacle upon the howling **Phlegethon** below ... it ap-

peared to me, in fact, a self-evident thing, that the largest ships of the line in existence, coming within the influence of that deadly attraction, could resist it as little as a feather the hurricane, and must disappear bodily and at once." –EDGAR ALLAN POE, *A Descent into the Maelström*

Phoebe (FEE BEE) - (from Greek mythology) *n.* another name for Artemis or Diana, the goddess of the moon, 2. a personification of the moon.

> "The Egyptians called her Isis; the Phoenicians gave her the name Astarte; the Greeks worshipped her under the name of **Phoebe,** daughter of Latona and Jupiter, and they explained her eclipses by the mysterious visits of Diana to the handsome Endymion." –JULES VERNE, *From the Earth to the Moon*

Phoebus (FEE buhs) - (from Greek mythology) *n.* a name for Apollo, the god of the sun, 2. a personification of the sun (see **Phaëthon**).

Pleiades (PLEE uh DEEZ, also PLAY uh DEEZ) - (from Greek mythology) *n.* the seven daughters of Atlas and Pleione, Zeus placed them among the stars, 2. a cluster of several hundred stars, only six of which are visible to the eye, in the constellation Taurus, the seventh being lost (representing the "Lost Pleiad," see **Electra**).

Poseidon (puh SY duhn) - (from Greek mythology) *n.* the god of the sea, water, earthquakes and horses; the brother of Zeus and Pluto, son of Cronos and Rhea, husband of Amphitrite. Identified with the Roman god Neptune.

*see **Daedalus** for citation, p. 154*

priapic (pry AY pik, also pry AH pik) - *adj.* phallic, 2. preoccupied with virility or masculinity.

*see other **priapic** entry for citation, p. 19*

Priapus (pry AY puhs, also pry AH puhs) - (from Greek and Roman mythology) *n.* the god of proceation, guardian of gardens and vineyards, personifying the erect phallus and the male procreative power; son of Dionysus and Aphrodite, 2. priapus—the phallus.

"'What about **Priapus**? Doesn't he have any say in all this?'" –TOM WOLFE, *A Man in Full*

Procrustes (pruh KRUHS teez) - (from Greek mythology) *n.* a legendary robber or highwayman of Attica, he captured travelers and tied them to his iron bed; he stretched the short ones and cut short the legs of the tall ones to make them fit its length. He was killed in the same manner by Theseus.

"Taft stands at the podium, fat and shaggy as ever. Seeing him, I think of **Procrustes**, the mythological highwayman who tortured his victims by stretching them on a bed if they were too short, or cutting them down to size if they were too

tall." –IAN CALDWELL AND DUSTIN THOMASON, *The Rule of Four*

Prometheus (proh MEE thee uhs, also proh MEE thyuhs) - (from Greek mythology) *n.* a Titan, a demigod; he made man out of clay and stole fire from Mount Olympus and gave it to man. He was punished by Zeus by being chained to a rock in the Caucasus where an eagle (or vulture) devored his liver, which grew back daily. He was ultimately rescued by Hercules.

*see **Achilles** for citation, p. 150*

Proserpine (Greek - **Persephone**) (PRAH suhr PYN) - (from Roman mythology) *n.* daughter of Ceres, wife of Pluto, she was carried off to Pluto's realm to become his wife and the goddess of the underworld. Identified with Persephone in Greek mythology.

*see **Ceres** for citation, p. 153*

protean (PRO tee un, also pro TEE un) - *adj.* of or pertaining to Proteus; characteristic of Proteus, 2. exceedingly variable; changeable; readily assuming different shapes or forms.

*see other **protean** entry for citation, p. 23*

Proteus (PROH tee uhs) - (from Greek mythology) *n.* a sea god, he could change his shape or appearance at will; an attendant to Poseidon, 2. (often p-) a person who changes his appearance or principles easily.

Psyche (SY KEE) - (from Greek mythology) *n.* a lovely young maiden, loved by Cupid (Eros) who visited her only at night, she personifies the human soul; through Cupid's prayers, Psyche was made immortal and came to symbolize immortality.

"'Used to call her Voluptas. **Psyche's** daughter. The personification to the Romans of sensual pleasure.'" —PHILIP ROTH, *The Human Stain*

Pygmalion (pig MAYL yuhn, also pig MAY lee uhn) - (from Greek mythology) *n.* a sculptor, he carved and then fell in love with a statue of a woman, which Aphrodite then brought to life as Galatea, 2. a play by George Bernard Shaw based on the same theme (1856–1950), which was the basis for the film *My Fair Lady.*

"Under the auspices of Aphrodite, in the guise of **Pygmalion**, and in the environs of Tanglewood, was the retired classics professor now bringing recalcitrant, transgressive Faunia to life as a tastefully civilized Galatea?" —PHILIP ROTH, *The Human Stain*

Rhadamanthus (RA duh MANT thus) - (from Greek mythology) *n.* son of Zeus and Europa, he was rewarded for his rigorous sense of justice by being made a judge of the underworld after his death, 2. an inflexible judge; a severe or rigorous master.

"He accordingly addressed a carefully considered epistle to Sue, and, knowing her emotional temperament, threw a **Rhadamanthine** strictness into the lines here and there." —THOMAS HARDY, *Jude the Obscure*

Saturn (SA tuhrn) - (from Roman mythology) *n.* the god of agriculture and vegetation, he was said to have devoured all his children except Jupiter (air), Neptune (water), and Pluto (the grave); identified with Cronus in Greek mythology.

"I told myself that after the war I'd get a real start, but I couldn't do it while the whole earth was busy in this hell-making project, or man-eating **Saturns** were picking guys up left and right around me." —SAUL BELLOW, *The Adventures of Augie March*

saturnalia (SA tuhr NAYL yuh, also SA tuhr NAY lee uh) - *n.* a celebration characterized by unrestrained merrymaking, revelry and often licentiousness, 2. Saturnalia—an ancient Roman festival of Saturn lasting for seven days beginning December 17.

*see other **saturnalia** entry for citation, p. 51*

Silenus (sy LEE nuhs) - (from Greek mythology) *n.* a satyr, son of Pan, chief of the sileni or older satyrs, he is usually depicted as jolly and drunken, having a bald head, pug nose and pimply face.

"'And **Silenus**, red of face, Upon his stumbling ass—You see, I haven't drunk a quarter of a bottle [of brandy] and I'm not **Silenus**.'" —FYODOR DOSTOYEVSKY, *The Brothers Karamazov*, transl. by David Magarshack (possibly quoting Schiller)

Sisyphean (SI suh FEE uhn) - (from Greek mythology) *adj.* of or relating to Sisyphus, 2. endlessly laborious or toilsome, useless, futile.

"... to dry [the wet pans and platters and utensils] seemed a task as **Sisyphean** as to repair the things wrong with his parents' house." —JONATHAN FRANZEN, *The Corrections*

Sisyphus (SI suh fuhs) - (from Greek mythology) *n.* a cruel, greedy king of Corinth, he was forever condemned in Hades to roll a huge stone uphill which always rolled back down.

Stentor - (from Greek mythology) *n.* a herald in the Trojan War, said to have the voice of fifty men; he died after losing a shouting contest with Hermes, 2. a person with an unusually loud voice.

stentorian (sten TOR ee uhn) - *adj.* extremely loud, a very loud voice.

> "At the Continental Congress, [John Adams] was a 'virtual secretary of war' and an impassioned advocate of independence, rivaling even Patrick Henry's **stentorian** voice." –JAY WINIK, *The Wall Street Journal, 3/24/05*

Tantalus (or **Tantalos**) (TAN tuhl uhs) - (from Greek mythology) *n.* a son of Zeus, a wicked king, a friend to the gods, he offended them by revealing their secrets to mortals. For this he was punished and condemned in Hades to stand in water that flowed from him when he tried to drink it and beneath fruit that wafted away in the wind when he tried to grasp it (hence the word tantalize).

> "**Tantalus** and his grapes had nothing on me: when I wanted Katie, all I got was Colonna; when I tried to focus on Colonna, all I could think of was sleep; and when, at last, I tried to sleep, the knock would come at our door, and it would be time for another jog with Katie." –IAN CALDWELL AND DUSTIN THOMASON, *The Rule of Four*

terpsichorean (TUHRP SI kuh REE uhn, also TUHRP suh KOHR ee uhn) - (from Greek mythology) *adj.* of or relating to the dance, or the Terpsichore, Greek Muse of dance, 2. *n.* a dancer.

> "She doesn't dance very well—it's her first day on the job as a tiki girl—but the quirky Becky ... can out-tiki Paul's rich fiancée ... in every department but the **terpsichorean**." –JOE MORGENSTERN, *The Wall Street Journal, 1/17/03*

Theseus (THEE SOOS, also THEE see uhs) - (from Greek mythology) *n.* a hero and King of Athens, he slew the Minotaur and united Attica, among his many other good deeds.

> "On the screen an actor in a bad wig appears. 'That's **Theseus**,' Milton explains. He's got this ball of string his girlfriend gave him, see. And he's using it to find his way back out of the maze.'" –JEFFREY EUGENIDES, *Middlesex*

Thesmophoria (thes moh FOH ree uh) - *n.* an ancient Greek festival in honor of Demeter, held by women.

> "As soon as the women signed [the union form] there was a wild excitement and uprush of indignation and they began to call out, as if it was a working woman's **Thesmophoria** of these pale people." –SAUL BELLOW, *The Adventures of Augie March*

Tiresias (ty REE see uhs) - (from Greek mythology) *n.* a blind Theban soothsayer; he revealed to Oedipus that he had killed his father and married his mother. One legend had Tiresias being turned temporarily into a woman.

> "(And I **Tiresias** have foresuffered all Enacted on this same divan or bed; I who have sat by Thebes below the wall And walked among the lowest of the dead.)" –T.S. ELIOT, *The Waste Land*

Titan (TY tuhn) - (from Greek mythology) *n.* any one of a family of giant deities, the children of Uranus and Gaea, they were overthrown by the Olympian gods, 2. the largest of Saturns ten moons, 3. titan—one of great size, strength or power.

> "... in the weird light they appeared less like natural cliffs and more like the ruins of cyclopean and **Titan**-reared battlements jutting from the mountain-slope." –ROBERT E. HOWARD, *Cthulhu*

Triton (TRY tuhn) - (from Greek mythology) *n.* a sea god, son of Poseidon and Amphitrite, he is portrayed as having the head and trunk of a man and the tail of a fish and carrying a trumpet made of a conch shell, 2. the larger of the two moons of Neptune.

"... like Greece in the mythological age before history began, men still share their world with beings that are not men, as the characters in Greek myths move through landscapes still inhabited by dryads and nymphs, **tritons**, fauns, satyrs, centaurs, and unearthly hybrid monsters." —LIN CARTER, *Tolkien*

Vesta (VES tuh) - (from Roman mythology) *n.* the virgin goddess of the hearth. She presided over the sacred fire, the central altar of family, city, tribe and race; the vestals were her priestesses; identified with Hestia in Greek mythology.

"He had brilliant ideas for Emma's tombstone. First he suggested a broken column with a drapery; then a pyramid, then a Temple of **Vesta**, a kind of rotunda, or perhaps a romantic pile of ruins." —GUSTAVE FLAUBERT, *Madame Bovary*, transl. by Francis Steegmuller

Voluptas (vuh LUHP chus) - (from Roman mythology) *n.* the goddess of pleasure.

*see **Psyche** for citation, p. 161*

Vulcan (VUHL kuhn) - (from Roman mythology) *n.* the god of fire and metalworking, son of Jupiter and Juno, husband of Venus. He had a forge on Mount Etna where Cyclops helped him make thunderbolts for Jove; identified with Hephaestus in Greek mythology.

"[In Turner's painting 'Rain, Steam and Speed'] A railway train careers through a tempest, its purpose unknowable, its creator a modern son of **Vulcan**." —TIM HILTON, *The New York Times Book Review*, 9/7/03

OTHER MYTHOLOGIES AND RELIGIONS

ISLAM

Caaba (kah BAH, also kah uh BAH) - *n.* the sacred edifice at Mecca; a small, cubical stone edifice containing the venerated "black stone," it is the Holy of Holies of Islam, the building in Mecca toward which all Muslims must pray.

"I return now to Temple No. 1, where new converts are consulting compasses. Tear-shaped, white with black numbers, the compasses have a drawing of the **Kaaba** stone at the center." —JEFFREY EUGENIDES, *Middlesex*

houri (HUR ee, also HOO ree) - *n.* one of the beautiful, dark-eyed virgins of the Muslim Paradise, among the rewards of faithful Muslims, 2. a voluptuously, seductively beautiful woman.

"... where the gardens of paradise may have been planted and the **houris** sung and danced." —P. SCHUYLER MILLER, *The Spell of Conan*

Mussulman (MUH suhl muhn) - Archaic *n.* a Muslim.

"... a thick mist in which every thing there was enveloped, and over which there hung a magnificent rainbow, like that narrow and tottering bridge which **Mussulmen** say is the only pathway between Time and Eternity." —EDGAR ALLAN POE, *A Descent Into the Maelström*

purdah (PUHR duh) - *n.* the practice observed by Hindus and some Muslims of secluding women.

*see other **purdah** entry for citation*

Shaitan (SHAY tahn, also SHY tahn) - (from Arab) *n.* the Devil, Satan, 2. an evil spirit, an evil jinni.

"'The Vatican denounced the [Illuminati] brotherhood as **Shaitan**.' ... 'It's Islamic. It means "adversary" ... God's adversary. The church chose Islam for the name because it was a language they considered dirty.' Langdon hesitated. '**Shaitan** is the root of the English word ... Satan.'" –DAN BROWN, *Angels & Demons*

sharif (also **shereef**) (shuh REEF) - *n.* a descendant of the prophet Muhammad by his daughter Fatima, 2. during Ottoman times, the chief magistrate or governor of Mecca, 3. a sovereign, prince or ruler of Morocco.

HINDUISM

ashram (AHSH ruhm, also ASH RAHM) - *n.* a secluded place for a community of Hindus leading a life of simplicity and religious meditation.

"'They don't have pay phones in California, only **ashrams**?'" –ROBERT MAILER ANDERSON, *Boonville*

avatar - (from Hindu mythology) *n.* the earthly incarnation of a deity or soul in a body, 2. a representation; exemplar, archetype.

*see other **avatar** entry for citation, p. 92*

chakra (CHAH kruh, also (SHAH kruh) - *n.* one of the seven centers of spiritual energy in the human body located along the spine.

"'You know negativity makes you tense. Look how clouded your crown **chakra** is. And your posture. You're so tight." –ROBERT MAILER ANDERSON, *Boonville*

Jain (JYN) - *n.* characteristic of or pertaining to the Jains, a non-Brahminical East Indian sect of Hinduism, established c. 6th century B.C., resembling Buddhism; it emphasizes asceticism and reverence for all living things, 2. a follower of Jainism.

"... he suggested visiting the hills at Udayagiri and Khandagiri, where a number of monastic dwellings were hewn out of the ground ... 'Built by a **Jain** king or something.'" –JHUMPA LAHIRI, *Interpreter of Maladies*

Kali (KAH lee) - *n.* in Hinduism, the mother-goddess Devi, esp. in her most terrible form as the goddess of death and destruction, often depicted as blackskinned, red-eyed, blood-smeared, wearing a necklace of skulls and a girdle of snakes.

"Go to the desert or tundra and wait for the visionary flash of light, the critical mass that will call down the Hindu heavens, **Kali** and Shiva and all the grimacing lesser gods.' –DON DELILLO, *Underworld*

kshatriya (also **kshatri**) (KSHA tree uh, also CHA tree uh) - *n.* a member of the military caste, the second of the four great castes or classes among the Hindus (second to the Brahmans).

"'I, whom the **Kshatriyas** know as Kerim Shah, a prince from Iranistan, am no greater a masquerader than most men.'" –ROBERT E. HOWARD, *The People of the Black Circle*

purdah (PUHR duh) - *n.* the practice observed by Hindus and some Muslims of secluding women.

"The Coblins belonged to this congregation too, and I had strung along with Cousin Anna in the oriental, modified **purdah** of the gallery while she wept for Howard amid the coorooing and smelling salts of the women in finery, sobbing at who would be doomed the coming year by fire or water—as the English text translated it." –SAUL BELLOW, *The Adventures of Augie March*

Shiva (also **Siva**) (SHI vuh, also SHEE vuh) - *n.* the third of the principal Hindu deities, worshipped for his powers of reproduction and dissolution, 2. a representation of this deity, 3. Judaism—[shiva]—the seven-day mourning period following the death of a loved one, freq. in the phrase "sit shiva."

see **Kali** for citation, p. 135

Surya (SOOR yah) - (from Hindu mythology) *n.* the sun god or god of light and warmth.

"Mr. Kapasi walked ahead, to admire, as he always did, the three life-sized bronze avatars of **Surya,** the sun god, each emerg-

ing from its own niche on the temple facade to greet the sun at dawn, noon, and evening." –JHUMPA LAHIRI, *Interpreter of Maladies*

BUDDHISM

koan (KOH AHN) - *n.* from Zen Buddhism, a puzzling or paradoxical statement or story often used to aid meditation and gain spiritual awakening.

"'The world's a **koan**,' he assured me just before I left, 'a **koan** from the very beginnin' and gettin' worse day by day.' A **koan**, as you probably know, is the paradox-invoking question Zen masters give their students to open up their minds; a famous one asks, 'Before your parents were, what is your original face?'" –MICHAEL MURPHY, *Golf in the Kingdom*

satori (suh TOR ee, also sah TOR ee) - *n.* from Zen Buddhism, a spiritual awakening or indescribable inner experience of enlightenment, often coming on suddenly.

"For an hour or so I was in Scotland again, walking the cobblestone streets of that little town, smelling the salt air, looking out in some kind of **satori** from the hill above hole thirteen." –MICHAEL MURPHY, *Golf* in the Kingdom

EGYPTIAN

Ammon (or **Amen** or **Amun**) (A muhn) - *n.* the supreme King of the Gods, depicted as a man with two long feathers rising straight up from his head; the patron of Thebes. He was identified by the Greeks with Zeus, and by the Romans with Jupiter (Jove) as Jupiter Ammon.

"In fact he was one of these powerful characters whose pictures don't even get into the papers because they're too strong to be named. And gradually this man, with whom she had taken up while still a high-school girl, built up to be about like Jupiter-**Ammon**, with an eye like that new telescope out at the Mount Palomar observatory, about as wicked as Tiberius, a czar and mastermind." —SAUL BELLOW, *The Adventures of Augie March*

Horus (HOHR uhs) - *n.* god of the sun, son of Osiris and Isis, depicted as having the head of a falcon or hawk. Adopted by the Greeks as Harpocrates, the god of silence.

"Saunière had helped the Louvre amass the largest collection of goddess art on earth— labrys axes from the priestesses' oldest Greek shrine in Delphi, gold caducei wands, hundreds of Tjet ankhs resembling small standing angels, sistrum rattles used in ancient Egypt to dispel evil spirits, and an astonishing array of statues depicting **Horus** being nursed by the goddess Isis." —DAN BROWN, *The Da Vinci Code*

ibis (EYE buhs) - *n.* a genus of wading stork-like birds found in warm and tropical regions, having a long, slender, downward-curving bill, 2. the Sacred Ibis of Egypt—a bird of the genus ibis having black and white plumage; worshipped by the ancient Egyptians.

"The men of the caravan know nothing of it, except that it had been placed with them by the men of a caravan from Stygia, and was meant for Kalanthes of Hanumar, priest of **Ibis**." —ROBERT E. HOWARD, *The God in the Bowl*

Isis (EYE suhs) - *n.* the moon goddess, the goddess of fertility, the principal goddess of ancient Egypt, wife and sister of Osiris, mother of Horus. The cow was her sacred object, its curved horns said to represent the cresent moon.

"The Egyptians called her **Isis**; the Phoenicians gave her the name Astarte; the Greeks worshipped her under the name of Phoebe, daughter of Latona and Jupiter, and they explained her eclipses by the mysterious visits of Diana to the handsome Endymion." —JULES VERNE, *From the Earth to the Moon*

see **Horus** *for additional citation*

Osiris (oh SY ruhs) - *n.* the god of the underworld and judge of the dead, one of the principal gods of ancient Egypt, husband and brother of Isis, father of Horus. His annual death and resurrection are said to personify the self-renewing vitality and fertility of nature; the constant foe of his brother (or son), Set, the god of evil.

"'By the way, December 25 is also the birthday of **Osiris**, Adonis, and Dionysus.'" —DAN BROWN, *The Da Vinci Code*

Set (SET) - *n.* the Egyptian god of evil, depicted with the head of an animal.

NORSE

Aesir (AY ZIR, also AY SIR) - *n.* pl. the chief group or race of Norse gods living at Asgard, including Odin, Thor, Balder, Loki, Freya, and Tyr.

"'This by Odin All-Father and by all the **Aesir** I swear.'" —ABRAHAM MERRITT, *The Ship of Ishtar*

Vanir (VAHN IR) *n.* pl. an early race of Norse gods, they preceded the Aesir.

ENGLISH/IRISH

geis (also **gaysh**, **geas**) (GESH) - (from Irish folklore) *n.* a taboo, a prohibition or solemn injunction; a moral obligation.

"'I could not learn your identity, Sir Holger. A **geas** has been laid on every being which might have told me.'" –POUL ANDERSON, *Three Hearts and Three Lions*

Puck (PUHK) - *n.* a mischievous sprite in English folklore, featured in Shakespeare's *A Midsummer Night's Dream*.

"'It's a swell book. It's the product of a scintillating brain, a **Puck** with tears streaming down his face, a golden-hearted clown holding for a moment the throne of God.'" –AYN RAND, *The Fountainhead*

puckish (puh KISH) - *adj.* whimsical, impish, mischievous.

OTHER

animism (A nuh MI zuhm) - *n.* the doctrine that all life is produced from a spiritual force separate from matter, 2. the attribution of a soul to all natural phenomena independent of their physical being, 3. a belief in the existence of a soul or spirit apart from physical matter; spiritualism as opposed to materialism.

"He was reminded of the second law of thermodynamics, the tendency of the physical universe toward disorder and level entropy [*sic*]. Perhaps here, that tendency found a more ... **animistic** ... expression." –POUL ANDERSON, *Three Hearts and Three Lions*

Ishtar (ISH tar) - *n.* the principal Babylonian goddess of love, sexuality, and fertility.

"'**Ishtar** the Mighty Goddess; Mother of the Gods and of men." –ABRAHAM MERRITT, *The Ship of Ishtar*

Davy Jones (DAY vee JOHNZ) - *n.* the personification of the spirit of the sea, depict-

ed as malevolent to sailors; Davy Jones Locker is a term for the grave of those who died at sea.

"'If you'll come up one by one, unarmed, I'll engage to clap you all in irons, and take you home to a fair trial in England. If you won't, my name is Alexander Smollett, I've flown my sovereign's colours, and I'll see you all to **Davy Jones**.'" –ROBERT LOUIS STEVENSON, *Treasure Island*

joss (JAHS) - *n.* a Chinese household divinity; a Chinese idol.

"With his grave face he resembled a booted and misshapen pagan burning incense before the oracle of a **Joss**." –JOSEPH CONRAD, *Typhoon*

joss house (JAHS HAUS) - *n.* a Chinese temple.

joss stick (JAHS STIK) - *n.* a fragrant, slender stick of incense burned by the Chinese before Joss.

kachina (kuh CHEE nuh) - (from North American Pueblo Indian mythology) *n.* any of the deified ancestral spirits believed to reside or periodically visit the pueblos, bringing rain, etc., 2. a masked and elaborately costumed dancer who seeks to invoke a particular spirit or kachina, 3. a carved doll representing a particular spirit or kachina presented to a child.

"I went down to my car and uncapped the tube of sunblock I'd spotted on a rack near the front desk in the mom-and-pop motel, next to the postcards and Indian dolls—the **kachina** dolls and snack packs of tortilla chips that are part of some curious neuron web of lonely-chrome America." –DON DELILLO, *Underworld*

Manichaeism (MA nuh KEE ih zuhm) - *n.* a dualistic religious philosophy taught from the 3rd to the 7th centuries A.D. by the Persian prophet Manes (Mani, Manichaeus) and his followers. The philosophy combines elements of Zoroastrain, Gnostic, Christian, and Pagan elements and divides the world between good and evil, believing in intrinsic evil (darkness, Satan, the body) and intrinsic good (light, God, the soul).

> "Like the most vitriolic of right-wing pundits …, Thomas Frank has a distinctly **Manichean** worldview. The political universe, for him, is divided between the good guys and the conservatives." —JOSH CHAFETZ, *The New York Times Book Review, 6/13/04*

Mithras (MITH ruhs) - *n.* the god of light and truth, a sun god; also a guardian against evil; One of the principal gods of ancient Persia. The worship of Mithras was introduced to Rome during the time of the Empire, and subsequently spread over most of northern and western Europe.

> "Rosslyn Chapel—often called the Cathedral of Codes—stands seven miles south of Edinburgh, Scotland, on the site of an ancient **Mithraic** temple." —DAN BROWN, *The Da Vinci Code*

Rosicrucian (ROH zuh KROO shuhn, also RAH zuh KROO shuhn) - *n.* a member of the Ancient Order Rosae Crusic, an international fraternity of religious mysticism devoted to the study of ancient mystical, philosophical and religious doctrines and their application to modern life, 2. a member of a secret society or order of the 17th and 18th centuries, founded by Christian Rosenkreuz in 1484. Members claimed secret and magic knowledge and powers such as the transmutation of metals, the pro-

longation of life, and power over the elements and elemental spirits.

> "'You see the eye that hangs over this pyramid here. What's pyramids doing on American money? You see this number they got strung out at the base of this pyramid. This is how they flash their Masonic codes to each other. This is Freemason, the passwords and handshakes. This is **Rosicrucian**, the beam of light. This is webs and scribbles all over the bill, front and back, that contains a message.'" —DON DELILLO, *Underworld*

OTHER RELIGIOUS TERMS

ablution (uh BLOO shuhn, also a BLOO shuhn) - *n.* a cleansing of the body, esp. a part of a religious ceremony or rite, 2. the liquid used for this washing.

> "He performed his **ablutions** after the manner of his kind, grunting lustily and splashing like a buffalo." —ROBERT E. HOWARD AND L. SPRAGUE DE CAMP, *Conan the Usurper*

apostasy (uh PAHS tuh SEE) - *n.* the renunciation of one's faith, religion or principles, 2. the renunciation of a belief or set of beliefs (an apostate is the person who apostatizes).

> "Any Muslim who sought to join [a secular society] or imitate them was an **apostate**." —BERNARD LEWIS, *What Went Wrong?*

apotheosis (uh PAH thee OH suhs, also a PUH thee uh suhs) - *n.* glorification, sometimes to a divine lever; deification, 2. a glorified example or ideal (the verb is apotheosize).

> *see other **apotheosis** entry for citation, p. 71*

beatitude (bee A tuh TOOD, also bee A tuh TYOOD) - *n.* supreme blessedness.

"There were probably half a dozen bands like the Royal Spades in every halfway-decent-sized city and rural area throughout the South, kids dreaming of some kind of transcendence, partly slumming, partly looking for an edge, but mostly looking for a nameless kind of **beatitude**, a future they couldn't quite envision but that was different from anything they knew." —PETER GURALNICK, *Sweet Soul Music*

catechism (KA tuh KI zuhm) - *n.* an instructional summary of the basic principles of a religion in question-and-answer form, 2. any similar handbook for teaching the basics of a subject.

"She spoke on a single, level tone, as if she were reciting an austere **catechism** of faith." —AYN RAND, *The Fountainhead*

censer (SENT suhr) - *n.* an ornamented vessel in which incense is burned, esp. during religious rites or services; thurible.

"Out in front of the building stood the priest and two altar boys. One of them was holding a **censer**, and the priest was leaning toward him, adjusting the length of its silver chain." —ALBERT CAMUS, *The Stranger*

doxology (DAHK SAH luh jee) - *n.* a short hymn or verse, a liturgical formula in praise of God.

"And virtually all the elements of the Catholic ritual—the miter, the altar, the **doxology**, and communion, the act of 'God-eating'—were taken directly from earlier pagan mystery religions." —DAN BROWN, *The Da Vinci Code*

eldritch (EL drich) - *adj.* unearthly, alien, supernatural.

"An instant later he had pushed through a screen of branches, and saw the source of that **eldritch** cry." —ROBERT E. HOWARD, *Conan the Conqueror*

empyrean (EM py REE uhn, also em PIR ee uhn) - *n.* the highest point of heaven and the abode of God, 2. the sky, the firmament, 3. *adj.* of the empyrean, heavenly, sublime (empyreal is also used as the adjective).

"There were times when they knew I was a burning boy, a dancing, roaring, skipping, brawling boy-moments of pure **empyrean** magic when the demon of sport was born in the howl of my bloodstream, when my body and the flow of the game commingled in a wild and accidental mating and I turned into something I was never meant to be: an athlete who could not be stopped, a dreaded and respected gamesmen loose and rambling on the court." —PAT CONROY, *The Lords of Discipline*

eschatology (ES kuh TAH luh jee) - *adj.* the branch of theology, or doctrines, dealing with death, resurrection, judgement, immortality, and the time preceeding the end of the world when the world will be judged.

*see other **eschatology** entry for citation, p. 117*

eschaton (es KUH tahn) - *n.* the end of the world, the end of time.

> "... even our theology depends on that Final Day, that **Eschaton** when the journey will finally arrive, to compel our belief in God." —MICHAEL MURPHY, *Golf in the Kingdom*

ethereal (i THIR ee uhl) - *adj.* of or like the ether, or upper regions of space, 2. highly refined; delicate; light; airy, 3. heavenly.

> "When I was a boy living in North Carolina, my father took me to see Selvy play, and his smoothness on the court seemed **ethereal**." —PAT CONROY, *My Losing Season*

execrable (EX si kruh bul) - *adj.* of the poorest quality, 2. hateful; abhorrent; detestable, abominable, atrocious, heinous.

*see other **execrable** entry for citation, p. 21*

execrate (EK suh KRAYT) - *v.* to declare as evil; to curse, 2. to denounce harshly, 3. to detest; to loathe; to abhor.

execration (EK suh KRAY shuhn) - *n.* an instance of execrating, the act of cursing; a curse dictated by violent feelings of hatred; imprecation; expression of utter detestation, 2. that which is execrated; a detested thing.

> "This called up a shout of **execration**." —JOSEPH CONRAD, *Typhoon*

expiate (EK spee AYT) - *v.* to atone; to make amends or reparations for.

> "Oedipus: What is the rite of purification? How shall it be done?
>
> Creon: By banishing a man, or expiation of blood by blood ..." —SOPHOCLES, *Oedipus the King*, introductory quote to Philip Roth's *The Human Stain*

glossolalia (GLAH suh LAY lee uh, also GLO suh LAY lee uh) - *n.* unintelligible, non-meaningful speech, often an ecstatic utterance associated with a trance state of a religious fervor, 2. non-meaningful speech associated with symptoms of schizophrenia (used in the definition of Pentecostal).

hagiography (ha gee AH grah fee, also ha jee AH grah fee) - *n.* the biography of a saint, 2. a biography which expresses extreme reverence and respect for its subject, 3. associated with iconography, or worship of an icon or person (related terms: hagiographer, hagiographic, hagiology, all stem from Hagiographa—the third and final part of the Jewish Scriptures, those books not in the Law or the Prophets).

*see other **hagiography** entry for citation, p. 170*

heretic (HER uh TIK) - *n.* a person holding unorthodox views or beliefs, esp. religious beliefs, 2. *adj.* of or pertaining to unorthodox views or beliefs.

*see other **heretic** entry for citation, p. 91*

heterodox (HE tuh ruh DAHKS) - *adj.* of or pertaining to creeds, beliefs or teachings, esp. religious ones that depart from the norm, 2. unorthodox but not to the extent of being heretical.

*see other **heterodox** entry for citation, p. 101*

idolatry (eye DOL uh tree) - *n.* the worship of idols, 2. blind admiration or devotion.

*see other **idoloatry** entry for citation, p. 91*

immanent (im UH nuhnt) - *adj.* existing within or restricted to the mind; inherent, 2. found within nature and in human nature or the human soul.

> "They were both deeply religious men; they both appreciated this possibility of God's

immanence in the world." –DAVID BODA-NIS, *E=MC Squared*

immolate (I muh LAYT) - *v.* to sacrifice by death; to kill as a sacrifice.

"... 'she has instituted human sacrifice, and since her mating with Constantius, no less than five hundred men, women and children have been **immolated**.'" –ROBERT E. HOWARD, *A Witch Shall Be Born*

inviolable (in VY uh luh buhl) - *adj.* safe from assault or trespass, 2. impregnable.

"The look on his face was her **inviolable** protection against the smirks, the Sarc 3 glances, and the mock **ruminations** of Nicole and Crissy." –TOM WOLFE, *I Am Charlotte Simmons*

inviolate (in VY uh lut) - *adj.* not violated or profaned; intact; safe.

"She went away terribly indignant, and I shouted after her again that the secret would remain sacred and **inviolate**." –FY-ODOR DOSTOYEVSKY, *The Brothers Kara-mazov,* transl. by David Magarshack

liturgy (LI tuhr jee) - *n.* set of forms prescribed for public religious worship; ritual.

"... it was not uncommon for these [visitors] to find themselves restless when confronted with hours of Hebrew **liturgy**." –DAVID LISS, *A Conspiracy of Paper*

mythopoeic (MI thu PEE ik) - *adj.* of or relating to the making of myths; productive in myth-making.

"... marking London as a **mythopoeic** genius who often wrote better than he knew." –EARLE LABOR, *Introduction, The Portable Jack London*

numen (NOO muhn, also NYOO muhn) - *n.* divinity, divine power, divine right.

"'The drugs and love and sex and craziness were crucial, but it was this lens-like quality of the music that gathered and focused the inner **numen** of the land, drew us back again and again and created among us a vortex of expectancy, obsession and ritual.'" –MAX LUDINGTON, QUOTED BY BRUCE BARCOTT, *The New York Times Book Review, 9/14/03*

numinous (NOO muh nuhs, also NYOO muh nuhs) - *adj.* of or pertaining to a numen; divine, supernatural, spiritual, 2. revealing or suggesting a supernatural presence.

"He staggered into the dazzling glare of the world spotlight, carrying the antimatter before him like some sort of **numinous** offering." –DAN BROWN, *Angels & Demons*

obsequy (AHB suh kwee) - *n.* a rite or ceremony performed at a funeral.

"Hadn't [Nixon] said that [Barbara Bush] really knew how to hate? Certain not-so-subtle sartorial signals at the recent seemingly endless Reagan **obsequies**—was that a silver jacket she had on?—suggest that she still does." –LARRY MCMURTRY, *The New York Times Book Review, 7/4/04*

preterhuman (PREE tuhr HYOO man) - *adj.* superhuman; more than human, that which is beyond human.

preternatural (PREE tuhr NA chuh ruhl, also PREE tuhr NACH ruhl) - *adj.* beyond or different from what is natural, or according to the regular course of things, but not clearly supernatural or miraculous; therefore something which is strange; inexplicable, extraordinary, uncommon. irregular, or abnormal.

"... as if his sight had become **preternaturally** acute." –JOSEPH CONRAD, *Typhoon*

propitiate (pro PI shee AYT) - *v.* to cause to become favorably inclined; to gain or regain another's good will or favor; to conciliate; to appease; (sacrifices made to propitiate the gods).

"Your brain would wither and crumble away were I to describe to you the incantations and spells and strange **propitiations** with which I drew a mewling, squalling, naked thing out of the Void." –ROBERT E. HOWARD, *Trails in Darkness*

reliquary (RE luh KWER ee) - *n.* a receptacle for holding or displaying sacred relics or texts.

"... the Papal Vault—the Pope's private **reliquary**, deep within his Borgia apartments." –DAN BROWN, *Angels & Demons*

sanctimonious (SANGK tuh mo nee us, also SANGK tuh mo nee yus) *adj.* affecting piousness or sanctity; hypocritically devout or religious.

supernal (su PUHR nuhl) - *adj.* celestial, heavenly, 2. of or coming from on high, the sky.

"By afternoon it was all over, and Wexler was on his way back to New York with the tape in his possession—one **supernal** song, with only background voices to add." –PETER GURALNICK, *Sweet Soul Music*

temporal (TEM puh ruhl) - *adj.* of or relating to time, 2. worldly; secular.

"In straining to recover our strength, he suggests, we have distanced ourselves from God. An overly **temporal** idea, perhaps, but a respectable one." –TUNKU VARADARAJAN, *The Wall Street Journal*

thaumatology (THO muh TOL uh jee) - *n.* the study of miracles, 2. a discussion of or account of miracles.

"In class a student mentioned the rumors to Father Paulus in the course of a discussion on the subject of **thaumatology**, or the study of wonders." –DON DELILLO, *Underworld*

theocracy (thee AH kruh see) - *n.* government by a god regarded as the ruling power or by officials claiming divine sanction, 2. a state so governed.

"Polynesian society is **theocratic** in structure. Chiefs, who are believed to be descended from the gods, in turn deified or supernatural forefathers, also hold the office of high priest." –JOHN KEEGAN, *A History of Warfare*

theosophy (THEE ah SAH fee) - *n.* a religious philosophy or system of beliefs and teachings dealing with the mystical apprehension of God.

thurible (THUR uh buhl, also THYUR uh buhl) - *n.* a container in which incense is burnt, especially in religious ceremonies; a censer.

9. SCENERY

PLANTS

acacia (uh KAY shuh) - *n.* any of various chiefly tropical trees of the legume family (genus Acacia) with feathery leaves and tight clusters of small yellow or white flowers, 2. the flower of this plant.

> "The jeep bucked and jumped, leaning badly at times, and when the track went narrow in thick bush she had to tell him to get his dangling arm back inside before the thorny **acacia** cut him up." –DON DELILLO, *Underworld*

acanthus (uh KANT thuhs) - *n.* any of a genus (Acanthus) of thistlelike plants of the acanthus family with lobed, often spiny leaves and long spikes of white or colored flowers, found in the Mediterranean region, Asia Minor, and India, 2. Archit. a motif or conventional representation of the leaf of this plant, used esp. on the capitals of Corinthian columns.

> "... a single ruby carved in the symbol of the **acanthus** ..." –ROBERT E. HOWARD, *Cormac Mac Art*

ailanthus (ay LANT thuhs) - *n.* any one of a variety of deciduous Asian trees with numerous pointed leaflets and ill-scented, greenish flowers.

> "On the West Side, she occupied three rooms with high ceilings; at the back there grew an **ailanthus** tree, and one of the front rooms contained a giant air-conditioner; it must have weighed a ton." –SAUL BELLOW, *Herzog*

amaranth (A muh RANTH) - *n.* any one of a variety of annuals of the genus Amaranthus, typically with tiny, dense green or purplish flowers, 2. an imaginary flower that never never fades(amaranthine—immortal, undying).

> "'I'll give you a tonic which you must make her take every day. By all that's **amaranthine** you really must." –MERVYN PEAKE, *Titus Groan*

anemone (uh NE muh nee) - *n.* any of various plants with white, purple, or red cup-shaped flowers; popular garden plants, 2. the sea anemone.

> "About [the glades] lay long launds of green grass dappled with celandine and **anemones**, white and blue, now folded for sleep." –J.R.R. TOLKIEN, *The Two Towers*

angelica (an JE li kuh) - *n.* a plant with edible stems, leaves or roots and aromatic seeds that are used as flavoring.

> "The second tier [of the wedding cake] was a mediaeval castle in gateau de Savoie, surrounded by miniature fortifications of **angelica**, almonds, raisins, and orange sections." –GUSTAVE FLAUBERT, *Madame Bovary*, transl. by Francis Steegmuller

arborvitae (also **arbor vitae**) (AHR buhr VY tee) - *n.* any one of a variety of North

American or Asian evergreen trees with small, scalelike leaves, flattened branchlets and small cones.

> "'Here, Will, take a little of this **arborvitae** to chew. It's a very pleasant taste.'" –SAUL BELLOW, *Herzog*

areca (uh REE kuh, also AR i kuh) - *n.* any one of the trees in the genus of pinnate— leaved palms, producing a thick-rinded fruit or egg-shaped nut, including the betel plam with produces betel nut (popular in southeast Asia).

> "... a small keepsake box made of carved sandalwood beside my bed, in which, long ago in India, my father's mother used to store the ground **areca** nuts she ate after her morning bath." –JHUMPA LAHIRI, *Interpreter of Maladies*

asphodel (AS fuh DEL) - *n.* any of a variety of Mediterranean plants having linear leaves and long clusters of white, pink or yellow flowers.

> "We got off in the outskirts of Algiers ... we had to cross a small plateau which overlooks the sea and then drops steeply down to the beach. It was covered with yellowish rocks and the whitest **asphodels** set against the already hard blue of the sky." –ALBERT CAMUS, *The Stranger*

aster (AS tuhr) - *n.* any of various plants having rayed, daisylike flowers that range in color from white to purplish or pink.

> "... the first and best of autumn, football weather, cold yellow **asters** in the fine air ..." –SAUL BELLOW, *The Adventures of Augie March*

auricula (o RI kyuh luh) - *n.* a central European primrose, also called Bear's ear, having large yellow flowers.

> "'One day I took it into my head to enter a mosque; there was ... a very pretty young devotee who was reciting her prayers; her breasts were entirely uncovered; between them she wore a bunch of tulips, roses, anemones, ranunculus, hyacinths and **auriculas**.'" –FRANCOIS VOLTAIRE, *Candide*, transl. by Richard Aldington

balsam (BOL suhm) - *n.* an aromatic resin flowing from various plants and trees, 2. a tree that produces balsam, 3. a plant cultivated to produce colorful flowers and a fragrant, resinous substance.

> "'**Balsam** and swansdown, Fuchsia dear, cygnets and eider bird, she must take it every day'." –MERVYN PEAKE, *Titus Groan*

belladonna (BE luh DAH nuh) - *n.* a poisonous perennial herb, having reddish-purplish flowers and small, glossy black berries, 2. an extract or tincture derived from the belladonna plant used as a medical preparation, especially in the treatment of asthma.

bergamot (BUHR guh MAHT) - *n.* a pear-shaped citrus fruit (Citrus bergamia) grown in southern Europe primarily for its rind, which yields a fragrant oil called Essence of Bergamot, much prized as a perfume, 2. the essence or perfume made from the fruit, 3. also any of several aromatic North American herbs of the mint family.

*see other **bergamot** entry for citation, p. 247*

bladder-wort (BLA duhr WUHRT, also BLA duhr WORT) - *n.* any of a variety of carnivorous aquatic plants of the genus Utricularia having leaves covered with small sacs filled with air to keep them afloat and shaped to trap aquatic animals and insects.

"Lowell ... fished out the ice-shocked devil by his water-logged apron, which was tangled in **bladderworts** and discarded horseshoes." –MATTHEW PEARL, *The Dante Club*

bole (BOHL) - *n.* the trunk or stem of a tree.

"A silver thread of a brook wound among great tree **boles**, whence hung large vines and gayly festooned creepers." –ROBERT E. HOWARD, *By This Axe I Rule!*

bracken (BRA kuhn) - *n.* a weedy fern with tough stems and large, triangular fronds, 2. an area dense with bracken.

"... the largest of the disturbed stones went bounding and spinning among the **bracken** and the pine-roots far below." –J.R.R. TOLKIEN, *The Hobbit*

bramble (BRAM buhl) - *n.* a tough prickly or throny bush including the raspberry and the blackberry.

"Then I came to a long thicket of these oak-like trees-live, or evergreen, oaks, I heard afterwards they should be called-which grew low along the sand like **brambles**, the boughs curiously twisted, the foliage compact, like thatch." –ROBERT LOUIS STEVENSON, *Treasure Island*

broom (BROOM, BRUM) - (among other definitions) *n.* a Eurasian shrub of the genus Cytisus, having compound leaves and showy, bright yellow or white flowers.

"I... crept back to the bank again, whence, sheltering my head behind a bush of **broom**, I might command the road before our door." –ROBERT LOUIS STEVENSON, *Treasure Island*

burdock (BUHR DAHK) - *n.* a weedy, biennial plant of the genus Arcticum having large leaves and pink or purplish flowers surrounded by prickly bristles.

"After carrying them along a little way openly an idea came to her, and, pulling some huge **burdock** leaves, parsley, and other rank growths from the hedge, she wrapped up her burden as well as she could in these, so that what she carried appeared to be an enormous armful of green stuff gathered by a zealous lover of nature." –THOMAS HARDY, *Jude the Obscure*

camellia (kuh MEEL yuh) - *n.* any of a genus (Camellia) of Asiatic evergreen shrubs and small trees of the tea family, with glossy evergreen leaves and waxy, rose-like flowers, 2. the showy, many-petaled flower.

campion (KAM pee uhn) - *n.* any of various plants of the genus Silene, having variously colored flowers, primarily white or pink, and fringed or notched petals.

"He gave a quick, reluctant glance [in Berlin] at what he had examined the night before, noted that the weeds among the bomb rubble were much the same as the London ones—**campion**, **dock**, and bracken—and then went into the kitchen." –IAN FLEMING, *The Living Daylights*

cardamom (also **cardamum** or **cardamon**) (KAHR duh muhm, also KAHR duh MAHM) - *n.* a pungent aromatic spice, the fruit of Elettaria caramomum, used in Asian cuisine, and in curry powder.

"Upon the altars of Shamash burn sandalwood and **cardamon** and verbena." –ABRAHAM MERRITT, *The Ship of Ishtar*

cassava (kuh SAH vuh) - *n.* a tropical American plant with a starchy, edible root, 2. this root, or a starch extracted from it, used in making tapioca and bread.

"On the platter were a dozen long pods and a heap of round cakes resembling the **cassava** bread the tropical folk press out and bake in the sun." —ABRAHAM MERRITT, *The Ship of Ishtar*

catalpa (kuh TAL puh, also kuh TOL puh) - *n.* any of the various deciduous trees of the genus Catalpa, usually with large leaves, showy clusters of flowers and long, slender pods.

"... those leafy nights of the beginning green in streets of the lower North Side ... when the white **catalpa** bells were opening and even the dust could have a sweet odor." —SAUL BELLOW, *The Adventures of Augie March*

catkin (KAT kuhn) - *n.* a drooping, dense cluster of scale-like flowers without petals, as of a birch, poplar, etc.

"All the grimy cottonwoods had sprung to life, released red **catkins** from their sheaths." —SAUL BELLOW, *Herzog*

celandine (SE luhn DYN, also SE luhn DEEN) - *n.* a weedy plant of the poppy family with yellow flowers, 2. a perennial plant of the buttercup family with yellow flowers (originally regarded as species of the same plant).

"About [the glades] lay long launds of green grass dappled with **celandine** and anemones, white and blue, now folded for sleep." —J.R.R. TOLKIEN, *The Two Towers*

cholla (CHOI yuh) - *n.* any one of the various spiny, shrubby or treelike cacti of the genus Opuntia, having cylindrical stem segments and being native to the southwestern United States and Mexico.

"... a dirt path that threaded among the clumps of **cholla** cactus ..." —MICHAEL CRICHTON, *Prey*

clematis (KLE muh tuhs, also kli MA tuhs) - *n.* a genus of vigorous climbing lianas of the buttercup family with bright colored flowers, found throughtout the temperate zones.

"Climbing roses, honeysuckle, **clematis** and the scarlet flame-flower scrambled up the wall." —E.R. EDDISON, *The Worm Ouroboros*

conifer (KAH nuh fuhr, also KOH nuh fuhr) - *n.* a cone-bearing, needle- or scale-leaved evergreen such as a pine, spruce or fir.

"Long shadows of crags and **conifers** fell across hills rough with gorse." —POUL ANDERSON, *Three Hearts and Three Lions*

cornel (KOR nuhl, KOR NEL) - *n.* any of the various plants of the genus Cornus, shrubs and small trees having very hard wood, including the bunchberry and dogwood.

"The spearshaft was wrist-thick **cornewood**, too sturdy to sever confidently with a swordblade." —DAVID DRAKE, *Cormac Mac Art*

corolla (kuh RAH luh, also kuh ROH luh) - *n.* the outer part or whorl of petals of a flower.

"'I still can't hear you,' Aarfy complained tolerantly, cupping his podgy hand behind the blanched **corolla** of his ear." —JOSEPH HELLER, *Catch-22*

deracinate (DEE RA suhn AYT) - *v.* to pull up or out by the roots; to uproot; to displace; to eradicate.

"Maugham's early experiences are mirrored in the career of Philip Carey in 'Of Human Bondage': the lonely and **deracinated** boy (Maugham had never visited England before his parents' death) was sent to a chilly boarding school where he

was handicapped not only by his poor English but by a painful stammer."
—Brooke Allen, *The New York Times Book Review*, 3/14/04

diatom (DY uh TAHM) - *n.* any of various minute, single-celled algae with delicate cell walls consisting mainly of silica.

"Around him spectators from the millions gowping at him ... the living fringe of a great number sunk in the ground, dead, and buzzing or jumping over Asia like **diatoms** of the vast bath of the ocean in the pins of the sun." —Saul Bellow, *The Adventures of Augie March*

dock (DAHK) - *(among other definitions) n.* a burdock plant, or the leaves of that plant, 2. any of the various plants of the genus Rumex of the buckwheat family, usually coarse weeds having small green or brown flowers, sturdy taproots and large leaves.

see **campion** *for citation, p. 176*

dulse (DUHLS) - *n.* a seaweed of a reddish brown color which is sometimes eaten, as in Scotland.

"'Last winter,' says the first girl, 'the island folk were reduced to eating **dulse**.'"
—Michel Faber, *The Crimson Petal and the White*

espalier (is PAL yuhr, also is PAL YAY) - *n.* a tree or shrub trained to grow horizontally in a flat plane, as against a wall, often in a symmetrical pattern.

"The long narrow garden ran back between two clay walls covered with **espaliered** apricot trees to the thorn hedge that marked it off from the fields." —Gustave Flaubert, *Madame Bovary*, transl. by Francis Steegmuller

euonymus (yu AH nuh muhs) - *n.* any of the various plants of the genus Euonymus, these plants are often cultivated for brightly colored, decorative foliage.

"Gary eased the car up the driveway past the bed of **hostas** and **euonymus** from which, just as she'd said, another SECURITY BY NEVEREST sign had been stolen."
—Jonathan Franzen, *The Corrections*

festoon (fes TOON) - *n.* an ornament such as a garland or chain which hangs loosely from two tacked spots, 2. any carved or molded decoration resembling this, as on furniture, 3. *v.* to adorn or hang with festoons.

"The fluffy, fair hair, soaked and darkened, resembled a mean skein of cotton threads **festooned** round his bare skull." —Joseph Conrad, *Typhoon*

flax (FLAKS) - *n.* a plant of the genus Linum which typically has a single, slender stalk, about a foot and a half high, with blue flowers, 2. a linen-like textile created from the fibers of the flax plant (flaxen being a pale yellow color, after the color of the fiber).

"'I was combing his hair before you came in; his hair's like **flax** and so thick! ...'"
—Fyodor Dostoyevsky, *The Brothers Karamazov*, transl. by David Magarshack

forsythia (fuhr SI thee uh) - *n.* any of the various plants of the genus Forsythia, cultivated for their branches of early-blooming, bright yellow, bell-shaped flowers.

"... this house, fully detached, was covered with wooden shingles, with a tangle of **forsythia** bushes plastered against the front and sides." –JHUMPA LAHIRI, *Inter preter of Maladies*

fuchsia (FYOO shuh) - *n.* a genus of shrub, of the Onagraceae family, with showy, drooping red, pink or purple flowers, 2. a vivid purplish-red color, 3. *adj.* of this color.

*see other **fuchsia** entry for citation, p. 205*

furze (FUHRZ) - *n.* a thorny evergreen shrub (Ulex Europaeus), with beautiful yellow flowers, very common upon the plains and hills of Great Britain; also called gorse and whin.

"Drawing nearer, she recognized the thickets, the trees, the **furze** on the hill, the chateau in the distance." –GUSTAVE FLAUBERT, *Madame Bovary*, transl. by Francis Steegmuller.

garland (GAHR luhnd) - *n.* flowers fashioned into a wreath or crown, 2. resembling a garland, 3. *v.* to decorate using a garland.

"The old woman, who was standing in the front, wore a capacious shift, apparently homemade, with no sleeves, so that the pitted gobs, the **garlands**, of fat that jiggled on the backs of her arms were exposed." –TOM WOLFE, *A Man in Full*

gentian (JENT shuhn) - *n.* any of the various plants of the genus Gentiana, having showy blue or variously colored flowers.

"... the range with the **gentian** flames under the pot." –SAUL BELLOW, *Herzog*

gorse (GORS) - *n.* any of the various plants of the genus Gentiana, having showy blue or variously colored flowers.

"... **gorse** slopes tilted crazily ..." –ROBERT E. HOWARD, *Bran Mak Morn*

greengage (GREEN GAYJ) - *n.* a type of plum with yellow-green skin and sweet-tasting flesh.

"... dishes heaped with fruit: **greengages**, peaches and green **muscat**-grapes ..." –E.R. EDDISON, *The Worm Ouroboros*

hawthorn (HO THORN) - *n.* any of the various plants of the genus Crataegus, usually thorny trees or shrubs with clusters of white or pink flowers and red fuit.

"In some such light as that glowed the last of the **hawthorns** that grew in the fields of men." –LORD DUNSANY, *The King of Elfland's Daughter*

hazel (HAY zuhl) - *n.* any of the various plants of the genus Corylus, shrubs or small trees bearing edible nuts in a leafy husk, esp. the hazelnut or filbert, 2. a yellowish or light brown, 3. *adj.* of this color.

*see other **hazel** entry for citation, p. 205*

heliotrope (HEE lee uh TROHP, also HEEL yuh TROHP) - *n.* any of the various plants of the genus Heliotrovium, native to Peru, with small very fragrant purplish flowers, 2. flowers that turn throughout the day to face the sun, 3. *n., adj.* reddish-purple.

*see other **heliotrope** entry for citation, p. 206*

horehound (HOHR HAUND) - *n.* an aromatic plant from the mint family, it yields a bitter extract that is used in flavoring and as a cough remedy.

"He would ... hand them **horehound** candy out the window to eat with the blue lint of his shirt pocket stuck in it and then drive away, not smiling once." –REYNOLDS PRICE, *A Long and Happy Life*

hosta (HOHS stuh, also HAH stuh) - *n.* any of the various plants of the genus Hosta, east Asian herbs including the plantain lily.

*see **euonymus** entry for citation, p. 178*

ilex (EYE LEKS) - *n.* any of the various plants of the genus Ilex, including holly, the holm-oak and the evergreen oak.

"A spilth of water fell from the bird as it climbed through the hot air to clear the lakeside trees, and a drop of lake water clung for a moment to the leaf of an **ilex**." —MERVYN PEAKE, *Titus Groan*

jute (JOOT) - *n.* either of two Asian plants that yield a coarse, strong fiber used to make rope, twine, mats, burlap, etc., 2. the fiber obtained from this plant.

"... cross-legged on a square of **jute** ..." —JHUMPA LAHIRI, *Interpreter of Maladies*

lanceolate (LANT see uh LAYT) - *adj.* narrow and tapering, as certain leaves.

liana (lee AH nuh, also lee A nuh) - *n.* any of various climbing, woody, tropical vines with roots in the ground that climb and grow luxuriantly often around the trunks of trees.

"It was sweltering; the close-set palm trunks, draped with loops and curves of flowering **lianas**, cut off the fresh sea breeze." —L. SPRAGUE DE CAMP AND LIN CARTER, *Conan the Buccaneer*

linden (LIN duhn) - *n.* deciduous shade trees of the genus Tilia with heart-shaped leaves and drooping clusters of yellowish, often fragrant flowers. The trees yield timber used to make crates, boxes and in millwork.

"... and they bore great kite-shaped shields of **linden** wood with iron rims ..." —ROBERT E. HOWARD, *Eons of the Night*

maguey (muh GAY) - *n.* any of the various fleshy-leaved agave plants, esp. the century plant and American aloe, found in the southwestern United States and Mexico.

[In the mountains of Mexico] "There were falls, though, and also thorns and cactuses, from huge **maguey** to vicious leg-tearing pads; and animals too." —SAUL BELLOW, *The Adventures of Augie March*

mandrake (MAN DRAYK) - *n.* a poisonous plant native to southern Europe having greenish-yellow flowers, very short stems, thick, fleshy, often forked, roots, and fetid lance-shaped leaves, 2. the forked root of the plant, which resembles the human body and was formerly thought to have magical powers and was said to utter a deadly shriek when pulled from the ground.

*see other **mandrake** entry for citation, p. 127*

mesquite (muh SKEET, also me SKEET) - *n.* any of the various plants of the genus Prosopis, small spiny or thorny trees or shrubs in the pea family native to southwestern United States and Mexico.

"... looked down on the **mesquite** flat wherein stood Lopez's squalid hut." —ROBERT E. HOWARD, *Trails in Darkness*

millet (MI luht) - *n.* a grass cultivated for its edible seed and for hay, 2. the white seeds of this plant.

"'In this tea we used to mix either roasted oaten flour or roasted **millet**-looking like canary seed, which in fact it was—stirring it into a thin slush and drinking it down.'" —OWEN LATTIMORE, QUOTED BY JOHN KEEGAN, *A History of Warfare*

mimosa (muh MOH suh, also my MOH suh) - *n.* any of the various plants of the genus

Mimosa, herbs, shrubs and trees growing in warm regions with compound leaves and globular heads of small white, yellow or pink flowers with protruding stamen.

"The camp [in Golden Gate Park] was located in a grove of **mimosa** trees." —JEFFREY EUGENIDES, *Middlesex*

muscat (MUHS KAHT, also MUHS kuht) - *n.* any of the various sweet white grapes native to Europe used to make muscatel wine and raisins.

see **greengage** *for citation, p. 179*

myrtle (MUHR TUHL) - *n.* any of the various plants of the genus Myrtus, an aromatic, evergreen shrub or tree native to the Mediterranean and western Asia, with pink or white flowers and bluish-black berries, 2. a vine having evergreen leaves and mostly blue flowers.

"... she began dragging the statue toward an oval bed of **myrtle**, beside the lamppost that flanked the brick pathway." —JHUMPA LAHIRI, *Interpreter of Maladies*

nasturtium (nuh STUHR shum) - *n.* a garden plant with bright, showy, trumpet-shaped red, orange or yellow flowers and pungent leaves and seeds.

"... the cool wind from the meadows ruffling the pages of his book and the **nasturtiums** on the arbor ..." —GUSTAVE FLAUBERT, *Madame Bovary*, transl. by Francis Steegmuller

nettle (NEH tul) - *n.* an herb covered with stinging hairs, 2. *v.* to pique, irritate, vex or provoke someone.

see other **nettle** *entry for citation, p. 36*

nosegay (NOHZ GAY) - *n.* a small, fragrant bunch of flowers.

"In her hands she holds the **nosegay** of white roses with which she lay in her coffin." —FYODOR DOSTOYEVSKY, *The Brothers Karamazov,* transl. by David Magarshack

ocote (oh KOH teh) - *n.* a resinous pine tree found primarily in Mexico or its wood.

"Two days it rained, and I was sunk in it while wet wood tried to burn and I tossed in whole bundles of resinous **ocote** to try to make a blaze." —SAUL BELLOW, *The Adventures of Augie March*

oleander (OH lee AN duhr) - *n.* a poisonous but ornamental chiefly tropical evergreen shrub having a cluster of white, pink or reddish flowers.

"I told myself how much I liked this place with its downtown hush and its office towers separated by open space and its parks with jogging trails and its fairy ring of hills and its residential streets of **oleanders** and palms and tree trunks limed white-white against the sun." —DON DELILLO, *Underworld*

palo verde (PA loh VER day, also PAH loh VER day) - *n.* any of the various plants of the genus Cercidium, the small trees or shrubs are small and spiny and nearly leafless, have showy yellow flowers and blue-green bark, found mainly in the southwestern United States and Mexico (Spanish for green tree).

"They came to flooded stretches [in the desert] where they had to leave the track and maneuver the jeep tenderly around the **palo verde** and cholla." —DON DELILLO, *Underworld*

panicle (PA ni kuhl) - *n.* a loosely and irregularly branched cluster of flowers.

the bibliophile's dictionary

"The golden leaves, the **panicles** of crimson and yellow blooms were etched against them as though upon some ancient Chinese screen." –ABRAHAM MERRITT, *The Ship of Ishtar*

parterre (pahr TER) - *n.* an ornamental flower garden in which the beds and paths are arranged to form a pattern (from French par terre, on the ground)

"Mansion after mansion claimed my gaze ... In Washington Street there was a row of four or five in excellent repair with finely tended lawns and gardens. The most sumptuous of these—with wide terraced **parterres** extending back the whole way to Lafayette Street—I took to be the home of Old Man Marsh." –H.P. LOVECRAFT, *The Shadow Over Innsmouth*

peony (PEE uh nee) - *n.* any of the various plants of the genus Paeonia, garden plants with large pink, red or white flowers.

"'And so do I!' the boy ... cried suddenly and unexpectedly from the crowd and blushed like a **peony** to the roots of his hair as he had done before." –FYODOR DOSTOYEVSKY, *The Brothers Karamazov*, transl. by David Magarshack

pergola (PUHR guh luh, also puhr GOH luh) - *n.* an arbor or passageway of lattice work that supports climbing plants.

*see other **pergola** entry for citation, p. 265*

periwinkle (PER i WING kuhl) - *n.* a light bluish color with purplish hues, 2. a blue-flowered myrtle, 3. an edible, small marine snail, 4. *adj.* of this color.

*see other **periwinkle** entry for citation, p. 207*

pippin (PI puhn) - *n.* any of several varieties of apple.

"He was very like Old King Cole of the nursery rhyme, even to that monarch's rubicund jollity, his apple round, **pippin** red cheeks." –ABRAHAM MERRITT, *The Ship of Ishtar*

pith (PITH) - *n.* the soft, spongy substance in the center of the stems of many plants and trees, 2. the essential or vital part of an idea or theory, 3. strength; vigor.

"Reed torches, their **pith** soaked in oil, burned in free-standing sconces of delicate bronze ..." –DAVID DRAKE, *Cormac Mac Art*

plane (PLAYN) - (among other definitions) *n.* a tree of the genus Platanus, 2. a sycamore or similar tree, having ball-shaped seed clusters, leaves similar to the maple and bark that comes off in large patches.

"When I think back about my immediate reaction to that redheaded girl, it seems to spring from an appreciation of natural beauty. I mean the heart pleasure you get from looking at speckled leaves or the palimpsested bark of **plane** trees in Provence." –JEFFREY EUGENIDES, *Middlesex*

polliniferous (POL uh NIF uhr uhs) - *adj.* yielding or producing pollen.

"... the grey-blue **polliniferous** body of the air ..." –MERVYN PEAKE, *Titus Groan*

primrose (PRIM rohs)- *n.* any of a genus of early-flowering plants, Primula, having white, red, or yellow flowers, 2. a flower of the primrose plant, 3. the light yellow color of some primroses, 4. *adj.* of this color.

*see other **primrose** entry for citation, p. 207*

privet (PRI vuht) - *n.* a shrub with small, dark-green leaves, widely used for hedges.

"The section of the court ... was walled off by shrubs planted in the inevitable tubs and trimmed so that they looked like seven- or eight-foot-high **privet** hedges."
—TOM WOLFE, *I Am Charlotte Simmons*

pullulate (PUHL yuh LAYT) - *v.* to put forth sprouts; to germinate; to bud, 2. to breed rapidly, 3. to move in large numbers; to teem; to swarm.

[referring to National Defence/Weather computers] "Everything and nothing (but mostly everything), a **pullulating** reality dependent upon thousands of assumptions, all of them untested, all of them untestable." —MARTIN AMIS, *Visiting Mrs. Nabokov*

ranunculus (RUH nung kyuh luhs) - *n.* any of the various shrubs of the genus Ranunculus, including the buttercup and crowfoot, found in temperate regions, most commonly having yellow flowers.

"'One day I took it into my head to enter a mosque; there was ... a very pretty young devotee who was reciting her prayers; her breasts were entirely uncovered; between them she wore a bunch of tulips, roses, anemones, **ranunculus**, hyacinths and auriculas'" —FRANCOIS VOLTAIRE, *Candide*, transl. by Richard Aldington

rick (RIK) - *n.* a stack or pile, as of grain, straw, or hay, in the open air, usually protected from rain with thatching.

"... the men gathered resinous firewood, piled it in **ricks**, lighted it, and collected the tar that ran out from under the piles."
—L. SPRAGUE DE CAMP AND LIN CARTER, *Conan the Buccaneer*

saguaro (also **sahuaro**) (suh WAHR uh, also suh GWAHR uh) - *n.* a very large, branching cactus native to southwestern North America with upward-curving, ribbed branches, white flowers and an edible red fruit.

"We were on a back road flanked by **saguaros** and wildflowers, notched **saguaros**, pecked by birds that nested there, and then we reached the interstate and edged into the windblast of streaming traffic." —DON DELILLO, *Underworld*

sargasso (sahr GA SOH) - *n.* a species of seaweed found floating in masses in the tropical waters of the Atlantic, esp. in the Sargasso Sea, 2. a confused or stagnant mass.

"Barquentine went off into a form of trance, the well-heads of his eyes appearing to cloud over and become opaque like miniature **sargassos**, of dull-chalky blue."
—MERVYN PEAKE, *Titus Groan*

satinwood (SA tuhn WUD) - *n.* a deciduous East Indian tree with lustrous, yellowish, close-grained wood, used for fine cabinet work and in making tools.

"She moved idly across the [boat's] cabin. A smear of reflection followed her on the lustrous surface of the pale **satinwood** paneling." —AYN RAND, *The Fountainhead*

scion (SY uhn) - *n.* a shoot or bud of a plant, esp. one for planting or grafting, 2. a descendant, offspring.

"'I have found it! Lo! Here is the **scion** of the Eldest of Trees!'" —J.R.R. TOLKIEN, *The Return of the King*

scorzenera (skor ZON er uh) - *n.* a plant of the genus Scorzonera, esp. S. Hispanica or black salsify, cultivated widely in Europe; its root is used as a vegetable, similar to the parsnip. Formerly called viper's grass, it was thought to be good against the bites of vipers and other venomous creatures.

"He had a taste for the bizarre, did Bertram, always trying to grow exotic vegetables for the table, which he'd give to the cook they had in those days. There are **scorzonera** growing here yet, half-hidden by weeds, and some strangled roots of salsify." –MICHEL FABER, *The Crimson Petal and the White*

sedge (SEJ) - *n.* any of the Cyperaceae family of grasslike plants often found in dense tufts in marshy places. They have usually triangular, solid stems, and long, grasslike, pointed leaves.

"His eyes were on the moorland, empty except for the **sedges** and heather which grew no higher than a man's knee." –ROBERT E. HOWARD, *Cormac Mac Art*

sloe (SLOH) - *n.* a North American plum tree, also called blackthorn, having tart dark purple or blue-black fruit, 2. the fruit of this tree.

"... on both shores there were steep slopes buried in deep brakes of thorn and **sloe**, tangled with brambles and creepers." –J.R.R. TOLKIEN, *The Fellowship of the Ring*

snapdragon (SNAP DRA guhn) -*n.* any plant of the genus Antirrhinum, with showy yellow, white or red flowers supposedly like the mouth of a dragon.

"... the **snapdragons** smell buttery in the sun." –DON DELILLO, *Underworld*

sorrel (SOR uhl, also SAHR uhl) - *n.* any of the various plants of the genus Rumex, having acid-flavored leaves, sometimes used as salad greens, 2. a light reddish brown color, 3. a horse of this color, 4. *adj.* of this color.

"He nibbled a bit of **sorrel**, and he drank from a small mountain stream." –J.R.R. TOLKIEN, *The Hobbit*

speedwell (SPEED WEL) - *n.* any of the various plants of the genus Veronica, a low-growing plant having clusters of small, usually blue flowers (see **veronica**).

sumac (also **sumach**) (SHOO MAK, also SOO MAK) - *n.* any of various shrubs or small trees of the genus Rhus with compound leaves and cone-shaped clusters of red fruit, including poison ivy and poison oak.

"It was one of those days in Central Park when there's a distilled sense of perception, a spareness, every line firm and unredundant, and the leaves were beginning to turn, the dogwoods and **sumacs**, and nothing was wasted or went unseen." –DON DELILLO, *Underworld*

tamarack (TA muh RAK, also TAM RAK) - *n.* a deciduous North American larch tree, usually found in swamps having short needles borne of spur shoots, 2. the wood from this tree.

"I crouched close among the dense **tamarack** and looked into a black-walled glade and the figures that moved therein. –ROBERT E. HOWARD AND L. SPRAGUE DE CAMP, *Conan the Usurper*

tamarisk (TAH muh RISK) - *n.* any of the various trees of the genus Tamarix, having small scale-like or needle-shaped leaves, slender branches and feathery clusters of small white or pinkish flowers, found mostly near salt water; often grown for windbreak.

> "We got off in the outskirts of Algiers. The beach wasn't far ... We walked between rows of small houses behind green or white fences, some with verandas hidden behind the **tamarisks**, others standing naked among the rocks." –**ALBERT CAMUS,** *The Stranger*

tare (TAR, also TER) - *n.* any of several weeds that grow in grain fields.

> "'I am incapable of receiving the slightest impression from the effort now made to plant thorns on the pillow of age, worth, and wisdom, and to sow **tares** between friends who have been such for nearly half a century.'" –**THOMAS JEFFERSON, QUOTED BY JOSEPH J. ELLIS,** *Founding Brothers*

tuber (TOO buhr, also TYOO buhr) - *n.* a short, thickened, usually underground stem, such as the potato, bearing buds from which new plants sprout.

> "And maybe it looked sinister because it was the left shoe, on the left foot, and this is what sinister means of course—unlucky, unfavorable, leftward—and the word was asserting its baleful roots, its edible **tubers** and stems, through the medium of someone's shoe." –**DON DELILLO,** *Underworld*

tuberose (TOO BROHZ, also TYOO BROHZ, TOO buh ROHZ) - *n.* a plant producing or bearing tubers, native to Mexico; this plant has grasslike leaves and is cultivated for its highly fragrant lilylike, waxy white flowers.

> "She pestered us for details of our own weddings: the jewels, the invitations, the scent of **tuberoses** strung over the nuptial bed." –**JHUMPA LAHIRI,** *Interpreter of Maladies*

tule (TOO lee) - *n.* any one of several bulrushes from the genus Scirpus; this plant grows abundantly in the marshy lowlands of the southwestern United States, 2. the land, usually marshy or swampy, where this plant is commonly found.

> "The Ohlone made canoes from **tule** reeds that grew on the shoreline and paddled out to Alcatraz Island where they collected pelican eggs [alcatraz means pelican in Spanish]." –**DANIEL BACON,** *The Official Guide to San Francisco's Barbary Coast Trail*

verbena (VUHR BEE nuh) - *n.* a genus of herbaceous plants of which several species are extensively cultivated for the great beauty of their flowers, including verbena, vervain and lantana.

> "Upon the altars of Shamash burn sandalwood and cardamon and **verbena**." –**ABRAHAM MERRITT,** *The Ship of Ishtar*

veronica (vuh RAH ni kuh) - *n.* the speedwell.

> "... and blooming, too, were **veronicas** and wild roses and nettles and the wild blackberries that thrust out their slender sprays from the thickets." –**GUSTAVE FLAUBERT,** *Madame Bovary,* transl. by Francis Steegmuller

vetch (VECH) - *n.* a climbing or twining plant with featherlike leaves and usually purple flowers, grown primarily for fodder or as a green manure.

> "[Jefferson's] descriptions of **vetch** as the ideal rotation crop." –**JOSEPH J. ELLIS,** *Founding Brothers*

whin (HWIN, also WIN) - *n.* the common furze or gorse, Ulex europæus.

> "The yard was overgrown with grass and **whins**." –**POUL ANDERSON,** *Three Hearts and Three Lions*

witch hazel (WICH HAY zuhl) - *n.* any of a variety of deciduous shrubs or trees of the genus Hamamelis; North American shrubs that bloom in late autumn or early winter with yellow flowers, 2. an alcohol-based solution containing an extract of the bark and leaves of this plant, a mild astringent used externally.

*see other **witch hazel** entry for citation, p. 249*

woad (WOHD) - *n.* an annual Old World plant from the mustard family, once cultivated for its leaves that produce a blue dye, 2. the dye made from this plant.

*see other **woad** entry for citation, p. 209*

zoysia (ZOI shuh, also ZOI zhuh, ZOI see uh, ZOI zee uh) - *n.* any of a variety of creeping grasses from the genus Zoysia, widely cultivated and used for lawns.

"Shadows lengthened on yellowing **zoysia**." —JONATHAN FRANZEN, *The Corrections*

WATER-BASED SCENERY

alluvium (uh LOO vee uhm) - *n.* sediment, clay or silt carried by flowing water and deposited in a river bed.

"... [he] continued to move downwards till the soil changed from its white dryness to a tough brown clay. He was now on the low **alluvial** beds." —THOMAS HARDY, *Jude the Obscure.*

archipelago (AHR kuh PE luh GOH, also AHR chuh PE luh GOH) - *n.* a large group of islands, 2. a sea containing a large number or group of islands.

"... we were not a team, we were much more like a lost **archipelago**, floating islands sharing straits and bays and rivers, but not linked together in a cohesive way." —PAT CONROY, *My Losing Season*

arroyo (uh ROI OH, also uh ROI uh) - *n.* a dry gully, 2. a rivulet or stream.

"The desert that had looked so flat and featureless in daylight was now revealed to have sandy dips, rock-filled beds, and deep **arroyos** that came up without warning." —MICHAEL CRICHTON, *Prey*

atoll (A TOL, also A TAHL, A TOHL, AY TOHL) - *n.* an island consisting of a ring-like coral reef and enclosing a lagoon.

"Lord Howe belongs to the Solomons neither geographically nor ethnologically. It is an **atoll**, while the Solomons are high islands; and its people and language are Polynesian, while the inhabitants of the Solomons are Melanesian." —JACK LONDON, *Mauki*

bight (BYT) - *n.* a curve or bend in a coastline or a bay formed by one, 2. a loop in a rope.

"... if you look on the west coast of the map of Norway you will see an indentation called Romsdal Fiord ... how they ever came to that bleak **bight** of land on the west coast I do not know." —JACK LONDON, *The Sea Wolf*

cataract (KA tuh RAKT) - *n.* a large waterfall, 2. any strong flood or rush of water; deluge, 3. an eye disease in which the crystalline lens or its capsule becomes opaque, causing partial or total blindness, 4. the opaque area of the eye created in this disease.

"... a deep pool under a smooth steep rock in a mountain **cataract** ..." —E.R. EDDISON, *The Worm Ouroboros*

dank (DANGK) - *adj.* unpleasantly damp; moist and chilly; clammy.

"A hulking oarsman ... struck up a chantey and others joined in, until the **dank** walls roared." —FRITZ LEIBER, *Swords Against Death*

estuary (ES chuh WER ee) - *n.* the wide lower course of a river where its current is met by the ocean tides, 2. an inland arm of the sea that meets the mouth of a river.

"San Francisco Bay is actually an **estuary**, mixing the cold Pacific Ocean with the fresh snow melt of the San Joaquin and Sacramento rivers." —DANIEL BACON, *The Official Guide to San Francisco's Barbary Coast Trail*

eyot (also **ait**) (AYT) - *n.* small island in a river or lake.

"That night they camped on a small **eyot** close to the western bank." —J.R.R. TOLKIEN, *The Fellowship of the Ring*

firth (FUHRTH) - *n.* a narrow inlet of the sea.

"... so they rode down at last to Mithlond, to the Grey Havens in the long **firth** of Lune." —J.R.R. TOLKIEN, *The Return of the King*

fount (FAUNT) - *n.* something from which water flows; a fountain; a source; a wellspring.

"'The creators were not selfless. It is the whole secret of their power—this it was self-sufficient, self-motivated, self-generated. A first cause, a **fount** of energy, a life force, a Prime Mover.'" —AYN RAND, *The Fountainhead*

freshet (FRE shuht) - *n.* the sudden overflowing of a stream due to weather, esp. a heavy rain or melting snow, 2. a fresh water stream emptying into the sea.

"The creek piercing the low corniche would be a torrent in spring when the snow melting in the uplands ... fed the **freshets**." —ROBERT E. HOWARD, *Cormac Mac Art*

gill (also **ghyll**) (JIL) - *n.* a narrow stream, a brook, 2. a deep rocky ravine, usually wooded, esp. one creating or directing a stream.

"... for there lay dark thickets, and a tumbled land of rocky **ghylls** and crags." —J.R.R. TOLKIEN, *The Return of the King*

hythe (also **hithe**) (HYTH) - *n.* a small port or haven, esp. a landing-place along a river.

"On the bank of the Silverlode ... there was a **hythe** of white stones and white wood. By it were moored many boats and barges." —J.R.R. TOLKIEN, *The Fellowship of the Ring*

levee (LE vee, also luh VEE) - *n.* an embankment to prevent inundation; as, the levees along the Mississippi; sometimes, the steep bank of a river, 2. a reception held by a sovereign or other high-ranking person upon arising, esp. one attended only by men, 3. a reception held by the president or other high-ranking official.

"St. Charles Avenue and the Mississippi River meet and the

187

avenue ends. Here an angle is formed, the avenue and its streetcar tracks on one side, the river and **levee** and railroad tracks on the other." –JOHN KENNEDY TOOLE, *A Confederacy of Dunces*

littoral (LI tuh ruhl) - *adj.* of or existing on a shore; *n.* a shore or coastal region.

"In short, Croker Global Foods is part of the engine room, the heavy plumbing, the industrial plumbing of this Elysian **littoral** known as the San Francisco Bay Area." –TOM WOLFE, *A Man in Full*

maelstrom (MAYUHL struhm, also MAYUHL strahm) - *n.* a large and violent whirlpool, 2. a situation that resembles a maelstrom in violence, turbulence, etc.

"'This,' said I at length, to the old man—'this can be nothing else than the great whirlpool of the **Maelström**.'" –EDGAR ALLAN POE, *A Descent Into the Maelström*

marge (MAHRJ) - (among other definitions) *n.* a border; margin; edge; verge (as of a river).

"'No, you will not drown, Olivia, daughter of confusion, for the **marge** is too shallow, and I can catch you before you can reach the deeps.'" –ROBERT E. HOWARD, *Shadows in the Moonlight*

mere (MIR) - *n.* a pool, pond, or lake.

"The long reeds and marsh grass waved in broken undulations and out across the desolation of the wastes a few still **meres** reflected the dull light." –ROBERT E. HOWARD, *Bran Mak Morn*

millrace (MIL RAYS) - *n.* a fast-moving current of water that drives a mill wheel, 2. the channel for this water.

"The Moskoe-ström whirlpool was about a quarter of a mile dead ahead—but no more like the every-day Moskoe-ström that the whirl, as you now see it, is like a **mill-race**." –EDGAR ALLAN POE, *A Descent Into the Maelström*

mucid (MU cid) - *adj.* characteristic of mucus; slimy; moldy; musty.

"Orr snickered with a slight, **mucid** sibilance and turned back to his work, squatting." –JOSEPH HELLER, *Catch-22*

pelagic (puh LA jik) - *adj.* of or pertaining to open oceans or seas (not to coastal or inland waters, Greek pelagos = sea).

"'I use Roman numerals to codify **pelagic** strata.'" –DAN BROWN, *Angels & Demons*.

rill (RIL) - *n.* a very small brook or stream.

"**Rills** of water began to run down; soon they grew to a **spate** that splashed and fumed on the stones, and spouted out over the cliff like the gutters of a vast roof." –J.R.R. TOLKIEN, *The Two Towers*

riparian (ruh PER ee uhn) - *adj.* of, relating to or situated on the bank of a watercourse; living or located along a body of water.

"Gary and Chipper, her fifth-grader and her first-grader, had the chlorination of the Y about them. With their damp hair they looked **riparian**. Muskratty, beaverish." –JONATHAN FRANZEN, *The Corrections*

rivulet (RI vyuh luht) - *n.* a small brook or stream.

"Blood dripped from his poniard and fingers, and trickled in **rivulets** down his thighs, arms and breast." –ROBERT E. HOWARD, *Rogues in the House*

roil (ROIUHL) - *v.* to make muddy or cloudy by stirring up sediment, 2. to irritate; agitate; vex.

*see other **roil** entry for citation, p. 214*

runnel (RUH nuhl) - *n.* a small stream; a rivulet; a brook, 2. a narrow channel for water; a narrow watercourse.

"The landfill showed him smack-on how the waste stream ended, where all the appetites and hankerings, the sodden second thoughts came **runneling** out, the things you wanted ardently and then did not." —DON DELILLO, *Underworld*

shoal (SHOHL) - *n.* a shallow place in a body of water, 2. a sandy, underwater elevation of the bottom of a body of water; a sandbar.

"... the navigation was delicate, the entrance to this northern anchorage was not only narrow and **shoal**, but lay east and west, so that the schooner must be nicely handled to be got in." —ROBERT LOUIS STEVENSON, *Treasure Island*

skerry (SKER ee) - *n.* a small, rugged or rocky island; a sea-rock or stretch of rocks typically covered at high tide; a reef.

"... the man in the story who went to sleep on the **skerry** thinking he had a spell that would hold back the tides." —L. SPRAGUE DE CAMP, *The Tritonian Ring*

spate (SPAYT) - *n.* a sudden flood, rush, overflow, inundation or outpouring.

*see **rill** for citation, p. 188*

tarn (TAHRN) - *n.* a small mountain lake, usually referring to one formed by glaciers.

"... a breeze had blown suddenly into their faces straight off the **tarns** of Elfland."

—LORD DUNSANY, *The King of Elfland's Daughter*

turbid (TUHR bid) - *adj.* having the sediment disturbed or roiled; muddy; thick not clear, 2. disturbed; confused; disordered; perplexed; muddled, 3. thick or opaque as with clouds or smoke.

"Add to that whitening of blackness [Michael Jackson's] undeniable androgyny, his epicene physique and manner, and his effeminate voice and the water is not so much muddied as made thoroughly **turbid**." —TUNKU VARADARAJAN, *The Asian Wall Street Journal*, 3/18-20/05

LANDSCAPE

acclivity (uh KLI vuh tee) - *n.* an upward slope or inclination of the earth, as the side of a hill; ascent.

"... sprang out into the road. Straight and white it showed to the **acclivity** by the Roman ruin." —SAX ROHMER, *The Insidious Dr. Fu-Manchu*

aiguille (ay GWEEUHL, also ay GWEE) - *n.* a sharp, slender, pointed peak of a rock or mountain, esp. the peaks of the Alps.

"... the rocks arose in fantasies of multicolored cone and peak, **aiguille** and minaret and obelisk, campanile and tower." —ABRAHAM MERRITT, *The Ship of Ishtar*

arbor (AHR buhr) - *n.* a place shaded by trees or by vines on latticework; bower, 2. a tree.

"... she sat in the dense shade of a grape **arbor** on a Chelsea roof, redwood posts and rafters and a latticework of cedar that was weathered bony gray." —DON DELILLO, *Underworld*

arborescence (AHR buh RE sents) - *n.* a treelike growth or formation (adjective is arborescent).

> "... knife in hand, we must cut away and deduct the needless **arborescence** of his nature, but the trunk and the few branches that remain we may at least be fairly sure of." —ROBERT LOUIS STEVENSON, *Introduction, Treasure Island*

arcadian (ahr KAY dee uhn) - *adj.* relating or belonging to the ancient Greek region of Arcadia, 2. rustic, peaceful and simple; pastoral, 3. *n.* a person of simple habits and tastes, 4. a native of Arcadia.

> "Only rarely, at the end of our century, does life offer up a vision as pure and peaceful as this one: a solitary man on a bucket, fishing through eighteen inches of ice in a lake that's constantly turning over its water atop an **arcadian** mountain in America." —PHILIP ROTH, *The Human Stain*

boskage (also **boscage**) (BAHS kij) - *n.* a thicket, a grove, a mass of growing trees or shrubs, 2. a decorative, pictorial representation of such a landscape.

> "The women melted within the flower spangled **boskage**; fainter and fainter came their voices; died away." —ABRAHAM MERRITT, *The Ship of Ishtar*

bower (BAU uhr) - *n.* a framework that supports climbing plants creating shade; a leafy recess; an arbor.

> "... [the cathedral] was not at all as I anticipated, not dark and libidinous and full of mystery; it reminded me in fact of a gigantic **bower**, full of springtime leaves and sunbeams streaming through the unstained glass." —MICHAEL MURPHY, *Golf in the Kingdom*

brake (BRAYK) - (among other definitions) *n.* an area dense with brushwood, briers, etc.; thick undergrowth; a thicket.

> "I lay down in the shelter of a cane **brake**." —H.G. WELLS, *The Island of Dr. Moreau*

butte (BYOOT) - (among other definitions) *n.* an area dense with brushwood, briers, etc.; thick undergrowth; a thicket.

> "... he looked across a narrow body of water to a terraced elevation on the other side. It was reddish brown, flat-topped, monumental, sunset burning in the heights, and Brian thought he was hallucinating an Arizona **butte**." —DON DELILLO, *Underworld*

coomb (KOOM) - *n.* a hollow in the side of a hill, 2. a valley along the side of a hill; a valley running inland from the sea, usually short and steep.

> "Still some miles away, on the far side of the Westfold Vale, lay a green **coomb**, a great bay in the mountains, out of which a gorge opened in the hills." —J.R.R. TOLKIEN, *The Two Towers*

coppice (KAH puhs) - *n.* a thicket of small trees, brushwood or shrubs; copse.

> "They went in single file along hedgerows and the borders of **coppices**, and night fell dark about them." —J.R.R. TOLKIEN, *The Fellowship of the Ring*

copse (KAHPS) - *n.* a thicket of small trees, brushwood or shrubs; coppice.

"North be south, east be west. **Copse** be glade and gully crest." —FRITZ LEIBER, *Swords and Deviltry*

dale (DAYUHL) - *n.* a valley; vale; dell.

"... [the railroad] goes up hill and down **dale**." –JULES VERNE, *From the Earth to the Moon*

declivity (dih KLIHV ih tee) - *n.* a steep downward slope, as that of a hill.

"He now paused at the top of a crooked and gentle **declivity**, and obtained his first near view of the city." –THOMAS HARDY, *Jude the Obscure*

defile (di FYL, also dee FYL) - (among other definitions) *v.* to march in a single line, 2. *n.* a narrow gorge or valley; a narrow mountain pass, 3. narrow gorge through which troops must pass, often restricting their movement.

"'Their flank is protected by the cliffs, but there is a **defile** left unguarded!'" —ROBERT E. HOWARD, *Conan the Conqueror*

dell (DEL) - *n.* a small, secluded valley; vale; dale.

"... raising my head to an aperture among the leaves, I could see clear down into a little green **dell** beside the marsh, and closely set about with trees, where Long John Silver and another of the crew stood face to face in conversation." —ROBERT LOUIS STEVENSON, *Treasure Island*

dingle (DING guhl) - *n.* a deep, wooded dell or hollow, a small wooded valley.

"In the meantime the supervisor rode on, as fast as he could, to Kitt's Hole; but his men had to dismount and grope down the **dingle**, leading, and sometimes supporting, their horses, and in continual fear

of ambushes." —ROBERT LOUIS STEVENSON, *Treasure Island.*

down (often **downs**) (DAUN) - *n.* an rolling expanse of grassy, treeless upland.

"And you are riding not on a road nor in a park nor even on the **downs**, but right across Narnia." –C.S. LEWIS, *The Lion, The Witch and The Wardrobe*

eminence (E muh nuhnts) - *n.* a position of high status, great distinction, or marked superiority, 2. a rise; a hill; an elevation of ground.

"Now, right before us, the anchorage was bounded by a plateau from two to three hundred feet high, adjoining on the north the sloping southern shoulder of the Spyglass, and rising again towards the south into the rough cliffy **eminence** called the Mizzenmast Hill." —ROBERT LOUIS STEVENSON, *Treasure Island*

escarpment (i SKAHRP muhnt) - *n.* a steep slope or long cliff, esp. that found in front of a fortification.

"The trail led them north along the top of the **escarpment**, and at length they came to a deep cleft carved in the rock by a stream that splashed noisily down." –J.R.R. TOLKIEN, *The Two Towers*

fell (FEL) - (among other definitions) *adj.* fierce, terrible, cruel, 2. *n.* a rocky or barren hill or ridge, 3. a moor; down; wild field.

"... the desolate lake and the great **fells** beyond it ..." –E.R. EDDISON, *The Worm Ouroboros*

fen (FEN) - *n.* low, swampy land; bog

"The thicket stretched down from the top of one of the sandy **knolls**, spreading and growing taller as it went, until it reached the margin of the broad, reedy **fen**, through which the nearest of the little rivers soaked its way into the anchorage." –ROBERT LOUIS STEVENSON, *Treasure Island*

fold (FOHLD) - (among other definitions) *n.* the earth's surface, the ground, 2. a hill, a dale, 3. a bend in a stratum of rock, 4. a fenced enclosure for domestic animals, esp. sheep (also used in a spiritual sense).

*see other **fold** entry for citation, p. 254*

glade (GLAYD) - *n.* an open space in a wood or forest, 2. an everglade.

"By this time the whole anchorage had fallen into shadow—the last rays, I remember, falling through a **glade** of the wood, and shining bright as jewels, on the flowery mantle of the wreck." –ROBERT LOUIS STEVENSON, *Treasure Island*

glen (GLEN) - *n.* a narrow, secluded valley; a dale; a depression between hills.

"The sides of the **glen** were shaggy with last year's bracken." –J.R.R. TOLKIEN, *The Two Towers*

grotto (GRAH TOH) - *n.* a cave; a cavern; a cavelike excavation.

"The next morning he climbed down into the basement on Hurlbut and went to work ... The Zebra Room was a neighborhood place with irregular hours ... Patrons ... descended out of the America of factory work and tyrannical foremen into an Arcadian **grotto** of forgetfulness." –JEFFREY EUGENIDES, *Middlesex*

heath (HEETH) - *n.* an extensive, uncultivated tract of land, esp. one covered with heather or other, similar low-growing plants, 2. a low-growing plant, esp. heather, that grows on such land.

"I am told there are people who do not care for maps, and find it hard to believe. The names, the shapes of the woodlands, the courses of the roads and rivers, the prehistoric footsteps of man still distinctly traceable up hill and down dale, the mills and the ruins, the ponds and the ferries, perhaps the Standing Stone or the Druidic Circle on the **heath**; here is an inexhaustible fund of interest for any man with eyes to see or twopence-worth of imagination to understand with!" –ROBERT LOUIS STEVENSON, *Introduction, Treasure Island*

hillock (HI luhk) - *n.* a small, natural hill; mound.

[watching Carter ride his motorcycle] "He disappeared behind a clutch of oak trees. A moment later he was in plain sight again. On a rise behind a **hillock** planted with daffodils, he had turned and was puttering back toward them." –GLEN DAVID GOLD, *Carter Beats the Devil*

hogback (HOG bak) - *n.* a sharp ridge with steeply sloping sides and a sharp crest, formed by the erosion of the broken edges of steeply dipping rock strata, 2. a steep, narrow ridge of hills.

"Few western wonders are more inspiring than the beauties of an Arizona moonlit landscape; the silvered mountains in the distance, the strange lights and shadows upon **hog back** and arroyo, and the grotesque details of the stiff, yet beautiful cacti form a picture at once enchanting and inspiring." –EDGAR RICE BURROUGHS, *A Princess of Mars*

hummock (HUH muhk) - *n.* a low, rounded mound of earth; a knoll; a hillock, 2. a ridge or hill in an ice field, 3. a tract of fertile, forested land, higher than an adjacent marshy area.

"Dog heard it too, and slowed her advance, crouching in the lee of a snow-**hummock**, a formless threat, invisible except for the metallic glint of her eyes." –Doug Allyn, *Icewater Mansions*

knoll (NOHL) - *n.* a low, rounded hill; a mound; a hillock.

see fen for citation, p. 192

laund (LAUND) - *n.* an open space among woods, a glade; a pasture.

"About [the glades] lay long **launds** of green grass dappled with celandine and anemones, white and blue, now folded for sleep." –J.R.R. Tolkien, *The Two Towers*

loam (LOHM) - *n.* a kind of soil; an earthy mixture of clay and sand, with organic matter to which its fertility is chiefly due, 2. any rich, dark soil.

"... almost completely burying herself in the soft **loam** of the ancient sea bottom ..." –Edgar Rice Burroughs, *A Princess of Mars*

march (MAHRCH) - (among other definitions) *n.* a boundary, frontier, 2. an area or region at a border or frontier, often governed by a marquess.

"They leave the passes and the waste land, And made their way to the Spanish **march**, Taking up their stand on a level plain." –*The Song of Roland,* transl. by Glyn Burgess

marish (MAR ish) - *adj.* marshy, resembling or having the characteristics of a marsh.

"At the first outset, heavy, miry ground and a matted, **marish** vegetation, greatly delayed our progress." –Robert Louis Stevenson, *Treasure Island*

mire (MYR) - *n.* a wet, soggy, muddy area; a bog, 2. deep mud or slimy soil, 3. *v.* to sink, to become stuck, as in the mire, 4. to soil with muck, mud or mire.

"The orcs hindered by the **mires** that lay before the hills halted and poured their arrows into the defending ranks." –J.R.R. Tolkien, *The Return of the King*

moor (MOOR) - (among other definitions) *n.* an extensive wasteland covered with patches of heath, and having a poor, light soil, but sometimes marshy, and abounding in peat; a heath.

"... you will come to a barren country. There the River flows in stony vales amid high **moors**." –J.R.R. Tolkien, *The Fellowship of the Ring*

moraine (muh RAYN) - *n.* boulders, stones and earth carried and deposited by a glacier.

"Snow-fields stretched down from the pass into the valleys of **moraine**." –Ursula K. LeGuin, *The Left Hand of Darkness*

morass (muh RAS, also mu RAS) - *n.* a tract of soft, wet ground; a marsh; a fen; a bog, 2. a difficult or perplexing situation.

"But where Silver stood with his lieutenant all was still in shadow, and they waded knee deep in a low, white vapour, that had crawled during the night out of the **morass**." –Robert Louis Stevenson, *Treasure Island*

palisade (PA luh SAYD) - *n.* a wall of wooden stakes, used as a defensive barrier, 2. a line of high, steep cliffs, esp. those along a river.

*see other **palisade** entry for citation, p. 269*

rank (RANGK) - (among other definitions) *adj.* having a very strong and bad odor or taste; rancid, 2. growing or grown profusely, with vigor; growing luxuriously, 3. producing a profuse, excessive crop; extremely fertile, 4. in bad taste, coarse, 5. complete; utter, as in rank deceit.

> "After carrying them along a little way openly an idea came to her, and, pulling some huge burdock leaves, parsley, and other **rank** growths from the hedge, she wrapped up her burden as well as she could in these, so that what she carried appeared to be an enormous armful of green stuff gathered by a zealous lover of nature." —THOMAS HARDY, *Jude the Obscure*

scarp (SKAHRP) - *n.* an escarpment.

> "[The town] has a unique position on the summit of a steep and imposing **scarp**, rising on the north, south, and west sides of the borough out of the deep alluvial Vale of Blackmoor." —THOMAS HARDY, *Jude the Obscure*

scree (SKREE) - *n.* a slope of loose rock forming a precipitous, stony mass upon a mountain-side, 2. the material making up such a slope.

> "... they went on up the ravine, until it ended in a sharp slope of **screes** and sliding stones." —J.R.R. TOLKIEN, *The Return of the King*

slough (SLUH, also SLAUGH) - *n.* a mud-filled bog or hollow; a mire, 2. a state or dejection or dispair.

> "'That comed—as you call it—of being arrant asses,' retorted the doctor, 'and not having sense enough to know honest air from poison, and the dry land from a vile, pestiferous **slough**.'" —ROBERT LOUIS STEVENSON, *Treasure Island*

spinney (SPI nee) - *n.* a small wood; thicket or grove; a copse.

> "Along the north shore there was fine grey sand which petered out among the **spinneys** of birch and elder." —MERVYN PEAKE, *Titus Groan*

steppe (STEP) - *n.* an extensive, semiarid, treeless, grass-covered plain; such as those found in southeastern Europe and Siberia.

> "The **steppe**-dry, treeless and offering good going in all directions—was unquestionably the main home of the wild horse." —JOHN KEEGAN, *A History of Warfare*

sump (SUHMP) - *n.* a swamp, marsh or morass, 2. a dirty puddle or pool or water; a cesspool, 3. low-lying land or a pit that receives and collects drainage water.

> "... they came to a wide almost circular pit ... It was cold and dead, and a foul **sump** of oily many-colored ooze lay at its bottom." —J.R.R. TOLKIEN, *The Two Towers*

swale (SWAYL) - *n.* a hollow, depression, or low tract of land, esp. such land in a wet or marshy area.

> "In a grassy **swale**, Conan halted and unsaddled his mount." —ROBERT E. HOWARD, *Conan the Conqueror*

sward (SWORD) - *n.* grass or turf covered land; a lawn or meadow, 2. *v.* to plant or to cover with grass or sward.

> "... he dropped to the **swarded** valley floor." —ROBERT E. HOWARD, *Conan the Warrior.*

swidden (*SWI duhn*) - *n.* an area cleared for cultivation using the methods of slashing and burning the previously existing vegetation.

> "... '**swidden**' (slash-and-burn) agriculturalists pursued their apparently feckless way of making a living because they found

themselves in forested areas where soil fertility was low but other people thin on the ground." –JOHN KEEGAN, *A History of Warfare*

sylvan (SIL vuhn) - *adj.* pertaining to the forest, or woodlands, 2. living, found, or carried on in the woods or forest, 3. wooded, or covered in forest.

> "… a girl … who is sometimes seen running through the trees and weeds, a shadow on the rubbled walls of demolished structures, unstumbling, a tactful runner with the sweet and easy stride of some creature of **sylvan** myth." –DON DELILLO, *Underworld*

talus (TAY luhs, also TA luhs) - *n.* a slope, 2. a pile of rock debris lying at the base of a cliff.

> "Their descent next morning was rapid, if precarious. Often Hugi yelped as Papillon's hoofs slipped on the **talus** and they teetered over a blowing edge of infinity." –POUL ANDERSON, *Three Hearts and Three Lions*

tor (TOR) - *n.* a prominent rock or pile of rocks, esp. those found on the top of a hill, 2. a rocky hill; a rocky peak.

> "There, peeping among the cloud-wrack above a dark **tor** high up in the mountains, Sam saw a white star twinkle for a while." –J.R.R. TOLKIEN, *The Return of the King*

tuffet (TUH fuht) - *n.* a hillock; a mound; a tuft or clump, esp. of grass, 2. a low seat or footstool.

> "Little Miss Muffet sat on a **tuffet.**" –CHILDREN'S NURSERY RHYME

tussock (TUH SUHK) - *n.* a tuft; a tuft of growing grass; a tuft of hair or feathers.

> "But this hindered them; for the grass was thick and **tussocky**, and the ground uneven, and the trees began to draw together into thickets." –J.R.R. TOLKIEN, *The Fellowship of the Ring*

vale (VAYUHL) - *n.* a valley, dale.

> "[The town] has a unique position on the summit of a steep and imposing scarp, rising on the north, south, and west sides of the borough out of the deep alluvial **Vale** of Blackmoor." –THOMAS HARDY, *Jude the Obscure*

wold (WOHLD) - *n.* an unforested rolling plain, especially a high one.

> "'I live upon the open **Wold** in days of peace.'" – J.R.R. TOLKIEN, *The Return of the King*

WINDS, SKY, AND HEAVEN

dust devil (DUHST DE vuhl) - *n.* a small whirlwind that swirls dust and debris.

> "I saw what appeared to be a small, swirling cloud of dark particles. It looked like a **dust devil**, one of those tiny tornado-like clusters that moved over the ground, spun by convection currents rising from the hot desert floor." –MICHAEL CRICHTON, *Prey*

empyrean (EM py REE uhn, also em PIR ee uhn) - *n.* the highest point of heaven and the abode of God, 2. the sky, the firmament, 3. *adj.* of the empyrean, heavenly, sublime (empyreal is also used as the adjective).

> "There were times when they knew I was a burning boy, a dancing, roaring, skipping, brawling boy—moments of pure **empyrean** magic when the demon of sport was born in the howl of my bloodstream, when my body and the flow of the game com-

mingled in a wild and accidental mating and I turned into something I was never meant to be: an athlete who could not be stopped, a dreaded and respected games-men loose and rambling on the court."
—PAT CONROY, *The Lords of Discipline*

ethereal (i THIR ee uhl) - *adj.* of or like the ether, or upper regions of space, 2. highly refined; delicate; light; airy, 3. heavenly.

"When I was a boy living in North Carolina, my father took me to see Selvy play, and his smoothness on the court seemed **ethe-real**." —PAT CONROY, *My Losing Season*

simoons (also **simoom**) (suh MOONZ, also sy MOONZ) - *n.* a strong, violent, hot wind carrying sand of the African and Asiatic deserts.

"Indeed, every appearance warranted me in apprehending a **simoon**. I told the cap-tain of my fears; but he paid no attention."
—EDGAR ALLAN POE, *The Fall of the House of Usher*

sirocco (suh RAH KOH, also shuh RAH KOH) - *n.* a hot wind from the south or southeast blowing across southern Italy and having originated in the Sahara as a dry, dusty wind becoming humid as it crosses the Mediter-ranean, 2. a warm southerly wind.

"I listened to the turboblades rattle in the wind and felt the **sirocco** heat come blow-ing in." —DON DELILLO, *Underworld*

squall (SKWOL) - *n.* a violent windstorm, coming on suddenly but lasting only briefly, often accompanied by rain or snow, 2. a harsh outcry or brief commotion.

"Sometimes **squalls** blew up, winds that suddenly swept in from the sea over the plateau of the pays de Caux and filled the countryside with fresh, salt-smelling air."
—GUSTAVE FLAUBERT, *Madame Bovary*, transl. by Francis Steegmuller

supernal (su PUHR nuhl) - *adj.* celestial, heavenly, 2. of or coming from on high, the sky.

"By afternoon it was all over, and Wexler was on his way back to New York with the tape in his possession—one **supernal** song, with only background voices to add."
—PETER GURALNICK, *Sweet Soul Music*

welkin (WEL kuhn) - *n.* the sky; the vault of heaven; the air above.

"Probably when a child he had attempted more than once to count [the cherubs on the painted ceiling] ... but however that might be, Lord Groan had not cast up his eyes to the old **welkin** for many years."
—MERVYN PEAKE, *Titus Groan*

OTHER SCENIC TERMS

agronomy (uh GRAH nuh mee) - *n.* soil and plant sciences applied to soil manage-ment and the raising of crops.

"'Do you think that to be an **agronomist** you must till the soil or fatten chickens with your own hands?'" —GUSTAVE FLAUBERT, *Madame Bovary*, transl. by Francis Steegmuller

---

arboretum (AHR buh ree tuhm) - *n.* a place for the cultivation, scientific study and exhibition of a variety of trees.

"He was escorted from the door to the **arboretum**, where Borax was taking lunch." —GLEN DAVID GOLD, *Carter Beats the Devil*

---

burr (BUHR) - (among other definitions) *n.* the rough edge remaing on a material, esp. metal, after is has been cut, cast or drilled, 2. a rough protuberance or outgrowth, esp. on a tree.

"... he was a man of fine appearance, as he had been a beautiful child ... his hair grew like chestnut **burr** the same as formerly, brown and gold, close bristles." —SAUL BELLOW, *The Adventures of Augie March*

---

commensal (kuh MENT suhl) - *n.* a companion at meals, 2. either of the organisms living in a relationship characterized by commensalism in which one species benefits and the other is neither harmed nor benefited; both organisms share the same food (unlike a parasite, which feeds off of its host), 3. *adj.* pertaining to, of, or like a commensal.

"Either there was soil deeper down, or this species of tree was a remarkable instance of a **commensal** or a parasite." —YANN MARTEL, *Life of Pi*

---

corniche (kor NEESH) - *n.* a road that winds alongside a cliff or steep slope, esp. a coastline.

"The creek piercing the low **corniche** would be a torrent in spring when the snow melting in the uplands ... fed the freshets." —ROBERT E. HOWARD, *Cormac Mac Art*

---

covert (KOH VUHRT, also KUH VUHRT) - *adj.* not openly practiced; concealed; hidden; disguised; surreptitious, 2. *n.* a covered or protected place; shelter, 3. a hiding place for game, as underbrush, a thicket, etc.

"Looking out from the **covert** he could see only a dun, shadowless world, fading slowly into a featureless, colorless gloom." —J.R.R. TOLKIEN, *The Two Towers*

---

debouch (di BAUCH) - *v.* to come forth from a narrow or confined area into the open, esp. in connection with the movement of military forces, 2. to emerge; to issue; to come forth.

*see other **debouch** entry for citation, p. 274*

---

fecund (FE kuhnd, also FEE kuhnd) - *adj.* prolific; fruitful; fertile; productive.

"'I am very busy with my work at the moment, and I feel that I am entering a very **fecund** stage.'" —JOHN KENNEDY TOOLE, *A Confederacy of Dunces*

---

fosse (FAHS) - *n.* a long, narrow ditch; a trench, 2. a moat or ditch dug as a fortification, usually filled with water, 3. a deep pit dug in the ground; a burying ground or grave.

"Beyond [a wide treeless space] was a deep **fosse** lost in soft shadow, but the grass upon its brink was green, as if it glowed still in memory of the sun that had gone." —J.R.R. TOLKIEN, *The Fellowship of the Ring*

---

fructify (FRUHK tuh FY) - *v.* to bear or cause to bear fruit, 2. to generate useful products or ideas.

"'As a boy of ten,' Dostoyevsky wrote ... 'I saw a performance of Schiller's Robbers and, I assure you, the powerful impression it made on me then had a very **fructifying** influence on my spiritual development.'" –DAVID MAGARSHACK, *Introduction, Fyodor Dostoyevsky's The Brothers Karamazov*

---

gutta-percha (GUH tuh PUHR chuh) - *n.* a tough rubbery or plastic substance derived from the latex of several Malaysian trees, used as electrical insulation, for waterproofing, for filling material (in dentistry) and formerly to make golf balls.

"... great fears were entertained regarding the brain of this worthy individual, which had hitherto been so well preserved within his **gutta-percha** cranium." –JULES VERNE, *From the Earth to the Moon*

---

hard scrabble (HARD SKRA bul) - *adj.* pertaining to a place barren of fertile soil, 2. working hard to derive a meager living from barren soil, poverty.

"Isabel Gervais answered in a gravelly voice out of the poor-born and **hardscrabble** South of my mother." –PAT CONROY, *My Losing Season*

---

harrow (HAR OH) - *n.* a farming tool made up of a heavy frame with sharp teeth or disks, used to break up or level off plowed ground, 2. *v.* to break up or level off with such a tool, 3. to cause or inflict great distress or torment.

"The fresh **harrow**-lines seemed to stretch like the channellings in a piece of new corduroy, lending a meanly utilitarian air to the expanse." –THOMAS HARDY, *Jude the Obscure*

---

hoar-frost (HOHR FROST) - *n.* ice crystals or frozen dew that form a white coating on a surface (of objects, esp. outside).

"Old Jonas McCrill, galloping back at the sound of the blast, found him where he lay, and wondered that his face should be that of an old, old man, his hair white as **hoar-frost**." –ROBERT E. HOWARD, *Trails in Darkness*

---

idyll (EYE duhl) - *n.* a carefree episode or experience, esp. in a rustic setting, 2. a short poem about a carefree episode or experience or rustic life, 3. a romantic episode.

"The year had been a fatherless **idyll** and I begged Mom to let me stay." –PAT CONROY, *My Losing Season*

---

lee (LEE) - *n.* a place sheltered from the wind, 2. shelter; cover; protection, 3. (Nautical) the side sheltered or away from the wind, 4. *adj.* of or on the side sheltered or away from the wind.

"Dog heard it too, and slowed her advance, crouching in the **lee** of a snow-hummock, a formless threat, invisible except for the metallic glint of her eyes." –DOUG ALLYN, *Icewater Mansions*

---

levin (LE vuhn) - *n.* (Archaic) lightning; a bolt of lightning, 2. any bright light or flame.

"In that second, Vakar came to life with the suddenness of a **levinbolt**." –L. SPRAGUE DE CAMP, *The Tritonian Ring*

---

rime (RYM) - *n.* a frost or granular ice coating; hoar-frost.

"April was cradling three **rimed** cartons [of gelati] against her corduroy jumper." –JONATHAN FRANZEN, *The Corrections*

---

shambles (SHAM buhlz) - *n.* (uses a singular verb) a condition of complete disorder or destruction, 2. a scene of great clutter, a jumble.

"'Ah, Mitra, we lay down to sleep among them, like sheep making their bed in the **shambles**!'" –ROBERT E. HOWARD, *Shadows in the Moonlight*

thatch (THACH) - *n.* straw, rushes, or other plant stalks, used for making or covering the roofs of buildings, 2. *v.* to cover with or as if with thatch.

"Then I came to a long thicket of these oaklike trees—live, or evergreen, oaks, I heard afterwards they should be called—which grew low along the sand like brambles, the boughs curiously twisted, the foliage compact, like **thatch**." –ROBERT LOUIS STEVENSON, *Treasure Island*

tilth (TILTH) - *n.* a tilling; the state of being tilled; the cultivation of land, 2. land that has been tilled; a ploughed field.

"The townlands were rich, with wide **tilth** and many orchards, and homesteads there were with oast and garner, fold and byre, and many rills rippling through the green from the highlands down to Anduin." –J.R.R. TOLKIEN, *The Return of the King*

topiary (TO pee ER ee) - *adj.* designating or of the art of clipping, trimming and training shrubs or trees into decorative, ornamental shapes, 2. *n.* topiary art or work, 3. a topiary garden.

"We rumble past privet hedges and under **topiary** arches to arrive at secluded lakefront homes where girls wait with satchels, standing very straight." –JEFFREY EUGENIDES, *Middlesex*

topography (tuh PAH gruh fee) - *n.* a detailed, precise representation or description of the physical features of a place or region, 2. the physical features of a region.

"Hamilton provides succinct summaries of the European journeys, together with maps. Here is a **topography** of a great artist's life and work. The narrative does not convey the precarious nobility of its subject's imagination." –TIM HILTON, *The New York Times Book Review, 9/7/03*

torrid (TOR id) - *adj.* intense dry heat, 2. passionate; ardent.

"... the crowd rushing like the billows of a raging sea under a torrential tropic sun that poured its **torrid** rays upon our fertile meadows." –GUSTAVE FLAUBERT, *Madame Bovary*, transl. by Francis Steegmuller

vegetal (VE juh tuhl) - *adj.* relating to or characteristic of plants; freq. used in contrast to animal, 2. relating to or producing growth.

"... the evocative **vegetal** smell coming familiarly off her fingers as she slides them up from her neck and across her warm ears and slowly from there over her cheeks to her lips ..." –PHILIP ROTH, *The Human Stain*

verdure (VUHR juhr) - *n.* the lush, vibrant greenness of flourishing vegetation, 2. vigorous green vegetation.

"... she would arrive breathless, rosy-cheeked, everything about her smelling of sap and **verdure** and fresh air." –GUSTAVE FLAUBERT, *Madame Bovary*, transl. by Francis Steegmuller

withe (WITH, also WITHE) - *n.* a tough, supple, slender twig or branch, as of a willow, used for binding things together; withy, 2. to bind with withes.

"Alianora set deftly to work building a shelter of plaited **withes**, while Hugi prepared supper and Holger felt useless." –POUL ANDERSON, *Three Hearts and Three Lions*

10. LOCAL AND FOREIGN

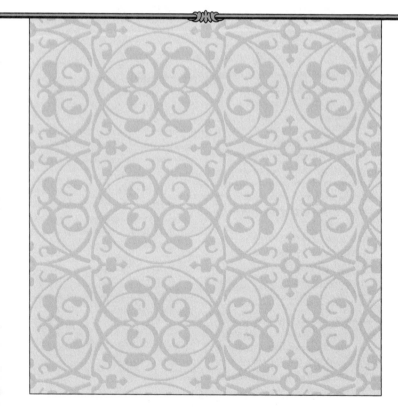

adventitious (AD VEN TI shuhs) - *adj.* added extrinsically; not inherent, 2. occurring accidently or spontaneously in an unusual or abnormal place.

> "So the planet was quickly settled by human beings, by their domesticated plants and animals, and by the parasites and other organisms that were **adventitiously** brought along." –ISAAC ASIMOV, *The Robots of Dawn*

autochthon (o TAHK thuhn) - *n.* one of the earliest known inhabitants of a specific location; aborigine, 2. an indigenous plant or animal.

> "Only human beings could live on this world and know that they were not **autochthonous** but had stemmed from Earthmen." –ISAAC ASIMOV, *The Robots of Dawn*

bourn (also **bourne**) (BOHRN) - *n.* a boundary; limit, 2. a goal or destination, 3. a domain.

> "And fresh and fair though it came from beyond the **bourn** of geography, and out of an age long lost and beyond history's ken, a dawn glowed upon Elfland that had known no dawn before." –LORD DUNSANY, *The King of Elfland's Daughter*

denizen (DE nuh zuhn) - *n.* an inhabitant; a resident; one who inhabits a particular place.

> "... the Bedouins are less citizens of the country than denizens of the land." –ANTHONY SWOFFORD, *Jarhead*

diaspora (dy AS puh ruh, also dee AS puh ruh) - *n.* The Dispersion; the dispersal of Jews outside of Isreal from the 6th century B.C. to the present, 2. a dispersal of people from their original homeland.

> "'Will the **Diaspora** head back?' Bush asked, referring to the Iraqis living out of the country." –BOB WOODWARD, *Plan of Attack*

ecumenical (E kyuh MEH ni kuhl) - *adj.* worldwide in scope or applicability, universal, 2. relating to the universal Christian Church, 3. relating to the promotion of accord among churches and religions.

*see other **ecumenical** entry for citation, p. 137*

ecumenism (also **ecumenicism**) (e KYOO meh NI zuhm) - *n.* a movement seeking to achieve unity among Christian churches or denominations, 2. a movement seeking accord among religions through cooperation and understanding.

*see other **ecumenism** entry for citation, p. 138*

endemic (en DEE mik, also in DEE mik) - *adj.* prevalent in a particular country, locality or region, 2. common in, but confined to, a certain country or locality, such as a disease.

> "Ego in movie land was like TB in a mining town. **Endemic** and ravaging but not necessarily fatal." –MARIO PUZO, *Fools Die*

immanent (im UH nuhnt) - *adj.* existing within or restricted to the mind; inherent, 2. found within nature and in human nature or the human soul.

*see other **immanent** entry for citation, p. 171*

omphalos (AHMP fuh LAHS, also AHMP fuh luhs) - *n.* the navel, 2. a central part, the heart of hub of a place, organization or sphere of activity, 3. (ancient Greek) the sacred rounded stone marking the center of the earth, located in Apollo's temple at Delphi; any sacred stone.

"'I believe that the sacred love I have borne these many years is a love that has sucked me straight into the vortex, the **omphalos** of the universe, and there I have seen such things my friends.'" –LOUISE ERDRICH, *The Master Butchers Singing Club*

pandemic (pan DEE mik) - *adj.* widespread; general, 2. epidemic over a wide geographical area and affecting a large proportion of the population, as a disease.

"In recent years, spam has become an annoyance **pandemic**." –MARSHALL SELLA, *The New York Times Magazine*, 12/15/02

peregrine (PER uh GRUHN, also PER uh GREEN) - *adj.* foreign; alien; belonging to another country; imported, 2. migratory or roaming.

"As soon as she had smiled her face altered again, and the petulant expression **peregrine** to her features took control." –MERVYN PEAKE, *Titus Groan*

Pisgah (PIZ guh) - *n.* a mountain summit east of Jordan from which Moses viewed the Promised Land.

"Going back to the yards, I climbed down a steep path, like a cliff of **Pisgah**." –SAUL BELLOW, *The Adventures of Augie March*

propinquity (pruh PIN kwe tee) - *n.* nearness, proximity, 2. kinship.

"... a big man himself but dwarfed by the **propinquity** of the giant." –JACK LONDON, *The Sea Wolf*

purlieu (PUHRL YOO, also PUHR LOO) - *n.* an outlying area, 2. purlieus—outskirts; environs; an adjacent district.

"He saw that his destiny lay not with these [buildings in the center of the city], but among the manual toilers in the shabby **purlieu** which he himself occupied, unrecognized as part of the city at all by its visitors and panegyrists, yet without whose denizens the hard readers could not read nor the high thinkers live." –THOMAS HARDY, *Jude the Obscure*

ultramontane (UHL truh MAHN TAYN) - *adj.* relating to the people or regions beyond the mountains, esp. the Alps, 2. supporting the supreme authority of the papal court.

*see other **ultramontane** entry for citation, p. 140*

Urheimat (ur HY maht) - *n.* a place, the location where a people or language originated.

*see other **Urheimat** entry for citation, p. 94*

11. VISUALS

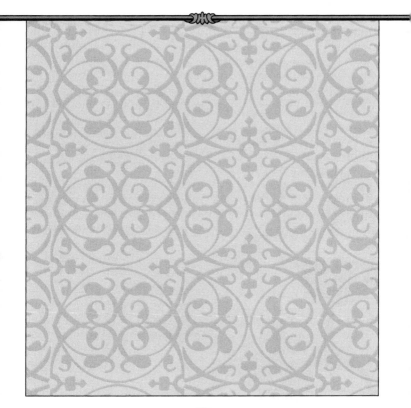

Colors

amber (AM buhr) - *n.* a hard yellow or brownish-yellow fossil resin, used for making ornamental objects and jewellery, 2. a brownish yellow, 3. *adj.* of this color.

> "Her shoulders were **amber**-toned, like the bathing odalisques he had seen in pictures; she was long-waisted like the feudal chatelaines." —GUSTAVE FLAUBERT, *Madame Bovary*, transl. by Francis Steegmuller

argent (AHR juhnt) - *n.* (Archaic) silver, 2. *adj.* of this color.

> "Some wore chain mail or plate, **argent** metal elaborately shaped and chased; others had robes and coronets." —POUL ANDERSON, *Three Hearts and Three Lions*

bay (BAY) - (among other definitions) *adj.* reddish brown, 2. n. a reddish brown, 3. a reddish-brown animal, especially a horse.

blanch (BLANCH) - (among other definitions) *v.* to bleach, 2. to take the color out of; to make or become pale or white.

> "Only the soundlessness of the dazed cats—the line of them—the undulating line as **blanched** as linen, and lorn as the long gesture of a hand." —MERVYN PEAKE, *Titus Groan*

carmine (KAHR muhn, also KAHR MYN) - *n.* a red or purplish-red pigment obtained mainly from the cochineal insect, 2. *n.*, *adj.* red or purplish-red; crimson.

> "Yet it looked both noble and knowing and its moist, long, generous lips, newly and carefully **carmined**, roused and tempted him." —FRITZ LEIBER, *Swords and Deviltry*

cerise (*suh REES*, also *suh REEZ*) - *n.* bright red; cherry red, 2. *adj.* of this color (cerise is French for cherry).

> "'Ohmygod, a **cerise** shirt. Cerise is such an in color this year.'" —TOM WOLFE, *I Am Charlotte Simmons*

cerulean (seh ROO lee uhn) - *adj.* sky-blue; azure.

> "Against a vague, pearl-and-**cerulean** morning sky floated the golden and scarlet flag of her house." —ROBERT E. HOWARD AND L. SPRAGUE DE CAMP, *Conan the Usurper*

chartreuse (shahr TROOS, also shahr TROOZ) - *n.* a pale yellowish green, 2. *adj.* of this color (Chartreuse is a trademark for a green or yellow liqueur).

> "He sat on the floor, his head resting against the edge of a couch, his bare feet stretched out, a pair of Guy Francon's **chartreuse** pyjamas floating loosely about his limbs." —AYN RAND, *The Fountainhead*

chlorotic (kluh RAH tik) - (among other definitions) *adj.* characterized as having chlorosis, an iron deficiency found mainly among young women causing a greenish-yellow discoloration to the skin.

> "And in the Stygian grotto I saw them do the rite, and adore the sick [greenish] pillar of flame, and throw into the water handfuls gouged out of the viscous vegetation which glittered green in the **chlorotic** glare." —H.P. LOVECRAFT, *The Festival*

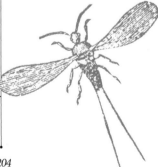

dun (DUHN) - *v.* to demand or persistently request payment, as for a debt, 2. *n.* a dull or neutral grayish-brown color, 3. a horse of such a color.

> "Then [the smoke] turned to **mauve** and yellow and **dun**." –JACK LONDON, *The Story of an Eyewitness*

ensanguine (in SANG gwuhn) - *v.* to stain with blood.

> "I pictured her socks in the air, her little tennis socks with the balls at the heels, those **ensanguined** balls, bouncing." –JEFFREY EUGENIDES, *Middlesex*

ethiopian (EE thee OH pee uhn) - *adj.* of, from, or pertaining to Ethiopia, the Ethiopian people, culture or language, 2. used allusively for black.

> "The raven on Lady Groan's shoulder awoke from his sleep and raised his **ethiopian** wing an inch or two, sleepily." –MERVYN PEAKE, *Titus Groan*

fawn (FON, also FAHN) - (among other definitions) *n.* a light brown or light yellowish brown, 2. adj. of this color.

> "Bond watched the blown golden hair and the **fawn** raincoat until it had vanished into the indigo dusk up the Wilhemstrasse." –IAN FLEMING, *The Living Daylights*

flax (FLAKS) - *n.* a plant of the genus Linum which typically has a single, slender stalk, about a foot and a half high, with blue flowers, 2. a linen-like textile created from the fibers of the flax plant (flaxen being a pale yellow color, after the color of the fiber).

> "Within the mullioned and transomed windows he could see the black, brown, and **flaxen** crowns of the scholars over the sills." –THOMAS HARDY, *Jude the Obscure*

fuchsia (FYOO shuh) - *n.* a genus of shrub, of the Onagraceae family, with showy, drooping red, pink or purple flowers, 2. a vivid purplish-red color, 3. *adj.* of this color.

> "I am nine years old and holding my father's meaty, sweaty hand ... I have come downtown for our annual lunch date. I am wearing a miniskirt and **fuchsia** tights. A white patent leather purse hangs on a long strap from my shoulder." –JEFFREY EUGENIDES, *Middlesex*

garnet (GAHR nuht) - *n.* any of several common, widespread silicate minerals, colored red, brown, black, green, yellow, or white, and used as gemstones and abrasives, 2. a dark to very dark red, 3. *adj.* of this color.

> "Her belt was a cord with large tassels, and her little **garnet**-colored slippers had rosettes of wide ribbons at the instep." –GUSTAVE FLAUBERT, *Madame Bovary*, transl. by Francis Steegmuller

glaucous (GLO kuhs) - *adj.* a dull or pale, grayish-, bluish- or yellowish-green.

> "To eyes accustomed to silver that shines like chrome, the surfaces of certain prize pieces in Indiana will look **glaucous**, dull and leaden." –MATTHEW GUREWITSCH, *The Wall Street Journal*, 12/10/01

hazel (HAY zuhl) - *n.* any of the various plants of the genus Corylus, shrubs or small trees bearing edible nuts in a leafy husk, esp. the hazelnut or filbert, 2. a yellowish or light brown, 3. *adj.* of this color.

> "The same fine head, and those soft **hazel** eyes." –SAUL BELLOW, *Herzog*

heliotrope (HEE lee uh TROHP, also HEEL yuh TROHP) - *n.* any of the various plants of the genus Heliotrovium, native to Peru, with small very fragrant purplish flowers, 2. flowers that turn throughout the day to face the sun, 3. *n., adj.* reddish-purple.

> "'Yes,' said Cora, who had reached the edge of the chair and was stroking her smooth **heliotrope** knees in quick, continual movements which Clarice emulated." –MERVYN PEAKE, *Titus Groan*

hoary (HOR ee) - *adj.* gray or white as if from age, 2. having white or gray hair due to aging, 3. extremely old, ancient.

> "Speculative philosophers drew along, not always with wrinkled foreheads and **hoary** hair as in framed portraits, but pink-faced, slim, and active as in youth." –THOMAS HARDY, *Jude the Obscure*

incarnadine (in KAHR nuh DYN, also in KAHR nuh DEEN, in KAHR nuh DUHN) - *n., adj.* pink or a very pale red, 2. blood-red; crimson.

> "The chaplain glanced at the bridge table that served as his desk and saw only the abominable orange-red pear-shaped plum tomato he had obtained that same morning from Colonel Cathcart, still lying on its side where he had forgotten it like an indestructible and **incarnadine** symbol of his own ineptitude." –JOSEPH HELLER, *Catch-22*

iridescent (IR uh DE suhnt) - *adj.* producing a display of brilliant, lustrous, rainbowlike colors: iridescent butterfly wings.

> "I had one last impression that was both ordinary and unforgettable: a pyramid of turtles; the **iridescent** snout of a mandrill; the stately silence of a giraffe ..." –YANN MARTEL, *Life of Pi*

jet (JET) - (among other definitions) *n.* a dense black coal that takes a high polish

and is used for jewelry, 2. a deep black, 3. adj. of this color.

lamp-black (LAMP BLAK) - *n.* a fine black soot created by the incomplete burning of carbonous materials; used as a pigment in paint, ink, etc.

> "Already today he has indulged in one furious outburst against a **lampblack** manufacturer in West Ham, and now slumps on the ottoman, snoring stertorously through his swollen, blood-clogged nose." –MICHEL FABER, *The Crimson Petal and the White*

limed (LYMD) - (among other definitions) *adj.* of wood, esp. oak, that is bleached with lime.

> "I told myself how much I liked this place with its downtown hush and its office towers separated by open space and its parks with jogging trails and its fairy ring of hills and its residential streets of oleanders and palms and tree trunks **limed** white-white against the sun." –DON DELILLO, *Underworld*

madder (MAD uhr) - *n.* any of genus of plants, esp. a perennial vine with small yellow flowers, 2. the red root of this vine, 3. a red dye made from this root, 4. bright red; reddish-purple; crimson, 5. *adj.* of this color.

> "A madder orange moon hangs over the city ... But it is the [orange] juice [on the billboard] that commands the eye, thick and pulpy with a **ruddled** flush that matches the **madder** moon." –DON DELILLO, *Underworld*

maiden's blush (MAY duhnz BLUHSH) - *n.* a soft pink color.

"Maybe those are old French roses climbing the chimney pot, a color called **maiden's blush**." –DON DELILLO, *Underworld*

mauve (MOV, also MOHV) - *n.* a pale reddish or grayish purple, 2. *adj.* of this color.

*see **dun** for citation, p. 205*

murrey (MUHR ee) - *n.* a grayish-purple to dark purple; like the color of the mulberry, 2. also called mulberry, 3. *adj.* of this color.

"She wore a **murrey**-coloured gown with a little lace collar." –THOMAS HARDY, *Jude the Obscure*

ocher (also **ochre**) (OH ker) - *n.* a yellowish or brownish orange color, 2. a pigment made of iron oxides, clay and sand, 3. *adj.* of this color.

"They were dressed in finely dressed hides of rabbits and other small animals, and a kind of coarse cloth; and many were tattooed from head to foot in **ocher** and woad." –ROBERT E. HOWARD, *Bran Mak Morn*

periwinkle (PER i WING kuhl) - *n.* a light bluish color with purplish hues, 2. a blue-flowered myrtle, 3. an edible, small marine snail, 4. *adj.* of this color.

"... a collection of broths simmered over **periwinkle** flames on the stove." –JHUMPA LAHIRI, *Interpreter of Maladies*

primrose (PRIM ROHZ) - *n.* any of the Primula genus of early-flowering plants, having white, red, or yellow flowers, 2. a flower of the primrose plant, 3. the light yellow color of some primroses, 4. *adj.* of this color.

"The room was high and white and **primrose** gold, flanked by Greek columns that caught the lickety amber light of a thousand candles." –DON DELILLO, *Underworld*

puce (PYOOS) - *n.* a brownish-purple color, 2. *adj.* of this color. (French for flea).

"Lenny wore a white slim-line suit, well-pressed, and a **puce** pimp shirt with a roll collar, like a man trying to remind himself he is indestructible." –DON DELILLO, *Underworld*

roseate (ROH zee uht) - *adj.* rose-colored, 2. cheerful, optimistic, rosy.

"The abyss was now a seething chaos of **roseate** and cerulean splendor." –H.P. LOVECRAFT, *Celephaïs*

rubicund (ROO bi KUHND) - *adj.* having a healthy rosiness; reddish; ruddy.

"He was very like Old King Cole of the nursery rhyme, even to that monarch's **rubicund** jollity, his apple round, pippin red cheeks." –ABRAHAM MERRITT, *The Ship of Ishtar*

ruddle (RUH duhl) - *n.* red ocher, 2. *v.* to color or mark with red ocher, esp. to mark sheep in this manner, 3. to cause to flush; redden.

*see **madder** for citation, p. 206*

rufous (ROO fuhs) - *adj.* of a brownish-red color; rust-colored.

[describing a tiger] "Wavy dabs of black circled the face in a pattern that was striking yet subtle, for it brought less attention to itself than it did to the one part of the face left untouched by it, the bridge, whose **rufous** luster shone nearly with a radiance." –YANN MARTEL, *Life of Pi*

russet (RUH suht) - *n.* a coarse, reddish-brown, homespun fabric, 2. a reddish-brown color, 3. a winter apple having reddish-brown, rough skin, 4. *adj.* of this color.

saffron (SA fruhn) - *n.* the dried, orange-yellow stigmas of a kind of crocus, used to color and flavor food and as a dye, 2. an orange-yellow, 3. *adj.* of this color.

> "... tigerish princes in their rich tunics, green girdles, leathern sandals and **saffron** mantles caught with great golden brooches." –ROBERT E. HOWARD, *Eons of the Night*

sallow (SA LOH) - *adj.* of an unhealthy pale-yellow hue.

> "He wore a wig of the first quality, but it showed its age and wear in its stains and a dingy **sallow** color poorly hidden by powder." –DAVID LISS, *A Conspiracy of Paper*

sanguine (SANG gwuhn) - *adj.* having the color of blood; red, 2. ruddy, as the complexion, 3. optimistic; cheerful; anticipating the best.

> "'Most likely he'll ride a black stallion and bear arms either of an eagle, sable on argent, or of three hearts **sanguine** and three lions passant or ...'" –POUL ANDERSON, *Three Hearts and Three Lions*

sepia (SEE pee uh) - *n.* a dark, slightly reddish brown color or pigment (the pigment being made from the inky secretions of the cuttlefish), 2. a sepia-colored drawing or photograph, 3. *adj.* of this color.

> "... the apple core going **sepia** in the lunch tray ..." –DON DELILLO, *Underworld*

sienna (see E nuh) - *n.* a pigment containing iron and manganese oxides, naturally yellowish-brown, reddish-brown when burnt ("burnt sienna"), 2. either of these colors, 3. *adj.* of either of these colors.

> "Herzog with a beating heart but composed face entered, looked around with pale-faced dignity at the hangings (**sienna**,

crimson, green) and the fireplace stuffed with the wrappings of her latest purchases." –SAUL BELLOW, *Herzog*

sorrel (SOR uhl, also SAHR uhl) - *n.* any of the various plants of the genus Rumex, having acid-flavored leaves, sometimes used as salad greens, 2. a light reddish brown color, 3. a horse of this color, 4. *adj.* of this color.

> "... the glum, barrel-chested Indian, whose well-knit **sorrel**-red face had degenerated rapidly into a dilapidated, calcerous gray." –JOSEPH HELLER, *Catch-22*

subfusc (SUHB FUHSK) - *adj.* a somber, dark or dusky color, 2. clothing of this color.

> "There is no relief from **subfusc** utilitarianism until he reaches the French windows that open up onto the garden, where Nature has been permitted to embroider the bare earth ever so slightly." –MICHEL FABER, *The Crimson Petal and the White*

taupe (TOHP) - *n.* a dark brownish gray, 2. *adj.* of this color.

> "Eden was leaning over [her son] Anthony and letting him pull on the **taupe** lapels of her Italian suit and suck on her blouse." –JONATHAN FRANZEN, *The Corrections*

tawny (TO nee, also TAH nee) - *n., adj.* a light brown to golden brown color.

"None of them noticed a large, **tawny** owl flutter past the window." –J.K. ROWLING, *Harry Potter and the Sorcerer's Stone*

teal (TEEUHL) - *n.* any of various species of small, short-necked, freshwater duck, 2. a dark grayish or greenish blue, 3. *adj.* of this color.

"He chose the hard-top, **teal** blue, and drove off." –SAUL BELLOW, *Herzog*

titian (TI shuhn) - *adj.* a reddish yellow; auburn; often used to describe hair color, esp. the color of hair found in many paintings by Titian (Venetian painter, 1490–1576).

topaz (TOH PAZ) - *n.* a hard mineral consisting largely of aluminum silicate and valued as a gem, 2. any of various yellow gemstones, especially a yellow variety of sapphire, 3. *adj.* of the color of topaz.

"I walk in the door and see light strike the cool walls and bring out the color in the carpets, the apricots and clarets, the amazing **topaz** golds." –DON DELILLO, *Underworld*

umber (UHM buhr) - *n.* a brown or reddish pigment used in painting, containing clay, iron oxides and manganese, 2. *adj.* having a brownish hue.

"In the midst of all this the lamp still cast a smoky glow, obscure and brown as **umber**." –ROBERT LOUIS STEVENSON, *Treasure Island*

verdant (VUHR duhnt) - *adj.* green color; green from vegetation, 2. inexperienced in judgement or sophistication.

"... everyone had commented that the man seemed a bit rough around the edges, his **verdant** eyes a bit more intense than usual." –DAN BROWN, *Angels & Demons*

verdure (VUHR juhr) - *n.* the lush, vibrant greenness of flourishing vegetation, 2. vigorous green vegetation.

*see other **verdure** entry for citation, p. 199*

vermilion (vuhr MIL yuhn) - *n.* a bright red to reddish orange, 2. *adj.* - of this color.

"The setting sun broke through the clouds for a minute and smeared them with streaks of lurid **vermilion**." –L. SPRAGUE DE CAMP AND FLETCHER PRATT, *The Complete Compleat Enchanter*

viridescent (VIR uh DE suhnt) - *adj.* green or slightly green.

"... the reptilian gaze of those eyes which must haunt my dreams forever. They possessed a **viridescence** which hitherto I had supposed possible only in the eye of a cat." –SAX ROHMER, *The Insidious Dr. Fu-Manchu*

woad (WOHD) - *n.* an annual Old World plant from the mustard family, once cultivated for its leaves that produce a blue dye, 2. the dye made from this plant.

"They were dressed in finely dressed hides of rabbits and other small animals, and a kind of coarse cloth; and many were tattooed from head to foot in ocher and **woad**." –ROBERT E. HOWARD, *Bran Mak Morn*

PATTERNS

amorphous (also **amorphic**) (uh MOR fuhs) - *adj.* without definite form, 2. general or vague.

"Somewhere near by had been the pit, dark and awful, wherein screaming victims were fed to a nameless, **amorphic** monstrosity which came up out of a deeper, more hellish cavern." –ROBERT E. HOWARD, *Black Colossus*

calico (KA li KOH) - *n.* a rough, brightly printed cloth, 2. *adj.* made of calico, 3. having spots like calico, esp. a cat or other animal.

> "'No, I was not "playing" with the cat. I only picked it up to fondle it a bit. It was a rather appealing **calico.**'" –JOHN KENNEDY TOOLE, *A Confederacy of Dunces*

dapple (DA puhl) - *v.* to mark or mottle with spots.

> "About [the glades] lay long launds of green grass **dappled** with celandine and anemones, white and blue, now folded for sleep." –J.R.R. TOLKIEN, *The Two Towers*

harlequin (HAHR li kwuhn) - *n.* a clown, a buffoon, traditionally presented in mask and many colored costume, 2. having a pattern of parti-colored diamond shapes.

> "Here and there that woods **harlequin**, the madrone, permitting itself to be caught in the act of changing its pea-green trunk to madder-red, breathed its fragrance into the air." –JACK LONDON, *All Gold Canyon*

moiré (mwa RAY, also mor AY) - *n.* cloth, especially silk, with a watered or wavy pattern (from French moirer, to water).

> "The parasol was of rosy iridescent silk, and the sun pouring through it painted the white skin of her face with flickering patches of light. Beneath it she smiled at the springlike warmth; and drops of water could be heard falling one by one on the taut **moiré.**" –GUSTAVE FLAUBERT, *Madame Bovary*, transl. by Francis Steegmuller

piebald (PY BOLD) - *adj.* spotted or patched, esp. in black and white, 2. a spotted animal, esp. a horse.

> "A disorderly mop of black-and-white hair covered his head ... the eye that looked from under the **piebald** thatch was bright blue." –L. SPRAGUE DE CAMP AND FLETCHER PRATT, *The Complete Compleat Enchanter*

quincunx (KWIN KUHNGKS) - *n.* an arrangement of five objects set in a square or rectangle, one in each corner and one in the center.

stria (STRY uh) - *n.* a narrow groove or thin channel, 2. a thin band or line.

> "The bridge rose up over the river in a graceful parabola, its steel cables strung with red lights. The Cadillac's tires hummed over its **striated** surface." –JEFFREY EUGENIDES, *Middlesex*

tesselate (TE suh LAYT) - *v.* to form into a mosaic pattern.

> "The room was built of rose-colored marble excepting the floor which was **tesselated** in rose and gray." –ROBERT CHAMBERS, *The King in Yellow*

variegated (VER ee uh GAYT uhd, also VER i GAYT uhd) - *adj.* marked with different colors in spots, streaks, etc.; parti-colored, 2. having variety in character, form, etc.; varied; diversified.

> "... a pile of **variegated** fruits ..." –H.G. WELLS, *The Island of Dr. Moreau*

LIGHT AND SHADE

adumbrate (A duhm BRAYT, also a DUHM BRAYT) - *v.* to give a sketchy outline, 2. to foreshadow vaguely, 3. to obscure, overshadow, 4. *adj.* in a shadow or shadows.

> "... for Gormenghast [Castle], huge and **adumbrate**, out-crumbles all." –MERVYN PEAKE, *Titus Groan*

alpenglow (AL puhn GLOH) - *n.* the rosy glow of the rising or setting sun on mountaintops.

"The lobby crowd loved the mural. An enormous mystical vision ... with a sort of Lost Horizon motif ... Amber mists, a cloaked old man with a staff, a cluster of flamingos standing in the **alpenglow**—a vision so steeped in kitsch you could die just by buying the postcard." –DON DELILLO, *Underworld*

aureole (OR ee OHL) - *n.* a corona, 2. a circle of light or halo around the head of a deity.

"To his dizzy gaze she seemed to float in an **aureole** of golden light." –ROBERT E. HOWARD, *Trails in Darkness*

chatoyant (shuh TOI uhnt) - *adj.* possessing a changeable, undulating or floating luster, 2. a color that varies in different lights or at different angles, 3. *n.* a stone or gemstone such as the cat's-eye with such luster; a chatoyant stone.

corona (kuh ROH nuh) - *n.* a pale luminous ring encircling a celestial body, visible through a haze or thin cloud.

"Pale though the sun is, there's real warmth in it, as it lights up the tiles of Notting Hill's rooftops and brings a **corona** of brilliance to the church spire." –MICHEL FABER, *The Crimson Petal and the White*

coruscate (KOR uh SKAYT, also KAHR uh SKAYT) - *v.* to sparkle; to glitter; to give flashes of light.

"He was bright. He had a natural **coruscating** skepticism about baseball's traditional wisdom." –MICHAEL LEWIS, *Moneyball*

crepuscular (kri PUHS kyuh luhr) - *adj.* of or resembling twilight, 2. becoming active at twilight, esp. animals or insects.

"At the **crepuscular** age of 34, Andre Agassi had a legitimate chance to win his ninth major." –L. JON WERTHEIM, *Sports Illustrated,* 9/20/04

diaphanous (di A fuh nuhs) - *adj.* of such fine texture as to be translucent.

"In a while they lifted their eyes up from the valley, and there was the western sky still shining above the last of the gloaming, a little strip of colour and dying light, so lovely that they believed that another elfland lay the other side of the valley, two dim **diaphanous** magical elfin lands hemming in this valley and few fields of men close upon either side." –LORD DUNSANY, *The King of Elfland's Daughter*

dinge (DINJ) - *n.* dinginess; grime; squalor.

"The only ghosts I let in were local ones, the smoky traces of people I knew and the **dinge** of my own somber shadow." –DON DELILLO, *Underworld*

effulgent (i FUL juhnt) - *adj.* shining brilliantly; radiant; resplendent.

"... an **effulgent** flood of sunlight ..." –JOSEPH HELLER, *Catch-22*

etiolate (EE tee uh LATE) - *v.* to render (a person or plant) unhealthy or pale and colorless by excluding it from sunlight, 2. to deprive of vigor or strength; to weaken.

"In this (cinema-complex) warren the **etiolated** cineasts grope and blink about their business." –MARTIN AMIS, *Visiting Mrs. Nabokov*

evanescent (E vuh NE suhnt) - *adj.* tending to fade from sight; ephemeral; vanishing (*v.* evanesce, *n.* evanescence).

"**Evanescent** corridors of memory intervene between my writing and his talk, so there are gaps in this brief account." –MICHAEL MURPHY, *Golf in the Kingdom*

gloaming (GLOH ming) - *n.* twilight; dusk (from the Old English glom meaning dusk).

"... after the coming of men [the Wood-Elves] took ever more and more to the **gloaming** and the dusk ..." –J.R.R. TOLKIEN, *The Hobbit*

incandescent (IN kuhn DE suhnt) - *adj.* emitting light as a result of being heated, 2. shining very brightly, 3. showing intense emotion, as of a performance, etc.

*see other **incandescent** entry for citation, p. 38*

lambent (LAM buhnt) - *adj.* playing lightly over a surface; flickering, said of a flame, etc., 2. giving off a soft glow (as in a lambent sky), 3. playing lightly and gracefully over a subject: said of wit, humor, etc.

"She was no longer the same as in the independent days, when her intellect played like **lambent** lightning over conventions and formalities which he at the time respected, though he did not now." –THOMAS HARDY, *Jude the Obscure*

lightsome (LITE suhm) - *adj.* bright, well lighted, 2. lighthearted; free from care; without worry or sorrow, 3. moving lightly; lively, nimble, quick, graceful.

*see other **lightsome** entry for citation, p. 27*

limn (LIM) - *v.* to depict in painting or drawing, 2. to portray in words; to describe; to depict, 3. to illuminate, specifically a religious manuscript.

"He saw a great bulky shape **limned** faintly and briefly in the gray doorway." –ROBERT E. HOWARD, *Conan the Conqueror*

limpid (LIM pid) - *adj.* transparent; clear; serene, 2. clear or simple in style.

"... the Elf King ... sent over Elfland a melody all made of notes he had caught from wandering inspirations that sing and stray through **limpid** blue beyond our earthly coasts." –LORD DUNSANY, *The King of Elfland's Daughter*

livid (LIV ihd) - *adj.* discolored; bruised, 2. pallid or ashen, as from shock or anger, 3. furious, extremely angry.

"Below the hill the land stretched away featurelessly, cloud-mottled in the **livid** moonlight." –C.L. MOORE, *Jirel of Joiry*

lucent (LOO suhnt) - *adj.* giving off light; shining; luminous, 2. clear or transparent.

"The jewel gleamed like a fat, **lucent**, quivering drop of blood." –FRITZ LEIBER, *Swords Against Death*

lucid (LOO sid) - *adj.* easily understood, clear, 2. clear-headed, rational, 3. transparent.

*see other **lucid** entry for citation, p. 212*

lurid (LUR id) - *adj.* a ghastly pale or wan appearance, 2. glowing through a haze, as flames enveloped by smoke, 3. gruesome; sensational; harsh or shocking, 4. exhibiting violent passions.

"... one curiously carven gold lamp, swinging from the fretted ceiling, shed a **lurid** light over all." –ROBERT E. HOWARD, *Conan the Conqueror*

nimbus (NIM buhs) - *n.* a hazy or cloudy radiant light seen about the head in depictions of deities or saints; an aureole, 2. a rain cloud, uniformly gray, dark, and low.

"But sometimes, in the pale **nimbus** of the night lamp, Longfellow thought he could see her gentle face staring at him from the corner of the bedchamber." —MATTHEW PEARL, *The Dante Club*

occultation (AH KUHL TAY shuhn) - *n.* the state of becoming hidden or of disappearing from view; concealment, 2. a type of eclipse.

"Fard Muhammad was never seen again in Detroit. He went into **occultation** like the Twelfth Imam of the Shiites." —JEFFREY EUGENIDES, *Middlesex*

opalescence (OH puh LE suhnts) - *n.* a milky brightness or iridescence like that of an opal.

"... the bird ... with a wild screech of horribly human laughter, rushed away through the trees to vanish in the **opalescent** shadows." —ROBERT E. HOWARD, *Shadows in the Moonlight*

pallid (PA lid) - *adj.* pale; wan; faint in color.

"Slowly it grew to a little globe of **pallid** light." —J.R.R. TOLKIEN, *The Hobbit*

pallor (PA luhr) - *n.* paleness, lack of color, especially of the face.

"The pillars of the market cast long shadows, and the **pallor** of the road in the moonlight gave the effect of a summer night." —GUSTAVE FLAUBERT, *Madame Bovary*, transl. by Francis Steegmuller.

pellucid (puh LOO sid) - *adj.* transparent; translucent; clear; allowing for maximum passage of light, 2. clearly understood; of a clear or simple style.

"Meanwhile the girl had joined her companions, and she silently resumed her flicking and sousing of the chitterlings in the **pellucid** stream." —THOMAS HARDY, *Jude the Obscure.*

penumbra (puh NUHM bruh) - *n.* a partially shaded area around the edges of a shadow, especially an eclipse, 2. a region around the edge of a sunspot, darker than the sun's surface but lighter than the middle of the sunspot.

"At that hour the building was deserted ... Lights cast a bluish **penumbra** there, in which could be made out dark paintings, the marble banister and busts of Roman patricians watching from their niches." —ARTURO PEREZ-REVERTE, *The Flanders Panel*

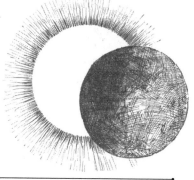

refulgent (ri FUHL juhnt) - *adj.* shining radiantly; resplendent; brilliant.

"For an instant, **refulgent** in his halo of media lights, the camerlengo looked celestial, like some kind of modern deity." —DAN BROWN, *Angels & Demons*

resplendent (ri SPLEN duhnt) - *adj.* shining with splendor.

"... **resplendent** in the background, the weathered copper dome of the grand church itself ..." —PHILIP ROTH, *American Pastoral*

roil (ROIUHL) - *v.* to make muddy or cloudy by stirring up sediment, 2. to irritate; agitate; vex.

"But in college there was a wide gulf between George W. Bush and John Kerry. As debates about civil rights and the Vietnam War **roiled** the campus, they went their separate ways." –JOHN TIERNEY, *The New York Times*, 3/21/04

scintillate (SIN tuhl AYT) - *v.* to throw off sparks; to sparkle; to flash; to shine, 2. to be lively, animated or brilliant.

"Spreading her arms wide, she swayed before him, her golden head lolling sensuously, her **scintillant** eyes half shadowed beneath their long silken ashes." –ROBERT E. HOWARD, *The Frost Giant's Daughter*

Stygian (STI jee uhn) - *adj.* of or relating to the River Styx, 2. gloomy and dark, 3. infernal; hellish, 4. totally binding or inviolable, as an oath sworn by the River Styx.

"I dreamed that I lay writhing on the floor in agony undescribable. My veins were filled with liquid fire, and but that **stygian** darkness was about me, I told myself that I must have seen the smoke arising from my burning body." –SAX ROHMER, *The Insidious Dr. Fu-Manchu*

swart (SWORT) - *adj.* swarthy, 2. having dark colored skin, 3. dark in color; black or blackish; dusky.

"He had not been there for some while, and it was with a kind of **swart** enjoyment that he surrendered to the sudden whim." –MERVYN PEAKE, *Titus Groan*

tenebrous (TE nuh bruhs) - *adj.* dark; gloomy: also tenebrious.

"I never sought to return to those **tenebrous** labyrinths." –H.P. LOVECRAFT, *He*

turbid (TUHR bid) - *adj.* having the sediment disturbed or roiled; muddy; thick not

clear, 2. disturbed; confused; disordered; perplexed; muddled, 3. thick or opaque as with clouds or smoke.

*see other **turbid** entry for citation, p. 189*

umbra (UHM bruh) - *n.* the darkest part of a shadow, a dark area from which all light is cut off, 2. the darkest part of the shadow cast by the moon onto the earth during a total solar eclipse.

"The springtime sun was setting behind St. Peter's Basilica, and a massive shadow spread, engulfing the piazza. Langdon felt an ominous chill as he and Vittoria moved into the cool, black **umbra**." –DAN BROWN, *Angels & Demons*

umbrage (UHM brij) - *n.* resentment; offense; a feeling of pique, 2. shade; shadow.

"Fierce births and deaths beneath **umbrageous** ceilings." –MERVYN PEAKE, *Titus Groan.*

wan (WAHN) - *adj.* pale, sickly-looking, 2. dim, faint, feeble or weak, 3. bland, uninterested.

"... a gray desert stretching flat and lifeless to the horizon, **wan** under the light of a dim red sun." –C.L. MOORE, *Jirel of Joiry*

SHAPES

annular (AN yuh luhr) - *adj.* ring shaped; forming a ring.

"They plodded around the **annular** harbor to the main canal." –L. SPRAGUE DE CAMP, *The Tritonian Ring*

annulus (AN yuh luhs) - *n.* a ringlike part, figure, structure, or marking.

"Langdon arrived behind her and eyed the peculiar donut-shaped hoop hanging where the doorknob should have been. 'An

annulus,' he whispered." —DAN BROWN, *Angels & Demons*

cruciform (KROO suh FORM) - *adj.* having the shape of a cross.

"We came from the Carolinas, the green hill country of the Blue Ridge, from **cruciform** towns with a single intersection." —PAT CONROY, *The Lords of Discipline*

Cyclopean (SI kluh PEE uhn, also SI KLOW pee uhn) - *adj.* of or pertaining to a Cyclops, 2. (c-) huge; gigantic; enormous; massive.

"And how my hatred for him grew and grew, during that fearful time, to **cyclopean** dimensions." —JACK LONDON, *The Sea Wolf*

falcate (FAL KAYT, also FOL KAYT) - *adj.* sickle shaped; curved and tapered to a point.

gibbous (GIB us) - *adj.* marked by a protuberance; rounded or bulging, 2. referring to the phase of the moon or a planet in which more than half but less than all of the disk is illuminated, 3. a humpback; having a hump.

"... grisly pre-Druidic oaks that fed unnameable monstrosities beneath a **gibbous** moon." —ROBERT E. HOWARD, *Cormac Mac Art*

gout (GOWT) - *n.* a disturbance of the uric-acid metabolism occurring predominantly in males and marked by arthritic attacks, 2. a blob, clot, or splash.

"The wind blew a **gout** of smoke into Sol's face as if trying to stop him from replying." —L. SPRAGUE DE CAMP, *The Tritonian Ring*

gyre (JY uhr) - *n.* a circular or spiral turning motion; whirl; revolution, 2. a circular or spiral form; ring; vortex.

"... circled about one another in ever-narrowing **gyres** ..." —MERVYN PEAKE, *Titus Groan.*

hank (HANGK) - *n.* a coil or loop, esp. of rope or yarn.

"... he sucks at a **hank** of his beard, which curls up and into his mouth through long training," —MERVYN PEAKE, *Titus Groan*

helical (HE li kuhl, also HEE li kuhl) - *adj.* in the shape or form of a helix or spiral.

"They turned in on the left by the church with the Italian porch, whose **helical** columns were heavily draped with creepers." —THOMAS HARDY, *Jude the Obscure*

homaloidal (HOHM ah LOID al) - *adj.* characteristic of a flat surface; a plane; flat; even.

"... 'we can see quite simply that this building is **homaloidal**, or—in the language of the layman—flat.'" —AYN RAND, *The Fountainhead*

infundibuliform (IN FUHN Di buh luh FORM) - *adj.* shaped like a funnel.

"The only end in sight was Yossarian's own, and he might have remained in the hospital until doomsday had it not been for that patriotic Texan with his **infundibuliform** jowls and his lumpy, rumpleheaded, indestructible smile cracked forever across the front of his face like the brim of a black ten-gallon hat." —JOSEPH HELLER, *Catch-22*

lenticular (len TI kyuh luhr) - *adj.* having the form of a biconvex lens; relating to or resembling a lens; shaped as or resembling a lentil.

"Right next to him, there's me, his sometime sister, my face already a conundrum, flashing like a **lenticular** decal between two images: the dark-eyed, pretty little girl I used to be; and the severe, aquiline-nosed, Roman-coinish person I am today." –JEFFREY EUGENIDES, *Middlesex*

lozenge (LAH zuhnj, also LAH zuhnj) - *n.* a flat, four-sided figure with a diamondlike shape, 2. a small, medicated candy, esp. of a lozenge shape.

"Ovoid and stiffened with whalebone, [the hat] began with three convex strips; then followed alternating **lozenges** of velvet and rabbit's fur, separated by a red band." –GUSTAVE FLAUBERT, *Madame Bovary*, transl. by Francis Steegmuller

meniscus (muh NIS kuhs) - *n.* a crescent-shaped body, 2. the curved upper surface of a liquid in a container.

moiety (MOI uh tee) - *n.* a half, 2. one of the two or more parts into which something has been divided; a part; a share; an interest.

"But, instead of paying him the **moiety** of my gains as I had promised, I denounced him to my own monarch." –ROBERT E. HOWARD AND L. SPRAGUE DE CAMP, *Conan the Usurper.*

ovoid (OH VOID) - *adj.* egg-shaped.

*see **lozenge** for citation*

rugose (ROO GOHS) - *adj.* having many wrinkles, creases or ridges; corrugated.

"If *Candide* is a masterpiece marking the climax of a thousand years of intellectual commerce between France and England, this is because it wedded the **rugosities** of thought then somewhat prevalent in

Britain with the formal elegance of French art." –PAUL MORAND, *Introduction, Francois Voltaire's Candide*

salient (SAY lyuhnt, also SAY lee uhnt) - *adj.* worthy of note, 2. standing out or projecting beyond a line or surface, 3. prominent; striking; conspicuous.

*see other **salient** entry for citation, p. 276*

spatulate (SPA chuh luht) - *adj.* spatula-shaped; having a broad, flat or rounded end.

"He was a sad, birdlike man with the **spatulate** face and scrubbed, tapering features of a well-groomed rat." –JOSEPH HELLER, *Catch-22*

Trinacrian (truh NA kree uhn, also try NA kree uhn) - *adj.* of or from Sicily; Sicilian, hence, three-pointed.

"'An eye inside a triangle.'

'It's called the **trinacria**.'" –DAN BROWN, *Angels & Demons.*

OTHER VISUALS

baroque (buh ROK, also ba ROK, buh RAHK, buh ROCK) - *adj.* (often Baroque) having an irregular shape, 2. flamboyant; outlandish, 3. an artistic style common in Europe from 1500 to 1700 exhibiting very elaborate and ornate forms, 4. a musical style common in Europe from 1600 to 1750 exhibiting strict forms and elaborate detail.

*see other **baroque** entry for citation, p. 104*

bas-relief (BAH ri LEEF, also BAS ri LEEF) - *n.* a term used in sculpture, also low-relief; forms projected only slightly from the background.

"The marble lintel over the door is a beautiful **bas-relief** from Italy depicting a woman holding poppies, wheat sheaves, and serpents." –DANIEL BACON, *The Official Guide to San Francisco's Barbary Coast Trail*

chiaroscuro (kee AHR uh SKYUR OH) - *n.* an artistic technique developed during the Renaissance, referring to the use of exaggerated light contrasts in order to create an image of volume, 2. a monochrome picture made by using several different shades of the same color (*The Oxford English Dictionary* states that clair-obscure is the same term; "claire-obscure" is used in Don DeLillo's *Underworld*).

> "In the delicately woven **chiaroscuro** of hearth, lamp, and wick, the ink seemed to lift off Longfellow's proofs, as if a page of Dante suddenly came alive under one's eyes." –MATTHEW PEARL, *The Dante Club*

cinquecento (CHING kwi CHEN TOH) - *n.* referring to the style of art, architecture and literature in Italy in the 1500s, characterized by a reversion to classical forms.

> "Acey had the calm and somber eye of a **cinquecentist**." –DON DELILLO, *Underworld*

efface (i FAYS, also e FAYS) - *v.* to obliterate or make indistinct by or as if by rubbing out.

> "Nevertheless, the Crusades left changes in the European military world that were never **effaced**." –JOHN KEEGAN, *A History of Warfare*

gesso (JE SOH) - *n.* a mixture of Plaster of Paris and glue used as a base for bas-relief or low-relief, sometimes used as a surface for painting, 2. a piece of art using this medium.

> "For a while she used house paint, radiator paint. She liked rough surfaces, flaked paint on metal, she liked puttied window frames, all the **gesso** textures, the gluey chalks and linseeds that get mixed and smeared, that get schmeered onto a weathered length of wood." –DON DELILLO, *Underworld*

incunabulum (in KYUH NA byuh luhm, also ing KYUH NA byuh luhm) (pl. -la) - *n.* a book printed before 1501 using movable type, 2. a work of art from an early period.

see other **incunabulum** *entry for citation, p. 87*

intaglio (in TAL YOH, also in TAHL YOH, in TA glee OH) - *n.* a design or form carved deep into the surface of a hard metal or stone.

> "Sergeant Claude Johnson, the only black WPA artist in Northern California, designed the green slate **intaglio** at the front entrance [of the National Maritime Museum] and the tile mural at the rear terrace, which was never completed." –DANIEL BACON, *The Official Guide to San Francisco's Barbary Coast Trail*

kitsch (KICH) - *n.* art, decorative objects, and other forms of representation of questionable artistic or aesthetic value; a representation that is excessively sentimental, overdone or vulgar.

see other **kitsch** *entry for citation, p. 84*

maquette (ma KET) - *n.* a small, preliminary sketch or small model to represent an intended art work, usually a sculpture, 2. used allusively for any model or template made to represent something to be built or produced.

> "There were bouquets from opening-night well-wishers, all of them gathered around the **maquette** for the 'Everywhere' poster." –GLEN DAVID GOLD, *Carter Beats the Devil*

putto (POO TOH) -*(pl. putti)* - *n.* the artistic representation of a small child-like angel or cupid, often nude or in swaddling clothes and having wings, as in baroque art.

> "Whereas its neighbors were hooded Arts and Crafts fortresses, One Hilgirt Circle was a **rococo** circus of archways, terracotta **putti**, gargoyles, and trellises strung with passion vines." –GLEN DAVID GOLD, *Carter Beats the Devil*

quattrocento (KWAH troh CHEN TOH) - *n.* the style of Italian art and literature in the fifteenth century.

> "A year of fellowship work in New York ensued, until Ohio State offered him a tenure-track position teaching **quattrocento** history, and he leapt at the chance to go home." –IAN CALDWELL AND DUSTIN THOMASON, *The Rule of Four*

rococo (ruh KOH KOH) - *adj.* of a style of art, architecture, and the decorative art marked by elaborate, asymmetric ornamentation, 2. an overly ornate style.

> *see **putto** for citation*

rotogravure (ROH tuh gruh VYUR) - *n.* a printing process using a rotary press in which an image is produced from an etched copper cylinder onto a surface, 2. the printed materials produced by this process.

> "In his father's pocket-sized dry-cleaning shop there had been a **rotogravure** picture of FDR framed on the wall above the pressing machine." –PHILIP ROTH, *American Pastoral*

scumble (SKUM buhl) - *v.* to soften or blur a picture or portion of a picture by covering it with an opaque or semi-opaque film for the purpose of softening hard lines or blending colors, 2. to produce an effect by the use of this process.

> "I used to half listen, listen with my face in a magazine, hearing **scumbled** voices coming from the back room, a cluster of words audible now and then above the dishwasher and the TV set." –DON DELILLO, *Underworld*

simulacrum (SIM yuh LA kruhm, also SIM yuh LAY kruhm) (pl. -ra) - *n.* an image, likeness, 2. a faint trace, vague representation, semblance, 3. a mere pretense, sham.

> "The smoke thickened and solidified and became a **simulacrum** of a tall, heavy woman, clad in wolfskin." –L. SPRAGUE DE CAMP, *The Tritonian Ring*

tincture (TINGK chuhr) - *n.* a substance used in dyeing, a pigment, 2. an imparted color; a stain; a tint, 3. a trace; evidence; a vestige, 4. a nonvolatile medicine, usually an alcohol solution, 5. *v.* to stain, to dye, to tint with color.

> "His fat, flabby, clean-shaven face looked as though it had been dyed with a faint **tincture** of licorice, and his white hair emphasized the piercing boldness of his small black eyes." –GUSTAVE FLAUBERT, *Madame Bovary*, transl. by Francis Steegmuller

trompe l'oeil (TROMP LUHI) - *n.* a deception or fooling of the eye; an illusion (from French, "deceives the eye"), 2. a style of painting intended to give the illusion of photographic reality.

> "In front of [St. Peter's Basilica], bordering the vast oval common, 284 columns swept outward in four concentric arcs of diminishing size ... an architectural **trompe l'oeil** used to heighten the piazza's sense of grandeur." –DAN BROWN, *Angels & Demons*

12. CLOTHING

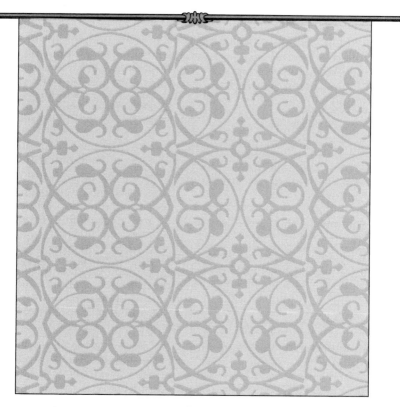

CLOTHING ITEMS

SHIRTS, DRESSES, ETC.

bodice (BAH duhs) - *n.* the fitted part of a dress from the waist up.

"He regarded the delicate lines of her profile, and the small, tight, apple-like convexities of her **bodice,** so different from Arabella's amplitudes." –THOMAS HARDY, *Jude the Obscure*

chemise (shuh MEEZ) - *n.* a loose, shirt-like undergarment worn by women, 2. a loosely fitting dress that hangs straight from the shoulders; a shift.

"He scored exactly once, with a young hippie from Oregon who had ketchup stains on her **chemise** and a scalpy smell so overpowering that he spent much of the night breathing through his mouth." –JONATHAN FRANZEN, *The Corrections*

cote-hardie (KOHT HAR dee) - *n.* a close-fitting, unisex garment with sleeves.

"His pointed shoes were satin, his **cote-hardie** of gold-broidered velvet." –ROBERT E. HOWARD, *Black Colossus*

dirndl (DUHRN duhl) - *n.* a dress having a tight bodice and a full skirt with a gathered waistband.

"... the boat came around to the west and picked up more speed. **Dirndls,** kerchiefs, and suit coats flapped in the breeze." –JEFFREY EUGENIDES, *Middlesex*

guayabera (GWEE uh BER uh) - *n.* a lightweight, open-necked cotton shirt, having large pockets and pleats in the front, usually worn untucked, outside the pants.

"Nearby, a group of Mexicans in cowboy hats conversed in Spanish, their accents sounding different to John than the Cubans in Miami. They weren't wearing **guayberas** either or playing dominoes." –ROBERT MAILER ANDERSON, *Boonville*

halter (HOL tuhr) - (among other definitions) *n.* a woman's top that ties behind the neck and across the back.

"Because now they pranced onstage: the chorus girls. Dressed in silver **halters,** robed in see-through shifts, they danced, reciting strophes that didn't scan to the eerie piping of flutes." –JEFFREY EUGENIDES, *Middlesex*

khilat (khil AHT) - *n.* a dress of honor given by a king or dignitary as an award of distinction to the recipient; any generous gift presented by an acknowledged superior.

"The other ... was dressed in a white, girdled **khalat** and a flowing head-dress." –ROBERT E. HOWARD, *A Witch Shall Be Born*

leg-of-mutton (LE guhv MUH tuhn, also LAYG uhv MUH tuhn) - *n.* like or resembling a leg of mutton in that said item tapers sharply from a large end to a much smaller end; used to described a sleeve (full and loose on the arm, close-fitting at the wrist) or a type of triangular sail.

> "... she hurried with me, swinging her arms in her short jacket of **leg-of-mutton** sleeves." –SAUL BELLOW, *The Adventures of Augie March*

middy (MI dee) - *n.* a middy blouse (named after midshipman); a loose blouse with a sailor collar, worn by women and children.

> "She wore a **middy** and a pleated skirt ... a proper, vain girl." –SAUL BELLOW, *Herzog*

muumuu (MOO MOO) - *n.* a long, loose dress.

> "Just as colorful as the flowers [in the salon] was Sophie Sassoon herself. In a purple **muumuu**, braceleted and begemmed, she glided from chair to chair." –JEFFREY EUGENIDES, *Middlesex*

pinafore (PI nuh FOOR) - *n.* a sleeveless, apron-like dress worn over other clothing.

> "... girls in white **pinafores** over red and blue frocks appeared dancing along the paths ..." –THOMAS HARDY, *Jude the Obscure*

shift (SHIFT) - (among other definitions) *n.* a loosely fitting dress that hangs straight from the shoulders, 2. a woman's loose fitting sleeveless undergarment; a slip; a chemise.

> *see **halter** for citation*

stomacher (STUH mi KUHR, also STUH mi CHUHR) - *n.* a woman's garment, heavily embroidered or embellished, and worn over the chest and stomach.

> "The once ivory muslin was now yellowish-brown, and her plain tan **stomacher** had grown so filthy as to almost want delousing." –DAVID LISS, *A Conspiracy of Paper*

LEGWEAR

bloomers (BLOO muhrz) - *n.* women's loose, wide pants gathered at or above the knee, 2. underpants of a similar design.

> "... her chicken-thin little sister in black gym **bloomers** cut paper with the big shears." –SAUL BELLOW, *The Adventures of Augie March*

breech-clout (BREECH KLAUT) - (more commonly, breech-cloth) *n.* a garment worn to cover the loins; a loincloth.

> "Olmec, naked but for a **breech-clout**, was fighting before his throne." –ROBERT E. HOWARD, *Conan the Warrior*

breeches (BRIH chuhz, also BREE chuhz) - *n.* trousers, 2. trousers ending just above or just below the knee, often tapered to fit closely.

> "... the platters of carved meat were brought round by the maître d'hotel himself, grave as a judge in silk stockings, knee **breeches**, white neckloth and jabot." –GUSTAVE FLAUBERT, *Madame Bovary*, transl. by Francis Steegmuller

breeks (BREEKS, also BRIKS) - *n.* britches; breeches.

> "He was naked except for his silken **breeks**, for, like the Hyrkanians, even the commoners and slaves of Stygia wore silk." –ROBERT E. HOWARD, *Conan the Conqueror*

culottes (KOO LAHTZ, also KYOO LAHTZ) - *n.* a split or divided skirt; a woman's knee-length full trousers cut to look like a skirt.

"... 'the girls are in danger of losing all of their cardigans and **culottes**.'" –JOHN KENNEDY TOOLE, *A Confederacy of Dunces*

jodhpurs (JAHD PUHRZ) - *n.* pants worn for riding horses, fitting loosely above the knee and tightly from the knees to the ankles.

"Something from Joseph Conrad sprang to my mind, although I cannot seem to remember what it was at the time. Perhaps I likened myself to Kurtz in *The Heart of Darkness* when, far from the trading company offices in Europe, he was faced with the ultimate horror. I do remember imagining myself in a pith helmet and white linen **jodhpurs**, my face enigmatic behind a veil of mosquito netting." –JOHN KENNEDY TOOLE, *A Confederacy of Dunces*

puttee (PUH TEE) - *n.* a strip of cloth wound around the leg from knee to ankle, 2. a leather gaiter to cover the lower leg.

"The lawn, the gardens, the gardener in **puttees** were all real." –TOM WOLFE, *A Man in Full*

trews (TROOZ) - *n.* tight-fitting trousers, esp. those made of tartan, usually combined with stockings and worn by Irishmen and Scottish Highlanders, 2. trousers.

"Highlanders in six different patterns of tartan, Lowlanders in plaid **trews** ..." –JOHN KEEGAN, *A History of Warfare*

OUTERWEAR

anorak (A nuh RAK) - *n.* a heavy jacket having a hood; a parka.

"Men in canvas **anoraks** are offering their jackets to undressed girlfriends." –IAN CALDWELL AND DUSTIN THOMASON, *The Rule of Four*

burka (bur KAH) - *n.* a long, loose garment that covers the entire body with veiled holes to allow for vision, worn by Muslim women to keep them from being viewed by men and strangers.

"Here [in Pakistan] it wasn't uncommon to see women dressed in **burkas**, and Wilson decided not to take any risks." –GEORGE CRILE, *Charlie Wilson's War*

burnoose (BUHR NOOS) - *n.* a long, hooded cloak worn by Arabs and Moors.

"His old sire, gruff and mocking, deeply tickled, lay like the Buffalo Bill of the Etruscans in the beach chair and bath towel drawn up **burnoose**-wise to keep the dazzle from his eyes—additionally shaded by his soft, flesh-heavy arm—his bushy mouth open with laughter." –SAUL BELLOW, *The Adventures of Augie March*

caftan (also **kaftan**) (KAF TAN) - *n.* a full-length tunic with long or elbow length sleeves, worn esp. in the Near East, 2. a type of woman's dress that imitates this look, usually worn loosely and made of brightly colored fabric.

"This younger son ... was clean-shaven and wore European clothes (Samsonov himself wore a **kaftan** and a beard)" –FYODOR DOSTOYEVSKY, *The Brothers Karamazov*, transl. by David Magarshack

chesterfield (CHES tuhr FEELD) - *n*. a single- or double-breasted overcoat, usually with a fly front and velvet collar, 2. a sofa, esp. one heavily stuffed and with upright armrests at either end.

see other chesterfield entry for citation, p. 279

doublet (DUHB luht) - (among other definitions) *n*. a man's close-fitting jacket, popular between the 15th and 17th centuries.

"'You look troubled, young Potter,' said Nick, folding a transparent letter as he spoke and tucking it inside his **doublet**." –J.K. ROWLING, *Harry Potter and the Chamber of Secrets*

jelab (JIL yab) - *n*. a Moroccan hooded cloak.

"Vakar, with an inaudible little sigh, walked towards the [big black stallion], pulling up his long Kernean **jelab** through his girdle." –L. SPRAGUE DE CAMP, *The Tritonian Ring*

jerkin (JUHR kuhn) - *n*. a closefitting, short jacket, collarless and often sleeveless, or a vest, usually made of leather; worn by men in the 16th and 17th centuries.

"The king and his allies moved westward at the head of fifty thousand men— knights in shining armor with their pennons streaming above their helmets, pikemen in steel caps and brigandines, crossbowmen in leather **jerkins**." –ROBERT E. HOWARD, *Conan the Conqueror*

jubbah (also **jibbah, djibba[h], djebba**) (JUB bah, also JUB beh) - *n*. a unisex, long outer garment worn in some Muslim countries.

"The door was opened, and the speaker burst into the room—a lean, wiry man in a white **djebbeh**, dark-skinned, the

whites of his eyes gleaming." –ROBERT E. HOWARD, *The Snout in the Dark*

kirtle (KUHR tuhl) - *n*. a man's tunic or coat, kneelength or slightly longer, worn in the Middle Ages, 2. a woman's long dress or skirt.

"Indifferent to the chill of the wind, she sat there, her only garments a scant **kirtle** which left her arms bare and came barely to her knees, and leather sandals on her feet." –ROBERT E. HOWARD, *Bran Mak Morn*

mantle (MAN tuhl) - (among other definitions) *n*. a loose, sleeveless coat or cloak worn over outergarments, 2. something that covers, envelops or conceals.

"... tigerish princes in their rich tunics, green girdles, leathern sandals and saffron **mantles** caught with great golden brooches." –ROBERT E. HOWARD, *Eons of the Night*

peignoir (payn WAHR, also pen WAHR) - *n*. a woman's loose-fitting dressing gown.

"She had on a lacy top, resembling a **peignoir**, with jeans, at the moment a fashionable teenage clash of chords deemed provocative." –TOM WOLFE, *I Am Charlotte Simmons*

raglan (RA gluhn) - *n*. a sleeve that extends from neckline to wrist with slanted seams from armhole to neck, 2. a garment with such a sleeve.

"He resembled a gentile lost in a fog, wearing a suede touring cap and a double-breasted raincoat with epaulets, gun flaps, **raglan** sleeves, he knows these terms from years in dry cleaning, broad-welt pockets, belt loops, sleeve straps and so

many buttons he felt dressed for life."
–DON DELILLO, *Underworld*

sarafan (SAHR ah FAN) - *n.* a long mantle, veil or sleeveless cloak, worn by Russian peasant women.

> "They follow her about with a **sarafan** or striped, home-spun skirt and beg her to get up so they can put it on and take her to church to be married." –FYODOR DOS-TOYEVSKY, *The Brothers Karamazov*, transl. by David Magarshack

surtout (SUHR TOO) - *n.* a man's great-coat or overcoat designed in the style of a frock coat and having pockets cut diagonally in front, popular in the late 19th century.

> "An anonymous letter informed the police that [the] murderer ... had boarded a ship to Liverpool in a **surtout** borrowed without permission." –MATTHEW PEARL, *The Dante Club*

tabard (TA buhrd, also TA bahrd) - *n.* a short, sleeveless cape made of coarse material and formerly worn by the lower classes or by monks and foot-soldiers, 2. a short-sleeved tunic worn by a knight over his armor and emblazoned with a coat of arms.

topper (TAH puhr) - (among other definitions) *n.* a lightweight, loose fitting coat or jacket worn by women and children.

> "She was wearing her short pink topper and the small red hat that tilted over one eye so that she looked like a refugee starlet from the Golddiggers film series ... Ignatius noticed hopelessly that she had added a dash of color by pinning a wilted poinsettia to the lapel of her **topper**." –JOHN KENNEDY TOOLE, *A Confederacy of Dunces*

tunic (TOO nik, also TYOO nik) - *n.* a loose-fitting garment reaching to the knees, worn by men and women, esp. in ancient Greece and Rome, 2. a plain, fitted outer garment, hip-length usually having a high, stiff collar and worn as part of a uniform, 3. a woman's long blouse, typically worn over a skirt or slacks.

> "He removed his light and shining hauberk And cut his **tunic** into strips. He placed the pieces in his great wounds." –*The Song of Roland*, transl. by Glyn Burgess

ulster (UHL stuhr) - *n.* a loose, long over-coat made of a heavy, rugged fabric, (from the name for Ireland).

> "She was wrapped in a long **ulster**, for the morning was raw; and I could see nothing but her face and a mass of light brown hair escaping from under the seaman's cap." –JACK LONDON, *The Sea Wolf*

weskit (WES kuht) - *n.* a vest (shortened from waistcoat).

> "'I can see he's been mixing in strange company. What's come of his **weskit**? I don't hold with wearing ironmongery.'" –J.R.R. TOLKIEN, *The Return of the King*

zoot suit (ZOOT SOOT) - *n.* a flashy suit popular in the 1940s, characterized by its extreme cut having high-waisted tapered trousers and a long, draped jacket with wide lapels and padded shoulders.

> "From the tender age of twelve, my mother had been unable to start her day without the aid of at least two cups of immoderately strong, tar-black, unsweetened coffee, a taste for which she had picked up from the tugboat captains and **zooty** bachelors who filled the boardinghouse where she had grown up." –JEFFREY EUGENIDES, *Middlesex*

HEADWEAR

Balaclava (BA luh KLAH vuh) - *n.* a warm, woolen hood covering the head and neck, worn by soldiers, mountain climbers and skiers (named after the Crimean village of Balaclava); helmet, also cap.

"Hagrid's face was entirely hidden by a wooly, snow-covered **balaclava**, but it couldn't possibly be anyone else." –J.K. ROWLING, *Harry Potter and the Chamber of Secrets*

boater (BOH tuhr) - *n.* a stiff braided straw hat with a flat crown and brim; originally one suitable to wear when boating.

"He tipped his **boater** back, observing the deck of the Charlie Mae." –GLEN DAVID GOLD, *Carter Beats the Devil*

Borsalino (bor suh LEE noh) - *n.* a type of man's wide-brimmed felt hat; a proprietary name for a hat made by Borsalino, an Italian company.

"Against the cold he had worn a hat, a gray felt **Borsalino**, with a red feather in the black band." –JEFFREY EUGENIDES, *Middlesex*

busby (BUHZ bee) - *n.* a tall fur hat worn by certain regiments of the British Army on ceremonial occasions.

"They were a fine lot of fellows, in the pale-blue, tight-fitting jackets, jaunty **busbys** and white riding breeches with the double yellow stripe, into which their limbs seemed molded." –ROBERT CHAMBERS, *The King in Yellow*

chaperon (SHA puh ROHN) - (French) *n.* hood, head covering or headgear, hence protector or protection.

"... something in the timbre of the voice caused the page to doff his feathered **chaperon** as he bowed and replied ..." –ROBERT E. HOWARD, *Conan the Conqueror*

chaplet (CHAP luht) - *n.* a wreath or garland worn around the head, 2. a string of prayer beads having one third the number of a rosary's beads, 3. a string of beads.

"She plucked the petals of the blossoms and fashioned them into a **chaplet** for her golden hair." –ROBERT E. HOWARD, *The Vale of Lost Women*

cloche (KLOHSH) - *n.* a woman's close-fitting, often bell-shaped hat (from the old French for bell).

"... a lady in a cream-colored suit, with a long scarf wound around her slender neck, a **cloche** pulled over her bobbed hair." –UMBERTO ECO, *Foucault's Pendulum*

cockade (kah KAYD) - *n.* an ornament, esp. a rosette or knot of ribbon, usually worn on the hat.

"That tall, fat old man, in an overcoat and a cap with a **cockade** was Mikhail Makarov, the police inspector." –FYODOR DOSTOYEVSKY, *The Brothers Karamazov*, transl. by David Magarshack

coif (KWOF) *n.* a tight, close-fitting cap, 2. a hair style.

"Her thin face, framed in a simple **coif**, was more wrinkled than a withered russet." –GUSTAVE FLAUBERT, *Madame Bovary*, transl. by Francis Steegmuller

coxcomb (also **cockscomb**) (KAHKS com) - *n.* one who is conceited, a dandy; a fop, 2. **cockscomb**—the fleshy red crest on the head of a rooster, 3. a cap worn by a court jester, adorned to resembly the comb of a rooster.

"In quick succession, each time without caring to look where he aimed, Carter threw a golfing cap, a flapper's cloche hat, a sombrero, and something quite silly, a **coxcomb**, onto the racks behind him, the coxcomb actually changing direction twice in midair before finding its place." –GLEN DAVID GOLD, *Carter Beats the Devil*

derby (DUHR bee) - (among other definitions) *n.* a hard, round, black hat with a narrow brim.

"He held his **derby** between his thighs ... and he looked into the hat as though debating whether it was wise to release his grasshopper on the lining for a while." –SAUL BELLOW, *The Adventures of Augie March*

diadem (DY uh DEM, also DY uh duhm) - *n.* a crown, 2. royal power; royal dignity, 3. an ornamental or jeweled cloth or headband, worn as a crown to signify sovereignty, 4. *v.* to put on a crown; to crown.

"The sky above is blue; the many clouds—sun-drenched, gilded, lively—have moved down, settled like a great **diadem** on the broad ring of the encircling mountains." –MILAN KUNDERA, *Ignorance*

fedora (fi DOHR uh) - *n.* a soft felt hat with a low, creased crown and a flexible brim.

"He is barely more than a silhouette, slender and elegant, wearing a **fedora** that shadows his face." –JEFFREY EUGENIDES, *Middlesex*

homburg (HAHM BUHRG) - *n.* a man's felt hat with a soft, dented crown and a slightly rolled, shallow brim.

"In the box seats across the field Edgar sets his hat at an angle on his head. It is a dark gray **homburg** that brings out the nicely sprinkled silver at his temples." –DON DELILLO, *Underworld*

kaffiyeh (kuh FEE uh) - *n.* a headdress worn by Arab men to protect them from dust and heat, usually made from a large square of cloth and fastened by a band around the crown.

"Only the headgear—the fez, the turban, the **kefiya**—remained, to symbolize their difference from the West." –BERNARD LEWIS, *What Went Wrong?*

Panama (PA nuh MAH, also PA nuh MO) - *n.* a stiff, hand-plaited, natural-colored hat with a flat crown, made from the leaves of a palmlike tropical American plant.

"He was still in his shirt, owing to sunburn, but wore his **panama**, the breeze molding the brim around." –SAUL BELLOW, *The Adventures of Augie March*

periwig (PER i WIG) - *n.* a men's wig fashionable in the 17th to 18th centuries, usually powdered with a ribbon to tie the hair in back; a peruke.

"I wore no **peruke**, and instead pulled my locks back in the style of a tie-**periwig**." –David Liss, A Conspiracy of Paper

peruke (puh ROOK) - *n.* a periwig, possibly referring to an earlier, simpler style of men's wig (from the old French, peruque, for wig).

*see **periwig** for citation*

Stetson (STET suhn) - *n.* a hat with a high creased crown and a broad brim, trademarked by the John B. Stetson Hat Company; most frequently associated with cowboys.

> "There he was able to see the celebrities in their furs or **stetsons** and alpacunas, going free in the midst of their toted luggage." –SAUL BELLOW, *The Adventures of Augie March*

tam-o'-shanter (TA muh SHAN tuhr) - *n.* a tight-fitting, flat-topped woolen cap of Scottish origin (named after the hero of Robert Burns' poem *Tam o'Shanter*).

> "She had no friends, and had always shambled around on her errands in her man's shoes and her black **tam**, thick glasses on her rosy, lean face, as a kind of curiosity in the neighborhood, some queer woman, not all there." –SAUL BELLOW, *The Adventures of Augie March*

toque (TOHK) - *n.* a woman's small, brimless tightly-fitting hat, 2. a chef's hat.

> "Her thick blonde hair, carefully smoothed back from her temples, was caught up beneath a **toque** of white gauze." –ARTURO PEREZ-REVERTE, *The Flanders Panel*

tricorn (TRY KORN) - *n.* a hat with the brim turned up on three sides, forming three points.

> "In among the spruces near the hedge the [plaster] priest in a **tricorn** reading his breviary had lost his right foot." –GUSTAVE FLAUBERT, *Madame Bovary*, transl. by Francis Steegmuller

trilby (TRIL bee) - (among other definitions) *n.* a soft felt hat having a deeply creased crown; similar to a homburg.

> "One evening a housemate brought a new boyfriend home; he was an older guy, a writer who wore a **trilby**, pretty intimidating in all sorts of ways" –NICK HORNBY, *Songbook*

SHOES AND SHOE PARTS

aglet (A gluht) - (among other definitions) *n.* the metal or plastic sheath over the end of a lace, esp. a shoelace, to facilitate threading it through the eyelet-holes, as of a shoe, and also to serve as ornamentation.

> "'And the metal sheath at each end of the lace.' ... 'The tag or **aglet**.'" –DON DELILLO, *Underworld*

alpargata (al PAHR gah tah) - *n.* a style of sandal.

> "He liked Spanish costumes, and when Herzog last saw him he was wearing white duck trousers of bull-fighter's cut and **alpargatas**." –SAUL BELLOW, *Herzog*

brogan (BROH guhn, also BROH GAN) - *n.* a thick, heavy, ankle-high shoe or work boot.

> "A pair of workman's **brogans** encased my feet." –JACK LONDON, *The Sea Wolf*

brogue (BROG) - *n.* a stout, heavy oxford shoe, 2. an Irish accent of a particular dialect or region.

> "Two men stood on the welcome mat. They wore gray suits, striped ties, black **brogues**." –JEFFREY EUGENIDES, *Middlesex*

buskin (BUS kin) - *n.* a thick-soled, laced half boot or high shoe that reaches halfway up to the knee, worn in Greek and Roman tragedies, 2. a tragic drama.

> "He drew on high, laced **buskins**." –ABRAHAM MERRITT, *The Ship of Ishtar*

counter (KAUN tuhr) - *n.* a piece of stiff leather around the back of the heel of a shoe or boot.

> "'And this stiff section over the heel. That's the **counter**.'" –DON DELILLO, *Underworld*

cuff (KUHF) - (among other definitions) *n.* defined in quote.

> "With his finger he traced a strip of leather that went across the top edge of the shoe and dipped down under the lace ... 'What is it?' ... 'It's the **cuff**.'" –DON DELILLO, *Underworld*

espadrille (ES puh DRIL) - *n.* a sandal with a rope or rubber sole and a cloth or canvas upper.

> "... the musicians entered ... casually dressed for the rehearsal ... a guest conductor, Sergiu Commissiona, an aged Romanian in a turtleneck shirt, white bush of hair up top, blue **espadrilles** below." –PHILIP ROTH, *The Human Stain*

eyelet (EYE luht) - *n.* a small hole, in cloth or leather, for the passage of a lace, cord or hook to fit through, 2. the metal ring surrounding such a hole used to strengthen it.

> "'You stick the lace through the what? ... The perforations at either side of, and above, the tongue.' ... 'The **eyelets**.'" –DON DELILLO, *Underworld*

gaiter (GAY tuhr) - *n.* a cloth covering or legging that provides protection from the instep to the knee, made of leather or cloth, 2. a smaller covering extending from instep to ankle and worn over a shoe, 3. an ankle-high shoe or boot with elastic sides, 4. an overshoe with a cloth top.

> "Behind the door hung a coat with a short cape, a bridle, and a black leather cap;

and on the floor in a corner lay a pair of **gaiters** still caked with mud." –GUSTAVE FLAUBERT, *Madame Bovary,* transl. by Francis Steegmuller

grommet (GRAH muht, also GRUH muht) - *n.* a reinforced eyelet, as in cloth, through which a fastener is passed, 2. the small metal or plastic ring used as reinforcement.

> "'And the little metal ring that reinforces the rim of the eyelet through which the aglet passes. We're doing the physics of language, Shay.' ... 'This is the **grommet**.'" –DON DELILLO, *Underworld*

hobnail (HAHB NAYL) - *n.* a short nail with a broad head used to protect the soles of boots or shoes.

> "... under it stood a row of heavy boots with shiny **hobnails**." –GUSTAVE FLAUBERT, *Madame Bovary,* transl. by Francis Steegmuller

huarache (wuh RAH chee, also huh RAH chee) - *n.* a flat-heeled, leather-thonged sandal worn by Mexican Indians.

> "Listening, I felt quite queer myself, in my bandages, cards and currencies in my pockets, my heart tight in my breast and toes free in the **huaraches**. I felt like someone who might come into the vision of a theosophist, that kind of figure." –SAUL BELLOW, *The Adventures of Augie March*

last (LAST) - (among other definitions) *n.* a foot-shaped form used to make or repair shoes.

> "'And when I take my shoe to the shoemaker and he places it on a form to make repairs—a block shaped like a foot. This is called what?' ... 'A **last**.'" –DON DELILLO, *Underworld*

mule (MYOOL) - *n.* a slipper or shoe that leaves the heel bare.

> "... seemed to be wearing, above her gray sweatpants, the top of a man's striped pajamas, and on her feet nothing but backless house slippers, those things called **mules**." –PHILIP ROTH, *The Human Stain*

oxford (AHKS fuhrd) - *n.* a sturdy, low, lace-up shoe.

> "They wore no veils, but as they came forward, Desdemona saw brown school **oxfords** on their feet." –JEFFREY EUGENIDES, *Middlesex*

quarter (KWOR tuhr, also KOR tuhr) - (among other definitions) *n.* a piece of leather that covers the heel of a shoe around to the vamp.

> "'And this piece amidships between the cuff and the strip above the sole. That's the **quarter**.'" –DON DELILLO, *Underworld*

sabot (sa BOH) - *n.* a wooden shoe made of a hollowed out piece of wood and shaped to fit the foot, 2. a sandal or shoe with a thick wooden sole and a band of leather across the instep.

> "... he enjoyed hearing Mademoiselle Emma's little **sabots** on the newly washed flagstones of the kitchen floor." –GUSTAVE FLAUBERT, *Madame Bovary*, transl. by Francis Steegmulle.

saddle shoe (SA duhl SHOO) - *n.* a flat, casual, lace-up shoe with a contrasting band of leather across the instep, usually black and white.

> "... passengers arriving and departing, having coffee in the Palm Court or getting their shoes shined, the wing tips of banking, the cap toes of parts supply, the **saddle shoes** of rum-running." –JEFFREY EUGENIDES, *Middlesex*

spat (SPAT) - (among other definitions) *n.* a cloth or leather gaiter covering a shoe upper and the ankle.

> "He had gone to a New Year's Eve party, leaving the house in his best: bowler hat, polka-dot muffler, **spats** on his two-tone shoes, pigskin gloves." –SAUL BELLOW, *The Adventures of Augie March*

vamp (VAMP) - (among other definitions) *n.* a piece of leather forming the upper part of a boot or shoe, covering the instep and often the toes.

> "'What's the frontal area that covers the instep?' ... 'It's called the **vamp**.'" –DON DELILLO, *Underworld*

welt (WELT) - (among other definitions) *n.* a narrow piece of leather stitched into a shoe between the sole and the upper.

> "'And the strip above the sole. That's the **welt**.'" –DON DELILLO, *Underworld*

ACCESSORIES

aigrette (AY GRET) - *n.* an ornamental tuft of long, white, showy plumes on an egret, 2. one of these plumes worn as ornamentation by a woman; any ornament such as this.

"A crown of **aigrettes** nodded above his head." —L. SPRAGUE DE CAMP AND LIN CARTER, *Conan the Buccaneer*

bandeau (ban DOH) - *n.* a narrow band worn around the head to hold the hair, 2. a narrow brassiere.

"Acey looked sensational in a white linen suit with a sequined **bandeau**." —DON DELILLO, *Underworld*

cincture (SINGK chur) - *n.* a belt; a girdle; something that encircles or surrounds.

"All the nuns at the convent wore plain blouses and skirts except for Sister Edgar, who had permission from the motherhouse to fit herself out in the old things with the arcane names, the wimple, **cincture** and guimpe." —DON DELILLO, *Underworld*

fichu (FI SHOO, also FEE SHOO) - *n.* a lightweight, triangular scarf worn over a woman's shoulders and fastened or tied at the breast.

"The ladies wore country-style headdresses and city-style gowns, with gold watch chains, tippets (the ends crossed and tucked into their belts), or small colored **fichus** attached at the back with pins and leaving the neck bare." —GUSTAVE FLAUBERT, *Madame Bovary*, transl. by Francis Steegmuller

fillet (FI luht, also fi LAY) - (among other definitions) *n.* a narrow strip of fabric; a band; a ribbon, 2. *v.* to bind or decorate as with a fillet.

"Her skin was dusky, her hair, a thick black mass, caught back and confined by a gold **fillet**." —ROBERT E. HOWARD, *The Snout in the Dark*

foulard (fu LAHRD) - *n.* a light weight, plain-weave or twill-weave fabric of silk or silk and cotton with a small printed design.

"... he saw himself reflected there in miniature down to his shoulders—his **foulard** on his head, his nightshirt open." —GUSTAVE FLAUBERT, *Madame Bovary*, transl. by Francis Steegmuller

gladstone (GLAD STOHN) - (among other definitions) *n.* a large leather traveling bag.

"I had to go and buy him a valise at the Army-Navy store—a tan, bulldog **gladstone**, the best I could get ... I taught him how to work the clasps and the key." —SAUL BELLOW, *The Adventures of Augie March*

lorgnette - (lorn YET) *n.* eyeglasses or opera glasses held to the eyes with a short handle.

"The ladies snatched up their **lorgnettes** and opera glasses, the men stirred in their seats, some getting up to have a better look at her." —FYODOR DOSTOYEVSKY, *The Brothers Karamazov*, trans. by David Magarshack

mantilla (man TEE yuh, also man TI luh) - *n.* a lightweight silk or lace scarf worn over the head and shoulders, often with a high comb, by Spanish and Latin American women.

"Lucille Kafkalis was standing exactly as she'd been told, half in and half out of the light, wearing a white hat sashed with glass cherries, a **mantilla** over bare shoulders, a bright green, décolleté dress, and high heels, in which she didn't move for fear of falling." —JEFFREY EUGENIDES, *Middlesex*

obi (OH bee) - *n.* a wide sash fastened in back with a large bow, worn as part of a Japanese kimono.

"She would tell him the latest scandals of the Tokyo press. A woman had mutilated her unfaithful lover and was found with the missing parts in her **obi**." –Saul Bellow, *Herzog*

panache (puh NASH, also puh NAHSH) - *n.* a plume of feathers, often used for a head-dress or helmet, 2. verve, flamboyance; flair.

"Save for these pansied dapplings, the island curved all glowing topaz, from its base in the opalescent shallows of the azure sea to its crest, where feathered trees drooped branches like immense **panaches** of ostrich plumes dyed golden amber." –Abraham Merritt, *The Ship of Ishtar*

parapluie (par ah PLEE) - *n.* an umbrella (a dated term, popular in the 19th century).

"She shelters under an umbrella that's ragged and skeletal, but holds in her free hand a much more substantial looking one, furled … William examines the **parapluie**, weighing it in his hands, running one gloved finger along its ivory handle, peeking into its waxy black folds." –Michel Faber, *The Crimson Petal and the White*

pince-nez (pans NAY, also pants NAY) - *n.* eyeglasses worn clipped to the bridge of the nose.

"… his former mother-in-law, handsome, autocratic, every inch the suffragist and 'modern woman' with her **pince-nez** and abundant gray hair." –Saul Bellow, *Herzog*

portmanteau (pohrt MAN TOH) - *n.* a large traveling bag of stiff leather with two hinged compartments.

"… when he left us he carried away the manuscript in his **portmanteau**." –Robert Louis Stevenson, Introduction, *Treasure Island*

rebozo (also **reboso**) (ri BOH ZOH, also ri BOH SOH) - *n.* a long scarf or shawl worn by Mexican women to cover the head and shoulders.

[in Mexico] "As for Thea, enfolded in the **rebozo**, she stared at me—hard, begging, firm and infirm, all together." –Saul Bellow, *The Adventures of Augie March*

reticule (RE tih KYOOL) - *n.* a drawstring purse or handbag, usually made of some woven material.

"A tuneless hum from the other side of the screen invites her to confess. Agnes has come prepared for this moment and removes from her new **reticule** a leaf of writing-paper onto which she has the previous evening noted all her sins, in order of appearance in her diaries for the last thirteen years." –Michel Faber, *The Crimson Petal and the White*

stole (STOHL) - (among other definitions) *n.* a long scarf, usually of embroidered silk or linen worn by some clergymen while officiating, 2. a long scarf, cloth or fur worn around the shoulders by women.

*see other **stole** entry for citation, p. 234*

tippet (TI puht) - *n.* a covering for the shoulders with hanging ends, often of fur and consisting of the whole animal.

"The ladies wore country-style head-dresses and city-style gowns, with gold watch chains, **tippets** (the ends crossed and tucked into their belts), or small colored fichus attached at the back with pins and leaving the neck bare."

—GUSTAVE FLAUBERT, *Madame Bovary*, transl. by Francis Steegmuller

valise (vuh LEES) - *n.* a small overnight bag; a piece of hand luggage.

*see **gladstone** for citation, p. 230*

RELIGIOUS CLOTHING

alb (ALB) - *n.* a long white linen robe worn by priests at Mass.

"You see, Monsignor, if you stand on television in the ancient **albs** and surplices of the Roman church there are at least enough Irishmen, Poles, Croatians watching in saloons to understand you." —SAUL BELLOW, *Herzog*

biretta (buh RE tuh) - *n.* a stiff, square cap with three or four ridges across the crown, worn esp. by Roman Catholic clergymen.

"The fake priest went past, Benedetti, wearing a lumber jacket and a black **biretta** and carrying a breviary." —DON DELILLO, *Underworld*

cassock (KA suhk) - *n.* a long, closefitting vestmest, usually black, worn as an outer garment or under the surplice by the clergy and those assisting in church services, 2. a member of the clergy or his position.

"My best friends, Tim and Rusty, were serving mass that Sunday, kneeling on each side of the priest in their **cassocks** and wayward purple socks." —CHRIS FUHRMAN, *The Dangerous Lives of Altar Boys*

chaplet (CHAP luht) - *n.* a wreath or garland worn around the head, 2. a string of prayer beads having one third the number of a rosary's beads, 3. a string of beads.

*see other **chaplet** entry for citation, p. 225*

chasuble (CHA zuh buhl) - *n.* a long, sleeveless vestment worn over an alb by a priest while celebrating Mass.

"He promised the Holy Virgin three **chasubles** for the church, and vowed to walk barefoot from the cemetery at Les Bertaux to the chapel at Vassonville." —GUSTAVE FLAUBERT, *Madame Bovary*, transl. by Francis Steegmuller

cilice (SIHL ihs) - *n.* a haircloth or coarse cloth, 2. a garment made of such cloth, typically worn as a robe of penitence.

"The spiked **cilice** belt that he wore around his thigh cut into his flesh, and yet his soul sang with satisfaction of service to the Lord." —DAN BROWN, *The Da Vinci Code*

crosier (also **crozier**) (KROH zuhr) - *n.* a staff with a crook or cross at the end; a bishop's staff.

"The Franks say: 'This is an act of great valour; In the archbishop's hands the **crozier** is truly safe.'" —*The Song of Roland*, transl. by Glyn Burgess

ephod (E FAHD, also EE FAHD) - *n.* a vestment worn by ancient Jewish priests, without sleeves, slit at the sides below the armpits and fastened with buckles at the shoulder and a girdle at the waist.

"... sent in your **ephod** before Eli to start service in the temple." —SAUL BELLOW, *The Adventures of Augie March*

fisherman's ring (FI shuhr muhnz RING) - *n.* one of the two seals used by the Pope, used in apostolical briefs and private letters; a large ring on which St. Peter is represented drawing in his net full of fish.

"Then he had sealed the Pope's bedroom, destroyed the papal **fisherman's ring**, shattered the die used to make lead seals, and arranged for the funeral." —DAN BROWN, *Angels & Demons*

guimpe (GAMP, also GIMP) - *n*. a blouse worn beneath a jumper or other low-necked dress, 2. a wide piece of cloth in some nuns' habits to cover the neck and shoulders.

> "All the nuns at the convent wore plain blouses and skirts except for Sister Edgar, who had permission from the mother-house to fit herself out in the old things with the arcane names, the wimple, cincture and **guimpe**." —DON DELILLO, *Underworld*

miter (also **mitre**) (MY tuhr) - *n*. the liturgical headdress worn by bishops at all solemn functions; it is a tall, pointed hat with peaks in both front and back.

> "And virtually all the elements of the Catholic ritual—the **miter**, the altar, the doxology, and communion, the act of 'God-eating'—were taken directly from earlier pagan mystery religions." —DAN BROWN, *The Da Vinci Code*

pallium (PA lee uhm) - *n*. the woolen vestment worn by the Pope and conferred upon archbishops and sometimes upon bishops.

> "'The box holds **palliums**—woven sashes that the Pope gives to newly elected cardinals.'" —DAN BROWN, *Angels & Demons*

rosary (ROH zuh ree, also ROHZ ree) - *n*. a series of prayers, 2. a string of beads on which these prayers are counted.

> "A long rosary of dark wooden beads hangs from her belt, a **rosary** she has not touched for some time." —ARTURO PEREZ-REVERTE, *The Flanders Panel*

sanbenito (SAN buh NEE toh) - *n*. a garment of sackcloth, resembling a scapular in shape, worn at the auto-da-fé of the Spanish Inquisition—yellow with a red St. Andrew's cross for the penitent and black with painted flames, devils, and other symbols for the impenitent.

> "... a week [after being imprisoned as potential victims of an auto-da-fé] each was dressed in a **senbenito** and their heads were ornamented with paper mitres; Candide's mitre and **sanbenito** were painted with flames upside down and with devils who had neither tails nor claws; But Pangloss's devils had claws and tails, and his flames were upright."—FRANCOIS VOLTAIRE, *Candide*, transl. by Richard Aldington

scapular (SKA pyuh luhr) - *n*. a short cloak or sleeveless outer garment covering the shoulders; worn by monks as prescribed by the Rule of St. Benedict, when doing manual labor and adopted by other religious orders as part of their ordinary costume.

> "He took care of his mother, a Catholic of the old eloquence, wearing a **scapular**, blessing herself and touching thumb-knuckle to her lips, and he loved her and watched her die." —DON DELILLO, *Underworld*

soutane (soo TAHN, also soo TAN) - *n*. a long gown that buttons up the front, worn by Roman Catholic priests as part of their ordinary outer garments and worn under the vestments in religious services; a cassock.

"Spanish pickpockets who were so clever they got to the priest's money through the **soutane**." —SAUL BELLOW, *The Adventures of Augie March*

stole (STOHL) - (among other definitions) *n.* a long scarf, usually of embroidered silk or linen worn by some clergymen while officiating, 2. a long scarf, cloth or fur worn around the shoulders by women.

"The elder stood on the top step, put on his **stole**, and began to bless the women who clustered round him." —FYODOR DOSTOYEVSKY, *The Brothers Karamazov*, transl. by David Magarshack

surplice (SUHR pluhs) - *n.* a white, loose-fitting, wide-sleeved ecclesiastical outer vestment worn by the clergy and choir in some churches.

"I think he plays in the large church there, and has a **surpliced** choir." —THOMAS HARDY, *Jude the Obscure*

vestment (VEST muhnt) - *n.* the ritual robes of the clergy worn as an indication of office or state, 2. the ritual robes worn by members of the clergy, acolytes or assistants at ecclesiastical ceremonies.

wimple (WIM puhl) - *n.* a headdress of cloth worn around the face and over the head, worn by medieval women and by certain nuns as part of their habit.

*see **guimpe** for citation*

FABRICS AND MATERIALS

appliqué (A pluh KAY) - *n.* a decoration cut from one piece of cloth and sewn to or applied to a larger piece of cloth.

"The blouse was decorated at chest-level with a calico **appliqué** in the shape of a strawberry." —JHUMPA LAHIRI, *Interpreter of Maladies*

astrakhan (AS truh kahn, also AS truh KAN) - *n.* a curly fur or wool from the young lambs of the Astrakhan region in Russia.

"We men also know how to display our bodies, which is to say we don't do it. The older we get the more clothes we wear until finally we appear in public in **astrakhans** and hats, gloves, mufflers and (identical) galoshes." —P.J. O'ROURKE, *The New York Times Book Review*, 12/22/02

baize (BAYZ) - *n.* a thick woolen or cotton cloth made to imitate felt, frequently dyed green, and used to cover billiard or gaming tables.

"Our cues bespeak us—both, coincidentally, presents from our wives (pious admirers, naturally, of their husbands' **baizecraft**)." —MARTIN AMIS, *Visiting Mrs. Nabokov*

barège (bah REJ) - *n.* a light, sheer fabric of silk or cotton, resembling gauze and used in making women's apparel, originally made at Baréges.

"He'd send her a piece of black **barège**— twelve meters, enough to make a dress." —GUSTAVE FLAUBERT, *Madame Bovary*, transl. by Francis Steegmuller

bast (BAST) - *n.* strong woody fibers from the inner bark of the lime or linden, cut into strips and coarsely plaited.

"At the table, finishing the fried egg, sat a man of about five and forty, of medium height, spare, weakly built, with reddish hair and a thin, reddish beard which bore a striking resemblance to a **bast**-sponge (this comparison and particularly the word '**bast**-sponge' for some reason flashed instantaneously through Alyosha's mind—he recalled it afterwards)." –FYODOR DOSTOYEVSKY, *The Brothers Karamazov*, transl. by David Magarshack

batiste (buh TEEST, also ba TEEST) - *n.* a fine, light, plain-woven fabric usually made from cotton or linen fibers and used to make clothing.

"His **batiste** shirt (it had pleated cuffs) puffed out from the opening of his gray twill vest at each gust of wind." –GUSTAVE FLAUBERT, *Madame Bovary*, transl. by Francis Steegmuller

bombazine (BAHM buh ZEEN) - *n.* a fine, plain woven fabric made from various fibers and often dyed black.

"Colonel Burr ... was elegantly attired in a silklike suit (actually made of a fabric known as **bombazine**) and carried himself toward the barge on the bank of the Hudson River." –JOSEPH J. ELLIS, *Founding Brothers*

broadcloth (BROD KLOTH) - *n.* a fine woolen cloth with a lustrous finish, 2. a closely woven silk, cotton or synthetic cloth with a narrow crosswise rib.

"He still wore the fine **broadcloth** suit in which he had fulfilled his mission, but it was bitterly the worse for wear, daubed with clay and torn with the sharp briers of the wood." –ROBERT LOUIS STEVENSON, *Treasure Island*

brocade (broh KAYD) - *n.* a thick heavy fabric with a raised interwoven design.

"... a hideous audience room, laden with overstuffed furniture with antimacassars on the plush **brocade** coverings." –KATHARINE GRAHAM, *Personal History*

bunting (BUHN ting) - (among other definitions) *n.* a light cotton or woolen cloth used to make flags, 2. flags, as a group, 3. long, colored strips of material used as holiday decoration.

"And so that glorious day arrived when Zanzibar and Yankee [our horses] came home. I suggested tricolored **bunting** and garlands of flowers, but Susan ignored my suggestions and kept the ceremony simple and dignified." –NELSON DEMILLE, *The Gold Coast*

calamanco (KAL uh MANG koh) - *n.* a glossy, woolen fabric with a checkered pattern on one side; popular in the 18th century.

"As Longfellow slipped into his **calamanco** dressing gown, the flowing silver tresses of his beard felt heavier than when he had put himself to bed." –MATTHEW PEARL, *The Dante Club*

calico (KA li KOH) - *n.* a rough, brightly printed cloth, 2. *adj.* made of calico, 3. having spots like calico, esp. a cat or other animal.

"She handed a new and absolutely plain garment, of coarse and unbleached **calico**." –THOMAS HARDY, *Jude the Obscure*

cambric (KAYM brik) - *n.* a finely woven cotton or linen fabric, usually white.

"He also maintained a less legal trade in French **cambrics** and other textiles." –DAVID LISS, *A Conspiracy of Paper*

chambray (SHAM BRAY, also SHAM BREE) - *n.* a lightweight cotton fabric with white threads woven across a colored warp.

"... he went for the big babes in leather jackets, low heels, berets, and **chambray** workshirts." –SAUL BELLOW, *The Adventures of Augie March*

chenille (shu NEEUHL) - *n.* a soft, tufted cord made of silk, cotton or worsted and used in embroidery, fringing or to make fabric, 2. a fabric made from chenille (from the French for caterpillar).

"Twinkle nodded, slouched on the floor in front of the fridge, wearing black stirrup pants and a yellow **chenille** sweater, groping for her lighter." –JHUMPA LAHIRI, *Interpreter of Maladies*

chiffon (shi FAHN) - *n.* a soft, filmy fabric of sheer silk or rayon.

"The women wore heels and sheer stockings, and short black dresses made of crepe and **chiffon**." –JHUMPA LAHIRI, *Interpreter of Maladies*

chintz (CHINTS) - *n.* a cotton fabric, printed and glazed, usually of bright colors.

"The fact that the yellow **chintz** armchair in the living room clashed with the blue-and-maroon Turkish carpet no longer bothered her." –JHUMPA LAHIRI, *Interpreter of Maladies*

cordovan (KOR duh vuhn) - *n.* a soft, fine-grained leather of goatskin or horsehide.

"My father nudged a haunch [of the dog] with the toe of his **cordovan** loafer." –RICHARD RUSSO, *Straight Man*

crepe (also **crape**, **crêpe**) (CRAYP) - *n.* a light, soft, crinkled fabric made of silk, cotton, wool, or other fibers.

*see **chiffon** for citation, p. 236*

crinoline (KRI nuhl uhn) - *n.* a coarse, stiff, heavily sized fabric used to line and stiffen hats and garments, of horsehair, cotton, linen, etc., 2. a petticoat made of this fabric, 3. a hoop skirt.

"Sweating in their **crinolines** and farthingales, in their flounced gowns of flame-coloured taffeta, like so many Queens of Hearts, the Moguls' Wives seem to comprise a suspended, forgotten enclave in this teeming town." –MARTIN AMIS, *Visiting Mrs. Nabokov*

damask (DA muhsk) - *n.* a fabric of cotton, silk, or wool having a woven pattern, 2. a fine, twilled table linen.

"... a silver bread gondola from which, beneath a cover of **damask** napkin, came the most delicious aroma of hot bread." –TOM WOLFE, *A Man in Full*

diaphanous (di A fuh nuhs) - *adj.* of such fine texture as to be translucent.

*see other **diaphanous** entry for citation, p. 211*

dimity (DI muh tee) - *n.* a thin, crisp cotton cloth with raised woven stripes or checks.

"His elbows on the ironing board, he would stare hungrily at all the feminine garments strewn about him—the **dimity** petticoats, the fichus, the collars, the drawstring pantaloons enormously wide at the waist and narrowing below." –GUSTAVE FLAUBERT, *Madame Bovary,* transl. by Francis Steegmuller

drugget (DRUH guht) - *n.* a strong cotton fabric with a raised pattern, used mainly for bedcovers, curtains, or table linens.

"'Oh, I know you would give me a tumultuary time beneath the **drugget**; but how about the long pull, when teeth decay and skins wrinkle and sag and tempers grow short?'" –L. SPRAGUE DE CAMP, *The Tritonian Ring*

farthingale (FAHR thun GAYL) - *n.* a hoop worn under a skirt to extend it horizontally, worn by women in the 16th and 17th centuries, 2. the skirt or petticoat worn over such a hoop.

*see **crinoline** for citation, p. 236*

frieze (FREEZ or free ZAY) - *n.* a decoration or series of decorations forming an ornamental band around a room, mantel, etc., 2. a heavy, coarse wool cloth with a shaggy or tufted uncut nap on one side.

"... a sullen fellow in **frieze** went around the hall with a long pole-torch, lighting the cressets." –C.L. MOORE, *Jirel of Joiry*

fustian (FUHS chuhn) - *n.* a kind of coarse twilled cloth, 2. pompous or pretentious speech or writing, 3. *adj.* relating to language that is pompous, bombastic or overly inflated.

*see other **fustian** entry for citation, p. 93*

gabardine (GA buhr DEEN) - *n.* a sturdy, tightly woven fabric of cotton, wool or rayon twill used to make dresses, suits, and coats.

"His face and his gray **gabardine** suit both seemed to be neat and freshly pressed." –JOHN KENNEDY TOOLE, *A Confederacy of Dunces*

gingham (GING uhm) - *n.* a light cotton fabric with a woven, checked pattern.

"She wore her **gingham** frock." –GLEN DAVID GOLD, *Carter Beats the Devil*

gossamer (GAH suh muhr) - *n.* a fine film of cobwebs, 2. a sheer, gauzy fabric, 3. anything delicate, light, or flimsy.

"Her body was like ivory to his dazed eyes, and save for a light veil of **gossamer**, she was naked as the day." –ROBERT E. HOWARD, *The Frost Giant's Daughter*

grisette (gri ZET) - *n.* a cheap grey fabric used to make dresses for the common, working girls in France, 2. a young girl of the French working class, esp. one employed as a seamstress or shop assistant.

"But now timidity gave way to impatience, and Paris beckoned from afar, with the fanfare of its masked balls, the laughter of its **grisettes**." –GUSTAVE FLAUBERT, *Madame Bovary,* transl. by Francis Steegmuller

gunny (GUH nee) - *n.* a coarse, heavy fabric made of hemp or jute, used for bags and sacks, 2. burlap.

gunnysack (GUH nee SAK) - *n.* a bag or sack made of gunny or burlap.

"A draggled muslin cap on his head and a dirty **gunny-sack** about his slim hips proclaimed him cook of the decidedly dirty

ship's galley in which I found myself."
—JACK LONDON, *The Sea Wolf*

haircloth (HAIR KLOTH) - n. a stiff, wiry fabric woven from cotton or linen with horse or camel hair, used for upholstery and for stiffening garments.

karakul (also **caracul[e]**, **carakul**, **karacul**) (KAR uh kuhl) - n. a breed of sheep from Central Asia having coarse, wiry fur; a sheep of the breed, 2. the curled and glossy coat of a karakul lamb, valued as fur, 3. a cloth imitation of the karakul fur.

"Hamid Karzai's **caracul** hat and green chapan became famous." —KHALED HOS-SEINI, *The Kite Runner*

kid (KID) (among other definitions) n. a young goat, 2. (also kidskin) — leather made from the skin of a young goat.

"He wore a pair of brand-new **kid** gloves and exquisite linen." —FYODOR DOS-TOYEVSKY, *The Brothers Karamazov*, transl. by David Magarshack

lamé (lah MAY) - n. a fabric interwoven with metallic threads, esp. gold or silver.

"Lana Lee got close to the man and reached into her gold **lamé** overalls." —JOHN KENNEDY TOOLE, *A Confederacy of Dunces*

lisle (LYUHL) - n. a strong, tightly twisted, fine cotton thread, esp. that using long-stapled cotton.

"A long, terribly thin neck rose up out of a pale, chalky blue T-shirt ... even Charlotte could tell it was one of those fine cottons, like **lisle**" —TOM WOLFE, *I Am Charlotte Simmons*

loden (LOH duhn) - n. a durable, water-proof coarse woolen fabric, 2. of a dark olive green color, often used for this cloth.

"He is wearing his **loden** coat, one of those hooded Tyrolean things of coarse cloth with wooden toggles for buttons." —DON DELILLO, *Underworld*

marten (MAHR tuhn) - n. a thick-furred, weasel-like mammal, 2. the fur of the marten.

"He throws down his great **marten** fur from his shoulders And stood there in his tunic of silk." —*The Song of Roland*, transl. by Glyn Burgess

merino (muh REE NO) - n. a breed of sheep from Spain, having fine, soft wool, 2. a fine, lightweight fabric made from merino wool.

"A young woman wearing a blue **merino** dress with three flounces came to the door of the house to greet Monsieur Bo-vary, and she ushered him into the kitchen, where a big open fire was blaz-ing." —GUSTAVE FLAUBERT, *Madame Bo-vary*, transl. by Francis Steegmuller

moiré (mwa RAY, also mor AY) - n. cloth, esp. silk, with a watered or wavy pattern (from the French moirer, to water).

"The parasol was of rosy iridescent silk, and the sun pouring through it painted the white skin of her face with flickering patches of light. Beneath it she smiled at the springlike warmth; and drops of water could be heard falling one by one on the taut **moiré**." —GUSTAVE FLAUBERT, *Madame Bovary*, transl. by Francis Steeg-muller

morocco (muh RAH KOH) - *n.* a soft, fine leather of goatskin, esp. that used for book bindings and shoes.

"[These books] can still be found today, often cased in boxes of brown **morocco**." –SIMON WINCHESTER, *The Professor and the Madman*

muslin (MUHZ luhn) - *n.* any of various plain-woven cotton fabrics, known to be sturdy and often sheer, used to make bedding.

*see **gunny sack** for citation, p. 238*

nankeen (also **nankin**) (NAN KEEN) - *n.* a durable yellow cotton fabric.

"... it seemed to him a strange sight, this elegant lady in her **nankeen** gown here among all this squalor." –GUSTAVE FLAUBERT, *Madame Bovary*, transl. by Francis Steegmuller

nap (NAP) - (among other definitions) *n.* the furry or hairy surface of a cloth formed by short fibers, esp. when raised by brushing.

Naugahyde (NO guh HYD, also NAH guh HYD) - *n.* an imitation leather, made in a trademarked process from fabric coated in vinyl, used for upholstery.

"After a breakfast of onion rolls and Nova Scotia, Simkin liked to lie down on the black **Naugahyde** sofa in his office, cover himself with an afghan knitted by his mother, listening to Palestrina, Monteverdi, as he elaborated his legal and business strategies." –SAUL BELLOW, *Herzog*

organdy (OR guhn DEE) - *n.* a crisp, sheer fabric made of cotton or silk, used for trim and to make curtains and apparel.

"Catherine wore a crisp **organdy** blouse, with sleeves standing stiffly, cheerfully about her shoulders," –AYN RAND, *The Fountainhead*

poplin (PAH pluhn) - *n.* a ribbed fabric, usually made of silk and worsted, used in making clothing, especially women's dresses, and upholstery (from the Italian papalino, papal).

"He had on an awful gray **poplin** cotton suit, the sort of thing that prisons issue when they set you free." –NELSON DE-MILLE, *The Gold Coast*

prunella (proo NE luh) - *n.* a sturdy, heavy fabric of worsted twill, used in making clerical and academic robes and women's shoe uppers.

"She had been charming, with her braids, her white dress, her **prunella**-cloth slippers." –GUSTAVE FLAUBERT, *Madame Bovary*, transl. by Francis Steegmuller

ruche (ROOSH) - *n.* lace, ribbon or muslin fashioned into a ruffle, fluting, or pleating, esp. at the wrist and neck for dresses and other women's garments.

"Even her neck was covered by a kind of unobtrusive **ruching**." –ISAAC ASIMOV, *The Naked Sun*

samite (SA MYT, also SAY MYT) - *n.* a heavy silk fabric, often interwoven with gold or silver threads, worn in the Middle Ages.

"All of them carried elegant black imitation **samite** briefcases." –MARIO PUZO, *Fools Die*

sateen (sa TEEN, also suh TEEN) - *n.* a cotton cloth with a smooth satin finish.

"About my cap I tied the red **sateen** pirate's scarf." –JOHN KENNEDY TOOLE, *A Confederacy of Dunces*

Savonnerie (SAV uhn REE) - *n.* a factory established in 17th century Paris as a soap works, later used to make hand-knotted pile carpets; now refers to the carpets made there and similar carpets made elsewhere in France.

> [In the Hotel Ritz Paris], "Uncertain, Langdon slid off the bed, feeling his toes sink deep into the **savonnerie** carpet." –DAN BROWN, *The Da Vinci Code*

serge (SUHRJ) - *n.* a sturdy twilled cloth made of worsted, wool, silk, rayon, etc. and having a diagonal rib; used in making suits and coats.

> "He was dressed in a dark blue **serge**." –H.G. WELLS, *The Island of Dr. Moreau*

sericulture (SER uh KUHL chuhr) - *n.* the practice of raising silkworms for the purpose of producing raw silk.

> "As a result, Byzantium became a center for **sericulture**. Mulberry trees flourished on Turkish hillsides. Silkworms ate the leaves." –JEFFREY EUGENIDES, *Middlesex*

shagreen (sha GREEN, also shuh GREEN) - *n.* the rough hide of the shark, ray or dogfish, used as an abrasive or polisher, 2. an untanned rough, granular leather made from the skin of a horse, seal, etc.

> "She gripped her sword in her free hand, but the feel of the **shagreen**-bound hilt inspired only a feeling of helplessness in her." –ROBERT E. HOWARD, *Conan the Warrior*

sisal (SY suhl, also SY zuhl) - *n.* the fiber of the Mexican agave plant used for cordage or rope.

> "... we didn't have doors. Instead we had long, accordion-like barriers, made from **sisal**, that worked by a pneumatic pump

located down in the basement." –JEFFREY EUGENIDES, *Middlesex*

taffeta (TA fuh tuh) - *n.* a crisp, glossy plain-woven fabric of silk, rayon, or nylon with a slight sheen used for women's garments.

see **crinoline** *for citation, p. 236*

tattersall (TA tuhr SOHL) - *n.* a cloth having dark lines on a light background that form a pattern of squares, 2. the cloth printed with such a pattern (named after a horse auction market established in the 18th century at Hyde Park Corner in London; this cloth being the traditional design of horse blankets).

> "She wore faded jeans and a pair of moccasins—as did Coleman—and, with the sleeves rolled up, an old button-down **tattersall** shirt that I recognized as one of his." –PHILIP ROTH, *The Human Stain*

tow (TOH) - *n.* coarse, broken flax or hemp fibers ready for spinning into cloth (note: this is the source for the term towhead referring to a person with white-blonde hair).

> "In this craft they found store of metal for the Viking's forge. Better still, balls of **tow** and oils to soak them in and flint to light them, strong shafts to carry the balls when blazing and oddly shaped crossbows to hurl the shafts with their heads of fire." –ABRAHAM MERRITT, *The Ship of Ishtar*

tricot (TREE KOH, TRY kuht) - *n.* a fabric, usually wool, that is knitted by hand, or by a machine in a fashion designed to resemble hand-knitting, 2. a style of tight-fitting knitted tights.

> "Emma was indeed charmed with his appearance when he came up to the landing in his velvet frock coat and white **tricot** riding breeches." –GUSTAVE FLAUBERT,

Madame Bovary, transl. by Francis Steegmuller

tulle (TOOL) - *n.* a fine starched net of silk, rayon, or nylon used for veils, gowns, etc.

"In the carriage Jude took from his pocket his extra little wedding-present, which turned out to be two or three yards of white **tulle**, which he threw over her bonnet and all, as a veil." –THOMAS HARDY, *Jude the Obscure*

twill (TWIL) - *n.* a fabric with parallel diagonal ribs.

"His batiste shirt (it had pleated cuffs) puffed out from the opening of his gray **twill** vest at each gust of wind." –GUSTAVE FLAUBERT, *Madame Bovary*, transl. by Francis Steegmuller

vair (VAR) - *n.* the fur of a squirrel, esp. one with a grey back and white belly, used in medieval times to line and trim robes.

"'Nay, Morgan will garb you in silk and **vair**.'" –POUL ANDERSON, *Three Hearts and Three Lions*

vicuña (or **vicuna**) (vi KOON yuh, also vy KOON yuh) - *n.* a llamalike ruminant mammal native to South America, having fine silky fleece, 2. the fleece of such an animal, 3. fabric made from this animal's fleece.

"His handsome stout white-haired brother in his priceless suit, **vicuña** coat, Italian hat, his million-dollar shave and rosy manicured fingers with big rings, looking out of his limousine with princely hauteur." –SAUL BELLOW, *Herzog*

wadmal (WAHD muhl) - *n.* a kind of thick coarse wool mostly used in winter clothing for the poor.

"He saw the peasants were a sturdy, fair-complexioned folk, bearded and long-haired, clad in rough **wadmal** coats and cross-gartered pants." –POUL ANDERSON, *Three Hearts and Three Lions*

warp (WORP) - (among other definitions) *n.* in weaving, the foundation or base; the threads running lengthwise in a loom and crossed by the woof.

whipcord (HWIP KORD, also WIP KORD) - *n.* a strong, twisted or braided cord used for whiplashes, etc., 2. a strong worsted fabric with a distinct, diagonally ribbed surface.

"... his topcoat—a Burberry all-weather that he loved like a brother and that went especially well with the suit he was wearing, a slate gray **whipcord** made for Charlie by a guy who did lapels for organized crime." –DON DELILLO, *Underworld*

worsted (WUS tuhd, also WUHR stuhd) - *n.* a firm-textured, tightly twisted woolen yarn made from long-staple fibers, 2. the fabic made from this yarn.

OTHER CLOTHING TERMS

accouter (uh KOO tuhr) - *v.* to outfit; to provide with equipment, esp. for military service.

"Then the Northerner and the gray one, moving like men in a dream, **accoutered** themselves, a shirt of light chain mail and a rounded, uncrested helmet for each." –FRITZ LEIBER, *Swords Against Death*

accoutrement (or **accouterment**) (uh KOO truh muhnt) - *n.* the act of being accoutered; an instance of accoutering, 2. a personal accessory, item of clothing or outfit, 3. a soldier's equipment other than weapons and uniforms.

"About his waist he wore an old brass-buckled leather belt, which was the one thing solid in his whole **accoutrement**." –ROBERT LOUIS STEVENSON, *Treasure Island*

array (uh RAY) - *v.* to set out for display; to place in order, 2. to dress in finery, in splendid attire, 3. *n.* an orderly, impressive arrangement or collection, 4. splendid attire or especially fine clothing.

"And next moment they all came tumbling out of a wardrobe door into the empty room, andy were no longer Kings and Queens in their hunting **array** but just Peter, Susan, Edmund and Lucy in their old clothes." –C.S. LEWIS, *The Lion, the Witch and the Wardrobe*

bespoke (bi SPOKE) - (among other definitions) *adj.* when said of goods—custom made or made-to-order, esp. clothing. 2. *n.* a bespoke item or article or clothing.

"Customers' responses are stored in a sort of **bespoke** database. All this for folks who probably have never shopped on Saville Row." –MARIA RUSSO, *The New York Times Magazine, 12/15/02*

bodkin (BAHD kuhn) - *n.* a small, sharply pointed tool used to make holes in fabric or leather, 2. a blunt needle used to pull tape or ribbon through a hem or loops, 3. (Archaic) a dagger.

"Long Beard laughed, too, the five-inch **bodkin** of bone, thrust midway through the cartilage of his nose, leaping and dancing and adding to his ferocious appearance." –JACK LONDON, *The Strength of the Strong*

caparison (kuh PAR uh suhn) - *n.* the richly ornamented covering for a horse; trap-

pings, 2. richly ornamented clothing, equipment or finery, 3. *v.* to cover a horse with such ornamentation, 4. to adorn in rich clothing.

"Because I am allegedly handling what Clyde calls 'the tourist trade,' I have been **caparisoned** in a costume of sorts." –JOHN KENNEDY TOOLE, *A Confederacy of Duces*

cochineal (KAH chuh NEEL, also KOH chuh NEEL) - *n.* a brilliant-red dye made from the dried bodies of a tropical American insect (the cochineal insect).

"'... for, if Columbus in an island of America had not caught this disease ... we should not have chocolate and **cochineal**.'" –FRANCOIS VOLTAIRE, *Candide*, transl. by Richard Aldington

décolletage (DAY KAH luh TAHZH, also DAY KOL luh TAHZH) - *n.* the low-cut neck of a woman's garment, esp. a dress, 2. a dress having a low neckline.

"There was a froth of lace around **décolletages**, a flashing of diamonds at throats; bracelets dangling medals and coins tinkled on bare arms." –GUSTAVE FLAUBERT, *Madame Bovary,* transl. by Francis Steegmuller

décolleté (DAY KAHL TAY, also DAY KOL TAY) - *adj.* having a low-cut neckline.

"He wore one of his favorite loose sports shirts, which opened on his big chest and slipped away from his shoulders softly. Male **decolleté**." –SAUL BELLOW, *Herzog*

dishabille (DIS uh BEUHL, also DIS uh BEEL) - *n.* the state of being partially undressed; carelessly or very casually dressed.

"... though she was not in bed, she was half-reclining on the settee in her boudoir

in an attractive but decorous **déshabillé**."
—Fyodor Dostoyevsky, *The Brothers Karamazov*, transl by David Magarshack

distaff (DIS TAF) - *n.* a staff that holds the unspun flax, wool, etc being used in spinning, 2. work or concerns mainly of importance to women, 3. a woman or women as a group; characteristic of women, 4. *adj.* female; specif., designating the maternal side of a family.

"By the fireplace in the large room at the foot of the stairs an old Breton woman sat spinning with a **distaff**." —Robert Chambers, *The King in Yellow*

doff (DAHF) - *v.* to take off: doffed his clothes, 2. to lift or tip (one's hat), 3. to discard.

"... something in the timbre of the voice caused the page to **doff** his feathered chaperon as he bowed and replied." —Robert E. Howard, *Conan the Conqueror*

fig (FIG) - (among other definitions) *n.* dress; equipment; array, primarily in the phrase in full fig, 2. physical condition; shape; form.

"Fussell turned up at his first Scout meeting in full **fig** right down to the official oxfords—and got laughed at." —P.J. O'Rourke, *The New York Times Book Review*, 12/22/02

floriated (FLOHR ee AY tuhd) - *adj.* adorned or decorated with floral designs.

"She wore long ruffled skirts, she wore denim skirts with **floriated** hems." —Don DeLillo, *Underworld*

flounce (FLAUNTS) - (among other definitions) *n.* a strip of decorative fabric, usually gathered of pleated along one edge, attached to a curtain or skirt.

"A young woman wearing a blue merino dress with three **flounces** came to the door of the house to greet Monsieur Bovary, and she ushered him into the kitchen, where a big open fire was blazing." —Gustave Flaubert, *Madame Bovary*, transl. by Francis Steegmuller

fob (FAHB) - *v.* to deceive or cheat another, 2. to dispose of goods through deception or fraud, 3. *n.* a short chain or ribbon attached to a pocket watch, often seen hanging in front of a vest or waist.

"In Rouen she saw ladies with charms dangling from their watch **fobs**." —Gustave Flaubert, *Madame Bovary*, transl. by Francis Steegmuller

frippery (FRI puh ree) - *n.* pretentious, showy dress, 2. a pretentious display; ostentation, 3. something trivial, nonessential.

"'But four thousand, my dear young lady, is a bit too much to throw away on such **frippery**, don't you think?'" —Fyodor Dostoyevsky, *The Brothers Karamazov*, transl. by David Magarshack

gird (GUHRD) - *v.* to encircle or bind, as with a band or belt, 2. to secure with a belt, 3. to prepare for action (p.t. girded or girt).

"All but one wore the scarlet tunic of the Numalian police, were **girt** with stabbing swords and carried bills—long-shafted weapons, half pike, half axe." –ROBERT E. HOWARD, *The God in the Bowl*

haberdasher (HA buhr DA shuhr) - *n.* a dealer in men's furnishings.

"Jimmy's father was a **haberdasher,** but Jimmy was mechanically inclined." –GLEN DAVID GOLD, *Carter Beats the Devil*

habiliment (huh BI luh muhnt) - *n.* the characteristic garb associated with a particular office, rank or occasion, 2. habiliment(s)—clothes.

"Nobody stared at Sue, because she was so plainly dressed, which comforted Jude in the thought that only himself knew the charms those **habiliments** subdued." –THOMAS HARDY, *Jude the Obscure*

jabot (zha BOH, also JA BOH) - *n.* a cascade of ruffles down the front of a blouse or shirt.

"... the platters of carved meat were brought round by the maître d'hotel himself, grave as a judge in silk stockings, knee breeches, white neckcloth and **jabot**." –GUSTAVE FLAUBERT, *Madame Bovary*, transl. by Francis Steegmuller

Jacquard (JA KAHRD) - *n.* a type of cloth with figures or designs woven into the fabric (made by a distinctive loom, the Jacquard loom, invented by J. M. Jacquard at the beginning of the 19th century).

"I selected the jewel-tone **jacquard** over the ivory because the weave went well with our carpets." –DON DELILLO, *Underworld*

layette (lay ET) - *n.* the clothing, bedding, and other accessories for a newborn child.

"But since she couldn't spend the money she would have liked and buy embroidered baby bonnets and a boat-shaped cradle with pink silk curtains, she resentfully gave up her own ideas about the **layette** and ordered the whole thing from a seamstress in the village without indicating any preferences or discussing any details." –GUSTAVE FLAUBERT, *Madame Bovary*, transl. by Francis Steegmuller

livery (LI vuh ree, also LIV ree) - *n.* a uniform worn by male household servants, 2. the board and care of horses for a fee, 3. the hiring out of horses and carriages.

"They were met at the airport by the **liveried** chauffeur and the limousine" –PHILIP ROTH, *American Pastoral*

milliner (MI luh nuhr) - *n.* a hat designer, hat maker or hat seller (derives from "Milan").

"He shopped for... ladies' bonnets from the **milliner** ..." –GUSTAVE FLAUBERT, *Madame Bovary*, transl. by Francis Steegmuller

mufti (MUHF tee) - *n.* a Muslim scholar or priest who interprets Muslim religious law, 2. plain clothing when worn by one entitled to a uniform, esp. military; primarily in the phrase in mufti.

"They go then, the Rescuers, all eight of them. United, as always, like soldiers in **mufti**." –MICHEL FABER, *The Crimson Petal and the White*

natty (NA tee) - *adj.* characterized by smart dress and manners; dapper.

"He had a dumpy figure, but wore **natty** clothes." –SAUL BELLOW, *Herzog*

panoply (PA nuh plee) - *n.* the complete armor of a warrior, 2. a covering that serves to protect, 3. a splendid or magnificent array.

"A collection of novellas that reflects the **panoply** of subjects, styles and literary modes that [Doris] Lessing has commanded for more than 50 years." –NOT ATTRIBUTED, *The New York Times Book Review, 6/6/04*

placket (PLA kuht) - *n.* a slit in a garment, 2. a pocket on a garment, esp. on a woman's skirt.

"When the **placket** of his shirt gave way, the stones tore freely into the skin on his chest and back." –GLEN DAVID GOLD, *Carter Beats the Devil*

raiment (RAY muhnt) - *n.* clothing: apparel; garments; attire.

"... the purpose of getting food, **raiment**, and house room for three people ashore." –JOSEPH CONRAD, *Typhoon*

ravel (RA vuhl) - *v.* to pull apart the fibers of cloth; unravel; fray, 2. to tangle or confuse, 3. *n.* a raveling, 4. a broken or loose thread, 5. a tangle or jumble.

"... she and Simon wore the same **ravelly** coat-sweaters." –SAUL BELLOW, *The Adventures of Augie March*

ruff (RUHF) - *n.* a high, stiffly starched round collar worn by men and women in the 16th and 17th centuries, 2. a projection of fur or feathers around the neck of an animal or bird looking like a collar.

"She was wearing a little blue silk scarf that held her pleated batiste collar stiff as a **ruff**." –GUSTAVE FLAUBERT, *Madame Bovary*, transl. by Francis Steegmuller

sachet (sa SHAY) - *n.* a small packet of perfumed powder placed in a drawer or trunk to scent the clothing.

"In this respect there was hardly anything he didn't get into, like ordering things on approval he didn't intend to pay for— stamps, little tubes of lilac perfume, packages of linen **sachet** ..." –SAUL BELLOW, *The Adventures of Augie March*

selvage (SEL vij) - *n.* the edge of a fabric woven to prevent raveling.

"... the buttonhole in the front that was frayed and needed **selvaging** ..." –TOM WOLFE, *A Man in Full*

skein (SKAYN) - *n.* a length of yarn wound into a loose coil, 2. something like or suggesting such a coil, 3. a group of geese (or goslings) when they are in flight.

"The fluffy, fair hair, soaked and darkened, resembled a mean **skein** of cotton threads festooned round his bare skull." –JOSEPH CONRAD, *Typhoon*

subfusc (SUHB FUHSK) - *adj.* a somber, dark or dusky color, 2. clothing of this color.

see other **subfusc** *entry for citation, p. 208*

treadle (TRE duhl) - *n.* a foot-operated pedal to drive a wheel, esp. a sewing machine or potter's wheel.

"He is sitting at his sewing machine, right shoe still on the foot **treadle**." –JEFFREY EUGENIDES, *Middlesex*

trousseau (TROO SOH) - *n.* the personal wardrobe, esp. clothing, accessories, and linens, that a bride assembles for her marriage.

"The enormous **trousseau** I'd bought spared me from worrying about clothes." –KATHARINE GRAHAM, *Personal History*

13. PERFUME
AND MAKE-UP

ambergris (AM buhr GRIS, also AM buhr GREES) - *n.* a waxy grayish substance produced by sperm whales and found floating at sea or washed ashore, used in the making of perfumes.

"And from these people of the west came caravans that brought finely tempered steel blades and the best chain mail—white cloth and red leather, **ambergris** and ivory, turquoise and rubies." –HAROLD LAMB, *Genghis Khan*

---

attar (A tuhr) - *n.* a fragrant essential oil or perfume obtained from flower petals.

"'Our bathwater was scented with petals and **attars**. Believe me, don't believe me, it was a luxury you cannot dream.'" –JHUMPA LAHIRI, *Interpreter of Maladies*

---

bergamot (BUHR guh MAHT) - *n.* a pear-shaped citrus fruit (Citrus bergamia) grown in southern Europe primarily for its rind which yields a fragrant oil, called Essence of Bergamot, much prized as a perfume, 2. the essence or perfume made from the fruit, 3. any of several aromatic North American herbs of the mint family.

"He goes by the red fires of civet and of **bergamot** that burn thereon!" –ABRAHAM MERRITT, *The Ship of Ishtar*

---

brilliantine (BRIL yuhn TEEN) - *n.* an oily, perfumed pomade for hair.

"... the man was otherwise unimaginable outside his barbershop ... he belonged completely to the massive porcelain chairs, two of them, to the hot-towel steamer, the stamped tin ceiling, the marble shelf beneath the mirror, the tinted glass cabinets, the bone-handled razor and leather strop, the horn combs, the scissors and clippers, the cup, the brush, the shaving soap, the fragrance of witch hazels and **brilliantines** and talcums." –DON DELILLO, *Underworld*

---

censer (SENT suhr) - *n.* an ornamented vessel in which incense is burned, esp. during religious rites or services; thurible.

*see other **censer** entry for citation, p. 169*

---

chignon (SHEEN YAHN) - *n.* a roll or knot of hair worn at the back of the head, esp. at the nape of the neck.

"Covering all but the very tips of her ears, [her hair] was gathered at the back into a large **chignon**, a toward the temples it waved a bit—a detail that the country doctor now observed for the first time in his life." –GUSTAVE FLAUBERT, *Madame Bovary*, transl. by Francis Steegmuller

---

citronella (SI truh NE luh) - *n.* a pale yellow oil obtained from a tropical Asian grass used to make perfumes and insect repellents.

"But when he saw the train, his heart sank—caked in last season's grime, it promised a smell in the compartments that would fade only after three weeks of **citronella**." –GLEN DAVID GOLD, *Carter Beats the Devil*

247

coif (KWOF) - *n.* a tight, close-fitting cap, 2. a hair style.

"Her thin face, framed in a simple **coif**, was more wrinkled than a withered russet." —GUSTAVE FLAUBERT, *Madame Bovary*, transl. by Francis Steegmuller

coiffure (kwah FYUR) - *n.* a hairstyle, 2. a headdress, 3. *v.* to arrange or style hair.

"Hair was sleek and shining in front, twisted and knotted behind; and every **coiffure** had its wreath or bunch or sprig—of forget-me-nots, jasmine, pomegranate blossoms, wheat-sprays, cornflowers." —GUSTAVE FLAUBERT, *Madame Bovary*, transl. by Francis Steegmuller.

depilatory (di PI luh TOHR ee) - *n.* a liquid or cream preparation used to remove hair.

"Perfumed, **depilated**, moist with **emollients**, wearing **kohl** around her eyes, Victoria let Lefty look upon her." —JEFFREY EUGENIDES, *Middlesex*

emollient (I MAHL yuhnt) - *adj.* producing the effect of softness, suppleness, and smoothness, esp. of the skin.

see depilatory for citation

enfleurage (AHN FLUHR AHZH) - *v.* the process of extracting perfumes from flowers by means of odorless fats absorbing the scents of these flowers.

"There's a man in Somerset who claims he's invented a method of **enfleurage** that requires no alcohol." —MICHEL FABER, *The Crimson Petal and the White*

frisette (frih ZEHT) - *n.* a band or cluster of small, tight curls (often artificial), worn across a woman's forehead.

"... 'the girl's hair is already out of style. She has her **frisette** gummed to her forehead instead of hanging soft and free. Women notice these things ... '" —MICHEL FABER, *The Crimson Petal and the White*

joss stick (JAHS STIK) - *n.* a fragrant, slender stick of incense burned by the Chinese before Joss.

kohl (KOHL) - *n.* a cosmetic worn by women in Egypt, Arabia, and the Middle East to line and darken the edges of the eyelids, typically prepared from antimony sulfide.

see depilatory for citation

lanolin (LA nuhl uhn) - *n.* the fatty, yellowish, sticky substance obtained from sheep's wool used in making soaps, ointments, and cosmetics.

"He could smell dust on her hands, and **lanolin**, and her vanilla and almonds." —GLEN DAVID GOLD, *Carter Beats the Devil*

maquillage (MA kee YAHZH) - *n.* makeup; cosmetics; theatrical make-up; the application of make-up.

"She gave [these vanities] all their due, and more. High heels, sheer hose, beautiful suits, hats, earrings, feathers, and the colors of pancake **maquillage**, plus electrolysis, sweet-sweats, and the hidden pinnings where adoration could come to roost." —SAUL BELLOW, *The Adventures of Augie March*

marcel (mahr SEL) - *n.* a hairstyle characterized by a series of even waves made by a curling iron (also called a marcel wave), 2. *v.* to style the hair in this fashion (named after Marcel Grateau, early 20th century French hairdresser who invented the style).

"... very near classical in an American way, a certain sort of old-fashioned way that doesn't stray drastically from plainness, like the face cut in raised relief on the old soap bar, maybe it was Camay, I'm not sure, the woman's head in profile, with **marcelled** hair, although Marian's was straight." –Don DeLillo, *Underworld*

orris root (OR uhs ROOT) - *n.* the fragrant root of a European iris; the fragrance resembling violets; used in perfumes and cosmetics.

"From a tall oaken cupboard facing the window came an odor of **orris root** and damp sheets." Gustave Flaubert, *Madame Bovary*, transl. by Francis Steegmuller

pomade (po MAYD, also po MAHD) - *n.* a perfumed ointment, esp. for the hair, 2. *v.* to apply pomade to.

"Little Richard... with his capes, spectacularly upswept **pomaded** hair, and heavy makeup was not the sort of person you were likely to overlook." –Peter Guralnick, *Sweet Soul Music*

pomander (POH MAN duhr) - *n.* a combination of aromatic substances balled together and worn on one's person, esp. as protection from infection.

"But, even above the soothing smell of the **pomander**, he could still detect the odor of snakes." –L. Sprague de Camp and Lin Carter, *Conan the Buccaneer*

quiff (KWIF) -(among other definitions) *n.* a young woman; specifically a female prostitute; a promiscuous woman; a "tart," 2. a lock or tuft of hair, esp. one plastered on the forehead, or one brushed or gelled upward over the forehead.

"His eunuch-like, dried-up face seemed to have become very small, the hair on his temples was tousled and, instead of his **quiff**, a thin tuft of hair stuck up on top of his head." –Fyodor Dostoyevsky, *The Brothers Karamazov*, transl. by David Magarshack

sachet (sa SHAY) - *n.* a small packet of perfumed powder placed in a drawer or trunk to scent the clothing.

"In this respect there was hardly anything he didn't get into, like ordering things on approval he didn't intend to pay for-stamps, little tubes of lilac perfume, packages of linen **sachet** ..." –Saul Bellow, *The Adventures of Augie March*

strop (STRAHP) - *n.* a flexible strip of leather or canvas used to sharpen a razor.

*see **brilliantine** for citation, p. 24*

thurible (THUR uh buhl, also THYUR uh buhl) - *n.* a container in which incense is burnt, especially in religious ceremonies.

titivate (TI tuh VAYT) - *v.* to make decorative alterations or additions to; to spruce up or to touch up, as to one's appearance or adornment.

"... really pure romance, **untitivated**, in our modern way, with satire or allegory." –James Branch Cabell, cited by Fritz Leiber, *The Blade of Conan*

witch hazel (WICH HAY zuhl) - *n.* any of a variety of deciduous shrubs or trees of the genus Hamamelis; North American shrubs that bloom in late autumn or early winter with yellow flowers, 2. an alcohol-based solution containing an extract of the bark and leaves of this plant, a mild astringent used externally.

*see **brilliantine** for citation, p. 247*

14. ARCHITECTURE

BUILDINGS

RELIGIOUS BUILDINGS

basilica (BUH si li kuh) - *n.* a rectangular building with a nave ending in an apse, with side aisles, used as a courtroom, public hall, etc., in ancient Rome, 2. a Christian church built in this style, 3. Roman Catholic Church—a church accorded certain ceremonial rights.

"Now he rested in the most sacred of tombs, buried five stories down, directly beneath the central cupola of the **basilica**." –DAN BROWN, *Angels & Demons*

campanile (KAM puh NEE lee, also KAHM puh NEE lee) - *n.* a bell tower, usually standing alone, but near a church.

"... the rocks arose in fantasies of multi-colored cone and peak, aiguille and minaret and obelisk, **campanile** and tower." –ABRAHAM MERRITT, *The Ship of Ishtar*

fane (FAYN) - *n.* (Archaic or Poetic) a place consecrated to religion; a temple or church.

"... above the shrine sounded a vague whispering. The trees which hemmed in and hid that mysterious **fane** spread long branches above it." –ROBERT E. HOWARD, *The Curse of the Golden Skull*

kirk (KIRK) - *n.* (Scottish) a church.

"True American-style democracy had its origins in this culture. Its values emanated from the Scottish **Kirk**, which had thrown out the top-down hierarchy of the Catholic Church and replaced it with governing councils made up of ordinary citizens." –JAMES WEBB, *The Wall Street Journal*, 10/19/04

manse (MANTS) - *n.* the house and land of a minister or cleric, esp. a Presbyterian minister.

"I was the only one with the key to this inn of interior peace that I had built on the other side of retinas and corneas and the soft tissues of my face. It is a **manse** of solitude and shade and refuge." –PAT CONROY, *My Losing Season*

pantheon (PANT thee AHN, also PANT three UHN) - *n.* all the gods of a people, 2. a temple dedicated to all the gods, 3. a monument or public building memorializing the dead, esp. the famous dead, heroes or heroines of a country, 4. Pantheon—a circular temple in Rome dedicated to all the gods, completed in 27 B.C.

priory (PRY uh ree) - *n.* a religious residence, specif. a monastery governed by a prior or a convent governed by a prioress.

rectory (REK tuh ree) - *n.* the residence of a rector, minister, or priest.

"... everyone was agreeable on that stretch of street leading up to the Episcopal **rectory** and church." –PHILIP ROTH, *The Human Stain*

tabernacle (TA buhr NA kuhl) - *n.* the portable sanctuary used by the Jews to carry the ark of the covenant through the desert, 2. a case or box on a church alter containing the consecrated elements of the Eucharist, 3. a large temple or place of worship.

"... the young woman's thoughts began to stray among old memories of girlhood and the convent. She remembered the tall altar candlesticks that soared above the vases full of flowers and the columned **tabernacle**." –GUSTAVE FLAUBERT, *Madame Bovary*, transl. by Francis Steegmuller.

teocalli (TEE uh KA lee, also TAY uh KAH lee) - *n*. in ancient Mexico or Central America, an Aztec temple or structure for the purpose of worship, built atop a truncated pyramid.

> "The treasure was there, heaped in staggering profusion—piles of diamonds, sapphires, rubies, turquoises, opals, emeralds; **zikkurats** of jade, jet and lapis lazuli; pyramids of gold wedges; **teocallis** of silver ingots; jewel-hilted swords in cloth-of-gold sheaths ..." —ROBERT E. HOWARD, *Black Colossus*

ziggurat (ZI guh RAT) - *n*. a temple tower of the ancient Assyrians and Babylonians, having the form of a terraced pyramid with each story smaller than the one below it.

*see **teocalli** for citation*

BUILDINGS RELATED TO DEATH

abattoir (A buh TWAHR) - *n*. a slaughterhouse for cattle, sheep, etc.

> "The horsecar at this hour, bound inward, packed people in like cattle headed for the **abattoir**." —MATTHEW PEARL, *The Dante Club*

barrow (BAR OH) - *n*. a large mound of earth or stones placed over a grave, graves, or an ancient burial site.

> "... [the flowers] grow where dead men rest. Behold! We are come to the great **barrows** where the sires of Theoden sleep." —J.R.R. TOLKIEN, *The Two Towers*

bier (BIR) - *n*. a stand on which a coffin or corpse is placed before burial.

> "King's remains reposed in a marble **bier** out in the middle of a reflecting pool within the center's walls." — TOM WOLFE, *A Man in Full*

cairn (KARN) - *n*. a mound of stones assembled as a memorial or landmark.

> "The dead men came out of their graves more frequently now, and rarely left him, waking or sleeping. He grew to wait and dread their coming, never passing the twin **cairns** without a shudder." —JACK LONDON, *In a Far Country*

cenotaph (SE nuh TAF) - *n*. a monument built to honor a dead person or persons whose remains are buried elsewhere, esp. soldiers.

> "I could distinguish a repellent array of antique slabs, urns, **cenotaphs**, and mausolean façades; all crumbling, moss-grown, and moisture-stained, and partly concealed by the gross luxuriance of the unhealthy vegetation." —H.P. LOVECRAFT, *The Statement of Randolph Carter*

charnel house (also just **charnel**) (CHAHR nuhl HAUS) - n. a building, room or vault in which corpses or bones are placed.

> "I was in the pit, the abyss, the human cesspool, the shambles and the **charnelhouse** of our civilization." —JACK LONDON, *What Life Means to Me*

funerary (FYOO nuh RER ee) - *adj*. relating to or suitable for a funeral or burial.

"... she was cremated ... A **funerary** urn was placed in a crypt in Marion, Ohio." —GLEN DAVID GOLD, *Carter Beats the Devil*

golgotha (GAHL guh thuh, also gahl GAH thuh) - *n.* a place or time of great suffering, 2. a graveyard; a place of interment; a charnel house, 3. another name for Calvary, the location where Christ was crucified outside Jerusalem.

"There have great things been done to mitigate the worst human sights and teach you something different from revulsion at them. All the **Golgothas** have been painted with this aim." —SAUL BELLOW, *The Adventures of Augie March*

inter (in TUHR) - *v.* to place in a grave; bury.

"So we buried George Allard ... As I said, George was **interred** in the Stanhope plot." —NELSON DEMILLE, *The Gold Coast*

necropolis (neh KROP uh lis) - *n.* a large and elaborate cemetery or burial land, esp. one found in an ancient city.

"Bursa looked—at least from a thousand feet up—pretty much as it had for the past six centuries, a holy city, **necropolis** of the Ottomans and center for the silk trade, its quiet, declining streets abloom with minarets and cypress trees." —JEFFREY EUGENIDES, *Middlesex*

obsequy (AHB suh kwee) - *n.* a rite or ceremony performed at a funeral.

"Hadn't [Nixon] said that [Barbara Bush] really knew how to hate? Certain not-so-subtle sartorial signals at the recent seemingly endless Reagan **obsequies**—was that a silver jacket she had on?—suggest that she still does." —LARRY MCMURTRY, *The New York Times Book Review*, 7/4/04

ossuary (AH shuh WER ee) - *n.* a container for receiving the bones of the dead; an urn, a vault.

"... if the church did not have space or funds to create tombs for an entire family, they sometimes dug an **ossuary** annex—a hole in the floor near the tomb where they buried the less worthy family members." —DAN BROWN, *Angels & Demons*

sepulcher (SEP uhl ker) - *n.* a burial vault; a tomb, 2. a chamber or receptacle for sacred objects or relics, 3. *v.* to place in a sepulcher, to inter.

"'I notice that no one in this whitened **sepulcher** of a room has so much as even looked at us.'" —JOHN KENNEDY TOOLE, *A Confederacy of Dunces*

tumulus (TYOO myuh luhs) - *n.* the mound of earth placed over an ancient tomb; a barrow.

"A resumption of this investigation was the outward and apparent hobby of Phillo—son at present—his ostensible reason for going alone into fields where causeways, dykes, and **tumuli** abounded." —THOMAS HARDY, *Jude the Obscure*

OTHER BUILDINGS

aerie (also **eyrie, eyry**) (AR ee, also ER ee, IR ee) - *n.* a bird's nest built up high, as on a cliff, esp. an eagle's nest, 2. a stronghold or house built on a high place, 3. the young birds in such a high nest.

"'You can't get the treasure,' Conan assured them from his **eyrie**." —ROBERT E. HOWARD AND L. SPRAGUE DE CAMP, *Conan the Usurper*

athenaeum (A thu NEE uhm) - *n.* an institution for the promotion of learning, 2. a library.

> "'And somewhere, born to the streets rather than the **athenaeum**, we will come upon the first true reader.'" —MATTHEW PEARL, *The Dante Club*

boite (BWAHT) - *n.* a small restaurant or night club (from French, literally box).

> "Jakob's Bierstube-Restaurant, a Zurich bar ... Jakob's is a dark, somewhat gloomy **boîte**, its low ceilings, 'even darker than the benches and booths, as if centuries of smoke and dust had become part of the wood.'" —DAVID LEAVITT, *The New York Times Book Review*, 6/20/04

boma (BOH muh) - *n.* a pen or stockade for herding beasts or for defensive purposes, 2. a police post, 3. a commissioner or magistrate's office, the center for administration associated with such an office.

> "We had pitched a camp in a sort of big glade and had built a thorn **boma**; for the lions were raising merry Cain in the bush." —ROBERT E. HOWARD, *Beyond the Borders*

byre (BYR) - *n.* a barn or shed for cows.

> "The townlands were rich, with wide tilth and many orchards, and homesteads there were with oast and **garner**, **fold** and **byre**, and many rills rippling through the green from the highlands down to Anduin." —J.R.R. TOLKIEN, *The Return of the King*

caravansary (also **-serai**) (KAR uh VANT suh ree) - n. a large inn or hostel, esp. one built around a large courtyard to accommodate caravans in the Near or Far East.

> "The zayats are the Burmese **caravanserais**, or rest-houses." —SAX ROHMER, *The Insidious Dr. Fu-Manchu*

cote (KOHT) - *n.* a shed or small building used to shelter domestic animals, esp. sheep, pigs or fowl; a shed used for storage.

> "'I get a piece of rock-salt, of which pigeons are inordinately fond, and place it in a **dovecote** on my roof.'" —THOMAS HARDY, *Jude the Obscure*

cromlech (KRAHM LEK) - *n.* a prehistoric structure having two or three upright stones and a large flat unhewn stone resting horizontally atop them; dolmen. Found mostly in Wales, Devonshire, Cornwall and Ireland; similar structures exist throughout the world.

> "I had seen their [the Pict's] **cromlechs** all over Britain, and I had seen the great rampart they had built not far from Corinium." —ROBERT E. HOWARD, *Bran Mak Morn*

deadfall (also dead-fall) *(DED FOL)* - *n.* a trap for animals in which a large weight falls on and kills or maims the prey, 2. a heap of fallen timber and tangled brush, 3. an uncivilized drinking or gambling establishment.

> [In the early 1850s] "Groggeries, beer and wine dens called '**deadfalls**,' melodeons, and brothels offered entertainment to any man with a few dollars." —DANIEL BACON, *The Official Guide to San Francisco's Barbary Coast Trail*

fold (FOHLD) - (among other definitions) *n.* the earth's surface, the ground, 2. a hill, a dale, 3. a bend in a stratum of rock, 4. a fenced enclosure for domestic animals, esp. sheep (also used in a spiritual sense).

*see **byre** for citation*

foundry (FOWN dree) - *n.* an establishment in which metals are cast and molded.

"... the dark old factories—Civil War factories, **foundries**, brassworks—were windowless now." –PHILIP ROTH, *American Pastoral*

garner (GAHR nuhr) - (among other definitions) *n.* a granary or storehouse for corn or grain, 2. a collection of something.

*see **byre** for citation, opposite page*

Gulag (GOO LAHG) - *n.* a prison, forced labor camp or similar establishment, 2. a name applied to the system of all Soviet prison camps.

"I had met the dark woman at last, the woman who let me in on the secret that the ferocity of tyrants could hide in the sweet flow of mother's milk, that the words 'I love you' could contain all the bloodthirsty despair of the abattoir, all the hopelessness of the most isolated, frozen **gulag**, all the lurid sadness of death row." –PAT CONROY, *My Losing Season*

hammam (also **hammaum**) (ha MEM) - *n.* an Oriental bathhouse; a Turkish bath.

"The air was already thick with incense. Moving back and forth, the priests looked like men at a **hammam**." –JEFFREY EUGENIDES, *Middlesex*

hermitage (HUHR muh tij) - *n.* the habitation of a hermit, 2. a retreat or hideaway.

"I kept my hatred of him in a tight **hermitage**—I was his Northern Ireland; he was my England." –PAT CONROY, *My Losing Season*

marquee (mahr KEE) - *n.* a large, often luxurious tent, used for outdoor entertainment, 2. a permanent canopy that projects over an entrance of a theatre, hotel, etc.

"It is the week of the Great Wessex Agricultural Show, whose vast encampment spreads over the open outskirts of the town like the tents of an investing army. Rows of **marquees**, huts, booths, pavilions, arcades, porticoes—every kind of structure short of a permanent one—cover the green field for the space of a square half-mile." –THOMAS HARDY, *Jude the Obscure*

melodeon (muh LOH dee uhn) - *n.* a small reed organ or harmonium, 2. a music hall.

"By 1857 it had become a Barbary Coast **melodeon**, presenting singers, dancers, comedians." –DANIEL BACON, *The Official Guide to San Francisco's Barbary Coast Trail*

quonset hut (KWAHNT suht HUT) - *n.* a prefabricated hut constructed of corrugated metal and having a semi-cylindrical roof bolted to a steel foundation.

[in Vietnam] "He worked in a **quonset hut**." –DON DELILLO, *Underworld*

souk (also **suk**) (SOOK) - *n.* an open-air marketplace in North Africa and the Middle East; a bazaar.

"'There is more gold in Pashkhauri than you ever saw.'

'You're a liar,' retorted Conan. 'I've seen the **suk** of the goldsmiths in Khurusun.'" –ROBERT E. HOWARD, *The People of the Black Circle*

superette (soop REHT) - *n.* a market, a small supermarket.

"He heard they went into the **superettes**, two women from the galleries. They went into the bodegas, the church, the firehouse." –DON DELILLO, *Underworld*

BUILDING PARTS

CHURCH PARTS

apse (APS) - *n.* a semicircular or polygonal projection from a building, esp. one at the east end of a church containing the altar, with a domed or vaulted roof.

> "Shaston ... was, and is, in itself the city of a dream. Vague imaginings of its castle, its three mints, its magnificent **apsidal** Abbey, the chief glory of South Wessex, its twelve churches, its shrines, **chantries**, hospitals, its gabled freestone mansions—all now ruthlessly swept away—throw the visitor, even against his will, into a pensive melancholy, which the stimulating atmosphere and limitless landscape around him can scarcely dispel."
> —THOMAS HARDY, *Jude the Obscure*

belfry (BEL free) - *n.* a bell tower, esp. one attached to a church, 2. the part of the tower or steeple where the bells hang.

> "The tall tower [of the Cathedral], tall **belfry** windows, and tall pinnacles of the college by the bridge he could also get a glimpse of by going to the staircase."
> —THOMAS HARDY, *Jude the Obscure*

chancel (CHANT suhl) - *n.* the part of a church around the altar, reserved for use by the clergy and choir, sometimes set off by a railing or screen.

> "High overhead, above the **chancel** steps, Jude could discern a huge, solidly constructed Latin cross—as large, probably, as the original it was designed to commemorate." —THOMAS HARDY, *Jude the Obscure*

chantry (CHAN tree) - *n.* an endowment to pay for the saying of Masses and prayers for the soul of a specified person, often the endower, 2. a chapel, altar, or other part of a church endowed for this purpose, esp. in the Middle Ages.

> *see **apse** for citation*

clerestory (KLIR STOHR ee) - *n.* the interior walls of a church rising above the adjacent roof and having windows for lighting the central part of the church, 2. any similar windowed wall supplying light to a building.

> "In the dim light and the baffling glare of the **clerestory** windows he could discern the opposite worshippers indistinctly only, but he saw that Sue was among them."
> —THOMAS HARDY, *Jude the Obscure*

minaret (MI nuh RET) - *n.* a tall, narrow tower attached to a mosque often having one of more projecting balconies.

> "Up the canyon rose far hills and peaks ... And far beyond, like clouds upon the border of the sky, towered **minarets** of white,

where the Sierra's eternal snows flashed austerely the blazes of the sun." —JACK LONDON, *All Gold Canyon*

narthex (NAHR THEKS) - *n.* a vestibule or entrance hall on the western end of an early Christian or Byzantine church or basilica, divided from the nave by a wall, railing, or screen.

"Unlike most churches, however, it had its entrance on the side, rather than the standard rear of the church via the **narthex** at the bottom of the nave." –DAN BROWN, *The Da Vinci Code*

nave (NAYV) - *n.* the middle or body of a church, extending from the chancel to the principal entrance.

"Saint-Sulpice, like most churches, had been build in the shape of a giant Roman cross. Its long central section—the **nave**—led directly to the main altar, where it was transversely intersected by a shorter section, known as the **transept**." –DAN BROWN, *The Da Vinci Code*

oculus (AH kyuh luhs) - *n.* an eye, 2. the large circular window at the west end of a church, 3. a round and hollow stone.

"The sun's rays, shining through the **oculus** on the south wall, moved farther down the line every day, indicating the passage of time, from solstice to solstice." –DAN BROWN, *The Da Vinci Code*

pronaos - *n.* the inner space in front of the body of a temple, esp. Greek or Roman, enclosed by the portico, similar to the narthex in some early Christian churches.

"The structure [of the Pantheon] seemed boxier from the outside than he remembered. The vertical pillars and triangular **pronaus** all but obscured the circular

dome behind it." –DAN BROWN, *Angels & Demons*

sacristy (SA kruh stee) - *n.* a room in a church holding sacred vessels and vestments; a vestry.

"Rusty and Tim carried cruets of water and wine into the **sacristy**." –CHRIS FUHRMAN, *The Dangerous Lives of Altar Boys*

solea (SOH lee uh) - *n.* specific to churches, the raised floor in the front portion of a chapel or the chancel.

"Father Mike ... crossed the **solea** and came down among the parishoners." –JEFFREY EUGENIDES, *Middlesex*

transept (TRANT SEPT) - *n.* either of two lateral arms of a cruciform church.

*see **nave** for citation*

tribune (TRI BYOON) - *n.* one chosen by the common people of ancient Rome as an officer to protect their rights, 2. a protector, a champion of the people, 3. the vaulted or domed apse of a basilica, 4. a platform or dais; a pulpit; a rostrum; the throne of a bishop, 5. a raised area for seating, esp. in a church.

"On a raised **tribune** facing Washington Park stood the Governor of New York". –ROBERT CHAMBERS, *The King in Yellow*

undercroft (UHN duhr KROFT) - *n.* a crypt used for burial under a church; an underground vault or chamber.

"'An **undercroft**?' Langdon asked. 'As in a crypt?'

'Yes, but a specific kind of crypt. I believe a demon's hole is an ancient term for a massive burial cavity located in a chapel ... underneath another tomb.'" –DAN BROWN, *Angels & Demons*

vestry (VES tree) - *n.* the room in a church where clergy place their vestments and sacred objects for storage; a sacristy, 2. a church room used for meetings or classes, 3. a committee administering temporal affairs of an Episcopal parish.

> "Some men would have cast scruples to the winds, and ventured it [a kiss], oblivious both of Sue's declaration of her neutral feelings, and of the pair of autographs in **vestry** chest of Arabella's parish church." —THOMAS HARDY, *Jude the Obscure*

ROOMS

atelier (A tuhl YAY) - *n.* a studio or workshop, esp. one used by an artist or fashion designer.

> "Five flights up are the **ateliers** of architects and painters, and the hiding-places of middle-aged students like myself who want to live alone." —ROBERT CHAMBERS, *The King in Yellow*

boudoir (BOO DWAHR, also BU DWAHR) - *n.* a woman's private sitting room, dressing room, or bedroom.

> "... though she was not in bed, she was half-reclining on the settee in her **boudoir** in an attractive but decorous déshabillé." —FYODOR DOSTOYEVSKY, *The Brothers Karamazov,* transl. by David Magarshack

garret (GAR uht) - *n.* the room or space on the top floor of a house just below the roof, esp. a pitched roof; an attic.

> "To a friend he confessed that he felt 'like a cat in a strange **garret**.'" —RON CHERNOW, *The House of Morgan*

kiva (KEE vuh) - *n.* a chamber built all or partially underground, used by the men of a Pueblo village for ceremonies, religious rites or councils.

> "Seeing her in such varied settings—laughing in the snow, dancing in the surf, crouching outside a **kiva** in New Mexico—buttressed rather than diminished his memories of her beauty." —GREG ILES, *Sleep No More*

oubliette (OO blee ET) -*n.* a dungeon, entered and exited only through a trapdoor in the ceiling (from the French oublier, to forget).

> "Wondering still, he heard the drone of Zachel's horn begin, and pitched, content, into the bottomless **oubliette** of sleep it opened." —ABRAHAM MERRITT, *The Ship of Ishtar*

pied à terre (pee AYD uh TER, also pee AYD ah TER) - *n.* a small town house, flat, or room used only part time or temporarily (from French, literally, foot on the ground).

> "Frightened, she hurried home to Gustaf's apartment (his company had bought a house in central Prague and he kept a **pied-à-terre** up under the eaves) and changed her clothes." —MILAN KUNDERA, *Ignorance*

privy (PRI vee) - *(among other definitions)* *n.* an outdoor toilet, a latrine, 2. an outhouse.

> "... at last they reached the height of refinement: they shut her up all night, in the cold and frost, in the **privy**." —FYODOR DOSTOYEVSKY, *The Brothers Karamazov,* transl. by David Magarshack

refectory (ri FEK tuh ree) - *n.* a dining hall, a room where meals are served, esp. in an institution.

> "... he ... ate heartily in the **refectory**." —GUSTAVE FLAUBERT, *Madame Bovary,* transl. by Francis Steegmuller

sanctum · sanctorum (SANGK tuhm SANGK TOHR uhm) - *n.* the innermost shrine, the Holy of Holies, of a Jewish temple and tabernacle, 2. one inviolably private place or retreat.

"She approaches the double doors and pushes her way into the **sanctum sanctorum**." –JEFFREY EUGENIDES, *Middlesex*

scullery (SKUH luh ree, also SKUHL ree) - *n.* a room adjoining a kitchen for washing dishes or other chores.

"... a **scullery**, where the goblin, a purple-skinned object with an oversized head and spindly little legs, was at his job of dishwashing." L. SPRAGUE DE CAMP AND FLETCHER PRATT, *The Complete Compleat Enchanter*

seraglio (suh RAL YOH) - *n.* the sequestered part of a Muslim's household where his wives or concubines live; harem, 2. the palace of a Turkish sultan.

"So she sat on her companion's — or captor's—knee with a docility that would have amazed Zarallo, who had anathematized her as a she-devil out of Hell's **seraglio**." –ROBERT E. HOWARD, *Conan the Warrior*

vestibule (VES tuh BYOOUHL) - *n.* a small entrance hall, chamber or passage between an exterior door and the interior of a building.

"He lingered awhile in the **vestibule**, and the service was some way advanced when he was put into a seat." –THOMAS HARDY, *Jude the Obscure*

zenana (zuh NAH nuh) - *n.* in India and Iran, the portion of a house reserved for the women of a family; an East Indian harem.

"'He even got into the king's **zenana**, guarded by a three-headed fiend of anthropophagous tastes, who nevertheless could not come near him, and reveled among the king's concubines for six days and fled before the king learned of his visit." –L. SPRAGUE DE CAMP, *The Tritonian Ring*

WINDOWS

casement (KAYS muhnt) - *n.* a casing, covering, 2. a window frame that opens outward on hinges along the side, 3. casement window—such a window, often with two such frames, opening like French doors.

"She would have liked to live in some old manor, like those long-waisted chatelaines who spent their days leaning out of fretted Gothic **casements**, elbow on parapet and chin in hand, watching a white-plumed knight come galloping out of the distance on a black horse." –GUSTAVE FLAUBERT, *Madame Bovary*, transl. by Francis Steegmuller

defenestration (dee FEN uh STRAY shun) - *v.* the act of throwing something out of a window (fenestre is window in French; San Francisco has a Defenestration Building).

"The **Defenestration** of Prague, the action of the Bohemian insurgents who, on the 21st of May 1618, broke up a meeting of Imperial commissioners and deputies of the States, held in the castle of the Hradshin, and threw two of the commissioners and their secretary out of the window; this formed the prelude to the Thirty Years' War." –*The Oxford English Dictionary*.

dormer (DOR muhr) - *n.* a gable extending out from a sloping roof built to accommodate a window, 2. the window itself.

"Many of the thatched and **dormered** dwelling-houses had been pulled down of late years, and many trees felled on the green." —THOMAS HARDY, *Jude the Obscure*

fenestration (FEN uh STRAY shun) - *n.* the arrangement or design of windows, as in a building.

"'There's no **fenestration** in this building,' said Wisner Stroock, 'only glass walls.'"
—TOM WOLFE, *A Man in Full*

lancet (LANT suht) - *n.* a small lance, 2. a surgical knife, usually with two edges and a point, like a lance used esp. for small incisions, 3. Architecture - an acutely pointed arch, 4. a high, narrow window topped with a lancet arch.

"In the background to the right, next to a **lancet** window framing a landscape, a lady, dressed in black, was reading the book that lay in her lap." —ARTURO PEREZ-REVERTE, *The Flanders Panel*

mullion (MUHL yuhn) - *n.* a non-structural vertical strip dividing the panes of a window.

"Her father was shaving before a little glass hung on the **mullion** of the window."
—THOMAS HARDY, *Jude the Obscure*

oriel (OR ee uhl) - *n.* a bay window projecting out from a wall and supported by brackets.

"Down obscure alleys, apparently never trodden now by the foot of man, and whose very existence seemed to be forgotten, there would jut into the path porticoes, **oriels**, doorways of enriched and florid middle-age design, their extinct air being accentuated by the rottenness of the stones."
—THOMAS HARDY, *Jude the Obscure*

transom (TRANT suhm) - *n.* a small hinged window hung over a door or another window, 2. a horizontal crosspiece dividing a window.

"Within the mullioned and **transomed** windows he could see the black, brown, and flaxen crowns of the scholars over the sills."
— THOMAS HARDY, *Jude the Obscure*

OTHER BUILDING PARTS

abutment (a BUHT muhnt) - *n.* the weight-bearing part of a structure, such as at the end of a bridge, 2. the process or act of abutting.

"Etched in the clear evening sky we saw plainly the giant details of massive turret and grim **abutment**; of serrated tower and titanic wall." —ROBERT E. HOWARD, *Eons of the Night*

arabesque (AR uh BESK) - (among other definitions) *n.* an intricate, elaborate pattern or design, esp. a design incorporating interwoven flowers, foliage and geometric forms.

> "They paused outside a tent whose yellow sign announced The World's Smallest Horse, with **arabesques** and filigree designs suggesting the idea was most attractive indeed." –GLEN DAVID GOLD, *Carter Beats the Devil*

architrave (AHR kuh TRAYV) - *n.* the lowest part of an entablature, a beam set directly on the capitals of the columns, also called an epistyle, 2. the molding around a window or a door.

> "You had to walk up three steps to the portico and pass between the two great white Doric columns to reach the front door, which was a colossal thing, painted dark green, with all sorts of raised panels and **architraves** a foot wide, plus window lights running down either side." –TOM WOLFE, *A Man in Full*

ashlars (ASH luhrz) - *n.* a square block of stone used for building, 2. a thin, dressed stone used for facing masonry walls, 3. masonry made of ashlar.

> "Wherever Jude heard of freestone work to be done, thither he went ... sometimes **ashlaring** an hotel in Sandbourne, sometimes a museum at Casterbridge." –THOMAS HARDY, *Jude the Obscure*

baluster (BA luh stuhr) - *n.* any of the small posts that support a railing, as on a staircase.

> "Crouching down behind the stone **balusters**, with every nerve tingling, Valeria glared down at the stealthy figure." –ROBERT E. HOWARD, *Conan the Warrior*

balustrade (BA luh STRAYD) - *n.* a row of balusters topped by a rail, as on a staircase or on the edge of a balcony.

> "... she decided to go back to the steps and the **balustrade** overlooking the square and the market's main street." –ARTURO PEREZ-REVERTE, *The Flanders Panel*

breezeway (BREEZ WAY) - *n.* a covered, open-sided passageway between two buildings, esp. a house and garage.

> "She set to work in the kitchen now, listening all the while for the reassuring sound of her men coming home, car doors closing in the **breezeway**, the solid clunk of well-made parts swinging firmly shut." –DON DELILLO, *Underworld*

capital (KA puh tuhl) -(among other definitions) *n.* the top part of a pillar or column.

cartouche (kahr TOOSH) - *n.* a structural ornament in the shape of an oval shield or oblong scroll to hold a design or inscription; a drawing or figure of the same, for the title or a map, etc., 2. a corbel, mutule, or modillion.

> "It has, however, everything: the mezzanine with the **colonnade** and the stairway with a goitre and the **cartouches** in the form of looped leather belts." –AYN RAND, *The Fountainhead*

caryatid (KAR ee A tuhd, also KAR ee uh TID) - *n.* a supporting column sculpted in the form of a female figure.

> "He was a man of about forty-two years of age, of large build, but slightly round-shouldered, somewhat like those **caryatids** that carry balconies on their shoulders." –JULES VERNE, *From the Earth to the Moon*

chevron (SHEV ruhn) - *n.* a badge or insignia consisting of stripes meeting at an angle, worn on the sleeve of a military, naval, or police uniform to show rank and service, 2.(rare) rafters or beams meeting at an angle at the peak of a roof.

> "She stood at parapets and wondered who had worked the stones, shaped these details of the suavest nuance, **chevrons** and rosettes, urns on balustrades, the classical swags of fruit, the scroll brackets supporting a balcony, and she thought they must have been immigrants, Italian stone carvers probably, unremembered, artists anonymous of the early century, buried in the sky." –DON DELILLO, *Underworld*

clerestory (KLIR STOHR ee) - *n.* the interior walls of a church rising above the adjacent roof and having windows for lighting the central part of the church, 2. any similar windowed wall supplying light to a building.

> "... purple-green light streamed through the pillared side-aisles and **clerestory** windows of a vast building." –DAVID DRAKE, *Cormac Mac Art*

coaming (KO ming) - *n.* a raised rim around a roof opening or ship's hatchway to keep out water.

coffering (KAH fuhr ing) - *n.* a strongbox, 2. a treasury, 3. Architecture - a sunken panel in a ceiling, dome or vault used for decoration.

> "Cormac had missed the hinged panel in the **coffering** which ornamented the walls." –ROBERT E. HOWARD, *Cormac Mac Art*

colonnade (KAH luh NAYD) - *n.* a series of columns placed at regular distances.

> *see **cartouche** for citation, p. 261*

coping (KOH ping) - (among other definitions) *n.* the top layer of a masonry wall, often having a slanting upper surface to shed water.

> "[The wall] was high, but he could leap and catch the **coping** with his fingers." –ROBERT E. HOWARD, *The Tower of the Elephant*

corbel (KOR buhl) - *n.* a bracket of brick or stone projecting from the side of a wall to support a cornice or arch.

> "But the saints and prophets in the window-tracery, the paintings in the galleries, the statues, the busts, the gargoyles, the **corbel**-heads—these seemed to breathe his atmosphere." –THOMAS HARDY, *Jude the Obscure*

cornice (KOR nuhs, also KOR nish) - *n.* a decorative, horizontal molding along the top of a wall, building, etc., 2. the topmost part of an entablature, 3. a decorative framework above a window designed to conceal curtain fixtures.

> "'... couldn't you give her a cornice, Mr. Roark, to keep peace in the family? Just a kind of crenelated **cornice**, it wouldn't spoil anything. Or would it?'" –AYN RAND, *The Fountainhead*

cramp (KRAMP) - (among other definitions) *n.* a metal frame with both ends bent to a right angle to hold pieces together, 2. a device to clasp or fasten things together; a clamp.

> "The shaft was constructed of separate cylinders connected internally by lead **cramps**." –DAVID DRAKE, *Cormac Mac Art*

crocket (KRAH kuht) - *n.* a small, projecting ornament usually in the form of curling leaves, buds or cusps placed along the outer angles of roofs, gables, etc., esp. in Gothic architecture.

"High against the black sky the flash of a lamp would show **crocketed** pinnacles and indented battlements." —THOMAS HARDY, *Jude the Obscure*

culvert (KUHL vuhrt) - *n.* a sewer or drain in a pipelike construction that crosses under a road, railroad, or path or through an embankment.

"A wall, too, the men of old had made from the Hornburg to the southern cliff, barring the entrance to the gorge. Beneath it by a wide **culvert** the Deeping Stream passed out." –J.R.R. TOLKIEN, *The Two Towers*

cupola (KYOO puh luh) - *n.* a small domed structure surmounting a roof, 2. a vaulted roof or ceiling, 3. a small dome resting on a base or pillars.

"Now he rested in the most sacred of tombs, buried five stories down, directly beneath the central **cupola** of the basilica." –DAN BROWN, *Angels & Demons*

dado (DAY DOH) - *n.* the section of a pedestal between the base and crown, 2. the lower portion of a wall, decorated differently from the upper section.

"The upper parts of the walls, seamed with a **dado** rail, are painted lurid peach, and crowded with framed miniatures; the lower parts are papered with a dense design of strawberries, thorns and red roses." –MICHEL FABER, *The Crimson Petal and the White*

eaves (EEVZ) - *n.* the lower edge of a roof projecting beyond the side of a building.

"Frightened, she hurried home to Gustaf's apartment (his company had bought a house in central Prague and he kept a pied-à-terre up under the **eaves**) and changed her clothes." –MILAN KUNDERA, *Ignorance*

entablature (in TA bluh CHUR) - *n.* a horizontal superstructure resting on columns and composed of architrave, frieze and cornice, found in classical architecture.

"[Detroit's] Grand Trunk Station, now a ruin of spectacular dimensions, was then the city's attempt to one-up New York. Its base was a mammoth marble neoclassical museum, complete with Corinthian pillars and carved **entablature**." –JEFFREY EUGENIDES, *Middlesex*

epistyle (EHP ih STYL) - *n.* same as architrave.

finial (FI nee uhl) - *n.* a decorative, ornamental projection at the tip of a spire, arch, or lamp shade support, or projecting upward from the top of a cabinet, etc.

"The vacant church was in a state of great decrepitude. Some of the high stone buttresses had fallen, and several delicate **finials** lay half lost among the brown, neglected weeds and grasses." –H.P. LOVECRAFT, *The Haunter of the Dark*

frieze (FREEZ or free ZAY) - *n.* a decoration or series of decorations forming an ornamental band around a room, mantel, etc., 2. a heavy, coarse wool cloth with a shaggy or tufted uncut nap on one side.

"Along the other three walls, shoulder to shoulder, arrows at strings, eyes fixed on the King of Emakhtila, ran an unbroken silver and scarlet **frieze** of archers." –ABRAHAM MERRITT, *The Ship of Ishtar*

gable (GAY buhl) - *n.* the triangular section of a wall under a pitched roof, 2. the wall at the end of a building having a pitched roof.

"The tank rolled past the affluent homes, the **gables** and turrets, the **porte cocheres**." – JEFFREY EUGENIDES, *Middlesex*

gadroon (guh DROON) - *n.* any of various oval-shaped patterns, usually continuous and joined at their ends, used to decorate moldings, silverware, etc.

"Just then the black maid, Carmen, arrived with a tray, a silver tray with **gadrooned** edges." –TOM WOLFE, *A Man in Full*

gambrel roof (GAM bruhl ROOF) - *n.* a roof having a double slope on each side with the lower slope being steeper that the upper.

"A house of stone such as he had always dreamed of, with a **gambrel roof** no less" –PHILIP ROTH, *American Pastoral*

gantry (GAN tree) - *n.* a frame or support, esp. a large vertical support used in assembling or servicing rockets, 2. any similar large vertical frame, including bridgelike frameworks over railroad tracks used to support signals.

"... the rattly ride up the **gantry** elevator; the awkward climb into the cockpit; and finally the slamming and sealing of the spacecraft hatch." –JIM LOVELL AND JEFFREY KLUGER, *Apollo 13*

garth (GAHRTH) - *n.* a small patch of enclosed ground, a yard, garden or paddock usually found beside a house or other building.

"This night, even the people must crowd within the walls; none dare be alone any more, on the outlying **garths**, when night's fallen." –POUL ANDERSON, *Three Hearts and Three Lions*

haha (HAH HAH) - *n.* a fence or wall set in a ditch around a garden or park, placed in this manner so as not to disrupt the view from within.

"... the edge of a steep walled gap which came without warning like the **haha** of an English park." –H.G. WELLS, *The Island of Dr. Moreau*

hasp (HASP) - *n.* a hinged metal fastening for a door, window, lid, etc., esp., a metal piece fastened by a padlock or pin.

"It took me twenty minutes to pry the **hasp** off with a tire iron." –DOUG ALLYN, *Icewater Mansions*

jamb (JAM) - (among other definitions) *n.* the vertical posts that form the sides of a door, window, or fireplace frame.

"Sprawling over the table with arrested pen, he glanced out of the door, and in that frame of his vision he saw all the stars flying upwards between the teakwood **jambs** on a black sky." –JOSEPH CONRAD, *Typhoon*

lintel (LIN tuhl) - *n.* a horizontal beam over the top of a door or window.

"The marble **lintel** over the door is a beautiful bas-relief from Italy depicting a woman holding poppies, wheat sheaves, and serpents." –DANIEL BACON, *The Official Guide to San Francisco's Barbary Coast Trail*

mansard (MAN SAHRD) - *n.* a roof having two slopes on all four sides each with the lower slope being steeper that the upper.

"They could look over the treetops to the buildings on Fifth Avenue, the unbroken taupe facade, and then to the **mansards** and temple-tops at the western edge of the park." –DON DELILLO, *Underworld*

muntin (MUHN tuhn) - *n.* a vertical framing piece between two panels, the side pieces being called stiles.

"Up a great curved window wall with white industrial **muntins** rose a series of curving ramps, one above the other, with white pipe railings and white wire grilles instead of balusters." –Tom Wolfe, *A Man in Full*

mutule (MYOO chool) - *n.* a projecting decorative bracket situated below and supporting the corona of a Doric cornice (modillion is the same, see **cartouche**).

ogee (OH JEE) - *n.* a molding consisting of an S-shaped curve, 2. any S-shaped curve or line, 3. an ogee arch—a pointed arch formed by the connection of two S-shaped sides.

"From his window he could perceive the spire of the Cathedral, and the **ogee** dome under which resounded the great bell of the city." –Thomas Hardy, *Jude the Obscure*

pediment (PE duh muhnt) - *n.* a triangular element, with a wide, low angle; frequently seen over the door of a building.

"After reading of how Jude sees the **pediments** over the Renaissance windows of Cardinal College as looking like superciliously raised eyebrows, one will forever see the façade of Christ Church as Jude saw it!" –John Bayley, *Introduction, Thomas Hardy's Jude the Obscure*

pergola (PUHR guh luh, also puhr GOH luh) - *n.* an arbor or passageway of lattice work that supports climbing plants.

[referring to Oakland's Lakeside Park] "Its maintenance budget resulted in a seedy and unkempt wilderness of overgrown trees and cracked paths interrupted by bandshells and **pergolas** that, even upon their dedication, looked to have been discarded by other cites." –Glen David Gold, *Carter Beats the Devil*

pilaster (pi LAS tuhr, also PY LAS tuhr) - *n.* a rectangular column projecting only slightly from a wall, typically ornamental.

"The mantelpiece was of the same heavy description, carved with Jacobean **pilasters** and scrollwork." –Thomas Hardy, *Jude the Obscure*

plinth (PLINTH) - *n.* the square block or slab at the base of a column, pedestal, statue, etc.

"An angel stands on a **plinth** nearby, gazing skyward." –Simon Winchester, *The Professor and the Madman*

porte-cochère (or **porte-cochere**) (port KO SHAR) - *n.* a roofed structure or porch over a driveway at the entrance to a building, providing shelter for those entering or leaving a vehicle.

*see **gable** for citation, p. 263*

portico (POHR ti KOH) - *n.* a covered walk, an open-sided walkway of which the roof is supported by columns.

"On the pavement, by the **portico** of Christ's Church, where the stone pillars rise toward the sky in a stately row, were whole rows of men lying asleep or drowsing, and all too deep sunk in torpor to rouse or be made curious by our intrusion." —JACK LONDON, *The People of the Abyss*

quoin (KOIN) - *n.* an exterior angle of a wall, or piece of masonry, 2. the stones or blocks forming this angle.

"... the enormous stone **quoins** at the entranceway ..." —PAT CONROY, *The Lords of Discipline*

sluice (SLOOS) - *n.* an artifical channel for moving water with a gate or valve regulating the flow, used in a canal or millstream, 2. the water held behind such a gate, 3. the gate or valve used in opening and closing such a canal, 4. a channel, esp. one to direct excess water, 5. a long sloping trough for separating and washing gold ore or for carrying logs, 6. *v.* to draw off or carry in a sluice, 7. to wash with water from a sluice, or with a similar rush of water, 8. to flow as in a sluice.

"The coolies lounged, talked, smoked, or stared over the rail; some drawing water over the side, **sluiced** each other; a few slept on hatches, ... and every Celestial of them was carrying with him all he had in the world." —JOSEPH CONRAD, *Typhoon*

stanchion (STAN chuhn) - *n.* a vertical beam or post used as a support, 2. a framework or two or more vertical bars fitted loosely around the neck of a cow to secure it in a stall or at a feedtrough, 3. *v.* to support by means of stanchions, 4. to confine (cattle) using a stancion.

stave (STAYV) - *n.* one of a number of narrow strips of wood, or narrow iron plates, placed edge to edge to form the sides, covering, or lining of a vessel or structure, 2. one of the cylindrical bars of a lantern wheel; one of the bars or rounds of a rack,

a ladder, etc., 3. a metrical portion; a stanza; a staff, 4. the five horizontal and parallel lines on and between which musical notes are written or pointed; the staff.

"Both above and below us were visible fragments of vessels, large masses of building-timber and trunks of trees, with many smaller articles, such as pieces of house furniture, broken boxes, barrels and **staves**." —EDGAR ALLAN POE, *A Descent Into the Maelström*

stele (STEE lee) - *n.* an upright stone slab bearing an inscription or having a sculpted surface, often used as a monument and applied to the surface on the face of a building.

"Vittoria slowed as the third niche loomed before them ... motioning with her head to the **stele** beside the apse. Carved in the granite block were two words: CAPELLA CHIGI" —DAN BROWN, *Angels & Demons*

stoa (STOH uh) - *n.* a portico or colonnade, esp. the great hall at Athens which has columns on one side and a wall on the other side (origin of the term stoics, who first studied in this hall).

trestle (TRE suhl) - *n.* a horizontal bar or beam held up by two pairs of divergent legs and used for support, 2. a supportive framework built of vertical, slanted supports and horizontal crosspieces, used for bridges.

"Frowsy kitchen scullions and a pair of unwashed girls were carrying in the planks and **trestles** for the table." —C.L. MOORE, *Jirel of Joiry*

volute (vuh LOOT) - *n.* a spiral, scroll-like ornament.

"It offered so many columns, pediments, friezes, tripods, gladiators, urns and **volutes** that it looked as if it had not been built of white marble, but squeezed out of a pastry tube." –AYN RAND, *The Fountainhead*

wainscot (WAYN skuht, also WAYN SKOHT) - *n.* a paneling or facing, usually wood, affixed to the walls of a room, 2. a panel forming the lower part of an interior wall finished in a different material from the upper part.

"... this front parlour or sitting-room, whose walls were lined with **wainscoting** of panelled oak reaching from floor to ceiling ..." –THOMAS HARDY, *Jude the Obscure*

wattle (WAH tuhl) - (among other definitions) *n.* a framework constructed of sticks, twigs or branches interwoven, used to make fences, walls, or roofs, 2. the material used in such a framework.

"When they reached the place, Holger saw a cottage of the most primitive sort, **wattle** and clay walls, a sod roof." –POUL ANDERSON, *Three Hearts and Three Lions*

wicket (WI kuht) - (besides the cricket and croquet terms) *n.* a small door or gate, especially one built into or near a larger one, 2. a small window or opening, usually fitted with a grating, as at a ticket window.

"The girl ... knocked cautiously at an arched door. Almost instantly a **wicket** opened in the upper panel, and a black face glanced out." –ROBERT E. HOWARD, *The Conan Chronicles*

DEFENSIVE ARCHITECTURE

barbican (BAHR bi kuhn) - *n.* a tower or other outdoor defensive fortification outside a castle or town.

"... something leaped upon the back of one of the arquebusiers, tore the leather jerkin from his shoulders and pursued him to the **barbican**." –ROBERT E. HOWARD, *Eons of the Night*

bastion (BAS chuhn) - *n.* that portion of a fortification that is projecting, 2. a well-defended or well-fortified position; a bulwark; often used figuratively.

"In fifty paces, with a swift bend round a jutting **bastion** of the cliff, it took them out of sight of the Tower." –J.R.R. TOLKIEN, *The Return of the King*

battlement (often -ments) (BA tuhl muhnt) - *n.* a parapet on top of a wall having indentations or notches used for defensive or decorative purposes.

"High against the black sky the flash of a lamp would show crocketed pinnacles and indented **battlements**." –THOMAS HARDY, *Jude the Obscure*

berm (or **berme**) (BUHRM) - *n.* a narrow ledge between the ditch and parapet in a fortification, 2. the usually unpaved shoulder or ledge along the edge of a paved road.

"Tall **berms** of snow rise like ramparts along the brick wall that surrounds the club." –IAN CALDWELL AND DUSTIN THOMASON, *The Rule of Four*

bivouac (BI vuh WAK, also BIV WAK) - *n.* a temporary, often unsheltered encampment, esp. of soldiers, 2. *v.* to camp in the open.

"We hump until past dark and form a combat **bivouac** within about two hundred yards of ten burning oil wells." –ANTHONY SWOFFORD, *Jarhead*

bulwark (BUL WUHRK) - *n.* a defensive wall; a fortified wall, 2. a breakwater, 3.

something or someone serving as a defense or safeguard, 4. (usually plural) the portion of a ship's side that extends above the deck.

cantonment (kan TOHN muhnt) - *n.* temporary living quarters built for housing troops, 2. the assignment of troops to these or other temporary quarters.

"Within an army whose backbone was supplied by a body of professional soldiers on whose tongues circulated from generation to generation the litany of the legions' **cantonments** and the lore of the life lived there, it is impossible that the soldiers' consciousness did not eventually come to be circumscribed by the geography of the frontiers." –JOHN KEEGAN, *A History of Warfare*

castellated (KAS tuh LAY tuhd) - *adj.* built in the style of a castle; having turrets and battlements, etc.

"... the **castellation** of England by the Normans—900 castles may have been built between 1066 and 1154 ...—was undertaken as a deliberate means of enforcing Norman rule on the Anglo-Saxons." –JOHN KEEGAN, *A History of Warfare*

chevaux-de-frise (singular is **cheval de frise**) (shuh VO duh FREEZ) - *n.* a defensive structure composed of barbed wire, spikes, or nails affixed along the top of a railing, wall, or wooden frame, used to halt enemy advancement, esp. cavalry charges, 2. a row of spikes, nails, jagged glass, etc., fixed into the top of a railing or wall to prevent trespass or escape.

"Across the horizon ran a far flung line of towers and minarets, turrets and spires and steeples, skyscrapers and mosques; a huge **chevaux-de-frise**." –ABRAHAM MERRITT, *The Ship of Ishtar*

circumvallation (SUHR KUHM VA LAY shuhn) - *n.* the process of surrounding with a rampart, a raised, wall-like structure or a trench, esp. used in besieging a fortress.

"Since the city had ample water supply within its massive walls, it managed to hold out against the Egyptians—who constructed a line of **circumvallation** around it against any relief operation—for seven months." –JOHN KEEGAN, *A History of Warfare*

citadel (SI tuh duhl, also SI tuh DEL) - *n.* a fortress or stronghold in a position of command in or near a city, 2. a stronghold used for shelter during battle.

crenelation (KRE nuhl AY shuhn) - *n.* a series of indentations or loopholes around the top of a castle, battlement or wall (each indentation being a crenel or crenelle).

"... as they approached that monstrous city and as its towers, spires, fanes, and great **crenelated** wall emerged ..." –FRITZ LEIBER, *Swords Against Death*

crenelle (also **crenel**) (kre NEHL) - *n.* the embrasures or indentations in an embattled parapet used for shooting or launching projectiles toward the enemy.

"An adjacent parapet was a shadowy line, and further **crenelles** and **embrasures** were barely hinted at in the dim starlight." –ROBERT E. HOWARD, *The People of the Black Circle*

embrasure (im BRAY zhuhr) - *n.* an opening or recess for a door or window, 2. a flared opening for a gun in a wall or parapet.

*see **crenelle** for citation*

hoochie (also **hootch**) (HOO CHEE) - *n.* (military slang) a temporary or insubstantial dwelling or shelter.

"We finish the bottle and return to the **hootch**." –ANTHONY SWOFFORD, *Jarhead*

machicolation (muh CHI kuh LAY shuhn) - *n.* a projecting gallery or parapet supported by corbels, or an opening in the roof over an entrance, through which heavy stones or boiling hot liquids can be dropped upon attackers by the defenders of a fortress.

"Four gates broke the circle of this wall, each flanked by guard towers with slits for archers and **machicolations** for the abuse of besiegers." –L. SPRAGUE DE CAMP AND LIN CARTER, *Conan the Buccaneer*

mantelet (also **mantlet**) (MANT luht, also MAN tuh luht) - *n.* a short cape or cloak; a short mantle, 2. a mobile screen or shield, 3. a movable screen used to protect besieging soldiers, 4. a bulletproof shield.

"'They're making a **mantlet**, curse them!' he raged." –ROBERT E. HOWARD AND L. SPRAGUE DE CAMP, *Conan the Usurper*

merlon (MEHR luhn) - *n.* the solid part of a battlement or parapet, between two openings, embrasures or crenels.

"As I came under the castle wall, treading on remnants of red petals and snaky stalks, I unwound my rawhide rope, swung it and sent its loop shooting upward to catch on one of the **merlons** of the crenellated parapet." –ROBERT E. HOWARD, *Eons of the Night*

motte (MAHT) - (among other definitions) *n.* a large artificial mound of earth with a flat top, often surmounted by a castle or fort.

"Castles, however, could be built very quickly—a hundred men might throw up a small **motte** in ten days." –JOHN KEEGAN, *A History of Warfare*

multivallation (muhlt uh va LAY shun) - *n.* the practice of using two or more ramparts to form multiple lines of defense.

"... defensive features [of strongholds] ... Outer walls were to be set around inner ones—**multivallation** ...'" –JOHN KEEGAN, *A History of Warfare*

paling (PAY ling) - *n.* one of a row of pointed sticks making a fence, 2. such a fence, 3. a pale; a picket.

"All round this they had cleared a wide space, and then the thing was completed by a **paling** six feet high, without door or opening, too strong to pull down without time and labour, and too open to shelter the besiegers." –ROBERT LOUIS STEVENSON, *Treasure Island*

palisade (PA luh SAYD) - *n.* a wall of wooden stakes, used as a defensive barrier, 2. a line of high, steep cliffs, esp. those along a river.

"This [whole town of huts] they enclosed with **palisades** ..." –JULES VERNE, *From the Earth to the Moon*

parapet (PAR uh puht, also PAR uh PET) - *n.* a wall or bank used to shield soldiers from frontal enemy fire, sometimes placed on top of a rampart, 2. a low wall or railing, as along a balcony.

"As I came under the castle wall, treading on remnants of red petals and snaky stalks, I unwound my rawhide rope, swung it and sent its loop shooting upward to catch on one of the merlons of the crenellated **parapet**." –ROBERT E. HOWARD, *Eons of the Night*

portcullis (pohrt KUH luhs) - *n.* a heavy iron grating lowered into place to bar the gated entry to a castle or fortified town.

"There the rocky roof came down close to the surface of the stream, and from it a

portcullis could be dropped right to the bed of the river to prevent anyone coming in or out that way." –J.R.R. TOLKIEN, *The Hobbit*

postern (POHS tuhrn, also PAHS tuhrn) - *n.* a small gate or back door, esp. a private entrance at the side or back of a fort or castle, 2. *adj.* situated in the back or rear, resembling a postern.

"He entered secretly, through the **postern**, wrapped in his cloak." –ROBERT E. HOWARD, *Conan the Conqueror*

rampart (RAM PAHRT) - *n.* an embankment of earth with a parapet on top, surrounding a castle or fort, for defensive purposes, 2. a means of defense or protection; a bulwark.

"Tall berms of snow rise like **ramparts** along the brick wall that surrounds the club ..." –IAN CALDWELL AND DUSTIN Thomason, *The Rule of Four*

revetment (re VET muhnt) - *n.* a layer of stone, concrete, sandbags, etc., supporting a wall or the side of an embankment, 2. such an em-

bankment or wall designed to protect against incoming attack, 3. a retaining wall.

"It took three weeks to shore up the stone **revetment**, build a support beneath it and restore the wheel to its previous stable condition." –JULES VERNE, *From the Earth to the Moon*

tourelle (TU RELL) - *n.* a turret.

"The bright blue Euskerian sun flashed on the gilding of dome and spire and **tourelle**, and flags bearing the owl of Tartessia flapped lazily in the faint breeze." –L. SPRAGUE DE CAMP, *The Tritonian Ring*

turret (TUHR uht) - *n.* a small tower or tower-shaped projection extending above a building, 2. a low, heavily armored structure projecting from a warship or tank, usually rotating horizontally and holding mounted guns and their gunners, 3. the attachment for a lathe including a rotating cylindrical block that holds various tools for cutting.

"Etched in the clear evening sky we saw plainly the giant details of massive **turret** and grim abutment; of serrated tower and titanic wall." –ROBERT E. HOWARD, *Eons of the Night*

BUILDING ACCESSORIES

arras (AR uhs) - *n.* a tapestry, 2. a wall hanging (named after Arras, a city in France).

> "... the **arras** hangs ..." —MERVYN PEAKE, *Titus Groan*

athanor (ATH ah nor) - *n.* a self-feeding furnace maintaining a uniform temperature, used by alchemists.

> "Now if you will lend a hand with this **athanor**, I shall finish compounding this mixture and we can retire for the night." —L. SPRAGUE DE CAMP AND FLETCHER PRATT, *The Complete Compleat Enchanter*

banquette (bang KET) - *n.* a long, upholstered bench, set against or built into a wall, 2. a platform within a trench or parapet on which soldiers stand when firing.

> "As I was wearing the soles of my desert boots down to a mere sliver of crepe rubber on the old flagstone **banquettes** of the French Quarter in my fevered attempt to wrest a living from an unthinking and uncaring society, I was hailed by a cherished old acquaintance." —JOHN KENNEDY TOOLE, *A Confederacy of Dunces*

censer (SENT suhr) - *n.* an ornamented vessel in which incense is burned, esp. during religious rites or services; thurible.

> *see other **censer** entry for citation, p. 169*

cistern (SIS tuhrn) - *n.* a large receptacle for holding water, esp. an underground tank for collecting and storing rainwater for use.

> "There was always **cistern** water to fall back on." —SAUL BELLOW, *Herzog*

cresset (KRE suht) - *n.* a metal cup or container, suspended from a pole, containing burning oil, wood or pitch and used as a torch or lantern.

> "The moon had not risen, and the garden was lighted with torches aglow in silver **cressets** when Kull sat down on the throne before the table of Ka-nu, ambassador of the western isles." —ROBERT E. HOWARD, *The Shadow Kingdom*

escutcheon (is KUH chuhn) - *n.* a shield or shield-shaped surface or emblem displaying a coat of arms, 2. something of this shape, 3. (Nautical) the surface on the stern of a ship bearing the ship's name, 4. "a blot on one's escutcheon"—a disgrace to one's reputation; a stain on one's honor.

> "Luckily, Charles remembered the address of his employer, and he hastened there ... He made out some **escutcheons** over a door, and knocked." —GUSTAVE FLAUBERT, *Madame Bovary*, transl. by Francis Steegmuller

festoon (fes TOON) - *n.* an ornament such as a garland or chain which hangs loosely from two tacked spots, 2. any carved or molded decoration resembling this, as on furniture, 3. *v.* to adorn or hang with festoons.

> "The fluffy, fair hair, soaked and darkened, resembled a mean skein of cotton threads **festooned** round his bare skull." —JOSEPH CONRAD, *Typhoon*

floriated (FLOHR ee AY tuhd) -*adj.* adorned or decorated with floral designs.

> *see other **floriated** entry for citation, p. 243*

gnomon (NOH muhn, also NOH MAHN) - *n.* a sundial; a pillar, rod, or other object that creates a shadow to indicate the time of day.

"... a golden line slanting across the church's floor. The line bore graduated markings, like a ruler. It was a **gnomon**, Silas had been told, a pagan astronomical device like a sundial." –DAN BROWN, *The Da Vinci Code*

lath (LATH) - *n.* a narrow, thin strip of wood or metal nailed in rows used as a backing for plaster, shingles, or tiles, 2. any similar building material.

"Where he lived was a little stale-air flat in a tenement. The plaster stuck on the **laths** mostly by the force of the paint." –SAUL BELLOW, *The Adventures of Augie March*

newel (NOO uhl, also NYOO uhl) - *n.* the vertical support at the center of a spiral staircase, 2. the post at the top or bottom of a flight of stairs supporting a handrail.

"Phillotson, horrified, ran downstairs, striking himself sharply against the **newel** in his haste." –THOMAS HARDY, *Jude the Obscure*

oast (OHST) - *n.* a kiln used for drying hops or malt, or for drying and curing tobacco.

"The townlands were rich, with wide tilth and many orchards, and homesteads there were with **oast** and garner, fold and byre, and many rills rippling through the green from the highlands down to Anduin." –J.R.R. TOLKIEN, *The Return of the King*

portiere (or **portière**) (pohr TYER, also POHR tee uhr) - *n.* a heavy curtain hanging across a doorway.

"In passing through the lobbies of swank places, the Palmer Houses and **portiered** dining rooms, tassels, tapers, string ensembles, making the staid bouncety tram-tram of Vienna waltzes, Simon had

absorbed this." –SAUL BELLOW, *The Adventures of Augie March*

rosette (roh ZET) - *n.* an ornament, as of ribbon or silk, that resembles a rose.

"She stood at parapets and wondered who had worked the stones, shaped these details of the suavest nuance, chevrons and **rosettes**, urns on balustrades, the classical swags of fruit, the scroll brackets supporting a balcony, and she thought they must have been immigrants, Italian stone carvers probably, unremembered, artists anonymous of the early century, buried in the sky." –DON DELILLO, *Underworld*

sconce (SKAHNTS) - *n.* a decorative bracket hung on a wall for holding a candle, candles or other objects.

"**Sconced** candles lit the place fairly well, showing it empty down to a doorway at the end." –POUL ANDERSON, *Three Hearts and Three Lions*

stile (STYUHL) - *n.* the series of steps for crossing a wall or a fence; a turnstile.

"The road passed between green fields, and coming to a **stile** Sue paused there, to finish the page she was reading." –THOMAS HARDY, *Jude the Obscure*

thurible (THUR uh buhl, also THYUR uh buhl) - *n.* a container in which incense is burnt, especially in religious ceremonies; a censer.

tracery (TRAY suh ree, also TRAYS ree) - *n.* ornamentation consisting of an open pattern of interlaced and branching lines.

"He asked for the foreman, and looked round among the new **traceries**, mullions, transoms, shafts, pinnacles, and battlements standing on the bankers half

worked, or waiting to be removed."
—THOMAS HARDY, *Jude the Obscure*

trefoil (TREE FOIL, also TRE FOIL) - (among other definitions) *n.* an ornamental form resembling a triofiate leaf, such as a clover.

"... the walls of the Gothic buildings across the way were built to withstand any threat ... with an imperious confidence ... O tre-foil tracery! O ye buildings such as will never be built again!" —TOM WOLFE, *I Am Charlotte Simmons*

valance (VA luhnts, also VAY luhnts) - *n.* a short, ornamental drapery hung from the edge of a bed, table or canopy, 2. a short, ornamental drapery or board mounted across the top of a window and serving to conceal structural features such as curtain rods, etc.

"... he found owls in his bedroom, perched on the red **valances**, which they had streaked with droppings." —SAUL BELLOW, *Herzog*

OTHER BUILDING TERMS

acanthus (uh KANT thuhs) - *n.* any of the genus (Acanthus) of thistlelike plants of the acanthus family with lobed, often spiny leaves and long spikes of white or colored flowers, found in the Mediterranean region, Asia Minor, and India, 2. Archit. a motif or conventional representation of the leaf of this plant, used esp. on the capitals of Corinthian columns.

*see other **acanthus** entry for citation, p. 174*

caisson (KAY SAHN, also KAY suhn) - *n.* a watertight chamber in which construction takes place underwater, 2. a watertight compartment used to repair damage to a ship's

hull or to raise sunken ships, 3. a large container used to hold ammunition, 4. a horse-drawn, two-wheeled cart carrying ammunition.

"It seemed to him that every corner of New York was flooded with celebration and that he alone, hidden in the watertight **caisson** of his room, was cold and lost and horrified." —AYN RAND, *The Fountainhead*

capacious (kuh PAY shuhs) - *adj.* able to hold or contain a great deal; spacious; roomy.

"... pockets as **capacious** as bags ..." —GUSTAVE FLAUBERT, *Madame Bovary*, transl. by Francis Steegmuller

chthonic (THAH nik) - *adj.* relating to the underworld; living beneath the earth's surface.

"You enter and are stunned by a conspiracy in which the sublime universe of heavenly ogives and the **chthonian** world of gas guzzlers are juxtaposed." —UMBERTO ECO, *Foucault's Pendulum*

cloacal (klo A kuhl) - *adj.*- relating to or characterized by a cloaca (a sewer or latrine).

"No, he is not unreasonably fastidious, and not the claustrophobic sort, although naturally he has a preference for bright, airy brothels (who wouldn't?). However, he's so smitten with Sugar that, to be honest, he'd willingly follow her into the rankest **cloaca**." —MICHEL FABER, *The Crimson Petal and the White*

Corinthian (kuh RIN thee uhn) - *adj.* pertaining to Corinth, its people or culture, 2. dissolute and loving luxury, as the people of Corinth were said to be, 3. in the style of the art of Corinth; gracefully elaborate, 4. designating or of the most elaborate of the three orders of Greek architecture (the others being Doric and Ionic), distinguished by a slender, fluted column and bell-shaped capital decorated with a design of acanthus leaves and volutes, 5. *n.* a native of Corinth, 6. a lover of elegantly luxurious living; sybarite.

> "... a rooming house with a **Corinthian** portico ..." –AYN RAND, *The Fountainhead*

---

debouch (di BAUCH) - *v.* to come forth from a narrow or confined area into the open, esp. in connection with the movement of military forces, 2. to emerge; to issue; to come forth.

> "The tunnel **debouched** into a wide room ..." –ROBERT E. HOWARD, *Conan the Warrior*

---

demesne (di MAYN, also di MEEN) - *n.* the grounds belonging to an estate or country house, 2. an estate; an extensive piece of landed property, 3. a district; a territory; a domain.

> "'I fear me I never heard of your **demesne**, good sir, but then I am from the far southwest and ignorant of these parts.'" –POUL ANDERSON, *Three Hearts and Three Lions*

Doric (DOR ik, also DAHR ik) - *adj.* the name of the oldest, strongest, and simplest of the three Grecian orders of architecture (Doric, Ionic, Corinthian), 2. of or pertaining to the ancient Greek region of Doris.

> "At ten minutes past four, the wagons pulled up in front of the Olympic Club's **Doric** columns, and the police, all in black tie, ran together—or as 'together' as they could, for they were quite snockered—into the club." –GLEN DAVID GOLD, *Carter Beats the Devil*

---

fug (FUHG) - *n.* a heavy, close, stuffy atmosphere, esp. that found in an overcrowded, poorly ventilated room.

> "The walls of the corridor are concave on one side and convex on the other; striped wallpaper bulges and wrinkles like ill-fitting clothing, medallioned with framed prints whose glass is opaque with **fug**." –MICHEL FABER, *The Crimson Petal and the White*

---

hamlet (HAM luht) - *n.* a small village.

> "He painted sea vistas he'd never seen and forest **hamlets** he'd never visited, complete with a pipe-smoking figure resting on a log." –JEFFREY EUGENIDES, *Middlesex*

---

immure (i MYUR) - *v.* to lock up, to confine, to imprison, 2. to build into or entomb within a wall.

> "No matter that [Saddam Hussein] almost never appeared anywhere that made him accessible to ordinary Iraqis, sending out a team of doubles to maintain the pretense of being the people's tribune, while sparing him from assassins' threats; **immured** in his palaces, he was ever the grim but inaccessible colossus." –JOHN BURNS, *The New York Times*, 7/4/04

---

inviolable (in VY uh luh buhl) - *adj.* safe from assault or trepass, 2. impregnable.

> "The look on his face was her **inviolable** protection against the smirks, the Sarc 3 glances, and the mock ruminations of Nicole and Crissy." –TOM WOLFE, *I Am Charlotte Simmons*

Ionic (eye AH nik) - *adj.* the name of one of the three orders of Grecian architecture (Doric, Ionic, Corinthian), characterized by the ornamental scrolls (spiral volutes) on the capitals of columns, 2. of or pertaining to the ancient Greek region of Ionia.

> "The town hall ... is a kind of Greek temple ... Its lower story has three **Ionic** columns; above is a row of arched windows; and the culminating pediment is filled with a figure of the Gallic cock, one of its claws resting on the Constitution and the other holding the scales of justice." –GUSTAVE FLAUBERT, *Madame Bovary*, transl. by Francis Steegmuller

Jacobean (JA kuh BEE uhn) - *adj.* of or pertaining to the reign of James I of England (1603–1625), esp. the style of his times, 2. of or pertaining to Henry James (1843–1916), American novelist and critic, 3. *n.* a prominent figure, a statesman or writer during the time of James I.

> "The mantelpiece was of the same heavy description, carved with **Jacobean** pilasters and scrollwork." –THOMAS HARDY, *Jude the Obscure*

jerry-builder (JER ee BILD uhr) - *n.* a speculative builder known for constructing cheap buildings made of poor materials for a quick profit.

> "But I already knew what she thought the academy would look like: a beaten-up frame house of dead-drunk **jerry-builders** under dusty laborious trees, laundry boiling in the yard, pinched chickens of misfortune, rioting kids, my blind mother wearing my old shoes and George cobblering, me with a crate of bees in the woods." –SAUL BELLOW, *The Adventures of Augie March*

kraal (KROL, also KRAHL) - *n.* in Southern or Central Africa, a rural village consisting of a collection of huts within an enclosure or stockade, 2. an enclosure for livestock; a stockade; a pen; a fold.

> "A previous [Zulu] chief had abolished the system by which warriors, when called to serve their chief in war, went with others from their locality to muster at his **kraal**." –JOHN KEEGAN, *A History of Warfare*

macadam (muh KA duhm) - *n.* a type of pavement made of layers of compacted, broken stone, usually bound together with tar or asphalt (named after John L. McAdam [1756–1836]).

> "... until the development of **macadamisation** in the early nineteenth century, roads generally lacked an all-weather surface." –JOHN KEEGAN, *A History of Warfare*

marquetry (MAHR kuh tree) - *n.* small pieces of material such as wood, ivory or metal, laid piece by piece into a wooden surface to create an intricate design which is applied to another surface, such as furniture, for ornamentation or decoration.

> "... the famous Herter Bed ... a fabulous creation in ebonized cherry inlaid with light woods, rosewood, brass, and Japanese **marquetry**, a veritable monument to Victorian dignity, solidity, respectability, and grandeur." –TOM WOLFE, *A Man in Full*

mews (MYOOZ) - *n.* (used with a singular verb) the royal stables at Charing Cross, London, built on the location where the royal hawks were mewed (caged, particularly while molting), 2. a small court or alley, once containing private stables, now mostly converted into residences.

> "We took the bird away. The toilet became his **mews**; he perched on the waterbox or cistern where the sound of trickling seemed to please him." –SAUL BELLOW, *The Adventures of Augie March*

mortise (MOR tuhs) - *n.* a hole, cavity, or space, in a piece of wood, stone, or other material that holds a tenon and forms a joint, 2. *v.* to join or fasten securely using mortise and tenon, 3. to make a hole in.

> "'From a builder's viewpoint it's terrific. Imagine what it would cost today. The foundations would hold the Empire State Building. And I'll show you the hand-hewn chestnut beams. Old **mortice** and **tenon**. No metal at all.'" –SAUL BELLOW, *Herzog*

Portland cement (POHRT luhnd si MENT) - *n.* a cement made by heating limestone and clay and pulverizing the resulting matter; this mixture then hardens under water (named after Portland, England).

> "In the moment he'd looked away, Carter had sprung the bookcase away from the wall, revealing a small, grey room with **portland cement** walls." –GLEN DAVID GOLD, *Carter Beats the Devil*

rococo (ruh KOH KOH, also roh kuh KOH) - *adj.* of a style of art, architecture, and the decorative art marked by elaborate, asymmetric ornamentation, 2. an overly ornate style.

> "Whereas its neighbors were hooded Arts and Crafts fortresses, One Hilgirt Circle was a **rococo** circus of archways, terracotta putti, gargoyles, and trellises strung with passion vines." –GLEN DAVID GOLD, *Carter Beats the Devil*

salient (SAY lyuhnt, also SAY lee uhnt) - *adj.* worthy of note, 2. standing out or projecting beyond a line or surface, 3. prominent; striking; conspicuous.

> "His words were falling down a well, hitting stone salients on their way, and each **salient** refused to stop them, threw them farther, tossed them from one another, sent them to seek a bottom that did not exist." –AYN RAND, *The Fountainhead*

tenon (TE nuhn) - *n.* the projection of the end of a piece of wood inserted into a corresponding hole (mortise) in another piece of wood to make a joint, 2. *v.* to make or provide using a tenon, 3. to join or fasten securely using mortise and tenon.

*see **mortise** for citation*

15. HOUSEHOLD OBJECTS

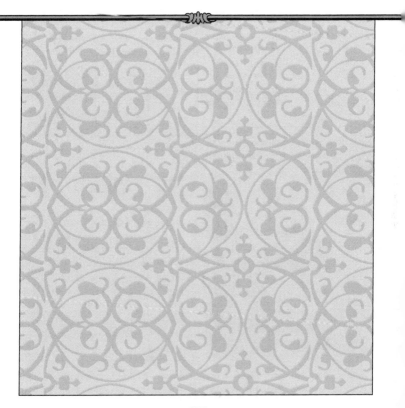

TOOLS

adz (or **adze**) (ADZ) - *n.* an axlike tool, having a curved blade set at a right angle to the handle; used to cut and shape wood.

> "... the ... appearance of a new sort of stone tool, fashioned from heavy basalt or granite, and ground by abrasion—the magnificent 'polished' axes and **adzes** of the New Stone Age." –JOHN KEEGAN, *A History of Warfare*

Archimedean Screw (or **Archimedean drill**, or **Archimedes' Screw**) (AHR kuh MEE DEE uhn SKROO) - *n.* an ancient instrument for raising water, made by winding a tube around a long cylinder in the form of a screw.

> "'It was at this juncture that Mr. Monck Mason ... conceived the idea of employing the principle of the **Archimedean screw** for the purpose of propulsion through the air." –EDGAR ALLAN POE, *The Balloon Hoax*

auger (O guhr) - *n.* a carpenter's tool with a spiral cutting edge for boring holes larger than those bored by a gimlet.

> "The drilling device consisted of a metal shaft about four feet long ending in a wide,

cylindrical length of corkscrew blade, a strong, serious boring tool whose imposing bit—rotated by turning the cranked handle at the top—glittered like new in the sunlight. An **auger**." –PHILIP ROTH, *The Human Stain*

awl (OL) - *n.* a small pointed tool used for making holes, as in leather or wood.

> "The treasures in the bunkers—correspondence, a bayonet, a beret, a helmet, homemade Iraqi dog tags with the information scrawled by hand with an **awl**—the worthless treasures call." –ANTHONY SWOFFORD, *Jarhead*

gimlet (GIM luht) - *n.* a small spiral-pointed tool used for boring, (gimlet eyed - *adj.* having a piercing glance).

> "While no one is spared Perrotta's **gimlet** eye, not a single character is left outside the pale of his wry affection, either." –WILL BLYTHE, *The New York Times Book Review, 3/14/04*

lathe (LAYTH) - *n.* a machine for shaping a piece of wood, metal, etc., in which the material is held and turned rapidly against a cutting or abrading tool.

> "His hobby was making napkin rings on his own **lathe**." –GUSTAVE FLAUBERT, *Madame Bovary*, transl. by Francis Steegmuller

mattock (MA tuhk) - *n.* an agricultural tool for loosening soil, digging up and cutting roots, etc.; like a pickax but with a flat blade on one or both sides of the handle.

> "In battle [the dwarves] wielded heavy two-handed **mattocks**." –J.R.R. TOLKIEN, *The Hobbit*

maul (MOL) - *n.* a heavy, long-handled hammer or mallet, often of wood, used to drive stakes, piles, or wedges, 2. *v.* to beat, bruise, or tear, 3. to handle roughly; mishandle.

> "Khosatral Khel was towering above him, his arms lifted like **mauls**, but as the blade caught the sheen of the sun, the giant gave back suddenly." –ROBERT E. HOWARD, *The Devil in Iron*

FURNITURE

angareb (-eeb, -ep) - *n.* a stretcher or lightweight bed used by the Arabs and Egyptians and in the Sudan.

> "As she lay on the **angareb** in the great hut, her state bordered between delirium and semi-unconsciousness." –ROBERT E. HOWARD, *The Conan Chronicles*

antimacassar (AN ti muh KA suhr) - *n.* a small cover to protect the backs or arms of furniture from soiling (anti + Macassar, a brand of hair oil).

> "... a hideous audience room, laden with overstuffed furniture with **antimacassars** on the plush brocade coverings." –KATHARINE GRAHAM, *Personal History*

bolster (BOHL stuhr) - *n.* a long, narrow cushion or pillow, usually set across a bed, 2. *v.* to prop up; to support, as with a bolster.

> "The room had been refurnished for him and Charlotte with silk-shaded reading lamps, bedside fleeces, drapes against the alley view and its barbarity—as in a palazzo against the smell of the canals-a satin cover on the bed, and auxiliary pillows on the roll of the **bolster**." –SAUL BELLOW, *The Adventures of Augie March*

chaise longue (SHAYZ LONJ, also SHAYZ LOWNJ) - *n.* a chair with a long seat for reclining; a chair with a seat long enough to support one's outstretched legs.

> "... looking at a wax figure exquisitely contorted on a satin **chaise longue** in a shop window ..." –AYN RAND, *The Fountainhead*

chesterfield (CHES tuhr FEELD) - *n.* a single- or double-breasted overcoat, usually with a fly front and velvet collar, 2. a sofa, esp. one heavily stuffed and with upright armrests at either end.

> "Fourteenth Street bargains filled the apartment—an overstuffed **chesterfield**, bronze screens, lamps, nylon drapes, masses of wax flowers, articles of wrought iron and twisted wire and glass." –SAUL BELLOW, *Herzog*

cheval-glass (sheh VAL GLAS) - *n.* a full-length, swiveling mirror mounted on a frame.

> "Edgar sometimes managed to angle the mirrors in such a way that he could catch a glimpse—by taking the free-standing antique in an old inn, the **cheval glass**, for example, and simply moving it to another part of the floor." –DON DELILLO, *Underworld*

commode (kuh MOHD) - *n.* an often elaborately decorated low-standing cabinet or chest of drawers, 2. a moveable stand holding a washbowl, 3. a toilet.

> "I was scandalized by the filth of men's rooms ... Urine was forever puddled on the floors. Scraps of soiled toilet paper adhered to the **commodes**." –JEFFREY EUGENIDES, *Middlesex*

coverlet (KUH vuhr luht) - *n.* a bedspread; a decorative bedspread.

> "... some high mountain ledge upon a valley whose cloudy **coverlet** had just been touched by rays of morning sun." –ABRAHAM MERRITT, *The Ship of Ishtar*

credenza (kri DEN zuh) - *n.* a sideboard or buffet, esp. one not having legs, 2. a long piece of office furniture, usually containing file drawers.

"... a smudged baseball balanced on the rim of a coffee mug that sat on the **credenza** ..." –DON DELILLO, *Underworld*

davenport (DA vuhn POHRT) - *n.* a large sofa, esp. one that converts to a bed, 2. a small, decorative writing desk, often with a hinged lid.

"She walked to the **davenport** and sat down; she let her back press against the cushions." –AYN RAND, *The Fountainhead*

divan (di VAN, also DEE VAN) - (among other definitions) *n.* a long couch or backless sofa, esp. one set against a wall with pillows in lieu of a back support (from the Turkish).

"As he sat on the plush **divan** and positioned the photo album on his lap, he felt a carnal hunger stir." –DAN BROWN, *Angels & Demons*

escritoire (ES kruh TWAHR) - *n.* a desk or table for writing, often having a top section for books.

"He went over to a mahogany **escritoire**, opened one of its drawers and took out a fat sealed envelope." –ARTURO PEREZ-REVERTE, *The Flanders Panel*

hassock (HA suhk) - *n.* a thick cushion used as a seat, a footstool, or for kneeling.

"'Sit here on this **hassock**.'" –NELSON DEMILLE, *The Gold Coast*

pallet (pa LUHT) - *n.* a platform used to store or move cargo or freight, 2. a narrow, hard bed or mattress filled with straw.

"... sitting in the dimness across from her **pallet**." –PHILIP ROTH, *American Pastoral*

palliasse (or **paillasse**) (pal YAS) - *n.* a thin mattress or pad, esp. one filled with straw or saw dust.

"Covering his feet and heaped about his slender body on all sides was a cold, dark, undulating **palliasse** of pine needles, broken here and there with heavy, weary-headed ferns and grey fungi." –MERVYN PEAKE, *Titus Groan*

tabouret (also **taboret**) (TA buh RET) - *n.* a low, drum-shaped stool; a low stool with back or arms; a small tabor (a kind of small drum).

"The man was sitting cross-legged on a low **taboret** with his eyes closed." –L. SPRAGUE DE CAMP, *The Tritonian Ring*

tansu (TAN SOO) - *n.* a Japanese chest of drawers or cupboard.

"Some people inherit houses; others paintings or highly insured violin bows. Still others get a Japanese **tansu** or a famous name." –JEFFREY EUGENIDES, *Middlesex*

tuffet (TUH fuht) - *n.* a hillock; a mound; a tuft or clump, esp. of grass, 2. a low seat or footstool.

"Little Miss Muffet sat on a **tuffet**" –CHILDREN'S NURSERY RHYME

CANDLES AND LANTERNS

lanthorn (LAN tuhrn) - *n.* an archaic term for a lantern.

"Hakon looked livid in the **lanthorn** light." –ROBERT E. HOWARD AND L. SPRAGUE DE CAMP, *Conan the Usurper*

tallow (TA LOH) - *n.* hard fat obtained from the bodies of livestock and used to make candles, soaps, and lubricants.

> "Israel Hands propped against the bulwarks, his chin on his chest, his hands lying open before him on the deck, his face as white, under its tan, as a **tallow** candle." –ROBERT LOUIS STEVENSON, *Treasure Island*

taper (TAY puhr) - (among other definitions) *n.* a long, slender candle; a waxed wick used to light candles.

> "... a strange conclave was taking place in the small velvet-hung **taper**-lighted chamber of Atalis, whom some called a philosopher and others a rogue." –ROBERT E. HOWARD, *The Hand of Nergal*

FIREPLACES

andiron (AN DY uhrn) - *n.* one of a pair of metal supports used to hold up logs in a fireplace.

> "Beneath the Egyptian goddess, inside the fireplace, two stone gargoyles served as **andirons**, their mouths gaping to reveal their menacing hollow throats." –DAN BROWN, *The Da Vinci Code*

fender (fen DUHR) - (among other definitions) *n.* a screen placed in front of a fireplace.

> "They went back, and found Thorin with his feet on the **fender** smoking a pipe." –J.R.R. TOLKIEN, *The Hobbit*

OTHER HOUSEHOLD OBJECTS

battledore (BAT uhl DOHR) - *n.* a flat paddle or racket used to hit a shuttlecock back and forth over a net in a game similar to badminton, 2. the name of this game, 3. a similarly shaped, typically wooden, paddle used in laundering to smooth out clothes; also used to put bread loaves, pizzas, etc., into an oven or glassware into a kiln.

> "The rudder was a light frame of cane covered with silk, shaped somewhat like a **battledore**, and was about three feet long, and at the widest, one foot." –EDGAR ALLAN POE, *The Fall of the House of Usher*

ferrule (also **ferule**) (FER uhl) - *n.* a metal cap or band attached at the end of a wooden pole or cane to prevent splitting and provide reinforcement.

> "Zim strode up to the man who had sneezed, shoved the **ferrule** of the swagger cane an inch under his nose and demanded, 'Name?'" –ROBERT HEINLEIN, *Starship Troopers*

piggin (PI guhn) - *n.* a small wooden pail, tub, or dipper having only one stave extended above the rim for a handle.

> "I told him my dingey was nearly swamped, and he reached me a **piggin**." –H.G. WELLS, *The Island of Dr. Moreau*

potsherd (PAHT SHUHRD) - *n.* a piece of broken crockery or pottery.

> "... elevating every chance visitor to its shores on a pedestal, seemingly for the purpose of casting **potsherds** at him." –JACK LONDON, *from a letter to the "Comrades of the Mexican Revolution," February 4, 1911*

spall (SPOL) - *n.* a piece of broken crockery or pottery.

> "He cleaned the kitchen windowsill, dust, hair, fly heads, flakes of plaster—stony little **spalls**." –DON DELILLO, *Underworld*

INDEX

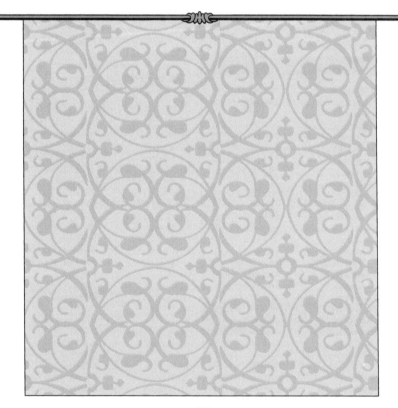